To Be a Pilgrim

TO BE A PILGRIM

The Anglican Ethos in History

by
Frederick Quinn

A Crossroad Book
The Crossroad Publishing Company
New York

The Crossroad Publishing Company
481 Eighth Avenue, Suite 1550
New York, NY 10001

Cataloging-in-Publication data is available from the Library of Congress.

ISBN: 0-8245-1900-0

1   2   3   4   5   6   7   8   9   10   05   04   03   02   01

For
the late Charles P. Price,
the late Charlotte Smith Quinn,
and
David Booth Beers and Margaret Graham Beers

"The Church's one foundation . . ."

Contents

Readings: *St. Patrick's Breastplate;* Bede of Jarrow, *A History of the English Church and People;* unknown, *Twelve Advent Lyrics from the Old English;* John of Salisbury, *The Statesman's Handbook;* Julian of Norwich, *Revelations of Divine Love*

Readings: C. S. Lewis, excerpts from *The Screwtape Letters, The Narnia Chronicles;* T. S. Eliot, "Journey of the Magi"; Evelyn Underhill, *Worship;* Charles Williams, *Descent into Hell,* selection from chapter "The Doctrine of Substituted Love"; Dorothy L. Sayers, *The Nine Tailors;* William Temple, *Christianity and the Social Order;* Michael Ramsey, *The Gospel and the Catholic Church*

Acknowledgments

M ANY PEOPLE have helped make this work possible. I want to thank the library of Virginia Theological Seminary, whose excellent collection is rivaled only by its attentive, professional staff. Several clergy have shown me glimpses of an Anglican ethos through their lives and in conversations, including Nathan D. Baxter, William F. Creighton, Barbara Duncan, Sanford Garner, Jr., Peter A. Grandell, James L. Green, Rona R. Harding, John A. Hind, Carolyn Tanner Irish, Howard A. Johnson, E. Felix Kloman, Ernest A. Lister, Murray F. Newman, Elizabeth Orens, H. Boone Porter, Edgar D. Romig, Paul B. Schwartz, Frederick B. Schmidt, William B. Swing, Samuel P. Van Culin, John David Van Dooren, C. Alfred Vogeli, and Francis H. Wade.

Several parishes heard sections of this book in sermons, courses, or conversations. I am grateful to the Anglican congregations in Warsaw, Poland, and Prague, the Czech Republic, and to the parishioners at St. John's, Georgetown; St. Columba's, All Saints', Chevy Chase; Grace Church, Silver Spring; Church of the Epiphany, All Souls' Memorial Church, Church of the Holy Communion, St. Paul's Church, Rock Creek; St. James' Chapel, Bowie; Christ Church, Accokeek; Christ Church (Ironsides), St. Andrew's, Leonardtown; and the Cathedral Church of St. Peter and St. Paul, all in the Diocese of Washington unless otherwise indicated, for their thoughtful comments. Members of the staff of National Cathedral, Washington, D.C., provided stimulating ideas or encouragement at various times. Judith Cecelia Dodge made useful suggestions on the music sections. Rowan Greer, H. Boone Porter, and Charles P. Price read and commented on versions of this manuscript and shared with me their lively and diverse insights; for such errors of fact or interpretation as remain, I am responsible.

My thanks go as well to Paul McMahon of Crossroad, to Maurya P. Horgan and Paul J. Kobelski of The HK Scriptorium, Inc., and to my agent, Priscilla Palmer, for their high professionalism and personal thoughtfulness.

I dedicate this work to Charles P. Price, whose Renaissance interests include long seasons as Professor of Systematic Theology at Virginia Theological Seminary and Preacher to the University at Harvard University; to Charlotte Alison Smith Quinn, spiritual and temporal companion of thirty-five years; and to David Booth Beers, attorney, classicist, and successively chancellor to the Diocese of Washington and the Protestant Episcopal Church in the United States, and his wife, Peggy, a writer-editor, fellow travelers on the highroads and byroads of Anglicanism.

Finally, I am grateful to the Right Reverend Jane Holmes Dixon, Bishop of Washington *pro tempore*, for her wise counsel, prayers, and friendship over many years.

Introduction

IT WAS THE EASTER DAWN in a small southern Maryland church, framed by ancient chestnut trees overlooking the Potomac River, a late-seventeenth-century chapel-of-ease, a day's carriage ride from the next small brick church. On the wall outside was a faded plaque commemorating an early vicar, expelled to England for declining to support the American Revolution. Inside, the rarely used colonial-era communion set of heavy-plated silver was polished and sitting on the chancel's small central table. While the altar setting represented the churchmanship of a starkly simple, earlier era, the celebrant wore eucharistic vestments, added during a more recent rector's tenure. The scent of spring flowers was everywhere, and soon a congregation of old farm families and workers in recently established high-technology industries gathered in the hazy dawn. The organist struck up "Welcome, Happy Morning! Age to Age Shall Say" and the ancient-yet-ever-new Easter service began. The communion setting, used by the church since before any present parishioner could remember, was by Merbecke, and someone sang an Appalachian folk tune for an offertory. A family from Sierra Leone, new to the neighborhood, appeared in traditional African dress, bringing the elements to the altar. The disparate strains of an Anglican heritage came together once more, and a new paschal season was launched in a small community, as it was all over the world and had been for centuries. I was aware of these currents as I led the service, and later wrote this book to share its heritage with a new generation.

The genesis of this volume lay in teaching adult parish courses on Anglicanism and speaking with devout Episcopalians who have had few opportunities to explore the historical uniqueness of the branch of the Christian church which they have chosen, among all others, as the place to come for worship, fulfillment, and service. Parishes want to know about the Bible and church beliefs and to have programs to instruct young people in the faith. Seminaries, in addition to teaching these topics, respond to contemporary interests in politics, race, gender, and sex. Meanwhile, the tenor of contemporary religious discourse is often ahistorical and asocial, concerned primarily with personal betterment or individual salvation. As a result, what is uniquely Anglican is often ignored or incompletely understood, yet deeper understanding of the Anglican past can prepare contemporary Christians to respond to many issues facing the church and society.

But believers must be Christians first and Anglicans second, as the works selected for this volume attest. The great drama of salvation—the life, death, and resurrection of Christ—and its continued relevance to the world are the cornerstones of our faith, as we wrestle with the unending task of interpreting life situations. We approach these challenges from a particular Anglican ethos, with historical roots in Christianity as it came to the British Isles, but which became a worldwide presence by the late nineteenth century and is an international Christian presence now, increasingly influenced by experience in Asia, Africa, North and South America, and Europe.

The study of a religious ethos does not hang on fixed dates as much as does conventional political history with the death of a monarch or the loss of a battle as a defining event. It is more like tracing the strands of a tapestry through time. The spirituality of Julian of Norwich, seemingly a product of the English Middle Ages, reappears in the twentieth century. Lancelot Andrewes, who sprang to life during the English Reformation, becomes a pivotal figure in the Oxford Movement three centuries later. Such strands do not exist in isolation, but are interwoven with others as anyone will conclude who has tried to work their way through the multiple prayer book studies tracing the origins of new liturgical rites. Events, such as the death of Henry VIII, that are supposed defining points in the evolution of an ethos are more important as beacons than as boundaries. The understanding of the evolution of a religious ethos is more than a study of white hats versus black hats in any age, more like tracing the interacting parts of a Bach fugue.

In studying the Anglican past, it is important to focus on what is vital and not rest in the byways of eccentricity and quirky irrelevance that make Anglican vicars and parishes such ready subjects for British film directors.

The spiritual can live close to the marginal, but they are not the same. Moreover, the flow of Anglican history is not logical. At times, as in the Reformation and in the Cromwellian era and its aftermath, it is as if a tornado had struck, uprooting trees here, diverting streams there. There are reasons why the new landscape emerged as it did, but there is not always an evident, smooth link with the immediate past. An additional cautionary note: the Anglican ethos should be looked at across its entire history, and not through a single person, decade, or event. Continuity runs through the centuries of Anglican history, with themes modified and restated, such as the ever-changing relationship between church and state, between Catholic and Reformation traditions, between three magnetic fields, generally called "high," "low," and "broad" church, and between the pull of an English past and a global present. Today's issues are usually generated by positions the church took in an earlier period and should be seen in such a context. Otherwise, the result is like studying a single triptych panel or piece of ancient stained glass and attempting to discern the spirit of an age from it.

How should the Anglican ethos be studied? A definition serves only as a point of departure. Anglicanism, a word not used until the 1830s, is about the unique characteristics of the Church of England, which has became a global federation of churches, loosely organized as the Anglican Communion. "Ethos" means the church's fundamental character reflected through its basic institutions, personalities, and movements. I have avoided using Anglican "genius" because that may seem boastful, "tradition," because it appears too overly wedded to the past; and "spirit" because the word is too vague. Although following a chronological order, this is not a volume of church history. Nor is it primarily a study of doctrine or theology, for doctrine in the Anglican tradition is both changing and porous, built on the Nicene and Apostles' Creeds, but even these are differently interpreted. Of course the Anglican tradition has produced excellent theologians, but among its best minds are also sensitive laity or skilled pastors, poets and narrative writers on religion. Anglicanism's most enduring works are characteristically synthetic, gaining inspiration from writers such as Augustine, Aquinas, Luther, Calvin, and many contemporary Continental theologians. Given Anglicanism's historic openness to foreign influences and its proclivity to meld them into its own culture, such a tendency has contributed to the institution's evolution in the way an organism's adaptability to its environment assures its continued growth. Anglican theology is usually situational and pragmatic, created in response to specific crises, rather than being systematic, as in the

German tradition. In this regard, it resembles the English common law tradition building on individual precedents derived from specific cases.

The Anglican ethos begins with a church based on the Bible as its basic source of belief, the Prayer Book as the wellspring of its liturgy, and an individual's faith and reason as the main instruments through which belief is interpreted. At the same time, it is a historic church, emerging from the Catholic tradition, retaining the ancient threefold order of bishops, priests, and deacons. From its traditions, and the complex, diverse issues they represent, it offers a richness to contemporary Christians and a way of looking at life and worship.

BIBLE

"the divine intervention . . . interpreted from several viewpoints"

Anglicans, like most Protestants, read the Bible and reflect and act on what they find there to be the word of God. However, few Anglicans can be called biblical literalists, arguing, as fundamentalists do, that every word in the Bible is infallibly true. Most see the Bible in its historical setting, the subject of many authors over many years, reflecting the divine intervention in history interpreted from several viewpoints. The Bible has been available in English translation from at least the 1530s and was widely circulated and read in homes and churches; for generations it was the basic written account around which people built their understanding of life's larger questions. Anglican sermons have generally been biblically based and for personal devotion many church members study each Sunday's Gospel selection and sometimes the daily cycle of lessons as well. Biblical quotations and images have worked their way into popular culture, and biblical scholarship, translation, and printing remain a prodigious enterprise. Most homes own a Bible, often passed from generation to generation, revered as a family heirloom, listing births, deaths, marriages, and other important events.

REASON

"a box of quicksilver"

Reason also plays a role in forming the Anglican ethos. Reason is not only logical, rational, analytical thought, but emphasizes the individual's rational choice of what to believe and how to interpret belief. Beyond acceptance of a few basic articles of faith, such as contained in the historic creeds, Anglicanism is notoriously short on doctrine. Church doctrine undergoes continual evolution, and Anglicanism never adopted anything like the infallibility of its chief bishop speaking for the whole church, nor the elaborate denominational statements of some Confessional churches, although in its time the Thirty-Nine Articles served as a doctrinal statement. Likewise, there never was an Anglican Calvin or Luther; hence doctrine is not tied to the thought of any founding figure and is diffuse, the work of many hands in many places over several centuries. The use of reason in religious thought is described by Jeremy Taylor (1613–1667): "Scripture, tradition, councils, and fathers, are the evidence in a question, but reason is the judge." Taylor believed that, unlike mathematical or philosophical reason, religious reason resembles "a box of quicksilver"; it "does not consist in a mathematical point: and the heart of reason, that vital and most sensible part . . . is an ambulatory essence, and not fixed."[1]

TRADITION

"Tradition is not wearing your father's hat,
it is in giving birth to a son."

Tradition is important in Anglican decision making; Anglicans look to their denomination's history, recalling important past events and how the church dealt with them, and past crises to see how they were resolved, looking to historic figures, lay and clerical, for inspiration. This is not a dead past, a funereal garden in which antiquarians can forage, but a source of riches and useful precedent for today's decisions. At its best, the living presence of the past provides an inspiration to contemporary searchers, the way the Communion of Saints, the living memory of those who have entered the larger life, can fortify and comfort contemporary Christians. A person or parish can become dangerously mired in the past, taking a roseate view of their denomination's history, or of their parish, as a snug harbor unaffected by change. Once as a student I asked a clergy leader to preach on a Christian perspective on race relations during a particularly troubled period. "I would," he said, "except I have my sermons planned for the rest of the year." In this case, and in others like it, "traditional parish" became a code word to avoid linking gospel to life. A Hasidic saying gives the issue perspective, "Tradition is not wearing your father's hat, it is in giving birth to a son."

Prayer Book
1549, 1552, 1662, 1928, 1979 . . .

The Anglican tradition of worship finds its fullest written expression in the Book of Common Prayer, first disseminated in English in 1549, and in revised form in 1552, by the gifted writer-archbishop, Thomas Cranmer. By placing the same book, in the vernacular language, in the hands of priest and people, the centuries-old gulf between celebrant and congregation was narrowed. This book reflects its era's literary heights and was designed for year-round corporate and individual use, with morning and evening prayer, and a eucharistic rite based on ancient traditions and drawing as well on Continental Protestant and English sources. The liturgical calendar was observed with changing short prayers, collects, and seasonal prefaces to the Eucharist. Psalms, canticles, and biblical readings changed with the liturgical year. Baptism, confirmation, marriage, and burial services covered most of life's seasons, and there was an ordinal as well. The 1662 Prayer Book remains the authorized text in England; the 1979 version is the official text of the Episcopal Church in the United States of America, although supplemental texts are widely used in both countries. Each province of the Anglican Communion has its own Prayer Book, often translated into several languages as well.

While the Prayer Book is the central guide to worship, it is usually accompanied by a hymnal. It would be a misreading of the Anglican ethos to limit it to books, prayers, and creeds, for chanting psalms and singing hymns and anthems, as well as reading hymn texts for meditation, is central to Anglican worship. "Whoever sings prays twice," St. Augustine may have said, and the progression of church music through the centuries is central to Anglican spirituality.

Catholic, Protestant, and English

The Anglican tradition is both Catholic and Protestant, with deep roots in its Celtic past and in Catholicism as it evolved in the British Isles; from this tradition Anglicanism retained a heritage of prayer, liturgy, and scholarship, as well as the historic threefold ministerial order of bishops, priests, and deacons. But the Reformation brought unique contributions as well, some violently introduced. The centralized claims of a pope to be the primary source of church doctrine, not accepted in England until the seventh century, were resolutely rejected by the Church of England in the sixteenth century, although the historic episcopate was retained as a sign of continuity with the church from apostolic times. Instead of waiting passively for doctrine to be handed them, the faithful were encouraged to read and study the Bible and assume personal responsibility for their conduct after prayer to God in fellowship with the church. This twin heritage, Catholic and Protestant, results in a church both sacramental and evangelical, biblical and liturgical, institutional yet prophetic, committed to prayerful worship and social action. What at first appear to be contradictions are complementary polarities, producing, at best, a harmonious, creative whole, and at worst, the friction and disorder church bodies frequently display. Measured, balanced, and tolerant, Anglicanism's ecstatic moments are generally framed in the controlled liturgical setting of the Book of Common Prayer.

THE PROTECTIVE INFLUENCE OF ENGLISH GEOGRAPHY

Geography influenced religion in important ways. The British Isles, separated from yet connected to the European continent gave English institutions a distinctive stamp. The "salt-water girdle" surrounding England left it protected from the sweeping conquests that feature in much European history. (Writers about the church in England compared it to a tranquil isthmus between two turbulent seas.) There was always close contact with the Continent, from which political and religious ideas made their way to England; but usually new ideas came to Britain after they were developed, and cautious, insular Britons took time to examine them, meld them with local traditions, and accept what they found most meaningful. English respect for the past vied with a fierce desire to be free from external authority, and there developed a respect for church, country, and king that served as a buffer against too sharp a break with the past. There is truth in Timothy Finn's observation: "At the core of all small villages of the Anglo-Saxon foundation there is a primal reverence—neither wholly Christian, nor yet quite pagan—for an inseparable blend of God, antiquity, and the king, which is really the true religion of the people."[2] Thus English religious institutions differed from Continental ones, and when the Reformation spread across sixteenth-century Europe, its reception in England was filtered and selective. While many Reformation beliefs were accepted, the church structure remained what it had been for centuries, although by now it was a distinctly national church severed from any connection with Rome.

The Anglican ethos, rooted in multiple sources, is thus the product of a distinct historical evolution, described below, with a chapter for each century from the Middle Ages to contemporary times. Given the multiplicity of sources and richness of information, I have been selective, but the bibliography suggests other avenues readers with special interests might pursue. Spelling and punctuation have been modernized as appropriate, and readings shortened as the length of sermons has shrunk from over an hour to under twenty minutes.

TWO PERSONAL CONCLUSIONS
We have a violent past, but one filled with beauty.

As I studied the Anglican past, two conclusions recurred: how violent is our religious heritage, despite its emphasis on balance and moderation, and how enduring are its contributions to literature, liturgy, the fine arts, and the spiritual journey. Conflict and disagreement can be destructive, but can also be sources of creativity—some of the church's most perceptive spiritual writings emerged from the violence-wracked seventeenth century through figures such as Lancelot Andrewes and Jeremy Taylor, able to reconcile the disparate strains of an age.

To be sure, mechanisms were in place for conciliation, reconciliation, and the irenic resolution of disputes, and a polity as porous as ours must seek consensus and accommodation or come unglued. The church has held together despite acrimonious differences, the most obvious being the American Episcopal Church during the Civil War. Still, book and sword interact closely for most of Anglican history. Religious controversy and disputes were often white-hot, leading to bitter conflict and spilt blood. Compromise and conciliation are not frequent features of religious discourse, even now. Books and martyrs were burned, churches pulled down, monasteries destroyed, heretics expelled, and dissenters scoffed at—the internal conflicts endure, albeit in verbal rather than physical form. Externally, news reports describe church burnings in northern Nigeria and the flogging of an Anglican bishop in Sudan. The letters-to-the-editor pages of *The Living Church* or *Church Times* are not always sources of civil discourse on disputatious issues.

Conversely, many of the most enduring contributions to the Anglican ethos are the work of poets, mystics, and proponents of the spiritual life, inviting others to share in personal experiences within a community of believers. Churches of the Anglican tradition are thus not comfortable places for those who seek crystal clear doctrine and black-and-white statements of belief on each issue. Those whose primary interest is in doctrine, refined by the paring knives of moral theology and canon law, will find the Anglican Church an uncomfortable home. Doctrine in the Church of England emanates from scripture and the creeds, but beyond basic doctrinal statements, there are numerous possibilities for refinement and personal interpretation and experience. The beauty of church architecture and music, the poetry of the Book of Common Prayer, the delicacy of much Anglican spiritual writing, sermons, essays, plays, and poems, the power of the various biblical translations in English, all shape the Anglican ethos. It contains an essentially poetic consciousness, episodic and impressionistic, lacking, for instance, the heavy doctrinal overlay of much Lutheran thought or the sharply honed legalism of some Calvinist traditions.

Finally, the Anglican middle way does not stand as "an invisible equatorial line between Romanism and Protestantism": it is more a union of opposites than a balance of opinions, Anglicanism's greatest nineteenth-century voice reminds us. F. D. Maurice, preaching at Lincoln's Inn, said it would be a dying church if it became a church reducing its message to the least common denominator among factions, or became locked in conflict among its warring parties. He urged the church to avoid:

> that tone of speaking dangerous and disgraceful . . . which appears to indicate that our condition is most safe when we can keep the elements of which our body politic consists, the Protestant and the Catholic, feeble, each balancing and counteracting the other; whereas in very deed we need them both in their fullest vitality, in their utmost concentration, that we may accomplish the tasks which have been committed to us, that we many not utterly lose what we have inherited.[3]

At a time when many persons understandably find fulfillment by widening their vision to the offerings of comparative religions, my desire was to head the other way and probe more deeply into Anglican history and the resultant ethos, which remained a partly undiscovered country I wanted to revisit. Like precious metal deposits mined the first time through with an older technology, there are hidden treasures found in revisiting Hooker and Andrewes, Gore and Maurice, and many similar

figures. Sunday sermons and courses allow only a glimpse of individual
issues and periods, and the world around them is often left like a bulletin
board with snapshots of Henry VIII as a villain and Elizabeth as a hero-
ine, the eighteenth century as decadent, the nineteenth century as sentimental, and the twentieth century as a lost age. Stepping through the
looking glass into the Anglican past will not lead to a crepuscular mon-
tage of dead clerics, institutions, and ideas preserved under glass and left
on a darkened parlor table—what a nineteenth-century American cleric,
William Reed Huntington, called "a flutter of surplices, a vision of village
spires and cathedral towers, a somewhat stiff and stately company of
deans, prebendaries and choristers." Quite the opposite, Anglicanism has
produced more than its share of martyrs, musicians, holy women and
men who endured with faith and works of mercy and justice through trying times. Such a study leads to a resurrection dawn, opening contemporary persons to the pull of the future, drawing them toward that eternal
Pentecost where the Spirit dwells, where warring religious bodies bend
their swords into plowshares.

1

From Earliest Times to the Middle Ages

It behoved that there should be sin; but all shall be well, and all shall be well, and all manner of things shall be well.
—*Julian of Norwich, English mystic (c. 1373)*

C ELTICS VERSUS ROMANS to the modern ear might suggest a basketball game, but this was a different sort of rivalry, a grudging clash between rivals that extended over centuries. In the end, the Romans won, the Celts capitulated, scattered, or went underground, preserving their stories, prayers, and rimes, which emerged a thousand years later in recognizable form. The encounter is played out in clashes of organizational bureaucrats versus mystics, those who habitually sucked power to themselves versus those for whom the religious quest was a more solitary journey. Although the contest began in the earliest centuries of the last millennium, its ramifications are with us still.

Christianity first came to Britain in two waves, one Celtic, one Roman. By the third century a scattered Christian presence was established through Celtic migrations in Wales, Ireland, and Scotland. Christians were among the Roman colonists as well, and by the fifth century, as Rome's political-military empire waned, scattered Christian communities remained where the Romans had been. The arrival of Augustine, the pope's representative, in A.D. 597, strengthened Rome's position. As the Romans moved outward from settled communities, they encountered representatives of earlier Celtic Christianity; the two distinct strains of Christian practice competed until the Synod of Whitby in 644, and their rivalry was formative to the Christian presence in Britain.

11

No separate Celtic church ever existed, and the Celtic–Roman rivalry was conducted within the arena of the one, holy, Catholic church, which made it all the more intense, as is true with most family feuds. The Celtic influences on church life we experience today may not be the ones that actually existed in the Middle Ages, but the residual strains show amazing continuities. Compare, for instance, these two journey prayers, one tenth-century, later Middle Irish, the second collected in rural Scotland in the early twentieth century:

> May this journey be easy, may it be a journey of profit in my hands!
> Holy Christ, against demons, against weapons, against killings!
> May Jesus and the Father, may the Holy Spirit sanctify us!
> May the mysterious God be not hidden in darkness, may the bright King
>   save us!
> May the cross of Christ's body and Mary guard us on the road!
> May it not be unlucky for us, may it be successful and easy![1]

The second example, also a hymn for a traveler, comes from a remarkable work, the *Carmina Gadelica,* by Alexander Carmichael, a Scottish revenue agent and collector of the folklore of the rural people of Scotland during the 1920s. The hymn was sung by the traveler, who might be accompanied by family and friends for part of a journey from which the prospect of return was risky:

> Life be in my speech,
> Sense in what I say,
> The bloom of cherries on my lips,
> Till I come back again.
>
> The love Christ Jesus gave
> Be filling every heart for me,
> The love Christ Jesus gave
> Filling me for every one.
>
> Traversing corries, traversing forests,
> Traversing valleys long and wild.
> The fair white Mary still uphold me,
> The Shepherd Jesu be my shield,
> The fair white Mary still uphold me,
> The Shepherd Jesu be my shield.[2]

The Celtic tradition, rich in prayer life and centered in large and small monasteries, was most visible among peoples on the margins of the empire, such as the Irish, Welsh, and Highland Scots. Celtic Christianity flourished from the fourth century for several hundred years, then lay dormant in isolated pockets of Great Britain until enjoying a recrudescence in modern times. Its attractive features included a closeness to nature and God, and a rich poetic side, with music, manuscript illumination, and carved stone crosses and metal objects containing filigreed, intertwining lines reflecting the interrelatedness of all creation. Celtic spirals, knots, and geometric designs have neither beginnings nor endings, as God is the Alpha and Omega and all creation is linked with its creator. Such forms had power as well to ward off the devil and all demonic forces. The prototype of the early Celtic monk as a craggy-faced, red-bearded, harp-carrying bard is only partially correct. Less attractive in Celtic belief was its emphasis on a starkly ascetical life and on endless rounds of penance. Fasting, constant deprivation of worldly attractions, and a morbid fixation on sin vied with a hope of the resurrection. Celts, like most Christians of that era, were biblical literalists, and the movement, despite its poetic richness, failed to produce a theologian of note. Governance was through a loose network of monasteries resembling tribal organizations ruled by abbots. Bishops were often part of monastic establishments but had no administrative powers or territorial responsibilities. Government by dioceses and parishes came later with Rome and was more congenial to urban settings than to the Celtic church's scattered rural congregations.

John T. McNeill, a historian of the Celtic period, writes:

> We are not familiar with men who choose to subsist on one meal a day, who sleep on hard floors with their heads on pillows of stone, who spend many hours of the day and night singing psalms and hymns, and yet with unfailing energy exercise creative leadership, changing society in which they move and schooling barbarous people. Few of these strange characters can be thought of as men of genius; rather they were remarkable for moral stature and rectitude.[3]

Such Celtic asceticism is depicted in "All Alone in My Little Cell" (Old Irish, eighth or ninth century):

> All alone in my little cell, without the company of a single person;
> Precious has been the pilgrimage before going to meet death.
> . . . .
> Sanctifying the body by good habits, trampling like a man upon it:
> With weak and tearful eyes for the forgiveness of my passions.
> . . . .
> A cold and anxious bed, like the lying down of a doomed man:

A brief, apprehensive sleep; invocations frequent and early.
. . . .
All alone in my little cell, all alone thus; alone I came into the world,
Alone I shall go from it.[4]

It is difficult to establish many hard facts about Celtic Christianity, and Celtic life is garlanded with charming legends and anecdotes, added to with their retelling over centuries. Such folklore, which includes many of the feats attributed to Patrick or Columba, has a spirituality of its own, making it valuable in creating a total picture of Celtic life. Religious belief is vulnerable to the historian's scrutiny, unless the subject matter is taken on its own terms, that of the faith community illustrating its deepest aspirations through myth and legend. There is a difference between traditional "hard" history—chronologies, facts, documents, and precise conclusions—and "softer" history, the folk beliefs, myths, and legends people believe and how they interpret such beliefs. Attention to both sorts of historical interpretation is needed to understand the religious ethos of a people. For example, the following account will be considered apocryphal by some, yet it vividly illustrates the point that St. Brigid, a major figure of the late-fifth- or early-sixth-century Celtic tradition, could invoke divine power over the elements:

> Once a solitary wild boar which was being hunted ran out from the woods, and in its headlong flight was brought suddenly into the herd of pigs that belonged to the most blessed Brigid. She noticed its arrival among her pigs and she blessed it. Thereupon it lost its fear and settled down among the herd. See how brute beasts and animals could oppose neither her bidding nor her wish, but served her timely and humbly.[5]

The Celtic tradition is alive today and enjoying a global revival. Go to the music section of any large book and record emporium. There, along with Jazz, Country and Western, and Classics, will be a large bin marked "Celtic"—with bards, singers, harpists, and players of ancient instruments singing of lost love, lost battles, wars, windy nights, bonfires on the hills and, interlarded with the romance and mystery, some of the religious songs that have survived centuries. Celtic spirituality has also been a source of growing interest among contemporary Christians, as suggested in the writings of A. M. Allchin and Ester De Waal. Despite the obstacles, Celtic spirituality survives—because it so deeply infuses every aspect of life. For example, consider this prayer about the most fundamental of all human actions for centuries, covering the fire at night. Should the fire go out, the family could freeze, be without food, and require a trip to a distant neighbor, island, or village for live embers to rekindle it. Each evening the peat fire was ritually smothered for the night. In this prayer, embers were formed in a circle and peat laid down in three sections, one each for the God of Life, the God of Peace, and the God of Grace, after which the circle was covered with enough ashes to smother but not extinguish the fire. When this smooring operation, as it was called, was complete, a blessing was intoned by the family member completing the operation:

> The sacred three
> To save,
> To shield,
> To surround,
> The hearth,
> The house,
> The household,
> This eve,
> This night,
> And every night,
> Each single night. *Amen.*[6]

PATRICK AND COLUMBA

The Celtic tradition, characterized by tireless missionaries moving as far as ships or roads would take them, was exemplified by St. Patrick (c. 390– c. 461), the son of a well-placed Roman administrator in northwest Britain. As a youth Patrick was kidnapped by Irish slave raiders, who sold him as a shepherd in Ireland. After escaping, Patrick went back to England and became a Christian monk and bishop. Later he returned to Ireland, and in a thirty-year period, created monasteries, preached to local chieftains, carved crosses over pagan symbols, and converted important local high kings to Christianity. As was the custom, if a king converted, the tribe followed, adding to the number of new Christians. Patrick baptized thousands of converts, ordained many clergy, and created a diocese at Armagh, from which he ruled and based his missionary journeys.

Equally important was the work of a figure of the next century, St. Columba (c. 521–597). Columba, whose temper ignited easily, left Ireland around 563 after an armed dispute over ownership of a manuscript in which many persons were killed; he spent over thirty years on the island of Iona off Scotland's west coast. Iona has long been considered "holy ground" for Christians, beginning during Columba's day and continuing to the present; its rebuilt abbey is visited by thousands of pilgrims each year. Columba both built a thriving monastic community and traveled widely in Scotland and the distant Hebrides, where, with a "voice of thunder," he challenged pagan peoples led by druids, non-Christian regional leaders who presided at religious sacrifices, divining the will of local nature gods. Columba confronted them with the cry, "Christ is my druid," and established a strong Christian presence among indigenous populations. The emotional Columba was described as "a typical Irishman, vehement, irresistible: hear him curse a niggardly rich man or bless the heifers of a poor peasant; see him follow a robber who has plundered a friend, cursing the wretch to his destruction, following him to the water's edge, wading up to the knees in the clear, green sea-water, with both hands raised to heaven."[7] Patrick and Columba and their followers were part of a scattered, vibrant indigenous Christian community. In Wales the isolated church was kept alive by figures like the Celtic abbot-bishop St. David (c. 520–588), who founded several monasteries and organized local clergy synods. These scattered churches, however, soon came into conflict with Rome, when Pope Gregory the Great, alarmed at the spread of barbarism and paganism, sent missionaries to England.

THE ROMAN PRESENCE

As Roman legions withdrew, the Roman church's presence in Britain solidified in 597 with the arrival of Gregory's envoy, Augustine of Canterbury, and expanded until ninth-century Viking invasions devastated the land. Augustine spent seven years in Britain, dying in 604. He appears to have been a competent, colorless administrator, who carried out his organizational mandate successfully, rather than being driven by the inner fire of a Columba. Augustine's monks made many conversions, but friction soon developed between the newcomers and the scattered local bishops who had kept the Christian faith alive, and who were now expected to submit to the newly arrived papal envoy's authority.

If the dispute was primarily over where authority lay, a classic power struggle, its surface manifestations were quarrels over liturgy and the correct date of Easter, greatest of the Christian feasts. (If the date was not agreed upon, some members of a family might be in the midst of a Lenten fast while others held their Easter meal.) It was not an idle dispute; the Celts had put their best mathematical and exegetical minds to calculating the date of Easter. And their calculations were no less accurate, they believed, than Roman ones. The larger question was alignment with the universal church and the powerful political presence behind it, or support of scattered local churches. Loosely organized, small in numbers, and widely scattered, the disparate Celtic churches were less-than-equal adversaries to the centrally organized, hierarchical Roman church.

The dispute came to a head in 664 when a synod was convened at Whitby. Oswy, the shrewd but illiterate king of Northumbria, ruled in favor of the Roman position instead of the Celtic one, saying he preferred to be in the favorable graces of the Keeper of Heaven's Gate than with St. Columba. Oswy covered his bets. His siding with the stronger Roman forces brought British Christianity into active alliance with mainstream Roman Catholicism, but left the vital strain of Celtic Christianity without institutional support, although it continued to exist on the margins of empire. The Synod of Whitby thus solidified the church–state alliance for several centuries. Once a Roman-led ecclesiastical organization was established throughout the country, it became a force for political unity by supporting royal government in alliance with the pope, making inseparable the union of church and state. At least for now.

"FROM THE FURY OF THE NORTHMEN, O LORD DELIVER US"

The century following the Synod of Whitby was a brief golden age of English religious culture, snuffed out by ninth-century Viking invasions. In the north, a Celtic monk-bishop, Aidan (d. 651), founded a center with monks from Iona at Lindisfarne, a rocky Northumbrian promontory from which Christianity spread to much of northeastern England. Elaborately carved stone crosses dotted England's north and monks produced magnificent illuminated manuscripts, like the Lindisfarne Gospels. The work of narrative secular bards was adopted by religious artists, such as Caedmon (d. c. 680), a monk from Whitby who turned a traditional hero's tale into a religious saga based on the biblical books of Exodus and Daniel. Later Cynewulf, a ninth-century poet, and other writers produced similar works, such as the *Dream of the Rood*, where the tree on which Christ was crucified recounts the event:

They swung me up on their shoulders, planted me into a hill,
Set me deep and straight. I saw the Lord of the world
Boldly rushing to climb upon me
And I could neither bend, nor break
The word of God. I saw the ground
Trembling. I could have crushed them all,
And yet I kept myself erect.[8]

With Viking raids on Lindisfarne in 793 began three centuries of Scandinavian conquest, pillages, slave raids, and the burning of monasteries and churches. The sea-roads, once used to speed missionaries about the English coast, became a dreaded place as sentinels watched for long-prowed Viking ships and raiders. To litanies was added the prayer, "From the fury of the northmen, O Lord, deliver us."

Initially, the Vikings were hit-and-run artists, sweeping along the English coast in small, swift wooden boats that could quickly slide up onto a beach or probe deeply into an inland waterway to surprise a village at work or a monastery at prayer. With names such as Ivar the Boneless, Bjorn Cripplehand, Halfdane, Inguar, Hubba, and Baeseg, the Vikings were Black September, Patet Lao, and Shining Path guerrillas rolled into one. Raiders and conquerors, they sought slaves and treasure. Loading their craft with sacred vessels, the illiterate Norsemen ripped illuminated manuscripts from their precious metal covers, burned libraries, and carted off as many chalices and sacred objects as their craft could hold. The plunder was there for the taking from vulnerable English and Irish churches built at the water's edge:

A hundred churches lapped by the wave, that is the number of . . . churches on the sea-coast. Or indeed, a hundred churches with perfect abundance. Mass-chalices in every church.[9]

We have only glimpses of their impact, but such accounts as survive are like glimpses into Dante's *Inferno,* as in this description of the destruction of Lindisfarne:

On the seventh of the ides of June, they reached the church of Lindisfarne, and there they miserably ravaged and pillaged everything; they trod the holy things under their polluted feet, they dug down the altar, and plundered all the treasures of the church. Some of the brethren they slew, some they carried off with them in chains, the greater number they stripped naked, insulted, and cast out of doors, and some they drowned in the sea.[10]

The Viking raids' impact has been called "an attack on both the body and soul of Christian England." Libraries, such as the extensive manuscript collection at York, were burned; shrines were destroyed, such as that of the venerated St. Cuthbert, who built Lindisfarne. The raiders, who came "like stinging hornets" or "fierce wolves," both prevented the English monks from expanding their activity and further struck fear for generations into the ordered life of the church and its members. Weakened by decades of raids and plunder, communities diminished in numbers and came apart. Discipline atrophied, and the peaceful ordering of their days became a memory of the past. The once tranquil sea-lanes, the "deep peace of running wave" of the bards along which missionaries sped or monks traveled freely, became dreaded lieus in which raiders might appear at any moment. An isolated monk in a monastery at the sea's edge reflected the spirit of the times:

> Bitter is the wind tonight;
> it tosses the white locks of the ocean;
> I fear not the coursing of a clear sea
> by the fierce warriors of the lochlann [Scandinavians—*ed.*].[11]

MONASTIC CHRISTIANITY

English religious life centered in various monasteries scattered about the country, although the monasteries would eventually decline in numbers and influence. Possibly there were thirty houses for men and six for women by the year 1000, all following the Benedictine rule. By 1066 more than fifty new monasteries were built.[12] Benedictines, modeled on the example of the great French monastery at Cluny, held sway until the twelfth century, after which a new and final wave of religious orders, mainly Cistercian monks and Dominican and Franciscan friars gained wide acceptance. An austere, purified version of the Benedictine rule was adopted by the Cistercians, who settled in desolate places and lived simplified lives. Dominicans were preachers and intellectuals; Franciscan friars lived and worked among the poor. At a time when the older, more established houses were large, complacent, and treasure-ridden, these new orders grew in numbers and influence, especially in centers like Oxford. By the fourteenth century the monastic clergy may have numbered seventeen thousand adherents in nine hundred houses.[13] Monks

and nuns took vows of poverty, chastity, and obedience to church superiors. A daily round of prayer and work was central to monastic life; occupants prayed together seven times throughout the day and night. As
centers of culture and learning, the monastic establishments enjoyed the
patronage of kings and rich bishops. Rich patrons, often in return for a
perpetual round of prayers for the dead or to win divine favor, bequeathed
large gifts of property and riches to the monastic establishments.

Originally the new orders came as strangers, lacking patrons and often
food and shelter. Enthusiasm and energetic preaching won them followers. Moving among the people, they performed good works, such as ministering to the sick, and gave lively sermons to combat heresy, convert the
unchurched, and arouse the spiritually sluggish. By the thirteenth century, the new clergy generation, enduring hardships, cheerful in countenance, and spiritual in demeanor, revived religious interest beyond what
had been seen in recent times. Path-breakers, however, soon became
sedentary establishment figures, and former prophets and preachers
evolved into administrators, collecting rents and fees. Spiritual disciplines
slackened, and monastic establishments became big businesses by the
standards of an earlier age, adding servants, farms, lands, and parish
churches under the monastery's control. Poorly managed and profligate,
most of the monasteries were in debt. They built when they should have
consolidated resources and continued extravagant lifestyles long after
their means were gone. Demands for hospitality, especially for passing
royal parties, were constant, and monks faced taxes, forced loans to the
crown, and bad harvests. Sheep were raised, and wool and farm products
sold for profit; monasteries became major economic influences in their
neighborhoods. The Benedictine abbey at Bury St. Edmunds once
owned 170 manors; the Cistercians at Fountains Abbey accumulated land
in 151 different parishes. While many monastic establishments declined,
the abbot's household at Bury St. Edmunds devoured six carcasses of
beef in one order for supplies, plus fifteen pigs, thirty-one geese, and 155
fowls. At Winchcombe the cook was ordered to serve each monk four
fried eggs at supper-time; at Newstead each canon was offered three eggs
or three herrings. Beer consumption was "on an heroic scale," and the
canons of Bolton put down 1,764 gallons of wine in a year.[14] A lot of
wine, but English water was mostly undrinkable.

Half of England's parishes were under monastic control by the mid-
thirteenth century, as landed patrons on whose property they were situated willed them to the monasteries.[15] Rivalries flared between orders and

between monks and the poorly paid secular clergy over such issues as funeral fees. By 1300 a system of licenses was introduced to control where and when friars could preach and to divide funeral fees with the poorly paid parish clergy. By the late Middle Ages, the waves of monastic settlements had spent their force in England; their greatest contributions had come earlier, and the large, moribund establishments were resented by secular clergy and laity.

THE PARISH

After the monasteries came parishes. There were possibly as many as forty thousand parish clergy in the thirteenth century, and most lived like serfs, often in small huts of wood and clay. They were usually poorly educated, although they were free and able to own land.

> [W]ithout stopping to think too deeply of why they were there or what was the real object of their work, they carried on according to the traditions they had inherited and were generally accepted by the people . . . . for the most part they gave the people what they needed and kept alive the rich heritage which later generations of churchmen have enjoyed.[16]

A small number of clergy who were born to rich households managed multiple parishes as sources of income.

Local parishes were usually controlled by local lords, who picked the clergy for them or turned them over to monasteries for management. Ecclesiastical appointments were sources of revenue for incumbents. Plural appointments increased revenues, one of the few ways of raising pitifully low salaries. However, multiple positions and nonresidence soon led to abuses that were rampant until the nineteenth century. Ten pounds a year was a standard salary for many parish clergy, but monasteries controlled the appointments and collected several times that sum from the landowner. While having work obligations and being under the local lord's jurisdiction, the parish clergy's only community obligation was generally to keep the bull and boar that serviced the parishioners' beasts. Clergy could harvest the glebe, the choice land reserved for the church, and claim the tithe, a tenth of the produce of a parishioner's land or beasts. Clerical tithes also included a tenth of all wages and produce, including milk, eggs, wax, and honey. Additionally, the priest could claim the second-best animal of anyone dying within the parish bounds, should that person's church payments be in arrears. Ecclesiastical authorities were as thorough and cunning in devising ways to collect their dues as parishioners were in avoiding them. Most clergy were married and parishes often passed from father to son. It was not until the late thirteenth century when, prodded by papal directive, married clergy gave way to celibate priests, but concubines remained common for some well-placed prelates. Many of the churches were dark and damp, for there was no central heating, no office space, toilets, or meeting rooms—all that came later if it came at all. *Humphrey Clinker,* written in a later century, described the setting:

> When we consider our ancient churches . . . may we not term them so many magazines of rheums [colds—*ed.*], created for the benefit of the medical faculty? And may we not safely aver that, in the winter especially (which in England may be said to engross eight months in the year), more bodies are lost than souls saved, by going to church?[17]

Villages were small, roads poor or nonexistent. Possibly a parish at this time covered four thousand acres, spread over farms and hamlets, with numerous chapels-of-ease. Peasants might spend lives within the ambit of a few hills and vales. Looming above any village would be the church, with its tower pointed skyward, to a world beyond the present. Sunday morning mass was widely attended, other services less so. People wandered about the church, as there were no seats, until bells called attention to the service's supreme moment, the consecration of the host. Communions were once a year, at Easter, and with bread only, wine being reserved for the priest. Preaching was rare until later in the Middle Ages, although some basic instruction was provided by the clergy, who were often uneducated themselves. Drama was used for instruction and entertainment; nativity scenes were widespread and easy to produce. Passion plays and resurrection dramas became increasingly popular and led to more elaborate pageants performed outdoors or in guildhalls. Some plays covered the drama of salvation, with characters such as Everyman, angels and devils, and by the fifteenth century comic or musical interludes were added. Equally popular were the widespread devotional books appealing to a gradually better-educated laity. A much-circulated work was Robert Manning's *Handlynge Synne* (1303), a long compendium of moral tales in poetic form with arresting titles such as "The Story of the Adulterous Wife Whose Skeleton Split in Two" and "The Sacrilegious Carolers Made to Dance Together for a Whole Year."[18]

THE WORLDVIEW OF A DISTANT TIME

The universe could be a frightening place if you thought much about it. The religious world of English women and men was not one of high scholarship, but a world in which devils and evil spirits lurked by night, saints and angels spoke to people, and the religious and secular, time and eternity were one. It requires a willing suspension of disbelief for a modern reader to enter such a world, and while it did not exist for all people over the millennium, it was the dominant worldview for many, echoed in the art, poetry, and theology of the English Middle Ages. Nowhere was this worldview more evident than in numerous wall paintings existing from Saxon times and, by the late Middle Ages, covering the walls, roofs, and chancels of many British churches. Lives of saints and biblical tales in vivid pigments predominated, often centered on Doomsday scenes, stark depictions of the Last Judgment with sinners in the hands of a stern God hauled off to hellfire and the saved led upward by angels. Such art illustrates an important aspect of early English spirituality, mirroring a religion whose most lasting insights were frequently expressed through the arts, more so than in doctrine. This side of English spirituality is demonstrated in many hymns and poems, including numerous examples from the Old English, such as "The Seafarer," "The Wanderer," and the "Twelve Advent Lyrics." There is both beauty and fatalism in such works, and the redemptive message does not come easily. Cheap grace is unknown to these early Christians. In "The Seafarer" the narrator's world is one where:

> Storms beat on the rocky cliffs and were echoed
> By icy-feathered terns and the eagle's screams;
> No kinsman could offer comfort there,
> To the soul left drowning in desolation.
> No man has ever faced the dawn
> Certain which of Fate's three threats
> Would fall: illness, or age, or an enemy's
> Sword, snatching the life from his soul.

> Fate is stronger
> And God mightier than any man's mind.
> Our thoughts should turn to where our home is,
> Consider the ways of coming there,
> Then strive for sure permission for us

To rise to that eternal joy,
That life born in the love of God
And the hope of Heaven.[19]

Typical of popular religious sentiment was William Langland's (c. 1332–c. 1400) "Piers Plowman," a long narrative poem that presents contemporary life through the eyes of a simple but virtuous plowman. Langland belonged to the clerical proletariat and, while eking out a modest living for self and family, keenly observed the lives of the urban and rural poor around him. The work's melancholy and discontent contrast with the more buoyant spirit of Chaucer's *Canterbury Tales*, another late-fourteenth-century composition. Langland presages criticisms that will come a century later with the Reformation. He is sharply critical of clergy corruption, injustice, the excesses of the rich, and the bitter round of the poor. Sloth was personified as a country parson who spent thirty years in a parish, never learned to read, but was skilled at hunting. The parade of low-life religious included money-grubbing monks, "Hermits, a heap of them, with hooked staves . . . were going to Walsingham, and their wenches too," and parish priests who keep the silver given for the poor. In "Piers Plowman" the king is asked to settle a dispute between Peace and Wrong. Reason says no pity should be extended to Wrong until "clerks and knights are courteous, and priests practice what they preach, till the custom of pilgrimages and of carrying money out of the land ceases," criticisms kings raised as well.

THE CATHEDRALS

No study of the Anglican ethos can ignore the architectural genius of the cathedral builders, who scattered across the landscape nearly twenty of the country's largest buildings. Imagine the effect, in an age with fewer people and no railroads or paved roads, of a voyager coming slowly upon the profile of the Salisbury or Durham cathedral looming above, yet part of their natural settings, equally connected with earth and sky. Most of these buildings were in place before the Reformation, with styles ranging from the strong, solid Norman to the lighter Gothic, and with numerous combinations of both. The cathedrals remained Britain's largest and most imposing buildings for centuries, until new technologies using structural steel and glass windows in the nineteenth century allowed for larger buildings, like the Crystal Palace. It is a tribute to the unknown architects and builders that these massive structures have endured. Fires swept through wooden parts; stone towers, pushing the latest technology too far, collapsed. Lightning hit lead roofs, melting them. One contemporary account of such a disaster at Canterbury Cathedral recalled:

> The grief and distress of the sons of the church were so great that no one can conceive, relate, or write them; but to relieve their miseries, they fixed the altar, such as it was, in the nave of the church, where they howled, rather than sang, matins and vespers.[20]

Monuments of the human spirit, cathedrals were a sublime expression of religious belief, funded often by wealthy merchants or nobility eager to assure safe passage from this world to the next. While cathedrals took centuries to build and pushed known technology to its limits, they also showed the range of religious expression through the grace of Lady chapels, the power of rood screens, the mystery of rose windows filled with the setting sun, the expanse of towers holding fog-enshrouded bells, biblical lessons and saints' lives starkly depicted on painted walls or, more subtly, through stained glass windows, carved friezes, and statues. Inside there were ceaseless rounds of prayer, processions, sung anthems, and chanted psalms in choirs before the high altar, or in side chapels commemorating different saints or members of the Holy Family. W. H. Auden described them:

> Cathedrals,
> Luxury liners laden with souls,
> Holding to the East their hulls of stone.[21]

The story of their governance, the rivalries between bishops and abbots, does not concern us here, nor does the shifting of architectural styles, nor the near destruction of many works of art at the hands of zealous Puritans. What endures, in Canterbury, Durham, York, Lincoln, and Salisbury is a living monument, frozen in stone, glass, metal, and wood, yet immediately accessible to prayerful and poetic spirits today as to peasants nearly a millennium ago. The cathedral was the visible counterpart of the episcopacy, the seat of the bishop, where ordinations and other important services in the diocese's life took place in addition to liturgical services built around the Christmas and Easter seasons. Given the resources of a choir school, it was possible to provide high standards of religious music for the nearby community. A Dean and Chapter could also offer a ministry of depth and variety unavailable in a small parish church, preserving the daily round of services, maintaining a library, and illuminating Psalters, Bibles, and missals.

The spirit of the age is reflected in the art of these early cathedrals. It was a world where "dragons were in the air," carved representations of angels vied with grotesque figures, "the snapping jaws are never far behind their heels." An art historian has written:

> [F]rail, naked humanity is for ever caught in the coils. They are the images of an eye hardened to unalleviated pain, to the wearing pangs of undiagnosed disease and its no less agonizing attempted cures, to wounds and blows, to the arrow that flieth by day and the pestilence that walketh in darkness.[22]

THE RIVALRY OF POPES AND KINGS

The conflict was over power. Rivalry between Rome and England was a constant in English church history from the Middle Ages to the Reformation, principally competition between popes and monarchs over a centralized church under Roman control or a national church ruled by the monarch. Illustrative of church–state conflict was the competition between Henry II (1133–1189) and Archbishop Thomas Becket (c. 1118–1170), whose prolonged disputes extended from 1162 until Becket's martyrdom in 1170. Henry, a humane, popular, and reform-minded monarch with a keen eye for details of running a kingdom, sought to establish order in the realm after a turbulent civil war and to introduce a modern legal system, which included trial by jury and common law replacing Roman law.

A stumbling block was the long-established provision for "Benefit of Clergy," allowing any person in religious orders to be tried by an ecclesiastical rather than a civil court for most charges. The system was subject to widespread abuse. Far more lenient than regular courts, ecclesiastical courts attracted miscreants, many claiming to be religious "clerks." Proof of their status was wearing a tonsure, a distinct clerical haircut, sometimes freshly obtained shortly before trial. Find someone with a pair of shears, get a new haircut, and your case was tried before a church rather than a civil court, with the prospect of a much lighter sentence. Litigants unhappy with the outcome of cases in England could appeal to Rome, further reducing the English courts' power. Clergy found guilty of blood crimes, like homicide, could only be punished with fines and short prison terms.

Henry, anxious to keep control at home, allowed appeals to Rome only with royal approval and prohibited clergy from leaving the country for trial. The church responded that the issue was not a question of legal jurisdiction but of basic authority. Who would predominate, church or state? A power struggle was brewing. If Henry was a calculating, self-confidant ruler, Becket, his chancellor, confidant, and drinking companion for eight years, was his match in brains and ego, causing the king to remark, "England is not a bush that can hold two such robins as the archbishop and myself." Originally Henry hoped Becket would retain the chancellorship as well, but the prosperous London merchant's son threw himself into his new charge diligently. Becket as archbishop was transformed into as ascetical, devout church leader. Matters came to a head in 1164 at a great council convoked at Clarendon. Henry proposed a compromise: clergy should be tried in ecclesiastical courts but, if found guilty, should be turned over to the king's justices for punishment. At the same time, the king held his ground: appeals to Rome were only allowed with royal consent, and election of bishops would originate in England, not Rome. As a ploy, Becket acceded to Henry, but then asked the pope to issue a dispensation releasing him from observing any of Henry's decrees conflicting with church law or custom. The king was furious; Becket fled to France and stayed six years. Negotiations continued intermittently, until Becket returned in 1170. Soon, however, he excommunicated several bishops who had sided with the king in the prolonged disputes. Henry was angry that once more his carefully brokered arrangement had been undercut by the strong-willed and crafty Becket. The king used ill-tempered words in the presence of some eager courtiers, asking: Why were there those who live off the royal bounty but will not avenge the king of this irksome priest?

Four of the king's overly zealous knights murdered the archbishop in a Canterbury Cathedral chapel. Becket's death sent shock waves throughout the country, and he became a renowned saint and martyr. Claiming the death of Becket was never his intention, Henry moved quickly to distance himself from the crime and sent a delegation to Rome to assure the pontiff of his innocence, but the damage was done. Far from tightening control over ecclesiastical courts, Henry watched as the numbers of cases transferred to Rome increased. Efforts to limit papal jurisdiction in English legal and ecclesiastical life were shelved until later centuries.

THE POLITICAL THEORY OF A RELIGIOUS EMPIRE

John of Salisbury tried to put it all together. The complex interplay between church and state is demonstrated in the writings of this close adviser of Becket. John of Salisbury (c. 1115–1180) was England's most distinguished theological mind of the twelfth century. John had studied law and literature in Paris and Chartres, where he eventually became bishop. Adviser to both Becket and the English pope Hadrian II, he sought a modus vivendi between church and state. In *Policraticus*, generally translated as *The Statesman's Handbook*, he portrayed the ideal state, where religious and temporal powers live in harmony because the king is God's agent, and from the divine monarch civil order flows. The work was in the vein of Machiavelli's *Prince*, written much later, or Castiglione's *Book of the Courtier*, works of theory and instruction for leaders. While Machiavelli's work was totally amoral, John's was a Christian document, expounding the theory of the divine right of monarchs and their necessary ties to the pope. It was not a revolutionary tract in any sense, but an articulate defense of the status quo. The body politic can be compared to a human body: the head equals the prince, the heart the senate, the hands the soldiers, etc. "The prince is the public power, and a kind of likeness on earth of the divine majesty," John wrote, arguing that the divine power of kings is conveyed through the intermediary of the church, which has no sword of its own, "but she uses it by the hand of the prince, upon whom she confers the power of bodily coercion, retaining to herself authority over spiritual things in the person of the pontiffs." Centuries later Henry VIII expounded a related theory, calling himself "the only supreme head in earth of the Church of England" (1534), arguing that this role belongs with a national monarch and not the pope in Rome. Throughout its history, the British monarch has remained titular head of the Church of England, although this role became increasingly ceremonial in later centuries.

THE NEW STATES ISSUE, A HEIGHTENED CONFLICT

England's conflict with the pope intensified during the Hundred Years' War, 1337–1453. The war was fought primarily against France, and since the popes were also French during much of this time, the British, never overly warm to their Gallic neighbors in the best of times, resented paying taxes to religious leaders they believed were in league with their mortal enemy. The rising tide of opposition to Rome and English political awareness—it is too early to use the word "nationalism"—produced the Statute of Provisors (1351), which said anyone accepting papal appointments in England should be fined and imprisoned until they renounced such provisions. By 1366 England was more than thirty years in arrears in annual payment to the pope. Parliament canceled the payments, arguing that they could not be made without consent of the lords and commons, and curbed papal courts' jurisdiction. Thus by century's end seeds of disputes crucial to the later Reformation were firmly planted in English soil. The church emerging from these conflicts would retain its Catholic nature, but it would be a national church, not one governed by Rome. The distinction is immensely important in following the gradual emergence of the Church in England toward independence from Rome.

"Poisonous Weeds" and "Fat Cows": The Attacks of Wycliffe the Reformer

Either you loved him or you detested him, depending if you were outside the established religious power structure looking in, or inside looking out. John Wycliffe (c. 1308–1384) was one of those loud, radical, hit-the-bull's-eye reformers who appear once or twice in a century and stir up the juices of the political, social, and religious establishment. Among the century's most articulate critics of the existing order, a quick-witted and sharp-tongued Oxford teacher, he mercilessly exposed the excesses of worldly prelates and comfortably living monks, calling the pope "a poisonous weed" and monks "fat cows." A satirist with an investigative journalist's gift of exposé, he turned his rapier-like wit on the excesses of an influential segment of society. Cutting close to the bone, he questioned the institutional sources of religious authority, arguing that each person is responsible to God alone—hence there is no distinction between clergy and laity and no need for ecclesiastical hierarchies. Most revolutionary of all, he believed the Bible, in English translation, should be freely available for all to read and interpret as guided by faith and reason, a position neither king nor archbishop accepted until much later.

Wycliffe argued for "civil dominion," by which he meant the right of civil authorities to confiscate holdings of clerics who abused their power. This was a direct, frontal attack and the pope ordered Wycliffe tried for heresy. Playing to a wider audience, Wycliffe switched from Latin to English, and his pamphlets with their inflammatory content were widely circulated. Monks were devoting their energies to property management, he argued; money payments replaced religious penance, and ecclesiastical courts intruded oppressively and corruptly into public and private life. Additionally, in his attacks on the papacy Wycliffe systematically attacked the Roman Catholic understanding of the sacraments, the doctrine of transubstantiation, and the right of popes to be the supreme arbiters of faith and morals. The papacy was angry but had difficulty in presenting a solid front since rival pontiffs in Rome and Avignon in 1378 claimed to be authentic descendants of Peter and concentrated their energies in displacing one another. Score one for Wycliffe.

THE MYSTICAL WAY

Although disputes with Rome were a feature of English political and religious life, and the number of reformers like Wycliffe and his followers grew gradually, devotional life continued in an orthodox manner. Popes found reason to be perturbed with English monarchs, chiefly over the collection of taxes, the role of ecclesiastical courts, and control of appointments, but evidence of traditional spiritual life remained strong. The English Middle Ages produced a rich flowering of mystical writers who left intensely personal accounts of encounters with God. Their numbers included Richard Rolle (c. 1300–1349), a Yorkshire hermit who wrote *The Fire of Love;* Walter Hilton (1330–1396), a Nottinghamshire monastic whose book *The Scale of Perfection* helped popular audiences find spiritual perfection in ordinary life; and the unknown author of *The Cloud of Unknowing* (c. 1360), in which "the sharp dart of longing love" pierces "the dark cloud of unknowing," where God is hidden. One of the best-known such writers was Lady Julian of Norwich (c. 1343–1413), who lived as a hermit isolated in a walled-off cell in the parish of St. Julian in Norwich, East Anglia. It was on May 8, 1373, the only certain date established in her life, that the thirty-year-old Julian fell seriously ill, entered a trance for five hours, and experienced sixteen overpowering revelations, about which she spent the next twenty years pondering and describing in *Revelations of Divine Love*, a major work of English mysticism. Julian's carefully constructed account is a personal statement of revelation within the context of traditional Catholic belief.

She is best known for the statement in her Revelation 13, "it behoved that there should be sin; but all shall be well, and all shall be well, and all manner of things shall be well." Julian wrote during a time when suffering and death were no strangers to England. The Black Death had decimated the population as had the Hundred Years' War with France, and England experienced the turbulence of the Peasants' Revolt of 1381, in which desperate but poorly organized peasant bands converged on London to protest high taxes and harsh working conditions. None of these events made their way into her writing, but readers, and those who visited Julian, could not help but be attracted to her serenity of vision offering an alternative to the darkness around them. Julian's mystical thought drew on the religious world of her time, a world depicted in the Doomsday paintings in village churches, where life was often brief and beset by illness and misfortune, and demonic and angelic forces were real and the Christian's duty clear. Her writing paints verbal pictures of the suffering Christ:

> with my physical eyes I saw heavy bleeding from the head. Great drops of blood, which looked as if they came from the veins, fell from the crown like pellets. When they appeared they were a brownish-red color for the blood was very thick, and as they spread they were bright red. Then when they reached the eyebrows they vanished. Yet the bleeding continued until I had seen and understood many things.[23]

The final revelation replaces suffering with majesty:

> Then our Lord opened the eyes of my spirit and showed me my soul in the middle of my heart. The soul was as large as a boundless world and seemed to be a blissfully happy kingdom. From its condition I could tell it is a glorious city. Enthroned in the midst I saw our Lord Jesus, God and Man, arrayed in majesty, beautiful and imposing, highest bishop, most majestic king, most glorious Lord.[24]

SUMMARY

We have come a long way, a thousand years at least, in our attempt to find the English church's unique traits. For the devout peasant working in the fields or small towns, little has changed. It is yet in the late Middle Ages a Catholic church, loyal to Rome, but that loyalty is increasingly contested by English kings for political reasons, as by the fourteenth century the idea of locally governed states emerges and the papacy's power declines, gradually making Rome one political competitor among many. It is a church with a deeply indigenous spirituality, Celtic and Anglo-Saxon, in addition to what foreign sources brought it over several centuries. A church of mystics and poets, its members included cathedral builders whose works are some of Western civilization's most enduring monuments. As well, it was a church ripe for the coming Reformation. For one thing, English monarchs coveted being masters of their own realm; other English cherished the national trait of independence from foreigners; and the shortcomings of monastic establishments that outlived their creative days were there for all to see. John-the-Baptist figures like John Wycliffe appeared on the horizon and more would follow. Strange new ideas came to England from the Continent; the stage was set for tumultuous happenings.

READINGS

The readings that follow display the richness of the Celtic and Catholic Christian past from which the Church of England emerged. This diverse heritage is often eclipsed in the Reformation's violence and in succeeding centuries' disputes, but the Middle Ages gave the church treasures of poetry, mysticism, and statescraft on which to build.

St. Patrick's Breastplate

Although the ancient hymn is called "St. Patrick's Breastplate," it cannot be linked accurately to the fifth-century British saint who spent much of his life in Ireland. Still, the work is typical of Celtic hymns, prayers, and poems. Repetition and enfolding one image into another characterize Celtic poetry, linking God with creation, nature, and humanity through encircling, weaving, and binding in a manner replicating the visual patterns of a Celtic stone cross or metal chalice.

> I bind unto myself today the strong Name
> of the Trinity, by invocation
> of the same, the Three in One, the One in Three.
>
> I bind this day to me forever, by power of
> faith Christ's Incarnation, his baptism in the
> Jordan River; his death on cross for my salvation;

his bursting from the spiced tomb, his riding
up the heavenly way; his coming at the
day of doom, I bind unto myself today.

. . . .

I bind unto myself today the virtues
of the starlit heaven, the glorious sun's
life-giving ray, the whiteness of the moon at even,
the flashing of the lightning free,
the whirling wind's tempestuous shocks, the stable earth,
the deep salt sea, around the old eternal rocks.

. . . .

Christ be with me, Christ within me, Christ behind me,
Christ before me, Christ beside me, Christ to
win me, Christ to comfort and restore me,
Christ beneath me, Christ above me, Christ in quiet,
Christ in danger, Christ in hearts of all that
love me, Christ in mouth of friend and stranger.

I bind unto myself the Name, the strong Name
of the Trinity, by invocation
of the same, the Three in One, and One in Three.
Of whom all nature hath creation, eternal
Father, Spirit, Word: praise to the Lord
of my salvation, salvation is of Christ the Lord.[25]

Bede of Jarrow

Among the scholar-monks of early English history, the most widely
known was Bede of Jarrow (673–735), whose *Ecclesiastical History of the
English People* is an important source of early British church history. Bede
wrote more than forty books, including sermons, poetry, and biblical
commentaries. As a youthful monk, he and the abbot were left alone in
the monastery when a plague swept the north of England, and they continued to sing the whole round of monastic services until others eventually joined their ranks. Bede led an outwardly uneventful life, moving
between the monastery at Jarrow and another within easy walking distance.

A sharp observer of the church and its personalities, Bede drew on
both Celtic and Roman traditions. His short sketches and carefully

crafted accounts are shaped like manuscript illuminations. A modern reader may be puzzled by how matter-of-factly Bede reports miracles alongside ordinary historical events. It was an age of faith in which he lived, and the presence of angels and demons, storms and meteors as divine auguries, recoveries of health caused by prayer or sudden death from sinful acts were interpreted as signs of divine intervention in human affairs.

Bede, in the selection below, describes a meeting between king and council discussing their acceptance of Christianity. Life's brevity and fatality are depicted in an often-cited image of a solitary sparrow flying from a storm into the fire-warmed banquet hall, then out again into the storm. "Man appears on earth for a little while; but of what went before this life or of what follows, we know nothing." Following the royal decision to accept Christianity, the pagan priest Coifi converts, borrows the king's stallion, and races off to destroy the non-Christian idols. The final selection describes two miraculous healings at the place where Edwin's successor, Oswald, was killed. (Edwin had been defeated and killed by the heathen king of Mercia in 633.) Such miracles elicit no special explanation from Bede; they were part of the ordinary round of living.

Edwin holds a council with his chief men about accepting the Faith of Christ. The high priest destroys his own altars.

When he heard this, the king answered that it was his will as well as his duty to accept the faith that Paulinus [Roman missionary, bishop of York, d. 644—ed.] taught, but said that he must still discuss the matter with his principal advisers and friends, so that, if they were in agreement with him, they might all be cleansed together in Christ the Fount of Life. Paulinus agreed, and the king kept his promise. He summoned a council of the wise men, and asked each in turn his opinion of this strange doctrine and this new way of worshipping the godhead that was being proclaimed to them.

Coifi, the Chief Priest, replied without hesitation: "Your Majesty, let us give careful consideration to this new teaching; for I frankly admit that, in my experience, the religion that we have hitherto professed seems valueless and powerless. None of your subjects has been more devoted to the service of our gods than myself; yet there are many to whom you show greater favor, who receive greater honors, and who are more successful in all their undertakings. Now, if the gods had any power, they would surely have favored myself, who have been more zealous in their service. Therefore, if on examination you perceive that these new teachings are better and more effectual, let us not hesitate to accept them."

Another of the king's chief men signified his agreement with this prudent argument, and went on to say: "Your Majesty, when we compare the present life of man on earth with that time of which we have no knowledge, it seems to me like the swift flight of a single sparrow through the banqueting-hall where you are sitting at dinner on a winter's day with your thanes and counselors. In the midst there is a comforting fire to warm the hall: outside the storms of the winter rain or snow are raging. This sparrow flies swiftly in through one door of the hall, and out through another. While he is inside, he is safe from the winter storms; but after a few moments of comfort, he vanishes from sight into the winter world from which he came. Even so, man appears on earth for a little while; but of what went before this life or of what follows, we know nothing. Therefore, if this new teaching has brought any more certain knowledge, it seems only right that we should follow it." The other elders and counselors of the king, under God's guidance, gave similar advice.

Coifi then added that he wished to hear Paulinus' teaching about God in greater detail; and when, at the king's bidding, this had been given, he exclaimed: "I have long realized that there is nothing in our way of worship; for the more diligently I sought after truth in our religion, the less I found. I now publicly confess that this teaching clearly reveals truths that will afford the blessings of life, salvation, and eternal happiness. Therefore, Your Majesty, I submit that the temples and altars that we have dedicated to no advantage be immediately desecrated and burned." In short, the king granted blessed Paulinus full permission to preach, renounced idolatry, and professed his acceptance of the Faith of Christ. And when he asked the Chief priest who should be the first to profane the altars and shrines of the idols, together with the enclosures that surround them, Coifi replied: "I will do this myself; for now that the true God has granted me knowledge, who more suitably than I can set a public example and destroy the idols that I worshipped in ignorance?" So he formally renounced his empty superstitions and asked the king to give him arms and a stallion—and, thus equipped, he set out to destroy the idols. Girded with a sword and with a spear in his hand, he mounted the king's stallion and rode up to the idols. When the crowd saw him, they thought he had gone mad; but without hesitation, as soon as he reached the temple, he cast into it the spear he carried and thus profaned it.[26]

Miraculous cures take place at the site of Oswald's death. A traveler's horse is cured, and a paralytic girl is healed.

Oswald's great devotion and faith in God was made evident by the miracles that took place after his death. For at the place where he was killed fighting for his country against the heathen, sick men and beasts are healed to this day. Many people took away the very dust from the place where his body fell, and put it in water, from which sick folk who drank it received great benefit. This practice became so popular that, as the earth was gradually removed, a pit was left in which a man could stand. But it is not to be wondered at that the sick received healing at the place of his death; for during his lifetime he never failed to provide for the sick and needy and give them alms and aid. Many miracles are reported as having occurred at this spot, or by means of the earth taken from it; but I will content myself with two, which I have heard from my elders.

Not long after Oswald's death, a man happened to be riding near the place when his horse suddenly showed signs of distress. It stopped and hung its head, foaming at the mouth, and as its pains increased, it collapsed on the ground. The rider dismounted, removed the saddle, and waited to see whether the beast was going to recover or to die. At length, having tossed this way and that in great pain for a considerable time, it rolled on to the spot where the great king had died. Immediately the pain ceased, and the horse stopped its wild struggles; then, having rolled on to its other side, as tired beasts do, it got up fully recovered and began to graze. The traveler, an observant man, concluded that the place where his horse was cured must possess especial sanctity, and when he had marked it, he mounted and rode on to the inn where he intended to lodge. On his arrival he found a girl, the niece of the landlord, who had long suffered from paralysis; and when members of the household in his presence were deploring the girl's disease, he began to tell them about the place where his horse had been cured. So they put the girl into a cart, took her to the place, and laid her down. Once there she fell asleep for a short while; and, on awaking, she found herself restored to health. She asked for water and washed her face; then she tidied her hair, adjusted her linen headgear, and returned home on foot in perfect health with those who had brought her.[27]

Twelve Advent Lyrics from the Old English

The lyrical, worshipful side of English spirituality is represented in numerous songs and poems, including a set of Old English Advent Lyrics found in manuscript form in Exeter Cathedral. The twelve lyrics were probably based on antiphons used in the medieval church during the Advent season, the four weeks before Christmas.

Oh vision of love, Holy Jerusalem,
Best of cities and birthplace of Christ,
Forever the home of kings, only
In you can the souls of the righteous rest
Exulting in endless glory. Your walls
Stand unstained; sin and evil
Shun you, hardship and crime and war
And punishment. You are wonderfully filled with a sacred
Hope, and with joy, according to your name.
Now look around you, across the wide world
And above you, at oceans and the great hanging
Arch of sky—see how Heaven's
King comes to you, longing for His death,
Embracing fate as, long ago,
Prophets' wise words announced, proclaiming
That marvelous birth, declaring, oh noblest
Of cities, your consolation and joy.
He has come, took flesh and left it to change
The Jews' pain, and yours, to happiness,
And to break the bonds of sin. And He has known
How the poor and suffering must seek mercy.[28]

John of Salisbury

John of Salisbury (c. 1115–1180) knew the corridors of power well. He studied law and logic in Paris and spent his life close to kings and bishops, in England and Rome, where he was close to the English pope Hadrian IV. An advisor to both Henry II and Becket, he ended his life as bishop of Chartres. One of the most articulate political theorists of his age, John here makes the case for a national monarch subservient to the pope, a position that held until reversed by Henry VIII four centuries later. From *The Statesman's Handbook*:

A commonwealth, according to Plutarch, is a certain body which is endowed with life by the benefit of divine favor, which acts at the prompting of highest equity, and is ruled by what may be called the moderating power of reason. Those things which establish and implant in us the practice of religion, and transmit to us the worship of God . . . fill the place of the soul in the body of the commonwealth. And therefore those who preside over the practice of religion should be looked up to and venerated as the soul of the body. For who doubts that the ministers of God's holiness are His representatives? Furthermore, since the soul is, as it were, the prince of the body, and has rulership over the whole of the body thereof. . . . The place of the head in the body of the commonwealth is filled by the prince, who is subject only to God and to those who exercise His office and represent Him on earth, even as in the human body the head is quickened and governed by the soul. The place of the heart is filled by the senate, from which proceeds the initiation of good works and ill. The duties of eyes, ears, and tongue are claimed by the judges and the governors of provinces. Officials and soldiers correspond to the hands. Those who always attend upon the prince are likened to the sides. Financial officers and keepers . . . may be compared with the stomach and intestines. . . . The husbandmen correspond to the feet, which always cleave to the soil, and need the more especially the care and foresight of the head, since while they walk upon the earth doing service with their bodies, they meet the more often with stones of stumbling, and therefore deserve aid and protection all the more justly since it is they who raise, sustain, and move forward the weight of the entire body.

Then and only then will the health of the commonwealth be sound and flourishing, when the higher members shield the lower, and the lower respond faithfully and fully in like measure to the just demands of their superiors, so that each and all are as it were members one of another by a sort of reciprocity, and each regards his own interest as best served by that which he knows to be most advantageous for the others.

> *That the Soldiery of Arms Is Necessarily Bound to Religion Like*
> *That Which Is Consecrated to Membership in the Clergy and the*
> *Service of God; and That the Name of Soldier is One of Honor*
> *and Toil*

What is the office of the duly ordained soldiery? To defend the Church, to assail infidelity, to venerate the priesthood, to protect the poor from injuries, to pacify the province, to pour out their blood for their brothers (as the formula of their oaths instructs them), and, if need be, to lay down their lives. The high praises of God are in their throat, and two-edged swords are in their hands to execute punishment on the nations and rebuke upon the peoples, and to bind their kings in chains and their nobles in links of iron. But to what end? To the end that they may serve madness, vanity, avarice, or their own private self-will? By no means. Rather to the end that they may execute the judgment that is committed to them to execute; wherein each follows not his own will but the deliberate decision of God, the angels, and men, in accordance with equity and the public utility. I say "to the end that they may *execute*," for as it is for judges to pronounce judgment, so it is for these to perform their office by executing it. Verily, "This honor have all His saints." For soldiers that do these things are "saints," and are the more loyal to their prince in proportion as they more zealously keep the faith of God; and they advance the more successfully the honor of their own valor as they seek the more faithfully in all things the glory of their God."[29]

Julian of Norwich

Although she claimed to be unlettered, Julian of Norwich's *Revelations of Divine Love* is a carefully composed and richly imaginative work whose depth and breadth of perception have assured it a lasting place in religious literature.

Chapter 27
The Thirteenth Revelation

After this the Lord reminded me of my earlier longing for him. I now saw that nothing stopped me but sin. This I saw to be generally true of us all. I thought to myself, "If there had been no sin, we should all have been pure and clean like our Lord, as he created us."

In my foolish way I had often wondered why, in God's foreknowledge, his wisdom could not have prevented the origin of sin. For if he had, I thought, then all would have been well. A question like this was best left well alone, but instead I senselessly and stupidly fretted and upset myself over it.

But Jesus, who in this vision told me about everything I needed to know, answered me with these words: "Sin is necessary, but all will be well, and all will be well, and all manner of things will be well."

In this bare word "sin," our Lord reminded me in a general way of all that is not good: the despicable shame and utter self-emptying he endured for us, both in his life and in his dying, and all the physical and spiritual suffering of his creation. For we have all experienced a little of this emptying, and we will know it completely, as we follow our master Jesus, until we are wholly cleansed. That is, until this mortal body and all unworthy inward desires are completely annihilated. After this I saw, together with all the suffering that ever has been or ever shall be. And I understood that deepest and greatest pain was the Passion of Christ. All this was revealed in an instant and was quickly transformed into encouragement, for our good Lord would not have the soul frightened by this terrible sight.

But I did not see *sin* itself. I believe that sin has no substance or reality and cannot be known except through the pain it causes. The pain is real enough, but, it seems to me, it lasts only for a while; it cleanses us and makes us know ourselves, and ask for mercy. The Passion of our Lord is our strength in all this and that is his blessed will. Because of his tender love for us all who are to be saved our good Lord quickly and sweetly comforts us saying, "It is true that sin is the cause of all this pain, but all will be well, and all manner of things will be well."

Chapter 60

[Julian develops the idea of God-as-Mother in the second person of the Trinity, along with God the Father and the Holy Spirit. Frequently the phrase "he is our Mother" is used, in Julian's perspective the Trinity's second person fully represents both masculine and feminine attributes, a theme more fully developed through the author's birthing and child-rearing imagery.]

Our Mother in nature, who is also our Mother in grace, wanted to become our Mother in everything, so he began at the bottom, in complete humility and gentleness, in the virgin's womb. (He revealed this in the first Revelation when he brought that gentle virgin before my mind's eye and I saw how simple and unpretentious she was when she conceived.) In this insignificant place our great God, the supreme wisdom of all things, arrayed himself in our poor flesh, and fully prepared himself for motherhood with all its work and service.

A mother's work touches us most nearly, is carried out with the greatest alacrity, and is the most reliable. Its nearness is because it is most natural, its alacrity is because it is most loving, and its reliability is because it is most true. No one could ever perform this service except Christ alone. We know that our own mother bore us for pain and for death. But what is it that Jesus, our true Mother, does? He who is all-love bears us for joy and eternal life! Praise him! So he carries us within himself in love, and he went into labor for full time, suffering the most agonizing pains and the sharpest birth pangs possible, until in the end he died. And when he had finished and given birth to us for our eternal happiness, even then his most wonderful love was not satisfied, as he revealed in his superlative words of love: "If I could suffer more I would suffer more."

He could not die any more, but he would not cease working! So he had to feed us, for the most precious love of motherhood has placed him under an obligation to us. The human mother suckles her child with her own milk, and with the utmost tender kindness our beloved Mother, Jesus, feeds us with himself through the blessed sacrament, which is my life's precious food. And through all the sweet sacraments he sustains us in the greatest mercy and grace. This is what he meant when he said, "I am the one whom Holy Church preaches and teaches." This to say, "All the health and life of the sacraments, all the virtue and grace of my word, all the goodness set apart for you in the Holy Church—it is I."

The human mother puts her child tenderly to her breast, and our tender Mother, Jesus, leads us intimately into his blessed breast, through the sweet open wound in his side, and there gives us a glimpse of the Godhead and the joy of heaven, with the inner certainty of eternal bliss. He revealed this in the tenth Revelation and also taught it to me though his sweet words: "See how I loved you," as he rejoiced over the wound in his side.

The lovely, loving word *Mother* is so sweet and so close to the heart of nature that it cannot really be used of anyone but him, and she who is his own true mother and mother of us all. Natural love, wisdom, knowledge, and goodness belong with motherhood. Though our physical birth is so small, insignificant, and simple compared to our spiritual birth, yet when God's creatures give birth, he is still the one who makes it happen. A natural, loving mother who understands and knows the needs of her child will look after him with the utmost tenderness—this is part and parcel of being a mother. As the child grows older she changes her methods but not her love and as he gets even older she allows him to be punished in order to break him of his faults and teach him to accept virtue and graces. This—along with everything that is lovely and good—is our Lord's work in those who are living in this way.[30]

2

The Sixteenth Century

Be of good comfort, Master Ridley, and play the man; we shall this day light such a candle by God's grace in England as I trust shall never be put out.

> —*Hugh Latimer, bishop of Worchester, to Nicholas Ridley, bishop of London, martyrs, as flames engulfed them (1555)*

I F THIS CENTURY'S RELIGIOUS HISTORY is viewed as a drama, stubborn Henry's long kingship yields to sickly Edward's short reign, then to vengeful Mary, who tries to reverse a half-century's irreversible changes in a few years, to be succeeded by cautious Elizabeth's long reign, where the Church of England is established as a *via media*, a middle way. If the century is considered as a play, Act One's dominant theme is the Catholic–Protestant conflict; Act Two, the equally acrimonious Anglican–Puritan dispute. The leading actors belong to an Elizabethan drama, a Shakespearean history or tragedy. Those without bloody hands perished as martyrs; few died in bed of old age. Imagine these characters' speeches as they, in costume and with the props of office, enter and exit. Kings and queens are surrounded by a host of scheming courtiers, politician-bishops, truly holy persons, monkish recluses, and blunt-spoken, energetic Puritans—and a stage full of printers, sailors, merchants, musicians, peasants, and gentry. The plot line was not tidy in this long, often bloody, sometimes heroic pageant. Anyone with even the most passing interest in this period should spend a morning on the second floor of London's National Portrait Gallery, where the cast of characters is assembled in all their finery and with stage looks of arrogance, cunning, confidence, or serene repose in "The Early Tudors" or "The Elizabethans" collections.

The English Reformation, or, more accurately, Reformations, unfolds early in the sixteenth century, when Luther's ideas gradually made their way from the Continent to port cities and to universities such as Oxford and Cambridge. Here they met a receptive climate primed by earlier and recent efforts at reform. Their audience was more widespread than an academic one. Unlike unquestioning peasants of the Middle Ages, reform ideas gained support from merchants and craftspersons whose growing economic independence had a corollary in their independence of spirit. Dissatisfaction over foreign control of British political and religious institutions was growing, as was criticism of Rome's financial exactions. In 1529 the English Church was part of the Roman Catholic Church; within three decades it would be a national church, with both strong Catholic underpinnings and new Protestant doctrinal overlays.

Their spread also coincided with the advancement of printing, the Bible's translation into English, and the gradual growth of popular protest in England, some of it fueled by the growth of a middle class in Britain. Most important for the future of the English church, this infusion of new ideas coincided with an impasse between king and pope leading to severed relations between the two powers. In this respect, the English Reformations of the sixteenth century had roots deep in the Middle Ages and were triggered by the English king and not the English church; this was a political, not a doctrinal, struggle, the main issues being power and authority rather than theology and belief.

A word of caution. The transformation of England from a Catholic to a Protestant nation did not occur overnight. The spread of Reformation ideas came not as a triumphal wave but as a steady flow, the rise and ebb of new forces, successively finding receptive ground, dissolving resistance, or avoiding too-strong opposition. If those near the throne and in universities were affected by the spread of Reformation ideas, most parish priests and parishioners went about their habitual worship until well into Elizabeth's time. In fact, it would be more accurate to speak of a "reforming" or "evangelical" church until the time of Mary, for the reformers did not see themselves as starting a new church.[1] But by the time of Mary the lines were clearly drawn and the differences between Catholics and Protestants sharply etched. Changes at the top took decades to reach the countryside, even though the geographic distances were not great; some did not accept the new religion, and others embraced it only reluctantly. But England at century's end was a vastly different place than in 1500.

FIRST STIRRINGS

Like goods from Dutch and German ports, Continental Reformation ideas made their way gradually into England and were assimilated by English intellectuals after long debate in places such as the White Horse Inn in Cambridge, also known as "Little Germany," since it was a center for discussion of German ideas. By 1517, when Martin Luther began to publicly challenge papal authority, England already had been exposed to reform ideas by Wycliffe's early teaching and by the Lollards, the fifteenth-century separatist minority of Bible-reading antihierarchical followers of Wycliffe. University students read Luther's criticism of the sale of indulgences, his emphasis on individual study of the Bible, and his assertion that in the death of Christ humanity was justified, and thus salvation could not be purchased through indulgences and the sale of masses for the dead. Revolutionary stuff, that, as subversive in its time as anything Karl Marx later ever wrote. Luther's books were burned in a London conflagration in 1521, presided over by Cardinal Wolsey (c. 1474–1530), the portly papal legate who gathered the country's political and religious leaders with him to watch the burning.

The conflict was more complex than a clear-cut Catholic–Protestant struggle, as reflected in the life of Thomas Bilney (1495–1531), one of the Cambridge Reformers, a circle of priests and academics who made a serious study of Luther's thought. Bilney was accused of heresy, and in a letter to the bishop of London, the trial judge, recalled his conversion in language resembling Luther's. With the excitement of youthful discovery, the young cleric described the importance of reading the New Testament and then disputed the value of good works as a way to salvation, thus putting him on a course bringing him into sure conflict with the church hierarchy.

> But at last I heard speak of Jesus, even then when the New Testament was first set forth by Erasmus. . . . I bought it even by the providence of God . . . and at the first reading I chanced upon this sentence of St. Paul . . . in I Tim. I "It is a true saying, and worthy of all men to be embraced, that Christ Jesus came into the world to save sinners; of whom I am the chief and principal." This one sentence . . . did so exhilarate my heart, being before wounded with guilt of my sins, and being almost in despair, that immediately I felt a marvelous comfort and quietness, insomuch "that my bruised bones leaped for joy."
>
> After this, the Scripture began to be more pleasant unto me than the honey or the honey-comb; wherein I learned, that all my travails, all my

fasting and watching, all the redemption of masses and pardons, being done without trust in Christ, who only saveth his people from their sins; these, I say, I learned to be nothing . . . or else much like to the vesture made of fig leaves, wherewithal Adam and Eve went about in vain to cover themselves.[2]

Such personal accounts became increasingly frequent during the Reformation, but were rarer in Roman Catholic times. Throughout his life Bilney questioned neither papal supremacy nor the church's authority, and in most respects was conventionally orthodox in belief. The young cleric was arrested, tried, and then recanted. Then—still suspect— he was executed for heresy in 1531, principally because he rejected the doctrine of purgatory and the need for intercession of the saints. His position, honestly arrived at as a matter of belief, struck at the core of papal fund-raising efforts through the sale of indulgences which liberated dead souls from purgatory for a price.

HENRY VIII

"Defender of the Faith" and "Supreme Head on Earth of the Church"

The English Reformation was shaped largely by the policies and personality of Henry VIII, king of England from 1509 to 1547, but the relationship is more complex than might first appear. Henry was headstrong and a bully; Charles Dickens called him "a blot of blood and grease upon the history of England," but emphasis on Henry's personality neglects what he tried to do as a ruler. While the Reformation gained irrevocable momentum during Henry's reign, the king never intended to tamper with the existing order in anything but a political manner. An eager, orthodox student of theology, he took his role as Defender of the Faith seriously, consistently upholding Catholic belief from Lutheranism's incursions. (This title was conferred on Henry at his request in 1521 by Pope Leo X to reward Henry for his treatise defending the traditional seven sacraments against Luther, who reduced them to three.) In faith and practice, Henry's religion was conventional, his approach to change cautious. The king's focus was principally on freeing the English crown from papal order, bringing the church under civil control and appropriating for his own use the sizable loads of church treasure being shipped to Rome as dues and offerings. Henry's actions brought religious institutions firmly under royal control in the 1530s. Land and treasure were confiscated for royal use, and church government passed into royal hands in 1532, when the convocation relinquished its right to be an independent legislative body for the church.

HENRY'S ANNULMENT
The Quest for a Male Heir

Henry and Pope Clement VII, whose pontificate extended from 1523 to 1534, represented two institutions on a collision course—the English nation and the papacy. Had British tabloids existed at this time, and had there been freedom of the press, Henry's marital life would have provided them with colorful copy. The king's frustration was driven by his failure to assure the Tudor dynasty's succession by producing a male heir with Catherine of Aragon, now forty years old, his wife of eighteen years. Alleging that this was divine retribution for marrying his deceased brother Arthur's wife, Henry sought to annul the marriage, something frequently arranged for European royalty, especially when an issue of dynastic succession was paramount. The legal grounds Henry used to press the annulment were straightforward: the marriage was a biblically forbidden (Lev. 20:21) union with a brother's widow, and Julius II, pope from 1503 to 1513, had exceeded his authority in allowing it. Henry, whose eye was now on Anne Boleyn, an attractive younger woman, told his Lord Chancellor, Cardinal Wolsey, to find ways to annul the marriage, something the worldly prelate could not do. The case was further complicated—this was decisive— because Catherine was the aunt of the Spanish king, Charles V, whose troops controlled Rome and whose enmity the pope could not afford. Spanish troops were quartered just down the street; England was a long way off. Clement stalled.

The breach with Rome became final between 1532 and 1534, when Henry pressed Parliament to pass several bills shifting power from Rome to England, including provisions that all future bishops should be consecrated in England, that only small amounts of English currency could be sent to Rome (instead of the large papal tithes), and that no new laws affecting the church could be promulgated by Rome without the king's permission. In a decree called the Act in Restraint of Appeals (1533), Parliament ruled that all ecclesiastical cases must be heard in English courts, instead of being automatically referred to Rome. The bill's preamble said "this realm of England is an empire," with the king as supreme head of church and state. The Defender of the Faith thus became Supreme Head on Earth of the Church in England as well. In 1536 an Act Extinguishing the Authority of the Bishop of Rome became law, and within a few years Henry consolidated both spiritual and temporal power in his hands. The dispute spun on; the pope avoided a decision on the annulment request, and Henry's frustration increased. It is doubtful Henry initially had any plan beyond a desire to dissolve the marriage and the perennial hope of English monarchs to increase their power at Rome's expense.

Events tumbled in swift succession. In May 1533 the Archbishop of Canterbury, Thomas Cranmer (1489–1556), declared the royal marriage null and void. Rome responded with an excommunication decree. Henry replied with additional laws eliminating all vestiges of ties with Rome, confirming the king as head of church and state, bringing the bishops and clergy under royal control, abolishing "Peter's pence," the dues sent annually to Rome, and giving the king power to establish doctrine and punish heresy. Cardinal Wolsey, the principal papal representative, was removed from any position of influence and accused of treason—that is, taking orders from a foreign power. Wolsey, a Renaissance condottiere, was a former Lord Chancellor who exerted great power at the royal court, and whose flamboyant lifestyle was a visible reminder of worldly excess. Unable to persuade the pope to grant Henry an annulment, Wolsey fell from power. His vast property holdings were forcibly ceded to the king, and Wolsey was indicted under statutes of Praemunire, laws protecting the crown against papal encroachments, which Wolsey's enemies invoked against the papal legate, who conveniently died on his way to trial. A few years earlier, the cardinal would have summarily dismissed the charges as being outside the court's jurisdiction, but times had changed and the English Parliament systematically eliminated any institutional traces of papal supremacy. A leading scholar of the period, A. G. Dickens, has written:

> Outside these eight years [1532–1540—ed.] the reign of Henry VIII has scarcely a single creative or revolutionary achievement to its credit. The King's will-power, his courage, his decisiveness, his immense capacity to inspire adulation, these preserved the way for the long Elizabethan peace which Englishmen were to enjoy amid a chaotic Europe. But otherwise his personal touch proved sterile; he was too egotistical, too emotional, too interested in kingly pleasures, too conservative to initiate new techniques of government, new paths of progress for English society.[3]

PLAYING OUT THE STRING
The Monasteries Are Dissolved

Between 1535 and 1539, Henry ordered the dissolution of the monasteries, with their vast holdings of land and wealth. Henry's costly wars and extravagant lifestyle left the royal treasury bare, and the king saw a rich source of income in the nearly nine hundred endowed religious institutions throughout the country. The monastic establishments, which may have housed twelve thousand women and men at this time, were a spent force, engendering neither artists nor scholars, living off their treasure, going through the motions of the religious life, although there were no doubt sincere souls in their numbers. Henry's Continental wars quickly absorbed the revenues amassed from the sale of monastic lands and treasures, but the king's action brought him no permanent financial gain. The monasteries' dissolution brought an end to one of England's most characteristic institutions of an earlier age. The device for dissolving these establishments was the finding of a royal commission headed by Henry's principal secretary and cabinet minister, Thomas Cromwell (1485–1540), a skilled lawyer, ambitious parliamentarian, and former Wolsey aide with few religious interests of his own, but with a strong desire to use religion to consolidate the monarchy's strength. Cromwell's commissioners, looking for dissipation and profligacy, found ample evidence, as government commissions usually do, and in 1536 Parliament transferred most monastic land to the king, who awarded some of it to trusted lieutenants and sold the rest to local gentry. This produced a class of loyal supporters, grateful to the Tudors and enthusiastic for the national episcopacy as a hedge against the return of papal forces, which would force them to relinquish their newly acquired wealth.

In a few short years, the thousand-year relationship of the Church in England with Rome was severed. Ironically, despite the substantial issues of doctrine and power conflicts between clerics in Rome and England, the Church in England had almost no role in this momentous happening. The revolution was triggered by a monarch desirous of finding a male heir, who was able to carry Parliament with him.

THOMAS CRANMER
(1489–1556)

Of the hundred-some Archbishops of Canterbury, the most remembered by most people is Thomas Cranmer, Henry's chief adviser on religious affairs who, after Henry's death, produced the Book of Common Prayer, which established norms for Church of England worship for succeeding centuries. Chance brought Cranmer into contact with the monarch. During 1529, Cranmer, a teacher of divinity, left Cambridge during a plague, traveling with one of his students to a family home in Essex, where two of Henry's closest counselors were staying. Conversation turned naturally to the king's marital plight, and Cranmer proposed a novel solution: let the universities of Europe and their experts decide the issues, thus avoiding an appeal to Rome. For Henry, who was staying nearby, this was fresh wind, a new approach, one that might work. He summoned the cleric and, after questioning Cranmer, commented enthusiastically, "This man, I trow, has got the right sow by the ear," and ordered the cleric to prepare a comprehensive written treatise on the annulment question, which was later presented to the pope in Rome, with Cranmer being a prominent member of the English delegation.

Next Henry asked Cranmer to be the emperor's ambassador to Germany to seek an alliance with the Lutheran princes. While in Nuremberg in 1531, Cranmer met his future wife, the niece of a German theologian. In 1532 William Warham, Archbishop of Canterbury, died and Henry named Cranmer as his successor, his married status notwithstanding. The papal bulls of confirmation arrived, and Cranmer, at his consecration on March 30, 1533, was expected to take two oaths, one supporting the pope, the second pledging fidelity to the king. Cranmer reworked the documents, swearing allegiance to the pope only insofar as this did not conflict with his duties to the king. Thus he avoided the dilemma of divided loyalties which had trapped Wolsey.

Much of Cranmer's initial time in office was spent sorting out the king's marriage problem. After detailed study and hearings, in late May the archbishop declared the marriage null and void. Five days later he affirmed the validity of Henry's marriage to Anne Boleyn, celebrated the previous January. Anne, great with child, was crowned queen on June 1, and on September 10 Cranmer became godfather to Henry and Anne's child, the future Queen Elizabeth. Three years later, at the king's insistence, the archbishop reversed himself and declared Henry's marriage to Anne invalid. The argument was that Anne's sister, Mary, had once been the king's mistress, and canon law thus enjoined against a marriage with Anne. If the finding was legal, it was hardly just, but the prelate had no choice but to follow Henry's dictates.

Neither Henry nor Cranmer was aware of what would be the archbishop's most enduring contribution—his authorship of the Book of

Common Prayer. The moment was right; the English language was being shaped in ways that would endure to modern times. By now Shakespeare's plays were available to a widespread public, as was the incomparable language of William Tyndale's English translation of the Bible, thanks to the spread of printing. Fortunately, Cranmer knew that his skills were as an editor and not as a creative writer, and his genius was to take the work of others and fashion it into a sonorous, cadenced language that would bear constant liturgical repetition in chantries for private prayer and cathedrals for collective worship. In fashioning the high language of English culture found in the Prayer Book, and so influential subsequently in English spiritual life, he resisted the movement of his time to load up his collects and eucharistic prayers with Greek and Latin phrases fashionable among humanist intellectuals, a circle in which he easily traveled. A linguistic conservative with a near-perfect ear for the patterns of speech and the mystery and meaning of language, in the midst of a political maelstrom, Cranmer, working largely alone in his study, turned out the achievement by which he is known to the ages, his English Prayer Book.

Despite his hesitancy, it would be wrong to view Cranmer as the king's rubber-stamp archbishop. Cranmer was an unqualified believer in the Lutheran idea of the "godly prince." The monarch's strong hand, he reasoned, was the only way to preserve domestic peace, prevent foreign invasions, and guard against heresy. That meant a national church headed by a king instead of a pope. Next is the question of temperaments. Henry was strong-willed and headstrong, intrinsically suspicious of those around him, usually with reason. Hans Holbein the Younger's (1497–1543) portrait of Henry is confirmed by contemporary accounts of a determined, pleasure-loving monarch who would let no one stand in his way. The archbishop was utterly loyal to the king, and his loyalty was rewarded by steady royal support in an era when the Tower of London was filled with once-powerful persons who opposed or miscalculated their relationship with the king. In one case, Henry allowed Cranmer to preside over an inquiry against himself brought by some scheming Kentish clergy and laity who went directly to the king in an effort to unseat the archbishop.

Cranmer was no Becket, no power politician, but he did intercede from time to time on behalf of persons who fell from the king's favor: Anne Boleyn, with whose family Cranmer once lived; John Fisher, the venerable scholar-bishop of Rochester, condemned to death as a traitor in 1535 because he opposed Henry's desire to rid himself of his wife; and

Thomas More, former Lord Chancellor, whose opposition to the Act of Supremacy led to his beheading in 1535. Cranmer's interventions did not save their lives, but he tried within the means available to him.

CRANMER AND EDWARD VI

Cranmer's impact on the larger church came only after Henry was safely in the tomb. Present at Henry's death in 1547, Cranmer also officiated at the coronation of the sickly youth Edward VI. It was during Edward's brief reign, 1547–1553, that his most lasting work was achieved. A book of *Homilies* to instruct clergy and laity was published in 1547. It would be republished, and its sermons often read verbatim by the clergy, until 1859. A translation of a German catechism was issued in 1548. The first Book of Common Prayer was completed in November 1548, the second in 1552. The Forty-Two Articles, later reduced to thirty-nine, appeared in 1553. Cranmer also compiled and codified existing canon law, but it was never ratified. In it he let stand provisions for the lawful persecution of heretics and acquiesced when Joan Bocher, also known as "Joan of Kent," was burned as an unrepentant heretic in May 1550 for denying the incarnation.

Edward was a remarkable youth, theologically astute beyond his years, and seriously committed to a path of reform. He also pursued a teenager's passion for deer hunting and followed the pageantry of English military display. The six years of his reign were a time of revolutionary change in English religious life, much of it directed by his godfather, Cranmer, and other evangelical advisers, but with the full participation and consent of the king.

With Edward's death, Cranmer again vacillated. An unwavering devotee of the divinely given monarchy, he supported Henry's decision that royal succession should pass to Mary, Henry's daughter with Catherine of Aragon. Notwithstanding, he signed a document giving the crown to sixteen-year-old Lady Jane Grey, whose tenuous claim to the throne was traceable to descent from Henry VII. Lady Jane made no personal claim to the crown and was beheaded, as was her husband, in the fury following the plot's failure. Cranmer was ordered confined to Lambeth Palace, then the Tower. He could have fled to the Continent, but chose to stay and defend himself instead.

CRANMER'S DEATH

Like many formative figures of the Church of England at this time, the gentle Cranmer died violently. During the reign of Mary Tudor, 1553–1558, Cranmer was ultimately tried for heresy, as were his colleagues Nicholas Ridley (c. 1500–1555), bishop of London, and Hugh Latimer (c. 1485–1555), bishop of Worcester. As flames engulfed him, Latimer said to his fellow martyr, "Be of good comfort, Master Ridley, and play the man; we shall this day light such a candle by God's grace in England as I trust shall never be put out." Cranmer, though also imprisoned at this time in Oxford, did not witness their procession to the stake or final moments.[4]

The archbishop was pressured to recant his doctrinal positions, which he did to an extent. Although an unequivocal supporter of the monarch, Cranmer could not accept Mary's religious beliefs, and his tormentors made the most of this apparent contradiction. In a statement shortly before his death on March 21, 1556, the sixty-five-year-old prelate acknowledged that he had changed his positions in hope of saving his life, but finally he could go no further in agreeing with his accusers. Subjected to a show trial that could have served as a model for later Nazi and Stalinist political trials, Cranmer was placed on a high stand by the Oxford church's rood screen, heckled by his interrogators, and led before the altar, where mockingly he was stripped of replicas of his priestly garments. Confounding his accusers, who had prematurely disseminated news of his repentance, shortly before his death he plunged his hand into the flames, saying, "This hand hath offended," after which he was consumed by fire without any visible signs of pain.

Dickens writes of Cranmer's death:

> Shortly before the execution the government decided to make capital out of Cranmer's recantations by printing them, together with the final one which he was due to pronounce at the stake. But this he failed to deliver. Instead, he managed before he was pulled down to repudiate all his recantations, to denounce the Pope as Antichrist and to repeat his Protestant doctrine of the Eucharist. . . . with their usual blend of bad luck and blundering, the Marians had failed to exploit the supreme opportunity they had so assiduously sought. To gain Cranmer's discrediting surrender rather than risk this appalling rebuff it would have been a thousand times preferable to have spared his life.[5]

A Balance Sheet

Cranmer was not a blameless hero, neither was he a villain. He made some clear mistakes, like not standing up to Henry as he rid himself of his wives, or letting Joan Bocher be burned. The signing of conflicting papal and royal oaths at the time of his installation and pledging support to both Mary and Lady Jane Grey can be attributed to his trying to pass unsuccessfully between the Scylla and Charybdis of competing loyalties. Cranmer won more skirmishes than he lost, but his losses were pivotal ones. In his defense, his temperament was a scholarly, self-critical one, with little taste for political combat, and even if he had the constitution of Becket, it would have done him no good to confront the headstrong monarch.

In his English Prayer Book, Cranmer made a lasting contribution to the ages. Not that his work was original—almost all of it was borrowed from other sources, Roman Catholic and Protestant. But he had an unwavering eye for the right phrase, a composer's ear for the musicality of language, and an artist's gift for pulling together disparate materials— all the more exceptional because of the age's sharp theological conflicts. Finally, his heroism at the hour of death assures him a permanent place in the company of martyrs. If Henry had the title "Defender of the Faith" and went peacefully to his grave, Cranmer's adult life was spent championing the faith as he knew it, for which he paid with his life.

Queen Mary

Edward VI, the male heir on whom Henry gambled so much, died in 1553, at age fifteen, from a pulmonary infection. This allowed Mary, Henry's eldest daughter, part-Spanish and a devout Roman Catholic, to assume the throne until her death five years later in 1558. Mary's brief reign ended disastrously. By marrying the king of Spain and making him king of England, she alarmed those fearful of becoming once again embroiled in Continental politics. Mary pushed a willing Parliament to repeal most of the last thirty years' reform legislation, but her efforts to reverse the Reformation's tides came too late. The reform ideas had been planted, and the institutions altered by the time she came to power. Given the change at the top, most clergy quickly swore loyalty to Mary; some two thousand priests abandoned wives in order to retain their posts. Married clergy were removed from parishes, as were heretics. Protestants fled to the Continent or were burned at the stake; more than three hundred persons paid for their beliefs with their lives. In her reign's final years, Mary's policies collapsed about her. A Spanish husband persuaded her to send English troops into a war against France, which the French won at Calais in 1558. The pope, for whom she had risked all, by now was closely aligned with France and expressed no gratitude to Mary for her efforts to restore England to the shepherd of Rome. Alienated from her subjects, who were stung by the losses to France, and with little to show for her religious efforts, she died a few months later, bitter and disappointed, and without any heir.

QUEEN ELIZABETH I

Queen Elizabeth I, monarch from 1558 to 1603, was twenty-five when she began to pick up the pieces of her half-sister Mary's disastrous reign. A promotion for the film *Elizabeth* downplayed the delicate political and religious aspects of the age, which it depicted as a "plush and bloody 16th-century thriller" in which the virgin queen emerges "from dewy-eyed girl to stone-faced icon amid assassination attempts and shadowy court intrigue. . . . Contains burning, bludgeoning, beheading, throats-slashing, torture, corpses, and sex," all of which was true. Elizabeth inherited a half-feudal and largely rural nation, with a strong Catholic religious presence despite Protestantism's incursions. Further, she had far fewer political options than her blustery father, nor was her temperament comparable to his. Lacking the power and money available to Henry VIII, her reform efforts during a forty-four year reign were characterized by cautious planning and application. Although in 1565 she decreed that the church should set standards for clerical ceremonies and dress, she was unable to prevent the introduction of clerical marriages and the removal of crucifixes. (She kept one in the royal chapel, to the chagrin of her opponents.) Elizabeth moved cautiously to restore power to the monarch as head of a national church through both retaining a clerical hierarchy and juggling its aspirations with those of growing numbers of squires and merchants. A skilled orator and author, Elizabeth was very much in charge of state and church, was articulate about her opinions, and was given to spontaneous responses to situations in which she found herself.

For example, following the English victory over the Spanish Armada, Elizabeth wrote a prayer in a psalm form that was sung as she made her way through London:

> Look and bow down Thine ear, O Lord.
> From Thy bright sphere behold and see.
> Thy handmaid and Thy handiwork,
> Amongst Thy priests, offering to Thee
> Zeal for incense, reaching the skies;
> Myself and sceptre, sacrifice.[6]

Although Elizabeth was respectful of the church, there was no mistaking who was in charge—as in her letter to a London bishop reluctant to let one of her courtiers build a house on land claimed by the bishop:

> Proud prelate,
>
> You know what you were before I made you what you are: If you do not immediately comply with my request by G—I will unfrock you.
>
> Elizabeth[7]

Elizabeth was a self-confident, decisive figure personally, but had first to consolidate power, for the old Tudor supremacy had been badly battered by Henry VIII's two successors. Prospects of civil war were real, and religiously the country was split into three factions: those loyal to Rome, those who remained Protestant but had either moved abroad or remained silent, and those who sought to preserve the Catholic tradition, reformed of its abuses and excesses yet combined with the Reformation's attractive features. In January 1559 a parliamentary Act of Supremacy restored the state church's position to what it had been during Henry's time, forbid the spiritual jurisdiction of any foreign prince, and legislated against anyone supporting a foreign authority against the queen. It also decreed that laity should receive the sacrament in both kinds, bread and wine, instead of bread only, and acknowledged Elizabeth as "supreme governor on earth" of church and state. A second Act of Uniformity completed the basic reforms, restoring the 1552 Prayer Book, with severe penalties for those who did not use it. The 1552 Prayer Book contained small but significant changes from its predecessors. The controversial Black Rubric was removed, with its denial of the real presence of Christ in the bread and wine. The sentences for administration were adroitly rearranged and altered, putting the 1549 language, "The body of our Lord Jesus Christ . . . preserve thy body and soul unto everlasting life" before the 1552 words, "Take and eat this in remembrance. . . ." Changes in the document reflect the Elizabethan Settlement's effort to combine traditional uniformity in public worship with an understanding of Protestant belief and practice.

In 1563, the Thirty-Nine Articles, a revision of Cranmer's Forty-Two Articles, were issued as a basic statement of church belief. A second book of *Homilies* was published in 1571, updating the 1547 book. As before, the collection's intent was to instruct unlettered clergy and illiterate congregations in the fundamentals of Christian belief. A final homily "Against Rebellion" (No. 21) was added following the Northern Rebellion of 1569 that sought to place Mary Queen of Scots on the throne. On balance, the statutes enacted during Elizabeth's time were less sweeping than those promulgated by her father but were more finely honed. In essence, church control now came not directly from the crown or its agent, a Wolsey or a Thomas Cromwell, but through church commissioners, representing a subtle but real shift in the locus of power. Richard Hooker (c. 1554–1600), one of the most lucid exponents for the emerging Church of England, expressed the formula providing an Elizabethan Settlement for relations between church and state, "We hold, that seeing there is not any man of the Church of England but the same man is also a member of the commonwealth; nor any man a member of the commonwealth which is not also of the Church of England . . . so with us, that no person appertaining to the one can be denied to be also of the other."[8]

If Henry was his own theologian, Elizabeth, schooled in languages, not theology, was an adroit politician, content to operate through laws and commissions, but to the same end, the consolidation of state power. Dickens described her:

> Elizabeth was an admirer but not a mental replica of her father. Theological tastes and learning were not hereditary in the family, and her education had been chiefly linguistic . . . perhaps no young woman of twenty-five has ever taken personal decisions having consequences so momentous. While intelligent and cautious to the point of indecision, she exuded an air of authority. . . . She had the inestimable advantage of understanding Englishmen . . . more clearly than other Tudors she perceived their hunger for romance without expense.[9]

Rome did not take the loss of England lightly, and in 1568 the pope supported Mary Queen of Scots (1542–1587), his preferred heir to the throne, hoping, as an outsider might, that a Catholic rebellion in the north would sweep southward. The pope excommunicated Elizabeth in

1570; a copy of the papal edict was smuggled into England and nailed to the bishop of London's palace door. The effort backfired; the northern rebellion fizzled and rebels were harshly put down. The excommunication edict forced Elizabeth to take action against papal supporters; in 1581 an act was passed declaring a "traitor" anyone joining the Church of Rome, and in 1587 Mary Queen of Scots, who had been in league with the Spanish plotters, was executed.

The gaps of Mary Tudor's era were now firmly sealed; the time was past when popes or foreign powers could tamper with English institutions, although one spectacular attempt remained in the Spanish Armada of 1588. This was to be Philip II's stunning victory for Spain and Catholicism, but it was doom-ridden from the start. The lumbering Spanish galleons were out-maneuvered by the smaller, faster English ships fighting in their own waters, and by what the Spanish called a "Protestant wind." Although the Spanish fleet began with 131 ships, only 65 returned to Spain. When the conflict ended, England had defeated Europe's largest power and an aggressive spirit of English nationalism was demonstrated. England would now become an international maritime presence, and within a century its settlers, merchants, and missionaries would journey to the earth's ends.

Protestantism emerged in England at the same time as merchant capitalism, and the two movements encouraged one another. "Men did not become capitalists because they were Protestants, nor Protestants because they were capitalists," the historian Christopher Hill has written. "In a society already becoming capitalist, Protestantism facilitated the triumph of new values. There was no inherent theological reason for the Protestant emphasis on frugality, hard work, accumulation; but that emphasis was a natural consequence of the religion of the heart in a society where capitalist production was developing."[10]

PURITANISM

Followers of the "Hot Party"

If, by the late sixteenth century, Catholic influence waned, a new religious force appeared—growing numbers of radical Protestants called Puritans for their desire to purify the church, to make it again the pure, simple institution they believed it once was. If the great theme in English church life from the early years until now was tension between the national church and Rome, and between Catholic and Protestant, for the next two centuries conflict between Puritan and royalist would be a central issue in English church life. Puritan beliefs differed little from what conventional church members believed at first, except for a growing distaste for bishops and ceremonies. Bent on reform of lives, Puritans attended lengthy church services on Sundays, plus lectures during the week, sometimes singing psalms as they walked from place to place. If Luther's thought provided its first wave in England in the early 1500s, Calvin's was the second wave by the 1540s, from which the enduring presence of English Puritanism emerged. Many English Protestant refugees, fleeing their country during Mary's persecutions, learned the Swiss reformer's ideas in cities like Zurich and Geneva.

Unlike Catholics, Puritans originally had no political agenda, nor did they seek to violate the law. Most supported the queen; their criticism was of what they regarded as lingering Catholic influences in the church, especially for its hierarchy and use of ceremony. Many Puritans had lived and studied in Calvin's Geneva and found church government by assemblies and councils more attractive than priesthood and episcopacy. While content to let the monarchy stand, their energies and loyalties were with a new system of government by presbyters. In addition, they replaced church vestments, the sign of the cross at baptism, ornaments, wedding rings, stained glass and music, choosing a starkly simple service, paying heavy attention to Bible readings, sermons, and, for music, metrical chanting of the psalms. For those who had endured a generation of seesawing between Rome and Canterbury, Puritanism's certainty was an undeniable attraction. As the movement grew in numbers and popularity, it became the breeding ground of zealots preaching civil disobedience and overthrowing the religious establishment. In their plainness and earnestness, Puritans were often prey to satire. Shakespeare's Malvolio in *Twelfth Night* and Ben Jonson's Mr. Zeal-of-the-land Busy are but two such characters. Puritanism began as a mainstream movement, deeply within the crucible of the Church of England, where it took shape and definition, and claimed a lasting place in the nation's political and religious life. It was dominated not only by an almost morbid moral sensitivity but also by outspoken opposition to usury, greed, and social injustice.

The Puritans opposed the use of "graven images," by which they meant almost all ceremonial objects. Iconoclasm, the destruction of icons and images, was extensive in the 1550s, with a parliamentary Act against Books and Images and the further sale of plate and church ornaments. The new bishop of Gloucester refused to wear cope and surplice at his consecration, saying he could find no New Testament precedent for them. The bishop of London ordered stone altars removed from churches. Clergy were enjoined against holding a "counterfeit popish mass in kissing the Lord's board, washing fingers after the Gospel, shifting the book from one place to another, licking the chalice . . . ringing sacring [consecration—*ed.*] bells or setting any light upon the altar."[11]

The reform-minded Archbishop of Canterbury Edmund Grindal (1519–1583) sought to rid the country of disorderly customs. One of his injunctions, while archbishop of York, was:

> That no innkeeper, alehouse-keeper, victualler, or tippler, shall admit or suffer any person or persons in his house or backside to eat, drink, or play at cards, tables, bowls, or other games in time of common prayer, preachings, or reading of homilies, on the Sundays or holy days; and that there be no shops set open on Sundays or holy days, nor any butchers or other suffered to sell meat or other things upon the Sundays or holy days.
>
> That the minister and churchwardens shall not suffer any lords of misrule, or summer lords and ladies, or any disguised persons or others in rushbearings . . . to come unreverently into any church or chapel or churchyard, and there dance or play any unseemly parts with scoffs, jests, wanton gestures, or ribald talk, namely in the time of divine service or of any sermon.[12]

THE CULTURAL CONTRIBUTION
OF THE ELIZABETHAN AGE

The cultural achievements of the Elizabethan Age were more properly evident in the secular sphere, and the Church of England, as a religious body supporting sacred music and art, made few contributions in this century. For one thing, struggles for independence were still fresh—there was not time enough for the subtleties of an independent fine arts tradition to develop yet, with a few signal exceptions. Active hostility to Catholic aesthetic traditions and iconoclasm were rampant; sincere Christians smashed ancient stained glass windows and pulled down historic rood screens and statues, believing they were destroying graven images forbidden in the Second Commandment. Priceless windows were destroyed for their lead; ancient wall paintings were scraped off or covered over; pipe organs were hacked apart. The statues and rood screens were replaced by royal and patronal coats of arts and tombs. Doomsday and other wall paintings gave way to boards containing the Decalogue, the Lord's Prayer, and the Creed, the unadorned essentials of Christian behavior, prayer, and belief. A royal decree of 1547 abolished what remained of fine arts in the churches:

> they shall take away utterly extinct and destroy all shrines, covering of shrines, all tables, candlesticks, trindles, rolls of wax, pictures, paintings, and all other monuments of feigned miracles, pilgrimages, idolatry, and superstition: so that there remain no memory of the same in walls, glass-windows, or elsewhere within their churches or houses. And they shall exhort all their parishioners to do the like within their several houses.[13]

In addition, there were few changes in church architecture. Altars were removed, replaced by freestanding tables—one critic called them "oyster boards"—placed lengthwise between two sides of the choir in the chancel. Church furniture was generally retained, but a reading desk was added, from which the morning prayer leader conducted most of the service, except when a sermon was preached from the pulpit. To the latter an hour-glass was attached, although some preachers reversed it midway through a sermon; a peg behind the pulpit held the preacher's black gown.

In the sixteenth century, a "two-room" concept of liturgical space developed. The celebrant came down among the people to read and preach during Morning and Evening Prayer; then communicants moved into the chancel for the eucharistic rite. Horton Davies, a liturgical scholar, observes:

> Though the one-room plan for an "auditory" church, which Wren was to use for his churches a century later, was more logical for Anglican worship, the Elizabethan arrangement had two advantages. . . . The first was that moving to the chancel for the Communion service seemed to give the Sacrament a special sacredness, which has been specially emphasized through most of Anglican history; the chancel screen helped separate the liturgy of the catechumens from the liturgy of the faithful, thus imparting to the climax of worship a sense of deep mystery.[14]

THE ROLE OF THE PRINTING PRESS IN THE ENGLISH REFORMATION

The English Reformation was not caused by, but was aided by, the spread of the printing press, which allowed the Bible to be disseminated in English and works by Lutheran and other Protestants to reach wider audiences, especially students, clerics, and the growing literate class of independent-minded merchants and traders important to English society from this time forward. In 1477 William Caxton (c. 1422–1491) established a movable-type printing press at Westminster; others soon followed and a vast literature of tracts and books was issued at prices affordable to many people. It was difficult to control the content and diffusion of printed matter, to the frustration of religious and political censors. England had only a handful of printers, but many more, with the latest equipment and able translators, worked in Protestant Germany and the Netherlands.

A brisk book trade between the Continent and England grew, and smuggling illicit religious works was well organized despite the long list of prohibited titles, such as Luther's works. Chests with false bottoms, flour sacks with packages of books as well as meal, cargoes of grain and bales of cloth with piles of flat printed sheets interlarded with the merchandise were means employed to spread the Reformation, not only through a large port like London, but through small ports along England's eastern seaboard as well. A great demand for popular devotional literature arose, and possibly 60 percent of such works came from overseas during the century's first half, despite periodic efforts to suppress such imports.[15]

THE BIBLE IN ENGLISH
"the salt of the earth"—"let there be light"

No force was more important to the English Reformation than the widespread dissemination of the Bible in English. Surprisingly, the Bible's translation into English came decades after its availability in other European languages. The first of many Bible translations had been printed in German by 1466, although Luther's New Testament, a landmark of German literature, did not appear until 1522. The whole or parts of the Bible appeared in Spanish, Portuguese, Italian, Dutch, and Czech by the late 1400s. Access to the Bible was fraught with difficulties. The Roman Catholic Church held that placing the Bible in the hands of people not properly educated was dangerous; it could lead to both errors in doctrine and questioning the church's authority. Thus, until 1536, possession of a Bible could result in the miscreant being burned to death at the stake. In 1543, at the prodding of conservative Henry VIII, the House of Lords passed a bill stating that "no woman, no artificers, prentices, journeymen, serving men of the degrees of yeoman or under, husbandman, nor laborers" could read the scriptures, the penalty being a month's wages. A shepherd lamented this restriction in a hand-lettered notation on the flyleaf:

> At Oxford, the year 1546, brought down to Saintbury [Gloucs] by John Darbye, price 14*d*, when I keep Mr. Latimer's sheep. I bought this book when the Testament was abrogated, that shepherds might not read it. I pray God amend that blindness. Writ by Robert Williams, keeping sheep upon Saintsbury Hill, 1546.[16]

Despite opposition, the English Bible was distributed widely during the 1530s and 1540s. First came Tyndale's New Testament, widely circulated in corrected form in 1535, and in the same year Miles Coverdale published the whole Bible in English. William Tyndale (1495–1536) an Oxford-educated English cleric, was the principal translator of the New Testament into English, and while later generations regard the King James Version of 1611 as the Authorized Version, much of it was Tyndale's work. Tyndale had an unrivaled ear for the rhythm and poetry of vernacular English. A long list of expressions now common in English originated with him, such as "the salt of the earth," "let there be light," "the burden and heat of the day," "a law unto themselves," and "the signs of the times." Tyndale's images, almost as much as Shakespeare's, have worked their way into English speech, with phrases such as "the birds of the air, the fish of the sea," "fight the good fight," "there may be one flock, and one shepherd." The story of Adam and Eve, the nativity and Easter accounts, so much a part of English culture, were disseminated as his translation spread throughout England. At the same time Tyndale, deeply aware of Luther's thought, replaced "elder" for "priest" and "congregation" for "church" and introduced other Protestant terms. His great desire was to place the Bible in the hands of a wide range of English readers. Rebuffed at home, he moved to Germany in 1524. Tyndale told an English church leader, "If God spare my life, ere many years I will cause a boy that driveth the plough shall know more scriptures than thou dost." Working in Antwerp with funds supplied by English merchants, Tyndale completed a translation of the New Testament and sections of the Old Testament. Henry VIII and Cardinal Wolsey feared the English Bible would threaten church order and pursued Tyndale to have his works destroyed. Betrayed by a supposed friend into moving from the safety of Antwerp's English house, he was seized, tried as a heretic, strangled, and burned at the stake in Brussels in 1536. His last words reportedly were, "Lord, open the King of England's eyes."

It was Miles Coverdale (1488–1568) who published the complete Bible in English. His first edition was printed in Germany in 1535; the Old Testament came from Italian Dominican sources, much of the New Testament from Luther's German Bible, and for the rest he took Tyndale's text with only minor alterations. Coverdale, still an Augustinian friar, had a gift for poetic speech, and his psalms were retained in the Book of Common Prayer as the Psalter until the 1928 Prayer Book revisions. Dickens observed, "Even in their obscure moments they have the mellow beauty of some ancient, familiar window with slightly jumbled glass; one would scarcely have the imperfections set right."[17] Coverdale married a Scottish gentlewoman, became bishop of Exeter, fled to Denmark and the Continent during Mary's reign, returned and eventually became an early leader of the Puritan movement.

Henry VIII, prodded by Thomas Cranmer, issued a royal order in 1536 that "the whole Bible of the largest volume, in English" should be placed in each parish church for individual reading and discussion. In 1538 Coverdale was asked to produce such a Bible, called the Great Bible, whose magnificently cadenced Psalter was retained even in the 1928 Book of Common Prayer. The volume was ready by April 1539, with a second edition and a preface by Cranmer appearing the following year. The work incorporated the century's latest biblical scholarship, drawing on Sebastian Münster's Latin translation of the Old Testament and the New Testament of Erasmus. By 1541 five editions had been printed, and the Bible in English was an accepted fact, although under Mary there would be efforts to collect the volume and burn it.

By the mid-1550s a small Bible could be bought for the price of a skilled worker's day's wages, and those who could not afford their own Bibles could hear excerpts read at Morning or Evening Prayer, or could leaf through the Great Bible placed in each parish church for public use. The English Bible was important to the development of both the Church in England and British culture and politics. All factions claimed it as their own; its imagery soon worked its way into the fabric of the English language, and its values, however distorted at times, became the norm for religious and civil conduct. It is difficult for later generations to imagine the importance of making the Bible available to a wider public, but the impact was revolutionary. The large volume was chained to a lectern in the rear of a church, and villagers came to hear the Bible read, or to read it themselves, and stayed to discuss the readings at length. Often they knew more about biblical characters and events than of nearby villages. In an era long before radio, television, and easy access to print media, biblical language and imagery penetrated the culture.

AN ENGLISH PRAYER BOOK

Nothing is more quintessentially Anglican than the Book of Common Prayer. Even those who no longer read it are drawn to the book, storing aging volumes with locks of ancestral hair and fading daguerreotypes. When periodic movements arise to suggest revising or updating its language, opponents appear from the wings, passionately arguing that the book is only slightly less hallowed than the tablets Yahweh gave to Moses, and therefore is not to be tampered with, under pain of deluges or plagues of locusts striking the would-be revisionists. In reality, the Prayer Book was a work of temporary historical compromise, drawn from numerous sources. Its emphasis shifted on key points as the church hammered out its beliefs, especially those concerning the Eucharist, the central act of Christian worship in which bread and wine are consecrated and consumed by priest and congregation. The English Prayer Book had its origins in Henry's reign. Cranmer worked assiduously on it, but did not go public with his results until Henry was safely in the grave.

In matters of personal and communal faith, Henry was largely a conservative Catholic. The king had no interest in liturgical reform, but in 1544 when war threatened with France and Scotland, he urged Cranmer to prepare an English-language litany for parish use. From 1540 to 1547 Cranmer also worked on an English Prayer Book, basing his work on the traditional Roman services and drawing also on Spanish Roman Catholic, Lutheran, Sarum, York, and Orthodox sources. The book brought together in a single volume the missals, breviaries, and manuals then in use, making them available to clergy and laity. Everyone, for the first time, was praying from the same book in the vernacular language. Multiple daily offices were reduced to two, laity received both bread and wine at communion, and baptism became a public rite, to be administered on Sundays and holy days. Saints days were limited to authentic New Testament characters, and rites were simplified. Only scriptural readings were used in the lectionary; pious commentaries on the lives of the saints were eliminated. The New Testament was read in its entirety every four months, the abridged Old Testament yearly, the Psalter monthly. The use of devotional objects such as holy water and ashes was eliminated, as in the minds of many such objects had taken on powers beyond their intended symbolism.

Above all, the book was in English. By placing in one book, in a language known to all, the entire range of church services, including the priest's parts, which previously were said privately by the celebrant alone from the altar missal, the distance between priest and congregation was reduced. Cranmer was a great English prose stylist, and sections of the book, including some of its shorter prayers and collects, are often included in anthologies of English literature. "He was a connoisseur of English who was not ashamed to borrow what he liked from other people's efforts," Diarmaid MacCulloch, a leading contemporary scholar on Cranmer has written, "so what we think of as Cranmer's Prayer Book English is in fact a patchwork of his adaptations of other writers." "If he were writing liturgy today he would face crippling lawsuits for breach of copyright," the Oxford historian stated, adding, "his motive was not sinister; it was an expression of his natural modesty and practicality, and his alterations of existing texts were almost invariably improvements."[18]

If the language was simpler than those previously employed in older liturgies, it was still vague in several important places, such as in the words of consecration during the communion rite; Cranmer planned it that way. As an ecclesiastical politician, he knew the possible boundaries of acceptable language; as a liturgical reformer, deeply influenced by Continental Protestantism, he wanted to present an essentially Protestant book, yet one acceptable to many Catholics. It almost worked—the Church of England's first Prayer Book lasted three years.

The English Prayer Book was introduced two years after Henry's death, on Whitsunday, June 9, 1549. Importantly, the Prayer Book's use was mandated by Parliament rather than the king, marking a shift in power from crown to Tudor laity. A law declared it the sole book to be used in English churches, under pain of imprisonment, although surely its spread was gradual. This was not an age of public toleration of diverse viewpoints. Sovereigns realized that control of churches, their rites, and sermons, was effectual control of the people. British monarchs made a stab at such control, usually through regulating the content of Prayer Books, and through licensing preachers or through censors regulating the substance of their sermons, but such measures never worked well for long.

Still, for all its beauty, the Prayer Book lasted only three years and never gained popular support. Reformers felt it did not go far enough; traditionalists thought that it went too far. There were public demonstrations on both sides, and in 1552 a more "Protestant" book was introduced which dropped the word "mass" from the communion service. The daily offices became Morning and Evening Prayer, to which were added opening sentences, a confession of sins, and an absolution or assurance of pardon. Liturgical vestments were no longer mandated, leaving priests with surplices, which to the uninitiated might be mistaken for a nightshirt of fine material, and bishops with rochets, long white robes with billowing sleeves. Kneeling was no longer required, except to receive communion; prayers replaced the use of oil in anointing the newly baptized or ill.

The greatest change was in the eucharistic rite. The communion table was just that, a table and not an altar, with the celebrant standing on the north side; parish congregational communion replaced private masses. Both bread and wine were offered communicants, a sharp departure from the earlier bread-only practice. Was the communion rite an act of remembrance or a recreating of Christ's body and blood, Transubstantiation, as it had been called in Roman Catholic belief? The new wording strongly suggests a memorial act, with the words, "Take and eat this in remembrance that Christ died for thee, and feed on him in thy heart by faith, with thanksgiving." Cranmer, in his own eucharistic beliefs, was distinctly Protestant, speaking of a "spiritual presence" in the bread and wine. God's presence came through faith, but faith came not from merit but as a gift of God to God's people. This was Luther's doctrine of justification by faith now expressed in liturgical language.

The Church of England's eucharistic belief in this period was clearly stated by Nicholas Ridley (c. 1500–1555), Cranmer's co-martyr. The bishop of London could not accept Christ's local physical presence in the communion bread and wine, but argued for the divine presence through grace. God remains in heaven, he argued, corporally separated from humanity until the Day of Judgment. But, as the sun sits high in the sky yet its rays shine on earth, so Christ, the Sun of righteousness, fills humanity with a divine radiance, giving to bread and wine the presence of God's grace. This is not Transubstantiation, as in the Roman rite, nor Memorialism, as some Protestants believed, but a different explanation for the Eucharist. Here, at a crucial juncture, the Church of England assumed a position it would often take, accommodating all sides to a point, while leaving the issue's resolution somewhat vague, in majestic, mystical language. Remember that these were formative years in which powerful opponents clashed and doctrine was being hammered out, often with the instruments of war close at hand.

At times, preaching in this age on topics such as the Eucharist was earthy, direct, and confrontational, as in this 1571 sermon by John Bridges attacking the Catholic doctrine of Transubstantiation. Bridges says:

> [Catholics] turned Christ out of his own likeness, and made him look like a round cake, nothing like to Jesus Christ, no more than an apple is like an oyster, nor so much, for there appears neither arms nor hands, feet nor legs, back nor belly, head nor body of Christ; but all is visored and disguised under the form of a wafer, as light as a feather, as thin as a paper, as white as a kerchief, as round as a trencher, as flat as a pancake, as small as a shilling, . . . as much taste as a stick and as dead as a door nail to look upon. O blessed God, dare they thus disfigure our Lord and Savior Jesus Christ?[19]

"FROM THE BISHOP OF ROME . . . GOOD LORD, DELIVER US"

In 1559, under Elizabeth, some vestments were restored and a prickly phrase in Cranmer's litany was removed, "From the Bishop of Rome and all his detestable enormities, Good Lord, deliver us." A catechism was added in 1604, and in 1662 editorial changes clarified how services should be conducted; but the book was basically the Elizabethan book of 1552 with small but significant changes. The English Book of Common Prayer thus remained for over two centuries until 1928, when a proposed revised version was narrowly defeated in the House of Commons.[20]

It is fortunate that Cranmer undertook his editorial work at a time when the English language, as it is known today, was in its formative stages. He thus stands alongside Tyndale, Shakespeare, and Milton as one of the shapers of modern English. A student of the period writes, "Through his connoisseurship, he created a prose which was self-consciously formal and highly-crafted, intended for repeated use until it was polished as smooth as a pebble on the beach. Yet he spared the users of the Prayer Book the worst pomposities of humanism and the sprawling sentence constructions which are only too common in the English prose writers of the sixteenth century."[21] In the long run, Cranmer's contribution to the church's life was not in formulating crystalline doctrine—no prelate of the age could do that—but in creating possibilities for worship for English women and men through widespread dissemination in English of the Bible and the Book of Common Prayer.

Writing of the Book of Common Prayer, C. S. Lewis said:

In the Prayer Book, that earnest age, not itself rich either in passion or in beauty, is matched in a most fruitful opposition and overwhelming material and with originals all but over-ripe in their artistry. It arrests them, binds them in strong syllables, strengthens them even by limitation as they in turn erect and transfigure it. Out of that conflict the perfection springs. There are of course many good, and different, ways of praying. Its temper may seem cold to those reared in other traditions but no one will deny that it is strong. It offers little and concedes little to merely natural feelings: even religious feelings it will not heighten till it has first sobered them; but at its greatest it shines with a white light hardly surpassed outside the pages of the New Testament itself.[22]

Later generations have treated the Prayer Book as if it were intended to be permanent, and absent doctrinal statements from councils, and lacking an Anglican pope, the Prayer Book's contents have assumed a status usually reserved for basic creeds. The wording of prayers and rubrics, the eucharistic canon, the Bible lessons selected for each Sunday, and the services of Morning and Evening Prayer were examined as sources of belief. A few years later, as Puritan conflicts sharpened, the defining element between opponents became adherence to the Prayer Book, and much artillery was expended over Prayer Book interpretation.

THE THIRTY-NINE ARTICLES

Anglicans, when asked what represents a concise statement of their church's beliefs, often reply "the Thirty-Nine Articles," then read them and are puzzled by their content. In arguments, church members sometimes consult the Articles, as others might a baseball rule book, then are puzzled by their archaic language. The Thirty-Nine Articles at first appear to stand alongside the Ten Commandments as a basic statement of Christian belief, but that is not the case. The Articles, reduced from forty-two, came about in 1563, fairly late in church history in response to a particularly thorny situation, the need to sort out a set of doctrinal statements acceptable to a spectrum of church opinion. The full title of the document suggests its purposes: *Articles Agreed upon by the Archbishops and Bishops of both Provinces, and the whole Clergy in the Convocation holden at London in the year 1562, for the avoiding of diversities of opinion and for the establishing of Consent touching true religion.*

In the mid-sixteenth century Reformation context, the Articles represent a judiciously worded compromise between more traditional doctrine and growing strains of Puritan thought. They make a minimal statement about the substance of faith and the church's structure, together with its ministry, sacraments, and relationship to the state. Drawn from Lutheran sources such as the Augsburg Confession and Wittenberg Concord, the Articles confirm allegiance to state rather than papacy. For example, Article XXXVII states, "The Power of the Civil Magistrate extendeth to all men, as well Clergy as Laity, in all things temporal; but hath no authority in things purely spiritual. And we hold it to be the duty of all men who are professors of the Gospel, to pay respectful obedience to the Civil Authority, regularly and legitimately constituted." Article VI states, "Holy Scripture containeth all things necessary to salvation: so that whatsoever is not read therein, nor may be proved thereby, is not to be required of any man, that it should be believed as an article of Faith, or be thought requisite or necessary to salvation." This Article gives the Bible and individual interpretation of its contents, as opposed to interpretations delivered *ex cathedra*, a place that would have been unacceptable in England a few years earlier.

The Lutheran expression of Paul's doctrine of justification by faith is expounded in Article XI, "We are accounted righteous before God, only for the merit of our Lord and Savior Jesus Christ by Faith, and not for our own works or deservings. Wherefore, that we are justified by Faith only, is a most wholesome Doctrine, and very full of comfort, as most largely expressed in the Homily of Justification." This Article, and the three that follow, clearly distance the Church of England from Catholic doctrine about salvation coming from good works and through the church as God's intermediary. The point is made explicitly in Article XXII, "The Romish Doctrine concerning Purgatory, Pardons, Worshipping, and Adoration, as well of Images as of Relics, and also Invocation of Saints, is a fond thing, vainly invented, and grounded upon no warranty of Scripture, but rather repugnant to the Word of God." The lengthy Article XVII, "Of Predestination and Election," is an eloquent statement of Protestant belief of that period, differing from Calvin's writings on the topic.

Transubstantiation is rejected in Article XXVIII: it "is repugnant to the plain words of Scripture, overthroweth the nature of a Sacrament, and hath given occasion to many superstitions," while the divine presence "after an heavenly and spiritual manner" is affirmed in the Eucharist.

"The Bread which we break is a partaking of the Body of Christ; and like-wise the Cup of Blessing is a partaking of the Blood of Christ," but "[t]he Sacrament of the Lord's Supper was not by Christ's ordinance reserved, carried about, lifted up, or worshipped," which disallows any veneration of the communion host.

Phrases such as "The Church has authority in Controversies of faith" in Article XX are vague. Did the authority find itself in pronouncements of councils, actions of bishops, or beliefs of individual Christians? The answer is not clear. The Articles should be considered short summaries of Church of England positions on specific issues, stated in general language responsive to contemporary controversies, their studied vagueness allowing various interpretations within a general statement of doctrine.

The Articles lack the tight coherence of a creed. Adherence to the Articles was never demanded of the laity, but clergy and members of Oxford and Cambridge universities were required to subscribe to them until the mid-nineteenth century. After 1865, Church of England clergy were required only to affirm that the church's doctrine as set forth in the Book of Common Prayer and Articles is agreeable to the Word of God and that they will not teach in contradiction of their contents.[23] In later centuries the Thirty-Nine Articles were generally relegated to an obscure corner of most theological libraries. F. D. Maurice associated them with "large wigs, afternoon slumber and hatred of all youthful eagerness and hope." Nevertheless, for the Church of England's leading nineteenth-century theologian, they were an authoritative model of how theology should be presented.[24]

DOCTRINE AND PREACHING

This century produced the English church's most original expositions of religious belief. Faced with periodic challenges to its existence, the church responded with enduring theological statements, such as those contained in the popular sermons of Hugh Latimer, John Jewel's *Apology for the English Church*, and Richard Hooker's *Of the Laws of Ecclesiastical Polity*, a work defying easy categorization. Latimer was the voice of popular reform, Jewel an apologist for the English Reformation, and Hooker the comprehensive theologian for the evolving Church of England. Although their works were crafted in response to particular crises of the moment, these writers and their contemporaries shaped a distinctly Anglican position on issues of church belief and structure which represent a point *in medias res* for the further growth of Church of England theology. Latimer was the foot soldier, Jewel the cavalry, and Hooker the heavy artillery in this contentious age. For this writer, the period of Jewel and Hooker, the second half of the sixteenth century, is one of two high points in the unfolding of Anglican religious thought, the other being the second half of the nineteenth century, the time of Maurice and Gore. In both instances, an unsettled era produced substantial writers who addressed questions of church and state, dogma and doctrine, and the spiritual life with freshness and originality only partially evident in authors who came before and after them.

Hugh Latimer

A major figure of the church between Catholic past and Protestant future was Hugh Latimer (c. 1485–1555), whose manner presaged a sort of emerging English preacher, blunt, rugged, simple, and to the point in expository style. Latimer was in and out of prison in the Tower and periodically defended himself against heated accusations of doctrinal deviation. The prelate, who successful fended off opponents for thirty years, and who was once a royal chaplain to Henry, and close associate of Cranmer, was burned at the stake when Catholicism returned under Mary. Latimer was burned at the same time as Ridley, on October 16, 1555. Cranmer soon followed.

Latimer's sermons, filled with earthy images, were crowd-pleasers, laced with rough humor and void of doctrinal subtleties. He attacked judicial corruption, the decline of charity among nobles, and other social ills, and satirized bishops, taken with "ruffling in their rents, dancing in their dominions . . . munching in their mangers and moiling in their gay manors and mansions" while the devil, "the most diligent prelate and preacher in all England" poisons peoples' hearts.[25] These were not scholarly sermons, but works for popular audiences, filled with homely illustrations, personal examples, proverbs, and words like "merit-mongers" or "brain-sick fools." The most famous was "Of the Plough," preached on New Year's Day 1548. Latimer compared the preacher to a farmer plowing who was "now casting them down with the law and with threatenings of God for sin; now ridging them up again with the Gospel and with the promises of God's favor; now weeding them by telling them their faults and making them forsake sin; now clotting them by breaking their stony hearts and by making them supple-hearted, making them to have hearts of flesh, that is, soft hearts and apt for doctrine to enter in." In a communion meditation Latimer compared the Eucharist to a great feast, "where there be great dishes and delicate fare, there be commonly prepared certain sauces, which shall give men a lust to their meats: as mustard, vinegar, and such like sauces. So this feast, this costly dish, hath its sauces: but what be they? Marry, the cross, affliction, tribulation, persecution, and all manner of miseries: for, like as sauces make lusty the stomach to receive meat, so affliction stirreth up in us a desire to Christ."[26]

Latimer stands with Richard Hooker, Lancelot Andrewes, and with later preachers like John Donne, John Wesley, John Henry Newman, and William Temple among the giants of Anglican preaching. Horton Davies has written, "Latimer's preaching was too courageous, too direct, and too compassionate ever to be mistaken for demagoguery. It was, whether in denunciation, retelling a biblical narrative, or in exposition, despite all its delightful divagations, prophetic and popular preaching at its best."[27]

John Jewel

An English response to the Roman Catholic Counter-Reformation came in a carefully reasoned, sharply worded polemic, the *Apology of the Church of England,* first published in 1562 in Latin. Its author was John Jewel (1522–1571), bishop of Salisbury, whose career reflected the age's doctrinal zig-zags. Jewel's formative years were spent at Oxford, where he was a student of the Continental reformer Peter Martyr, yet as public orator to the university, he composed congratulations to Mary on her accession to the throne. Jewel was present as a notary at the trials of Ridley and Cranmer and signed an anti-Protestant document in 1554. Notwithstanding, he prudently fled to the Continent, where he stayed until Mary's death. After being installed bishop of Salisbury in 1560, he became a major apologist for the Elizabethan Settlement in opposition to Rome.

Describing the state of religion in England, he wrote to Peter Martyr in late 1559, complaining about the lingering presence of Catholic ceremonial, of which the small silver cross in the Queen's chapel was a symbol:

> Religion among us is in the same state which I have often described to you before. The doctrine is every where most pure; but as to ceremonies and maskings, there is a little too much foolery. That little silver cross, of ill-omened origin, still maintains its place in the queen's chapel. Wretched me! This thing will soon be drawn into a precedent. There was at one time some hope of its being removed; and we all of us diligently exerted ourselves, and still continue to do, that it might be so. But as far as I can perceive, it is now a hopeless case. Such is the obstinacy of some minds. There

seems to be far too much prudence, too much mystery, in the management of these affairs; and God alone knows what will be the issue. The slow-paced horses retard the chariot.[28]

His *Apology*, a comprehensive defense of the Church of England and refutation of the Roman Catholic position, drew the line for subsequent controversy with Rome. Jewel challenged opponents to prove their case from the Bible or early church councils, defended a system of church government through regional synods, and argued that a general Reformation of the church was needed and not successfully provided for at the Council of Trent. An Oxford contemporary and cleric whom Jewel had deprived of his living in Salisbury for remaining a Roman Catholic wrote a bitter *Answer* in 1564; Jewel's *Reply* came the following year, Harding's *Confutation* in 1566, Jewel's *Defense* in 1567. By then the range of Anglo-Roman differences was aired, and Jewel's works were commended to the people by Archbishop of Canterbury Richard Bancroft (1544–1610) as a statement of the Church of England's positions in relation to Roman Catholicism.

The Council of Trent, which triggered the Church of England response, met on and off from 1545 to 1563 in the mountainous northern Italian town of Trento. Although it renewed spiritual life and church discipline within the Roman Catholic Church and made regular the standing of individual priests, the role of diocesan synods, and the manner of appointing bishops, it offered no conciliatory gestures to Protestants. The English were miffed at being invited as observers without being allowed to speak or argue in their defense. Scripture and tradition were given equal weight as sources of dogma, rebuffing Protestant arguments favoring the primacy of scripture. The Vulgate translation was proclaimed the authoritative biblical text, squelching the place of many emerging vernacular translations, and the church was declared the sole agent able to interpret the Bible. Traditional doctrines of purgatory, indulgences, and veneration of relics were left intact. There was nothing in the Council of Trent's outcomes for Protestants, who in turn consolidated anti-Roman positions that remained hardened for the next four centuries.

Jewel's conclusion was in sharp, unyielding language:

And in very truth we have tarried not for, in this matter, the authority or consent of the Trent council, wherein we saw nothing done uprightly nor by good order; where also everybody was sworn to the maintenance of one man; where our princes' ambassadors were condemned; where not one of our divines could be heard . . . we have restored our churches by a provincial convocation and have clean shaken off, as our duty was, the yoke and tyranny of the Bishop of Rome, to whom we were not bound, who also had no manner of thing like neither to Christ, nor to Peter, nor to an apostle, nor yet like to any bishop at all.[29]

Through figures like Jewel the English Church defined its doctrine in opposition to the positions taken at the Council of Trent. Conversely, no such reform council was ever convoked in England to ponder doctrines, nor discuss church–state relations, the place of bishops, clergy salaries and appointments, relations with Puritans and Presbyterians, or the place of the Prayer Book and liturgical reform. Such a gathering was never held in England for two reasons; first, when the Council of Trent was convoked, the Reformation was still new to England, and Reformation doctrines had just made their inroads. Also, no monarch or Archbishop of Canterbury would call such a council; its recommendations would threaten the carefully balanced relationship between church and state. Centralized control of church and state was a delicate issue, and examining questions of individual faith was less risky than taking on the institutional problems facing the church, the principal one being where authority lay.

Richard Hooker

The most comprehensive statement of Church of England religious belief and political theory about the relationship between church and state at the end of this century is provided in the writings of Richard Hooker (c. 1554–1600). The serenity and scope of Hooker's prose belie the acrimonious decades in which he wrote. Hooker fended off the once-dominant Catholic movement's smoldering embers, Calvin's encroaching influence, plus the fires of spreading Puritanism, while arguing that the Church of England was defined by more than opposition to these schools of thought. This he did in *Treatise on the Laws of Ecclesiastical Polity*, the first five books of which were published between 1594 and 1597. The work was an ambitious effort to state a theory of natural law, including the relationship of church and state. It tried to do what no previous Church of England apologist attempted, and if it succeeded brilliantly in places, it left many central issues unresolved.

Hooker grew up in an Exeter merchant's household. John Jewel, then bishop of Salisbury, was his sponsor during Hooker's student years, and, after teaching Hebrew at Oxford, Hooker became Master of the Temple, 1585–1591. The starkly simple Temple Church on Fleet Street, where

Hooker spent his formative London years, was a prestigious appointment, the gathering place for England's leading lawyers and royal counselors. It was an exhausting assignment. Hooker's Sunday morning
sermons were refuted that evening by a radical Calvinist cleric whose
intensity of preparation was fueled by having lost out to Hooker for the
prestigious appointment. An observer said, "the forenoon sermon spake
Canterbury, the afternoon Geneva." Then Hooker answered his opponent the following Sunday. The content of his sermons was closely
argued, but he was severely myopic and lacked a strong voice. A contemporary said of his preaching, "he may be said to have made good music
with his fiddle and stick alone, having neither pronunciation nor gesture
to grace his matter."

Hooker retired, at his own request, to a country rectorship in Bishops-
bourne, near Canterbury, where he said "I may keep myself in peace and
privacy, and behold God's blessing spring out of my mother earth, and
eat my own bread without oppositions." His home life was sedentary; a
visitor reported seeing Hooker in the fields, tending his sheep and reading the *Odes of Horace* while his shepherd was off having his meal. A later
composite description in the 1911 edition of the *Encyclopedia Britannica*
is "of a person of low stature and not immediately impressive appearance,
much bent by the influence of sedentary and meditative habits, of quiet
and retiring manners, and discolored in complexion and worn and
marked in feature from the hard mental toil which he had expended on
his great work" which can be compared, *mutatis mutandis*, to the most
creative, encompassing works of a musician like Bach or Beethoven.[30]
Despite being severely myopic, Hooker was cheerful, even humorous in
manner, his prose style expansive, encyclopedic in scope.

In the writings that poured from his pen in his life's last decade,
Hooker painted a vast canvas of natural law governing the universe. Law's
seat "is the bosom of God," its voice "the harmony of the world" (E.P.,
I.xvi.8). Law governs the universe, and both ecclesiastical and civil polities
come under it. There is both natural and positive law, the former lasting
and unchangeable, the latter subject to constant amendment. Political
societies fall under the second category and are subject to change, as are
church bodies. Hooker believed both civil and ecclesiastical society could
be modified. Membership in society is membership in a body organized
by laws, he answered. The theory of government by contractual relationship which Hooker outlined was later elaborated into a full-blown statement of political theory by John Locke.

Hooker, not surprisingly, articulated a political doctrine of church and state supporting Queen Elizabeth. Monarchy was the preferred form of political organization, Hooker believed. These were new times, but he stopped short of making a case for the divine right of kings. The author latched onto the constitutional monarchy as the ideal form of government. Without it, anarchy could reign and individual passions dominate politics; with it, order and stability would prevail. "What power the king hath, he hath it by law; the bounds and limits of it are known," Hooker wrote, without ever setting the bounds. He acknowledged a king could turn tyrannical, leaving undiscussed how a tyrant might be removed from office.

Once Hooker's theory was in place, it was easy to refute Puritans; after all, they rejected ecclesiastical law and thus undermined the whole society, so the argument went. While acknowledging great respect for Puritans, Hooker believed their government by the Elect falsely divided society into separate domains of church and state. The Elizabethan formula of an "ecclesiastical polity," the subject of his massive work, was more representative, a church governed by bishops and parliament. Not a biblical solution, but one in harmony with divine law and reason, by now verified by successful experience. Monarch and Parliament also had enduring religious as well as secular responsibilities, Hooker argued. "A gross error is to think that regal power ought to serve for the good of the body and not of the soul, for men's temporal peace and not for their eternal safety: as if God had ordained kings for no other end and purpose but only to fat up men like hogs to see that they have their mast" [Mast, Old English for pig's food—*ed.*].

Sections of Hooker's political and ecclesiastical canvas were left unpainted, as might be expected in the work of any theorist writing in such unsettled times. Hooker denied the necessity of the episcopacy, which he believed was required by tradition, but dispensable in extreme circumstances; his eucharistic doctrine was less developed than writers like Cranmer, his theory of church and state was a distinct response to the emerging English situation and far from the biblical idea of an Israel of God. Still, it would be wrong to exaggerate the incompleteness of his work, for Hooker tried to do what no comparable writer had attempted so far, sketch a comprehensive theory of church and state, and where he did not complete the edifice at least he boldly left outlines in place on which successors might build.

As a polemicist, Hooker avoided Latimer's direct confrontations, or Jewel's sharp language, coming at Puritan targets elliptically after building a strong foundation of argument. Unlike Jewel, his manner was conciliatory, seeking to find common ground among antagonists rather than provoke new controversy. In tackling the sensitive question of the Eucharist's meaning, he wrote, "What these elements are it skilleth not, it is enough that to me which take them they are the body and blood of Christ, his promise in witness hereof sufficeth, his word he knoweth which way to accomplish; why should any cogitation possess the mind of a faithful communicant but this, O my God thou art true, O my soul thou art happy!" (E.P., V.lxvii.7, 12).

In addition to the content of his works, Hooker earns a lasting place in English letters as a prose stylist. There is a spacious, architectural quality to his writing. He attacks major problems and builds carefully, slowly, in both explaining them and laying out solutions. Often his prose is laced with humor and irony, not always easily discernible in solid paragraphs with massive overlays of qualifying clauses. Here is Hooker summarizing the place of law: "all things in heaven and earth do her homage, the very least as feeling her care, and the greatest as not exempted from her power: both Angels and men and creatures of what condition soever, though each in different sort and manner, yet all with uniform consent, admiring her as the mother of their peace and joy" (E.P., I.xvi.8).

Lancelot Andrewes

If Jewel was the polemicist and Hooker the theorist, Lancelot Andrewes (1560–1626) was the author of some of the century's most lasting devotional literature. Andrewes represented the Arminian faction in Church of England belief, named for a Dutch anti-Calvinist theologian, Jacobus Arminius (1560–1609), who strongly opposed Calvin's doctrine of predestination. Andrewes is best known for his volume *Preces Privatae,* drawing on eastern and western liturgies, championing the origins of Anglican belief in the patristic period, Christendom's first five centuries. It is a jewel of a book, the product of a poetic mind and a deeply reflective religious temperament. For Andrewes, "one canon, reduced to writing by God himself, two testaments, three creeds, four general councils, and the series of fathers of that period—the centuries, that is, before Constantine, and two after—determine the boundary of our faith."[31]

Andrewes, dean of Westminster Abbey and bishop of Chichester, Ely, and Winchester, was a scholar of both scripture and liturgical traditions, a renowned preacher and liturgical specialist. Andrewes is remembered for his poetic sermons and a collection of prayers printed after his death. The manuscript was said to be frayed by his holding it and stained with the author's tears. It followed the model of contemporary devotional manuals, with prayers for each day, written in Greek, Hebrew, or Latin. Void of sentimentality, these are practical guides for the soul seeking Christ. There are prayers of penance, meditations on the nature of faith, intercessory prayers for all sorts and conditions of persons, and praises to God the world's creator and sustainer. John Henry Newman, who used the book for his devotions after mass, said of them three centuries later, "Never has the image of a bee going from flower to flower to gather a honey of fragrant simplicity been so apt."[32]

Andrewes's perspective was anything but insular. There is a generosity and spaciousness to his prayer life. He knew the Church in England needed God's help to make it whole and was aware of splits within the Eastern Church and of the dislocations between Rome and the reformers. He prayed, "For the Church Catholic, its confirmation and increase; Eastern, its deliverance and union; Western, its readjustment and pacification; British, the restoration of the things that are wanting, the strengthening of the things which remain."[33] T. S. Eliot, writing in 1928, at the time of his baptism in the Church of England, was deeply influenced by Andrewes's spirituality. Of his sermons, Eliot writes:

> In this extraordinary prose which appears to repeat, to stand still, but is nevertheless proceeding in the most deliberate and orderly manner, there are often flashing phrases which never desert the memory. In an age of adventure and experiment in language, Andrewes is one of the most resourceful of authors, in his devices for seizing the attention and impressing the memory.

Eliot's "Journey of the Magi" was influenced by Andrewes, as suggested in this passage:

> "Of the wise men come from the east, it was no Summer progress. A cold coming they had of it at this time of the year, just the worst time of the year to take a journey, and especially a long journey. The ways deep, the weather sharp, the days short, the sun farthest off, in *solstito brumali,* the very dead of Winter." Of the Word made flesh, again, "I add yet further; what flesh? The flesh of an infant. What *Verbum infans,* the Word an infant? The Word, and not able to speak a word. How evil agreeth this! This he put up. How born, how entertained? In a stately palace, a cradle of ivory, robes of estate? No: but a stable for His palace, a manger for His cradle, poor clouts [diapers—*ed.*] for His array."[34]

DEVOTIONAL LITERATURE

The growth of Protestantism in England resulted in an outpouring of popular devotional literature, much of it focusing on personal responsibility as a way to virtue. Works were aimed at students, sailors, and laborers with titles like *Plain Man's Path-way to Heaven* (1601), and *The Practice of Piety, Directing a Christian How to Walk That He May Please God* (1612). The latter volume, written by Bishop Lewis Bayly, went through fifty-eight editions within a hundred years. The book would maker sober reading for modern audiences, appealing as it does to the "sin-haunted," who will come before "the outraged Creator of the Universe, the divine, inflexible Judge" of humanity.[35] A later volume, *Four Birds of Noah's Ark* (1609), contained prayers for children, servants, apprentices, colliers, and galley slaves, and reflected the Protestant idea of the importance of the workplace as a setting for living a religious life.

There was an immense popularity to such books during the sixteenth century. Printed matter was now available, literacy was spreading, people wanted to make up their own minds on religious questions. The traditional church's authoritarian structure was severely weakened; the Protestant priesthood of all believers meant that responsible household heads needed to be both religiously informed on issues, and in turn inform others. Davies wrote, "They instructed all members of the household in their social duties and obligations, laying before them the virtues appropriate to their callings in the household, the town, and the state, affirming the duty to be generous toward the poor and handicapped, to overcome abrasive anger with the lenitives of patience and forgiveness, and to cultivate the prudential virtues of honesty, industry, and thrift."[36] Many of these books were compilations of prayers, psalms, and devotional readings, differing little from Roman Catholic counterparts except for a strong emphasis on the Bible and the absence of miracle stories.

JOHN FOXE'S *BOOK OF MARTYRS*

Equally popular during this century was John Foxe's *Acts and Monuments of the Christian Martyrs*, generally known as *Foxe's Book of Martyrs*, a lengthy compendium of accounts of the violent deaths of early Christians and of Protestants at the hands of Roman Catholics. Foxe (1516–

1587), after leaving Oxford, spent several years in Calvinistic enclaves in Europe, including Basel and Strasbourg. His multivolume work on the Christian persecutions was first published in English in 1563, while memories of the Marian persecutions were still fresh. A polemical, skillfully argued volume, its purpose was to document the endurance of Protestant martyrs during Mary's reign. Vividly argued, strong in drama, uneven in documentation, it gained enduring popularity as an encyclopedia of papal tyranny. Foxe based his accounts on trial documents, but he was, above all, a determined polemicist who produced one of the most effective works in the history of religious propaganda. Foxe was no streetcorner bigot; he wrote plays in Latin and published the Gospels in Anglo-Saxon. He wanted to believe the worse of opponents, and uncritically accepted reports of Catholic persecutions of Protestants. His bitter pages were the precursors of a strain of enduring intolerance manifest in groups like the Irish Orangemen of modern times.

Here is Foxe's account of the martyrdom of Hugh Latimer and Nicholas Ridley, two English bishops burned at the stake under Mary I in 1555:

Ridley went to the stake, kneeled down by it, kissed it, most effectiously prayed, and behind him Master Latimer kneeled, as earnestly calling upon God as he. After they arose, the one talked with the other a little while, till they which were appointed to see the execution, removed themselves out of the sun. What they said I can learn of no man.

Then Dr. Smith, of whose recantation in King Edward's time you heard before, began his sermon to them. . . . He ended with a very short exhortation to them to recant and come home again to the church, and save their lives and souls, which else were condemned. His sermon was scant in all a quarter of an hour.

Then the wicked sermon being ended, Doctor Ridley and Master Latimer kneeled down upon their knees towards my Lord Williams of Thame, the vice-chancellor of Oxford, and divers other commissioners appointed for that purpose. . . . Master Ridley said: I beseech you my lord, even as Christ's sake that I may speak but two or three words. . . . Doctor Marshall, vice-chancellor, ran hastily unto him, and with their hands stopped his mouth and said: Master Ridley, if you will revoke your erroneous opinions, and recant the same, you shall not only have liberty so to do, but also the benefit of a subject, that is, have your life. Not otherwise? Said Master Ridley. No, quoteth Doctor Marshall, therefore if you will not do so, then there is no remedy but you must suffer for your deserts. Well, quoteth Master Ridley, so long as the breath is in my body, I will never deny my Lord Christ and his known truth: God's will be done in me. And with that he rose up, and said with a loud voice: Well, then I commit my cause to Almighty God, which shall indifferently judge all.[37]

MUSIC

The emergence of a distinctly Church of England musical tradition was one of the contributions of the English Reformation. This, however, like much else, came about sporadically, exacerbated by Henry VIII's dissolution of the monasteries, which both replaced the centrality and mystery of the mass with Morning and Evening Prayer and left hundreds of skilled musicians unemployed. The Catholic tradition had resisted popular hymns, but metrical settings of psalms were introduced with Protestantism's spread. Little of this era's parish music is memorable other than for its purely historic interest. The influence of Lutheran chorales and Calvin's metrical psalms was considerable, but most indigenous music was drab, especially compared to other poetry and drama of the Elizabethan Age.

Some of the period's most enduring liturgical music was the communion settings of John Merbecke (d. c. 1585). Organist at St. George's, Windsor, Merbecke, a writer and theologian, was tried for heresy and sentenced to the stake in the mid-1540s, but was rescued by Stephen Gardiner, bishop of Winchester. In addition to church music, Merbecke wrote an English concordance to the Bible and an annotated Book of Common Prayer, to assure musical uniformity in parish singing. The composer's output was scant, and he is chiefly remembered for his communion setting contained in his *Book of Common praier noted* (1550), possibly commissioned by Cranmer. The work drew on existing Gregorian and Sarum musical sources and followed the "for every syllable a note" principle being introduced into English music. It was revived for parish use at the time of the Oxford Movement, considerably adapted for modern use. Merbecke, once a composer of promise, was a vacillating personality, and in later life turned from composing and joined those who condemned church music as "vanity."

It was in cathedrals, the private chapels of the wealthy, endowed churches, and Oxford and Cambridge colleges, places capable of retaining professional musicians, that a liturgical musical tradition flourished. By the later years of Elizabeth's reign a creditable collection of anthems, canticles, and other church music had been written; to earlier psalm and communion chant settings were added the polyphonic genius of composers like Thomas Tallis (c. 1505–1585), William Byrd (1543–1623), and Thomas Morley (1557–1604?), all of whom remained devout Roman Catholics. Thomas Tallis and William Byrd were the Elizabethan period's most important English-language composers. Tallis, whose employment included service at Waltham Abbey, Canterbury Cathedral, and as Gentleman of the Chapel Royal, founded a music publishing company with Byrd. Tallis's output included masses, motets, and numerous office hymns. His English church music set high standards for cathedral choirs, and his hymn tunes remain in modern hymnals, especially the enduringly popular "eighth tune" usually associated with Bishop Ken's hymn, "All Praise to Thee, My God, This Night."

Often called "an English Palestrina," William Byrd was a lifelong Roman Catholic who held the post of director of music of the Chapel Royal under Elizabeth. Byrd retained the sense of mystery of his Catholic heritage in his choral compositions, while employing Protestantism's new one-note-for-each-syllable dictum. Byrd was the author of three Latin masses and numerous motets, and his English works included two complete communion services, a full set of Preces and Responses generally used in matins or evensong, plus psalm settings and anthems. Byrd's Great Service, circa 1580 ("Great" in the sixteenth century meant "large" or "full-length"), was a setting of the canticles prescribed for matins and evensong, the *Venite* (Psalm 95), *Te Deum,* and *Benedictus* at the morning service, and the *Magnificat* and *Nunc Dimitis* used at evensong. Byrd's music employed new technical advances in composition, producing the rich, full-bodied, euphonious notes associated with an English "cathedral sound." Byrd reached maturity at a time when the range of recent French and Flemish polyphonic composition became available, giving him rich possibilities composers a generation earlier did not have at their disposal. Older forms of chanting gave way to new concepts of melody, harmony, and rhythm, and the use of instruments with choral compositions became widespread. Byrd's polyphonic music was written for as many as ten different voices, employing a variety of melodic lines. Rarely did Byrd use all of the voices together; he constantly added or subtracted for coloration and dramatic effect. Repetitions helped build intensity or emphasize a point, as in the anthem "Sing Joyfully unto God" and the lines "Blow the trumpet in the new moon," where various vocal combinations produce the sound of a trumpet at night under a new moon, and its startling effect on the assembled people. Byrd was to music what Shakespeare was to drama, a writer of originality and variety, borrowing heavily from predecessors, yet leaving the imprint of genius on an age. In his music the English Gothic "perpendicular" style of architecture found its musical counterpart.

SUMMARY

In the crucible of sixteenth-century politics, the broad outlines of what became an Anglican *via media* were hammered out. What emerged was a church both traditional and reformed, emphasizing word and sacrament, with a greater awareness of the place of the laity than had been the case in earlier centuries. Eventually the church tolerated opponents, but these were intolerant times and conflict was still often responded to with burnings at the stake, excommunications, and heated polemics. Two parties thus emerged during this century: what might be called the high church party of Elizabeth's reign and the anti-Calvinists, who emerged later, providing the poles around which others coalesced, upsetting the delicate Elizabethan Settlement of 1559.

The 1500s ended with the Church of England established as a national church, displaying worship styles and doctrinal tendencies not possible at the century's beginning. Roman Catholics remained in isolated pockets; Puritanism was on the rise. Edmund Grindal (1519?–1583), one of Elizabeth's Archbishops of Canterbury, was bishop of London, when in 1565 he described conditions not unlike those in many dioceses throughout the Anglican Communion today:

> Some say the service and prayers in the chancel, others in the body of the church; some say the same in a seat made in the church, some in the pulpit with their faces to the people; some keep precisely to the order of the book, others intermeddle psalms in metre; some say in a surplice, others without a surplice; the Table standeth in the body of the church in some places, in others it standeth in the chancel; in some places the Table standeth altarwise, distant from the wall a yard, in some others in the middle of the chancel, north and south; in some places the Table is joined, in others it standeth upon trestles; in some places the Table hath a carpet, in others it hath not; administration of the Communion is done by some with surplice and cap, some with surplice alone, others with none; some with chalice, some with communion cup, others with a common cup; some with unleavened bread, some with leavened; some receive kneeling, others standing, others sitting; some baptise in a font, others in a basin; some sign with the sign of the cross, others sign not; some with a square cap, some with a round cap, some with a button cap, some with a hat.[38]

Readings

The *First* and *Second Royal Injunctions* of Henry VIII (1536, 1538)

Thomas Cromwell, Henry's chancellor, was a skilled lawyer, who drew up these decrees establishing the king's supremacy over the church and ordering the clergy to periodically preach against "the Bishop of Rome's usurped power and jurisdiction." Preachers were to urge congregations to work hard and avoid superstitious habits; clergy should not frequent taverns and alehouses; and, in the 1538 injunction from Thomas Cromwell ("Crumwell" in the document) to Thomas Cranmer, an English Bible was ordered placed in every church. These documents were drafted with legal acumen, stipulating penalties for clergy who avoided enforcing them.

First Royal Injunction (1536)

In the name of God, Amen. In the year of our Lord God 1536, and of the most noble reign of our sovereign lord Henry VIII, king of England and of France, the twenty-eighth year, and the ___ day of _____, I, Thomas Crumwell, knight, Lord Crumwell, keeper of the privy seal of our said sovereign lord the king, and vicegerent unto the same, for and concerning all his jurisdiction ecclesiastical within this realm, visiting by the king's highness's supreme authority ecclesiastical the people and clergy of this deanery of _____ by my trusty commissary _____ lawfully deputed and consisted for this part, have to the glory of Almighty God, to the king's highnesses's honor, the public weal of this his realm, and increase of virtue in the same, appointed and assigned these injunctions ensuing, to be kept and observed of the dean, parsons, vicars, curates, and stipendiaries resident or having cure of souls, or any other spiritual administration within this deanery, under the pains hereafter limited and appointed.

The first is, that the dean, parsons, vicars, and others having cure of souls anywhere within this deanery, shall faithfully keep and observe, and as far as in them may lie, shall cause to be observed and kept of others, all and singular laws and statutes of this realm made for the abolishing and extirpation of the Bishop of Rome's pretensed and usurped power and jurisdiction within this realm, and for the establishment and confirmation of the king's authority and jurisdiction within the same, as of the supreme head of the Church of England, and shall to the uttermost of their wit, knowledge, and learning purely, sincerely, and without any color or dissimulation declare, manifest, and open for the space of one quarter of a year now next ensuing, once every Sunday, and after that at leastwise twice every quarter, in their sermons and other collations, that the Bishop of Rome's usurped power and jurisdiction, having no establishment nor ground by the law of God, was of most just causes taken away and abolished; and therefore they owe unto him no manner of obedience or subjection, and that the king's power is within his dominion the highest power and potentate under God, to whom all men within the same dominion by God's commandment owe most loyalty and obedience, afore and above all other powers and potentates in earth.

To the intent that all superstition and hypocrisy, crept into divers men's hearts, may vanish away, they shall not set forth or extol any images, relics, or miracles for any superstition or lucre, nor allure the people by any enticements to the pilgrimage of any saint, otherwise than is permitted in the Articles lately put forth by the authority of the king's majesty and condescended upon by the prelates and clergy of this his realm in Convocation, as though it were proper or peculiar to that saint to give this commodity or that, seeing all goodness, health, and grace ought to be both asked and looked for only of God, as of the very Author of the same, and of none other, for without Him that cannot be given; but that they do rather apply themselves to the keeping of God's commandments and fulfilling of His works of charity, persuading them that they shall please God more by the true exercising of their bodily labor, travail, or occupation, and providing for their families, than if they went about to the said pilgrimages.

Also, the said dean, parsons, vicars, curates, and other priests shall in no wise, at any unlawful time, nor for any other cause than for their honest necessity, haunt or resort to any taverns or alehouses, and after their dinner or supper they shall not give themselves to drinking or riot, spending their time idly, by day or by night, at tables or card-playing, or any other unlawful game.

Second Royal Injunction (1538)

Item, that you shall provide on this side of the feast of Easter next coming, one book of the whole Bible of the largest volume, in English, and the same set up in some convenient place within the said church that you have cure of, whereas your parishioners may most commodiously resort to the same, and read it; the charges of which book shall be reasonably borne between you, the parson, the parishioners aforesaid, that is to say, the onehalf by you, the other half by them.

Item, that you shall discourage no man privily or apertly from the reading or hearing of the said Bible, but shall expressly provoke, stir, and exhort every person to read the same, and that which is the very lively word of God, that every Christian man is bound to embrace, believe, and follow, if he look to be saved; admonishing them nevertheless, to avoid all contention and altercation therein, and to use an honest sobriety in the inquisition of the true sense of the same.

Item, that you shall every Sunday and holy day through the year openly and plainly recite to your parishioners twice or thrice together, or oftener, if need require, one particle or sentence of the "Pater Noster" or Creed, in English, to the intent they may learn the same by heart, and so from day to day to give them one like lesson or sentence of the same, till they have learned the whole "Pater Noster" and Creed, in English, by rote; and as they be taught every sentence of the same by rote, you shall expound and declare the understanding of the same unto them, exhorting all parents and householders to teach their children and servants the same, as they are bound in conscience to do.

Item, that you shall make, or cause to be made in the said church, and every other cure you have, one sermon every quarter of the year at least, wherein you shall purely and sincerely declare the very gospel of Christ, and in the same exhort your hearers to the works of charity, mercy, and faith, specially prescribed and commanded in Scripture, and not to repose their trust or affiance in any other works devised by men's phantasies beside Scripture; as in wandering to pilgrimages, offering of money, candles, or tapers to images or relics, or kissing or licking the same, saying over a number of beads, not understood or minded on, or in such-like superstition, for the doing whereof you not only have no promise of reward in Scripture, but contrariwise, great threats and maledictions of God, as things tending to idolatry and superstition, which of all other offenses God Almighty does.

Item, that you, and every other parson, vicar, or curate within this diocese, shall for every church keep one book or register, wherein ye shall write the day and year of every wedding, christening, and burying made within your parish for your time, and so every man succeeding you likewise; and also there insert every person's name that shall be so wedded, christened, or buried; and for the safe keeping of the same book, the parish shall be bound to provide of their common charges one sure coffer with two locks and keys.

All which and singular Injunctions I minister unto you, and to your successors, by the king's highnesses's authority to me committed in this part, which I charge and command you . . . to observe and keep, upon pain of deprivation, sequestration of the fruits, or such other coercion as [to] the king's highness, or his vicegerent for the time being, shall be seen convenient.[39]

Thomas Cranmer

Thomas Cranmer is remembered primarily for his Litany and Book of Common Prayer, but he was as well a skilled writer of sermons. In the excerpts chosen below, he defends the English church's position on baptism and the Lord's Supper, presenting a set of definitions different from those employed by the Roman church.

Bread Is Not a Vain and Bare Token

But how can he be taken for a good Christian man, that thinketh that Christ did ordain his sacramental signs and tokens in vain, without effectual grace and operation? For so might we as well say, that the water in baptism is a bare token, and hath no warrant signed by Scripture for any apparel at all: for the Scripture speaketh not of any promise made to the receiving of a token or figure only. And so may be concluded, after your manner of reasoning, that in baptism is no spiritual operation indeed, because that washing in water in itself is but a token.

But to express the true effect of the sacrament: as the washing outwardly in water is not a vain token, but teacheth such a washing as God worketh inwardly in them, that duly receive the same: so likewise is not the bread a vain token, but sheweth and preacheth to the godly receiver, what God worketh in him by his almighty power secretly and invisibly. And therefore as the bread is outwardly eaten indeed in the Lord's Supper, so is the very body of Christ inwardly by faith eaten indeed of all them, that come thereto in such sort as they ought to do: which eating nourisheth them unto everlasting life.

And this eating hath a warrant signed by Christ himself in the sixth of John, where Christ saith: "He that eateth my flesh and drinketh my blood hath everlasting life." But they, that to the outward eating of the bread joined not thereto an inward eating of Christ by faith, have no warrant by Scripture at all: but the bread and wine to them be vain, nude, and bare tokens.

An Expression in the Book of Common Prayer
Explained [The Holy Communion—ed.]

Christ is present, whensoever the church prayeth unto him, and is gathered together in his name. And the bread and wine be made unto us the body and blood of Christ (as it is in the book of Common Prayer); but not by changing the substance of bread and wine into the substance of Christ's natural body and blood: but that in the godly using of them, they be unto the receivers Christ's body and blood. As some of the Scripture saith, that their riches is their redemption, and to some it is their damnation: and as God's word to some is life, to some it is death, and a snare (as the prophet saith). And Christ himself to some is a stone to stumble at, to some is a raising from death; not by conversion of substances, but by good or evil use: that thing, which to the godly is salvation, to the ungodly is damnation.

So is the water in baptism, and the bread and wine in the Lord's supper, to the worthy receivers, Christ himself and eternal life; and to the unworthy receivers, everlasting death and damnation; not by conversion of one substance into another, but by godly or ungodly use thereof. And therefore in the book of the holy communion we do not pray absolutely, that the bread and wine may be made the body and blood of Christ, but that unto us in that holy mystery they may be so, that is to say, that we may so worthily receive the same, that we may be partakers of Christ's body and blood, and that therewith in spirit and in truth we may be spiritually nourished. And a like prayer of old time were all the people wont to make at the communion, of all such offerings, as at that time all the people used to offer, praying that their offerings might be unto them the body and blood of Christ.

Of the Efficacy of the Sacraments

I mean not, that Christ is spiritually either in the table, or in the bread and wine, that be set upon the table: but I mean, that he is present in the ministration and receiving of that holy supper, according to his own institution and ordinance. Like as in baptism, Christ and the Holy Ghost be not in the water, or font, but be given in the ministration, or to them, that be duly baptized in the water.

And although the sacramental tokens be only significations and figures, yet doth Almighty God effectually work in them, and duly receive his sacraments, those divine and celestial operations, which he hath promised, and by the sacraments be signified. For else, they were vain and unfruitful sacraments, as well to the godly as to the ungodly. And therefore I never said of the whole supper, that it is but a signification or a bare memory of Christ's death, but I teach, that it is a spiritual refreshing, wherein our soul be fed and nourished with Christ's very flesh and blood to eternal life.[40]

Justification by Faith

[From the 1538 Articles, based on the 1530 Lutheran Augsburg Confession.]

On justification, we teach that its proper meaning is remission of sins and acceptance or reconciliation of us into the grace and favor of God; that is, true renewal in Christ. And we teach that though sinners do not obtain this justification without repentance, and a good will and well inclined outgoing . . . of heart, wrought by the Holy Spirit, towards God and their neighbor, yet they are not justified in virtue of the worth or merit of their repentance, or of any of their works or merits; but they are justified freely for Christ's sake through faith, when they believe that they are received into grace and their sins are remitted for the sake of Christ, who by his death made satisfaction for our sins. This faith God imputes for righteousness in his sight. . . . But the faith we have in mind is not empty and idle, but is that "which worketh by love." For the true Christian faith, of which we speak here, is not only knowledge of the articles of the faith, or a mere historical belief of Christian doctrine; but, together with that knowledge and belief, it is a firm trust in the mercy God promised for Christ's sake, whereby we maintain . . . and conclude with certainty that he is merciful and propitious even to us. This faith truly justifies; it is truly saving; it is not feigned, dead, or hypocritical, but of necessity it has hope and love inseparably joined to it, and also zeal for good living; and it performs good works to suit each place and time. For good works are necessary to salvation, not because they make an ungodly man righteous, nor because they are a price for sins or a cause of justification; but because it is necessary that he who is already justified by faith and reconciled to God through Christ should have a care to do the will of God.[41]

Hugh Latimer

Son of a yeoman farmer, Hugh Latimer (1485–1555) was a new sort of preacher, attractive to widespread audiences with homely imagery, direct emotional appeal, and open attacks on injustice and greed. He was of little significance as a theologian, but important as a social reformer. Latimer's ideas became a rallying point for a generation of "Commonwealth Men," those opposed to covetous landlords, and for wider participation in government by an emerging generation of artisans and merchants. His famous sermon "Of the Plough" was preached on New

Year's Day 1548 at Paul's Cross, the preaching station outside St. Paul's
Cathedral, which Thomas Carlyle later called "a kind of *Times* newspaper
but edited partly by heaven itself." Latimer was burned to death at
Oxford in October 1555 for refusing to recant his positions against the
Roman Catholic Church.

From the Sermon of the Plough

For as the ploughman first setteth forth his plough, and then tilleth his
land, and breaketh it in furrows, and sometimes ridgeth it up again; and at
another time harrowth it, and clotteth it, and sometimes dungeth and
hedgeth it, diggeth it, and weedeth it, purgeth and maketh it clean: so the
prelate, the preacher, hath many divers offices to do. He hath first a busy
work to bring his parishioners to a right faith, as Paul calleth it, and not a
swevering faith, but to a faith that embraceth Christ, and trusteth to his
merits; a lively faith, a justifying faith, a faith, that maketh a man righteous
without respect of works. . . . He hath a busy work, I say; to bring his flock
to a right faith, and to confirm them in the same faith.

And now I would ask a strange question. Who is the most diligent
bishop and prelate in all England, that passeth all the rest in doing his
office? I can tell, for I know him, who he is, I know him well. But now, I
think, I see you listening and hearkening, that I should name him. There is
one that passeth all the others, and is the most diligent prelate and
preacher in all England. And will ye know who it is? I will tell you. It is the
devil, he is the most diligent preacher of all others, he is never out of his
diocese; he is never from his cure, ye shall never find him unoccupied; he
is ever in his parish, he keepeth residence at all times. . . . And his office is
to hinder religion, to maintain superstition, to set up idolatry, to teach all
kind of Popery. He is as ready, as can be wished, forto set forth his plough,
to devise as many ways, as can be, to deface and obscure God's glory.

Where the devil is resident and hath his plough going; there away with
books, and up with candles; away with Bibles, and up with beads; away
with the light of the Gospel, and up with the light of candles, yea, at noon-
day. Where the devil is resident, that he may prevail, up with all superstition
and idolatry, painting of images, candles, palms, ashes, holy water, and
new services of men's inventing, as though man could invent a better way
to honor God with, than God himself hath appointed. Down with Christ's
cross, up with purgatory, I mean. Away with clothing the naked, the poor,
the impotent: up with decking of images, and gay garnishing of stocks and
stones. Up with man's traditions and his laws, down with God's traditions

and his most holy word. . . . There must be nothing but Latin, not so much as, "Remember, man, that thou art ashes, and into ashes thou shalt return." Which be the words, that the minister speaketh to the ignorant people, when he giveth them ashes upon Ash Wednesday, but it must be spoken in Latin. God's word may in no wise be translated into English. Oh that our prelates would be as diligent to sow the corn of good doctrine, as Satan is to sow cockle and darnel! And this is the devlish ploughing, the which worketh to have all things in Latin.[42]

John Jewel

John Jewel's (1522–1571) *Apology of the Church of England*, first published in 1562, was the Church of England's answer to the Roman Catholic Church's Council of Trent, which launched the Counter-Reformation. The work was a gloves-off polemic, answering the Roman arguments in kind: many sections begin with a creedal "We believe"—in the authority of scripture, Christ as the sole mediator between God and humanity, and the Reformation concept of justification by faith without the intermediary of indulgences and the threat of purgatory. The lines were clearly drawn, excoriating "the tyranny of the Bishops of Rome, and their barbarous Persian-like pride."

Part II

We believe, that there is one church of God, and that the same is not shut up . . . into some one corner or kingdom, but that it is catholic and universal, and so dispersed throughout the whole world. So that there is now no nation which can truly complain that they be shut forth and may not be one of the church and people of God. And that this church is the kingdom, the body, and the spouse of Christ; and that Christ alone is the prince of this kingdom; that Christ alone is the head of this body; and that Christ alone is the bridegroom of this spouse.

. . . that there are in the church divers orders of ministers; that there are some who are deacons, others who are presbyters, and others who are bishops, to whom the instruction of the people, and the care and management of religion, are committed: and yet that there neither is, nor is it possible there should be, any one man who has the care of this whole catholic church, for Christ is ever present with his church, and needs not a vicar, or sole and perfect successor; and that no mortal man can in his mind contain all the body of the universal church, that is, all the parts of the earth; much less can he reduce them into an exact order, and rightly and prudently administer its affairs. . . . that the bishop of Rome, or any other person, should be the head of the whole church, or a universal bishop is no more possible, than that he should be the bridegroom, the light, the salvation, and the life of the church; for these are the privileges and titles of Christ alone, and do properly and only belong to him.

We say that the bread and wine are the holy and heavenly mysteries of the body and blood of Christ, and that in them Christ himself, the true bread of eternal life, is so exhibited to us at present, that we do by faith truly take his body and blood; and yet at the same time, we speak not this so as if we thought the nature of the bread and the wine were totally changed and abolished, as many in the last age have dreamt, and as yet could never agree among themselves about this dream. For neither did Christ ever design that the wheaten bread should change its nature, and assume a new kind of divinity, but rather that it might change us.

But then as to the fairs and sales of masses, and the carrying about and adoring the bread, and a number of such-like idolatrous and blasphemous follies, which none of them dare to affirm to have been delivered to us by Christ or his Apostles, our church will not endure them; and we justly blame the bishops of Rome for presuming, without any command of God, without any authority of the holy fathers, and without any example, not only to pro-pose the sacramental bread to be adored by the people with a divine wor-ship; but also to carry it about before them upon an ambling nag wherever they go, as the Persian kings did heretofore their sacred fire, and the Egyp-tians their image of Isis; and so have turned the sacraments of Christ into pageantry and pomp; that, in that very thing in which the death of Christ was to be celebrated and inculcated, and the mysteries of our redemption ought to be piously and reverently represented, the eyes of men should only be fed with a foolish show, and a piece of ludicrous levity.[43]

Richard Hooker

By the late sixteenth century Richard Hooker emerged as a major voice of the Church of England. His *Of the Laws of Ecclesiastical Polity*, which began to appear in 1593, was an eight-volume attempt to both refute Puritan beliefs and carve out a distinctly Church of England position on church structure and doctrine. Like John Locke a generation later, Hooker placed a high premium on reason as a way to ascertain the order of God's universe and the divine will for humanity. Hooker told Conti-nental Reformers they were wrong to reject totally the Roman Catholic heritage just because it had become corrupt. Likewise, he said Roman Catholics were absurd to reject the Reformers' legitimate grievances. The Church of England, having recently broken its ties with Roman Catholicism, set about defining the basis of a state church, hence the phrase "ecclesiastical polity." Hooker's style was clear and focused, avoiding the emotional polemics of many contemporaries, or their lengthy citations of ancient authors. The core of Hooker's argument is in chapters 50–56 of book V, dealing with religion and the social order, prayer, and the sacraments. In staking out his position, Hooker bypasses Reformation doctrines of election and predestination, and elaborate Roman Catholic arguments for papal government.

Of the Laws of Ecclesiastical Polity

True Religion Is the Root of All True Virtue and the Stay of All Well-Ordered Commonwealths

So natural is the union of religion with justice, that we may boldly assert that there is neither where there are not both. For how should they be unfeignedly just, whom religion doth not cause to be such; or they religious, who are not proved such by their just actions? If those employed about the public administration of justice follow it only as a trade, with an unquenchable and unconscionable thirst for gain, being at heart not persuaded that justice is God's own work, themselves His agents in this business, the sentence of right God's own verdict, and themselves His priests to deliver it, then the formalities of justice do but serve to smother right, and that which was necessary ordained for the common good is made, through shameful abuse, the cause of common misery. . . . Seeing, therefore that the safety of all estates appeareth to depend upon religion. . . . we have the reasons why true virtues should honor true religions as their parent and all well-ordered commonweals should love her as their chiefest stay.[44]

Tests of Church Power

Now touching the nature of religious services, and the manner of their due performance, thus much generally we know to be most clear; that whereas the greatness and dignity of all manner of actions is measured by the worthiness of the subject from which they proceed, and of the object whereabout they are conversant, we must of necessity in both respects acknowledge, that this present world affordeth not any thing comparable unto the public duties of religion. For if the best things have the perfectest and best operations, it will follow, that seeing man is the worthiest creature upon earth, and every society of men more worthy than any man, and of societies that more excellent which we call the Church; there can be in this world no work performed equal to the exercise of true religion, the proper operation of the Church of God.

That which inwardly each man should be, the Church outwardly ought to testify. And therefore the duties of our religion which are seen must be such as that affection which is unseen ought to be. Signs must resemble the things they signify. . . . Duties of religion performed by the whole societies of men, ought to have in them according to our power a sensible excellency, correspondent to the majesty of him whom we worship (2 Chr. ii.5). Yea then are the public duties of religion best ordered, when the militant Church doth resemble by sensible means, as it may in such cases, that hidden dignity and glory wherewith the Church triumphant in heaven is beautified.

Howbeit, even as the very heat of the sun itself, which is the life of the whole world, was to the people of God in the desert a grievous annoyance, for easy whereof his extraordinary providence ordained a cloudly pillar to overshadow them: so things of general use and benefit (for in this world what is so perfect that no inconvenience doth ever follow it?) may by some accident be incommodious to a few. In which case, for such private evils remedies there are of like condition, though public ordinances, wherein the common good is respected, be not stirred.

Let our first demand be therefore, that in the external form of religion such things as are apparently, or can be sufficiently proved, effectual and generally fit to set forward godliness, either as betokening the greatness of God, or as beseeming the dignity of religion, or as concurring with celestial impressions in the minds of men, may be reverently thought of; some few, rare, casual, and tolerable, or otherwise curable inconveniences notwithstanding (V.vi).

The Psalms

The prophet David having therefore singular knowledge not in poetry alone but in music also, judged them both to be things most necessary for the house of God, left behind him to that purpose a number of divinely indicted poems, and was farther the author of adding unto poetry melody in public prayer, melody both vocal and instrumental, for the raising up of men's hearts, and the sweetening of their affections towards God. In which considerations the Church of Christ doth likewise at this present day retain it as an ornament to God's service, and an help to our own devotion.

In church music curiosity and ostentation of art, wanton or light or unsuitable harmony, such as only pleaseth the ear, and doth not naturally serve to the very kind and degree of those impressions, which the matter that goeth with it leaveth or is apt to leave in men's minds, doth rather blemish and disgrace that we do than add either beauty or furtherance unto it. On the other side, these faults prevented, the force and efficacy of the thing itself, when it drowneth not utterly but fitly suiteth with matter altogether sounding to the praise of God, is in truth most admirable, and doth much edify if not the understanding because it teacheth not, yet surely the affection, because therein it worketh much. They must have hearts very dry and tough, from whom the melody of psalms doth not sometime draw that wherein a mind religiously affected delighteth (V.xxxviii.2, 3).

The Eucharist

The grace which we have by the holy Eucharist doth not begin but continues life. No man therefore receiveth this sacrament before Baptism, because no dead thing is capable of nourishment. That which groweth must of necessity first live. If our bodies did not daily waste, food to restore them were a thing superfluous. And it may be that the grace of baptism would serve to eternal life, were it not that the state of our spiritual being is daily so much hindered and impaired after baptism. In that life therefore where neither body nor soul can decay, our souls shall as little require this sacrament as our bodies corporal nourishment. But as long as the days of our warfare last, during the time that we are both subject to diminution and capable of augmentation in grace, the words of our Lord and Savior Jesus Christ will remain forcible, "Except ye eat the flesh of the Son of man, and drink his blood, ye have no life in you" (John 6:33).

Life being therefore proposed, unto all men as their end, they which by baptism have laid the foundation and attained the first beginning of a new life have here their nourishment and food prescribed for *continuance of life in them*. . . . Whereas therefore in our infancy we are incorporated into Christ and by Baptism receive the grace of his Spirit without any sense or feeling of the gift of God, that we know by grace what the grace is which God giveth us, the degrees of our own increase in holiness and virtue we see and can judge of them, we understand that the strength of our life began in Christ, that his flesh is meat and his blood drink, not by surmised imagination but truly, even so truly that through faith we perceive in the body and blood sacramentally presented the very taste of eternal life, the grace of the sacrament is here as the food which we eat and drink.

The real presence of Christ's most blessed body and blood is not therefore to be sought for in the sacrament, but in the worthy receiver of the sacrament.

And with this the very order of our Savior's words agreeth first "take and eat"; then "this is my Body which was broken for you": first "drink ye all of this"; then followeth "this is my Blood of the New Testament which is shed for many for the remission of sins" (Mark 14:22). I see not which way it should be gathered by the words of Christ, when and where the bread is His body and the cup His blood, but only in the very heart and soul of him which receiveth them. . . . If on all sides it be confessed that the grace of Baptism is poured into the soul of man, that by water we receive it although it be neither seated in the water nor the water changed into it, what should induce men to think that the grace of the Eucharist must needs be in the Eucharist before it can be in us that receive it?[45]

Lancelot Andrewes

Lancelot Andrewes (1555–1626) was a leading preacher of his age. Fluent in fifteen languages, the author was one of the translators of the Authorized Version of the Bible. His book *Private Prayers*, first published in 1648, is a major devotional work. Andrewes wrote the book in Greek, Hebrew, and Latin, copiously copying from the Bible and other sources. Very little of the work is original but, like Cranmer, Andrewes had an unerring eye for original prayers beautifully written. The *Preces Privatae* follows a distinct outline, a set of daily devotions based on the first chapters of Genesis, followed by Gospel narratives, such as the resurrection on Sunday, the crucifixion on Friday, and so on. A deeply personal confession of sin for each day is followed by an intercessory prayer and an act of thanksgiving.

Intercession

Let us pray God, for the whole creation; for the supply of seasons, healthy, fruitful, peaceful:

> for the whole race of mankind; for those who are not Christians; for the conversion of atheists, the ungodly, Gentiles, Turks and Jews:
> for the succor and comfort of all who are dispirited, infirm, distressed, unsettled, both men and women; for thankfulness and sobriety in all who are hearty, healthy, prosperous, quiet men and women:

for the catholic Church, its establishment and increase; for the Eastern, its deliverance and union; for the Western, its adjustment and peace; for the British, the supply of what is wanting in it, the strengthening of what remains in it; for the episcopate, presbytery, Christian people; for the states of the inhabited world, for Christian states, far off, near at hand, our own:

for our divinely-guarded king, the queen, and the prince; for those who have place in the court; for parliament and judicature, for army and police, commons and their leaders, farmers, graziers, fishers, traders and mechanics, down to mean workmen and the poor:

for all who for sufficient reasons fail to call upon Thee, from stress of engagements, for all who have no intercessor in their own behalf; for all who at present are in agony of extreme necessity or deep affliction; for all who are attempting any good work which will bring glory to the name of God, or some great good to the Church; for all who act nobly either toward things sacred or towards the poor; for all who have ever been offended by me either in word or in deed.

God have mercy on me and bless me; God show the light of his countenance upon me and pity me; God bless me, even our God. God bless me and receive my prayer.

Tuesday

God, Thou art my God, early will I seek Thee. Blessed art Thou, O Lord, who gatherest the waters into the sea, and broughtest to sight the earth, and madest to sprout herb and fruit-tree. There are the depths and the sea as on an heap, lakes, rivers, springs; earth, continent, and isles, mountains, hills and valleys; glebe, meadows, glades, green pasture, corn and hay, herb and flowers for food, enjoyment, medicine, fruit-trees bearing wine, oil and spices, and trees for wood; and things beneath the earth, stones, metals, minerals, coal, blood and fire, and vapor of smoke.

An Horology

Thou that hast put in Thine own power the times and the seasons, give us grace that we may pray to Thee in a convenient and opportune season; and save us.

Thou that for us men and for our salvation wast born in the depth of night, grant us to be renewed daily by the Holy Ghost, until Christ Himself be formed in us, to a perfect man; and save us.

Thou that very early in the morning, at the rising of the sun, didst rise again from the dead (Luke 24:1), raise us also daily to newness of life, suggesting to us, for Thou knowest them, habits meet for repentance; and save us.

O Thou that at the third hour (Acts 2:15) didst send down Thy Holy Ghost on the apostles, take not that same Holy Spirit from us, but renew Him every day in our hearts; and save us.

Thou that at the sixth hour of the sixth day (Matt. 27:45) didst nail together with Thyself upon the Cross the sins of the world, blot out the handwriting of our sins that is against us, and taking it away, save us.

Thou that at the sixth hour didst let down a great sheet from heaven to earth (Acts 10:9ff.), the symbol of Thy Church, receive into it us sinners of the Gentiles, and with it receive us into heaven; and save us.

Thou that at the ninth hour for us sinners and for our sins, didst taste of death (Matt 27:46), mortify our members which are upon earth, and whatsoever is contrary to Thy will; and save us.

Thou that at the tenth hour didst grant unto Thine apostle to discover Thy Son and to cry out with great gladness, We have found the Messiah (John 1:39-41), grant to us also, in like manner, to find the same Messiah and having found Him to rejoice in like manner; and save us.

Thou that didst even at the eleventh hour of the day of Thy goodness send into Thy vineyard those that have stood all the day idle, promising them a reward (Matt 20:6), give us the like grace, and though it be late, even as it were about the eleventh hour, favorably receive us who return to Thee; and save us.

Thou that at the sacred hour of the Supper wast pleased to institute the mysteries of Thy Body and Blood, render us mindful and partakers of the same; yet never to condemnation, but to the remission of sin, and to the acquiring of the promises of the New Testament; and save us.

Thou that at eventide was pleased to be taken down from the cross and laid in the grave (Matt 27:57), take away from us, and bury in Thy sepulcher, our sins, covering whatever evil we have committed with good works; and save us.

Thou that at midnight didst arouse David Thy prophet (Ps. 119:62) and Paul Thine apostle (Acts 16:25), that they should praise Thee, give us also songs in the night and to remember Thee upon our beds; and save us.

Thou that with Thine own mouth hath declared that at midnight the Bridegroom shall come (Matt. 25:6), grant that the cry may ever sound in our ears, Behold the Bridegroom cometh, that we may never be unprepared to go forth and meet him; and save us.

Thou that hast made the evening the end of the day, so that Thou mightest bring the evening of life to our minds, grant us always to reflect that our life passeth away like a day; to remember the days of darkness that they are many; that the night cometh wherein no man can work; by good works to prevent the darkness, lest we be cast out into outer darkness; and continually to cry unto Thee, Abide with us, O Lord, for it draweth towards evening and the day of our life is now far spent.[46]

3

The Seventeenth Century

His fare is plain, and common, but wholesome, what he hath is little, but very good; it consisteth most of mutton, beef and veal.
    —*George Herbert, in The Country Parson (1652)*

Religion and conflict are Janus-faced. Outside the hushed cathedral angry voices pierce the quiet; not far from the tranquil parish church, swords are angrily drawn, all in the Lord's name. England emerged from the Reformation's doctrinal and political battles only to plunge into a second devastating century of conflict. During the seventeenth century, the great issue was not the conflict with the papacy or contending eucharistic doctrines, but defining the power of kings and their relationship to the church, an issue with implications on where temporal loyalties would lie, but with few spiritual ramifications. Intolerance among Christian bodies was reflected in heavy polemics on all sides, often accompanied by violence. Ministers and laity were arrested and mutilated, many—Anglican and Puritan—fled abroad. Church symbols were hacked down in the mid-century wars, the Prayer Book was banned, and both sides outdid themselves in levying cruel restrictions on opponents. In the end, growing weariness of conflict led to a climate of uneasy tolerance at the century's end, but by then a chasm had grown between the Established Church and dissenters that endured centuries later. Despite the turbulence, possibly spurred by it, some of Anglicanism's most enduring voices emerged, like the poets George Herbert and John Donne and the philosopher John Locke, diamonds in the slag heap of an unsettled age.

The cast of characters changed rapidly, contributing to the century's unsettled character. During the first half-century two headstrong monarchs ruled, but both lacked Henry's sure hand and Elizabeth's deftness. From 1603 to 1625 James I of England (James VI of Scotland) reigned as successor to Elizabeth, succeeded by his son, Charles I, from 1625 to 1649. A brutal interlude, the Commonwealth and Protectorate, endured from 1649 to 1660. Then came the Restoration monarch Charles II, 1660–1685, the brief reign of James II, 1685–1688, the longer reign of the imported Dutch ruler, William, 1689–1702, and his English spouse, Mary, 1689–1694.

The precipitous changes and their impact are captured in a popular anonymous poem, "The Vicar of Bray":

> In good King Charles's golden days,
>   When loyalty no harm meant;
> A furious High-Church man I was,
>   And so I gained preferment.
> Unto my flock I daily preached,
>   "Kings are by God appointed,
> And damned are those who dare resist,
>   Or touch the Lord's Anointed."
>
> And this is Law, I will maintain
>   Unto my dying day, Sir,
> That whatsoever King shall reign,
>   I will be Vicar of Bray, Sir!
>
> When James possessed the Crown,
>   And Popery grew in fashion,
> The Penal Law I hooted down,
>   And read the Declaration:
> The Church of Rome I found would fit
>   Full well my constitution,
> And I had been a Jesuit
>   But for the Revolution.
>   And this is Law, etc.

The agile Vicar of Bray switched allegiances to "William our Deliverer," became a Tory under "glorious Anne," and a Whig under George. Explaining the rationale for five conversions in four decades, his summa was:

> The illustrious House of Hanover
>   And Protestant Succession,
> To these I lustily will swear,
>   Whilst they can keep possession:

> For in my Faith and Loyalty
>   I never once will falter,
> But George my lawful King shall be,
>   Except the times should alter.
>   And this is Law, etc.[1]

THE STUART MONARCHY,
THE FIRST PHASE (1603–1649)

James I (1603–1625)

James I, sometimes called "the wisest fool in Christendom," was not a prudent leader. Invited from Scotland to rule England, he consistently misjudged the tenor of the times. Now that the possibility of foreign invasions had diminished, English people chaffed at tight monarchical control. James, however, was propelled by a single idea, the divine right of kings, the belief that a monarch's power came from God and people had no rights, only such privileges as are granted by the king. Royal accountability was to God, not to a constitution or legislative branch and the king was above the law, responsible for the people's welfare, determining what was best for his subjects, who could not dispute their monarch's decrees. The role of the church was to support the king and make his will known to the people. "No Bishop, no King," James declared; his detractors, who would not return to the old order, turned the phrase to "No King, no Bishop." This idea of strong monarchical control was now resisted in England, where a growing number of entrepreneurs and squires were attracted to the power of parliamentary life and the Puritan party. Conflict was inevitable, disputes with an intransigent king led to civil war and to confrontation over the role of kings as well, triggered by a parliamentary "Apology" that was anything but. Under the guise of explaining their actions to the sovereign, Parliament told James their rights did not emanate from him and "that in Parliament they may speak freely their consciences without check and controlment," warning the king to make no laws affecting religion without their consent. The line between divine right and limited monarchy was now clearly drawn, and Parliament gradually extended its control; policy ceased to be "king's craft" and became a legislative initiative instead in ways never possible under Henry or Elizabeth. Times had changed, the locus of power had shifted away from the crown.

Catholic fortunes fell in 1605 with discovery of the Gunpowder Plot, a terrorist attempt by discontented Catholics to blow up king and government during Parliament's opening. Catholics had been repressed by Elizabeth and sought relief, which they believed James promised but failed to provide. After the plotters were seized, recusants—Roman Catholics who refused to attend services of the established Church of England—were required to take an oath repudiating papal claims, to attend Anglican services, and to receive the sacrament, something clearly unacceptable to them. Puritans fared little better. Originally they had high hopes, eagerly meeting the king in large numbers on his journey south from Scotland with a petition signed by over a thousand of their leaders. Reforms in church liturgy and government, and a new translation of the Bible were among their demands.

James invited the Puritans to debate issues with the bishops, with the king presiding over the session. A few Puritan demands were met, including introduction of the King James Bible in 1611, but the king suspected the Puritans of wanting to introduce a Presbyterian form of government, such as had been advocated in Scotland, and which he opposed. Instead of securing more favorable concessions, Puritans faced stringent royal controls.

While most of them remained within the Church of England, Puritans campaigned against government by bishops and against religious ceremony. A rigid Sabbatarianism, curbing frivolity and sports on Sunday, was part of their worldview, abolishing even ancient games and gamboling that had flourished on village greens for centuries. Puritans were indignant when the king issued a Declaration of Sports in 1618, supporting morris-dancing and the maypole. So unhappy with life in England were so many Puritans that they fled to hospitable countries of Protestant Europe and eventually to the new world to create their own political-religious society. On September 6, 1620, approximately one hundred Puritans set sail for America from Plymouth Harbor in a small ship, the *Mayflower*. Later came the Massachusetts Bay Colony in 1628, founded in part "against the kingdom of the Anti-Christ." More than a thousand persons settled there in the 1630s, and by 1640 their numbers had reached twenty thousand. England, a maritime nation with easy access to the world's waterways, began building an overseas empire. Other settlements followed in the West Indies, and by 1639 the East India Company was established in Madras, a foothold for what would later become a vast Continental empire. Missionaries sailed with the colonists; their primary purpose was to be a moral and educational presence to the overseas

English, but the seeds were planted for what would one day be a network of local dioceses leading eventually to a global Anglican Communion, centuries later fully in the hands of indigenous leadership.

Charles I (1625–1649)

James was succeeded by his son, Charles I, in 1625, perhaps the century's most inept ruler. The conflict between crown and Parliament heightened in Charles's reign, during which the king's mercurial personality and constantly shifting policies caused him to yield much of his power and gain nothing in return. Physically frail and affected with a speech impediment, Charles trusted no one and told everyone what they wanted to hear, then reversed himself. Deeply devout in his personal religious life, he was inept in managing foreign and domestic relations, and his word counted for nothing.

When he came to the throne in 1625, Charles encountered an enthusiastic body of clergy eager to throw over any traces of Calvinism infecting English religious life. Simultaneously, he met growing numbers of Puritans, still inside the Church of England, to whom Calvin's ideas were formative. Moreover, his French Roman Catholic wife, Henrietta Maria, insisted on greater toleration of Catholics as part of the marriage pact. Charles agreed, but never acted on his promises. Habitually short of money, his requests for funds were met by Parliament's Petition of Rights in 1628, prohibiting arbitrary arrest, forbidding taxes being levied without parliamentary approval, and outlawing royal declarations of martial law. The king kept asking Parliament for money; Parliament gave it to him, but always with the price of limiting royal power.

A court of star chamber, named for the room in which it met, was formed by Charles in 1629, with wide powers to inflict punishments on Puritans who criticized the Church of England. The court could levy fines or imprisonments, or have the ears cut off critics who wrote books or pamphlets against the church. Toleration and restraint were not features of the age, and attacks on differing viewpoints were severe by both sides. Charles did not call Parliament into session between 1629 and 1640, which only left the Puritans with their discontents unanswered.

By royal decree the king undid the austere work of Puritan reformers. He upheld the value of "honest mirth or recreation" in a 1633 *Declaration to His Subjects Concerning Lawfull Sports,* which he ordered read from pulpits across the country, and which helped sharpen growing tensions between Puritans and others. Among its strictures:

as for our good people's lawful recreation, our pleasure likewise is, that after the end of divine service our good people be not disturbed, letted [hindered—*ed.*] or discouraged from any lawful recreation, such as dancing, either men or women, archery for men, leaping, vaulting, or any other such harmless recreation, nor from having of May games, Whitsun ales, and morris dances, and the setting up of maypoles and other sports therewith used: so as the same be had in due and convenient time, without impediment or neglect of divine service; and that women shall have leave to carry rushes to the church for the decorating of it, according to their old custom.[2]

William Laud

The monarch's staunchest support in the 1630s came from William Laud (1573–1645), the Archbishop of Canterbury, who paid for it with his life. In 1633 Laud was named to head the church, after previously being president of St. John's College, Oxford, and bishop of St. David's and London. Intolerant Puritans met their match in unyielding Laud. The Archbishop championed a church "Catholic and reformed," but was a constant opponent of Calvinism and the Puritans, especially as a member of the inquisitorial star chamber and high commission court.

As strong-headed as he was energetic, Laud brooked no opposition to his wishes. A passionate stickler for all factions adhering to the letter of the law as he interpreted it, Laud was his own worst enemy, a secretive, quick-tempered prelate who played the corridors of power well, but who had no friends beyond his palace supporters. (When he moved to Lambeth Palace, it was with his two pets, a cat from Smyrna and a tortoise that survived him for over a century until killed accidentally by a gardener in 1753.)[3] Not an original thinker himself, Laud at times showed considerable breadth and comprehension of other viewpoints, especially of Roman Catholics. He maintained an abiding affection for Oxford, and as chancellor found funds for many benefactions, including a chair of Arabic and a rich collection of original manuscripts from the East. Although he held several profitable church positions simultaneously, Laud had no personal interest in money, food, or grand living. Laud was hard-working and a zealot for causes he believed in; when the party he supported went down, the archbishop fell from power with it.

Laud as archbishop inherited an unenviable situation. In addition to facing vocal opposition, he presided over a church with low educational and moral standards, contradictory worship practices, and lax discipline.

In quick succession, he issued decrees aimed at raising clergy standards, forbidding cockfighting in churches, cutting ears off pamphleteers who attacked his bishops, insisting all altars and baptismal fonts be restored to their rightful places, and Prayer Book worship be enforced. Moving church furnishings causes an uproar in parishes at any time, and one of Laud's most controversial rulings was to replace freestanding communion tables with stone or wooden altars, guarded by rails, and fixed firmly to the church's east wall. Laud's support of church ritual was based on his belief that the church constituted "the greatest place of God's residence upon earth." His was a vision of the ancient continuity between the contemporary church and its roots in the church's first centuries. He complained that in England's present political climate it was "superstition nowadays for any man to come with more reverence into a church than a tinker and his bitch come into an ale-house."[4]

Silk coverings adorned altars, falling in corner folds to the ground in what became known as a "Laudian throw"; lighted candlesticks appeared on altars, which in turn were surrounded by carved rails where communicants knelt to receive the consecrated bread and wine. Incense returned to the church, and a mixed chalice was employed, using wine with some water to symbolize blood and water flowing from Christ's body on the cross. Colorful, elaborately embroidered copes were worn by clergy in some places, and ornamentation spread to all aspects of worship.

The Puritans would have none of it. A Puritan lawyer with a caustic pen, William Prynne (1600–1669), whose ears were clipped and cheeks branded for causing controversy, satirized Laud presiding over a service:

> [W]hen the Bishop approached near the Communion Table, he bowed with his nose very near the ground some six or seven times; then he came to one of the corners of the Table, and there bowed himself three times; then to the second, third and fourth corners, bowing at each corner three times. . . . then after reading many prayers by himself and his two fat chaplains (which were with him, and all this while were upon their knees by him, in their surplices, hoods, and tippets) he himself came near the Bread, which was cut and laid in a fine napkin, and then he gently lifted up one of the corners of the said napkin, and peeped into it until he saw the bread (like a boy that peeped after a bird-nest in a bush) and presently clapped it down again. . . . after which more prayers being said, this Scene and Interlude ended.[5]

Laud missed nothing; he knew what to expect from allies, and what to look for from opponents. During a 1634 visit to Leicestershire in the

Diocese of Lincoln he paid equal attention to details of ceremony and peoples' conduct, as noted in entries of persons admonished during his episcopal visitation:

> *Pickwell*: John Ball, for working on the Sabbath day. Ball answered, that he did dress a lamb that was eaten with maggots upon a Sunday, which lamb was ready to perish, but that he did not otherwise work upon the Sabbath. (Dismissed with a warning.)
>
> *Easton Magna*: Mr. Black of Thorpe Langton, for reading divine service . . . in his cloak and without a surplice, being first desired by Bringhurst Wignail, one of the churchwardens, to wear the said surplice.
>
> *Somerby*: Thomas Hill, for being churchwarden and yet a very frequent sleeper in the church.
>
> *Garthorpe*: Michael Robinson, late churchwarden, for neglecting his office and suffering dogs to come into the church, which have defiled the church and disturbed the minister.
>
> *Bitteswell*: Edward and John Dillingham are notorious Puritans. Gone into New England.[6]

An autocratic nature and unwavering support of Charles's despotism made Laud fair game for the Long Parliament, which remanded him to custody in 1640 and condemned him to death four years later. A deeply devout person, supportive of the fine arts, Laud was solicitous of the poor as well, but his stubborn temperament worked against him. When the king fell, Laud, his unwavering clerical supporter, was lost as well. The American church, in casting a wide net in its definition of saints, includes William Laud, memorialized on the date of his martyrdom, January 10. "The utter collapse of the Laudian Church within five years of its most signal triumph invites a tragic interpretation," the historian H. L. Trevor-Roper writes, adding, "And yet there is nothing tragic in it. . . . In the height of his power, Laud remained what he had always been,—an industrious and conscientious official, too busy for personal pleasures, too businesslike for megalomania, and by nature averse from that splendor and ostentation which would have made his own fall as spectacular as that of his Church."[7] C. V. Wedgwood concluded, "Laud was more of a tidier-up and setter-in-order than a true reformer."[8] Much of Laud's work was violently reversed by the Long Parliament, which abolished the historic episcopate and banished the Prayer Book. The form of church government it adopted, the Westminster Assembly of Divines, never gained much following in the Church of England and was abolished when traditional church institutions were restored in 1660.

Civil War (1642–1648)

The century's middle years were a time of violent conflict, the ramifications of which took centuries to resolve. Fueled by religious disputes, the Civil War (1642–1648) led to lasting, bitter divisions. The king, many nobles, and the state church were on one side; Parliament and Puritans, whose numbers included artisans and merchants, were on the other, no less autocratic, but with power more widely diffused among presbyters and politicians. The war brought two contrasting positions into sharp focus, government by divine right of kings, and government by Parliament. The Puritan-led soldiers believed they were doing God's will as they systematically toppled churches, burned paintings, smashed stained glass windows, tore up books, and cut up liturgical garments, destroying such ancient treasures as the Reformation's iconoclasts missed. The destruction was systematic. A 1643 report by one Puritan group noted, "We brake down twelve superstitious pictures, and took two popish inscriptions, four cherubims, and a holy water font at the porch door. . . . At Little Mary's . . . We brake down sixty superstitious pictures, some popes and crucifixes, and God the Father sitting in a chair and holding a glass."[9] St. Paul's Cathedral was used as a cavalry stable, another cathedral's baptismal font became a watering trough for animals, other church buildings were turned into barracks and prisons. Bishop Joseph Hall (1574–1656), a moderate, watched in dismay in 1643 as his Norwich cathedral was trashed by Puritans:

> Lord, what work was here, what clattering of glass, what beating down of walls, what tearing up of monuments, what pulling down of seats, what wresting out of irons and brass from windows and graves, what defacing of arms, what demolishing of curious stone work that has not any representation in the world but only the coat of the founders and the skill of the mason, what tooting and piping upon destroyed organs, and what hideous triumph on the market day before all the country, when, in a kind of sacrilegious and profane procession, all the organ pipes, vestments, both copes and surplices, together with the leaden Cross which had been newly sawn down from over the green yard pulpit, and the service books and singing books that could be had, were carried to the fire in the marketplace, a lewd wench walking before the train, in his cope, trailing in the dirt, with a service book in his hand, the time, and usurping the words of the Litany, used formerly in the Church; near the public cross all these monuments of idolatry must be sacrificed to the fire. Neither was it any news, upon the Guild day, to have the Cathedral now open on all sides, to be filled with muske-

teers, waiting for the major's return, drinking and tobaccoing as freely as if it had turned ale-house.[10]

The war's first phase ended in 1645 with Oliver Cromwell's victory and the king's surrender. The old order was violently uprooted, the future was uncertain. The House of Commons was largely Presbyterian, and through the Westminster Assembly of 1643 tried to establish Presbyterianism as the state religion. The army, however, remained independent; the result was widespread toleration for all but Roman Catholics and Anglicans. The episcopacy was abolished in 1644, as were all forms of church structure, including cathedral chapters and deans. The Prayer Book was declared illegal, and possibly two to three thousand clergy out of ten thousand were thrown out of their parishes. Playhouses were closed in 1642; the observance of Christmas Day was forbidden, and only civil marriages were legal. However, government by presbyters, which the Puritans proposed, was seen by many to be as tyrannical as the episcopacy had ever been. John Milton, many would agree, was right, "New Presbyter is but old Priest writ large."[11] Enforcement of Puritan edicts was sporadic; besides, some clergy, agile as the Vicar of Bray, changed beliefs and practices with the times; others modified services enough to escape criticism, sometimes reciting forbidden prayers, such as the baptismal rite, by committing them to memory rather than reading them from a book. Meanwhile, affluent Church of England families hired their own chaplains, who used the Prayer Book rite behind closed chapel doors. Persecuted believers, in any time or place, are adept at surviving, determined to outlast their tormentors, and usually do so.

Meanwhile, Charles's fortunes plummeted. Having withdrawn to the Isle of Wight, in late 1647 the English monarch negotiated a secret treaty with Scotland. The Scots would invade England and restore the monarchy, after which Charles agreed to establish Presbyterianism for a three-year period. The Scots moved south, but into the hands of Cromwell's waiting troops. The string ran out for Charles.

On January 30, 1649, the King was tried for treason and beheaded outside the Whitehall banqueting house. The king's execution sent shock waves of revulsion among the English people. Preachers compared it to the crucifixion and Judah's ruin in the Old Testament. "The black act is done," wrote the Archbishop of Canterbury, William Sancroft (1617–1693), "which all the world wonders at, and which an age cannot expiate. The waters of the ocean we swim in cannot wash out the spots of that blood, than which never any was shed with greater guilt, since the son of God poured out his."[12] People were revolted by the sight of royal blood, and Cromwell's apparent victory carried with it the seeds of his cause's eventual defeat. Charles died with dignity and in death gained a following not otherwise secured during his turbulent reign. A despotic king was bad enough, but military despotism was never acceptable to the English. Charles was revered by many as a martyr and saint. Handkerchiefs dipped in his blood were reported to work miracles, and with the Restoration, January 30, the date of his death, became a fast day, a Prayer Book service commemorated by royal mandate until 1859.

War left the country religiously divided. Two staples of the Church of England's religious life, episcopacy and Prayer Book, were abolished. Many new religious bodies, offshoots of the Puritan era, sprang into being at this time, including Congregationalists, Baptists, and Quakers. Cromwell said, "I meddle not with any man's conscience," but his tolerance did not extend to Catholics and Church of England members, the latter of whom were divided between those loyal to the new regime and those clinging to the monarchy. Many of the monarchy's supporters went abroad or sought jobs as chaplains in homes of affluent courtiers. These high church followers of Laud worked for the day when the monarchy would be restored and with it the state church. Anglicans of a later age will not easily understand the violence and disruption of such a conflicted time. Later wars were destructive, but this was a bitter civil war fought over doctrine and power, protagonists on both sides clothing their actions in elevated religious language.

John Evelyn (1620–1706), a Church of England layperson, described a group that met clandestinely for worship during the Cromwellian period. On Christmas Day 1658 he and his wife were caught attending a Prayer Book service at Exeter Chapel on the Strand in London:

> Sermon ended, as he [the celebrant] was giving up the Holy Sacrament, the chapel was surrounded with soldiers, and all the communicants and assembly surprised and kept prisoners by them, some in the house, others carried away. It fell to my share to be confined to a room in the house. . . .
> In the afternoon came Col. Whaly, Goffe and others, from White-Hall to examine us one by one; some they committed to the Marshall, some to prison. When I came before them they took my name and abode, examined me why, contrary to an ordinance made that none should any longer observe the superstitious time of the Nativity (so esteemed by them), I did offend, and particularly be at Common Prayers, which they told me was but the mass in English, and particularly pray for Charles Stuart, for which

we had no Scripture. I told them we did not pray for Charles Stuart, but for all Christian Kings, Princes, and Governors. They replied, in so doing we prayed for the King of Spain too, who was their enemy and a Papist, with other frivolous and ensnaring questions and much threatening; and finding no reason to detain me, they dismissed me with much pity of my ignorance. These were men of high flight and above ordinances, and spoke spiteful things of our Lord's Nativity. As we went up to receive the Sacrament the miscreants held their muskets against us as if they would have shot us at the altar, yet suffering us to finish the office of Communion, as perhaps not having instructions what to do in case they found us in that action. So I got home, late the next day, blessed be God.[13]

Oliver Cromwell

The person most associated in the popular mind with Puritanism was Oliver Cromwell (1599–1658), a small estate owner elected to Parliament from Cambridge in 1628. His manner was passionate and argumentative, his "insolent behavior" and "imperious carriage" drawing adverse comment from contemporaries. Skilled as a military leader—his troops called him "Ironsides"—Cromwell's New Model Army successively defeated royal troops throughout England, and brutally put down insurrections in Ireland and Scotland. Cromwell believed he was a modern-day Moses, called to lead his people from the bondage of Laud and his followers to the promised land via the Red Sea of civil war.

On July 4, 1647, Cromwell and Charles I met; Cromwell submitted proposals to reduce, but not eliminate, royal power. They included governing through a council of state that would control the military and foreign policy, plus religious toleration. A vacillating yet cunning king, Charles stalled for time and tried to play Parliament off against the army, which resulted in Parliament making harsher demands, creating a Presbyterian form of church government, and denying toleration to the Church of England and the Roman Catholic Church. The equation turned with Charles's flight to the Isle of Wight, and by 1648 Cromwell believed only the king's execution would permit political stability. With characteristic bluntness Cromwell remarked, "I tell you, we will cut off his head with the crown upon it." When the king was executed on January 30, 1649, he said it was an act "which Christians in after times will mention with honor and all tyrants in the world will look at with fear."

Cromwell presided over first a quasi-democratic Commonwealth and then a more authoritarian Protectorate. He died in 1658, having secured a lasting place for popular government and independent churches and was buried in Westminster Abbey, but, characteristic of the age, during the Restoration his bones were removed and hung at Tyburn, a place of public hangings. The revolution produced no successor; Cromwell's son, Richard, lacked either the personality or skills to follow his father, and no other revolutionaries had a vision more lasting than keeping their adherents in power. Following the period's musical chairs, more than seven hundred Puritan clergy were dismissed from positions when Charles II, Charles I's son, came to power. The episcopacy was restored and Prayer Book worship again became the norm.

Several customs Puritans found obnoxious were revived, such as clergy wearing a white surplice over black cassocks, people kneeling for communion, clergy making the Sign of the Cross at baptisms, and bowing when the name of Jesus was uttered in a prayer. In addition, several parliamentary acts, collectively called the Clarendon Code, were passed, creating a permanent divide between establishmentarians and dissenters. The former were the Church of England clergy, the aristocracy, many of the gentry, and most of the people; the latter, the dissenting clergy, artisans, and merchants—traditional wellsprings of Puritan support. The acts required holders of civic office to be Church of England members; attendance at any non–Church of England "assembly, conventicle, or meeting" was forbidden, and nonconformist clergy were not allowed to live within five miles of places where they had previously worked. Access to universities was denied Catholics, Quakers, Presbyterians, Baptists, and Church of England members who would not swear allegiance to the throne's new occupants. The breach between church and state was thus politically resolved, and a victorious pro–Established Church House of Commons, remembering the excesses of its recent opponents, showed no magnanimity, piling on repressive legislation in swift succession, creating a permanent fissure between established church and dissenters.

CHARLES II, JAMES II

Charles died in 1685, a convert to Rome; his successor and brother, James, was an avowed papist, who fled to France after a brief reign (1685–1688), never able to successfully navigate England's shifting political climate. He was succeeded by William of Orange, a Dutch Calvinist, who jointly ruled with Mary, the English daughter of James II. The nuances of English religious life were foreign to William, but England was weary of religious wars and this century's final years were a stable, more tolerant time than before. An Act of Toleration in 1689 allowed most non-conforming and free churches to function, providing they kept doors unlocked and informed local Anglican bishops of their existence, although dissenters could not hold parliamentary office, become magistrates, or receive Oxford or Cambridge degrees.

The long-term implication of a more religiously tolerant atmosphere was that, while the Church of England remained the *established* church, it was no longer an all-powerful *national* church, and many talented clergy and laity were aligned with numerous newly formed denominations. The mid-seventeenth century thus represented a watershed for the Church of England, with the long tie between crown and altar irreparably changed. How could it be otherwise? Parliament was a rising political force and this, more than anything, contributed to the diminished crown–church tie. The church did not meet in convocation from 1664 to 1689, missing an opportunity to regulate its affairs and forfeiting control of its interests to Parliament. In the past, kings such as Henry VIII made a stab at being theologians; others, such as Elizabeth, showed an interest in religion. Charles II was a pious believer, but otherwise royal interest in religion waned. This was not a negative development, for it meant the church of the future would compete for support on its merits. Parliament, sometimes called a "a lay synod of the Church of England" would play a role in decreeing public morality and in ratifying issues of church governance, but the church's intellectual leadership would now come from clerics in the two main universities, Oxford and Cambridge. Further, by the late seventeenth century a close alliance was forged between Church of England clergy and the landed gentry. Battered by the Civil War, each found in the other an ally, resulting in a conservative church, suspicious of those who would tamper with its structure or practices.

Meanwhile, the piety and good works extolled by preachers were translated into action. The spread of lay religion was characteristic of the times. Believers no longer left direction of all religious activities to the clergy. The quest for personal salvation included good works. Thus, lay-led Bible societies and study groups formed, including those creating overseas missions, such as the Society for the Propagation of Christian Knowledge, founded in 1698 for "promoting Religion and Learning in any part of His Majesty's Plantations abroad, and to provide Catechetical Libraries and free schools in the parishes at home." Another well-known missionary group, the Society for the Propagation of the Gospel in Foreign Parts, was chartered in 1702. At home, Societies for the Reformation of Manners hauled blasphemers and profaners of the Lord's Day before local courts and protested the excesses of Restoration drama. Other groups undertook prison reform, built hospitals, or created centers for orphans and children. The era of Christian philanthropy had begun.

THE CHURCH IN AMERICA

Despite the vicissitudes of political and religious life in England during this time, the church in America led a relatively tranquil life. It was not until the mid-eighteenth century that the Anglican Church became a significant force in America. During the seventeenth century the church was hardly more than a hundred parishes scattered along the Atlantic coast from Massachusetts to the Carolinas. Among the earliest English religious presences was the Virginia Company's 1607 Jamestown settlement, with Pocahontas, an Indian princess, among the first native converts. Captain John Smith, in describing the first church service in Virginia on May 13, 1607, wrote:

> we did hang an awning (which is an old sail) to three or four trees to shade us from the sun, our walls were rails of wood, our seats unhewed trees, till we cut planks: our pulpit a bar of wood nailed to two neighboring trees. This was our Church until we built a homely [unpretentious] thing like a barn, set upon crotchets [brackets], covered with rafts, sedge [coarse plants], and earth; so was also the walls, that could neither defend wind nor rain. Yet we had daily Common Prayer morning and evening, every Sunday two sermons, and every three months the Holy Communion, with a homily on Sundays. We continued two or three years after until more Preachers came.[14]

New settlers carried the religious controversies of their native country with them, principally the acrimonious Puritan–Established Church dispute. In New England, Puritans dominated settler life from their arrival in the *Mayflower* in 1620. A persecuted minority in their own land, the Pilgrim's dreamed of founding a New Israel in the wilderness, a spiritual commonwealth where governance of church and state would replicate the Old Testament's legal codes. Meanwhile, the Church of England remained a minority church in New England, although its numbers grew in larger cities like Boston. It was not until the century's end that the Toleration Act of 1689 during the reign of William and Mary gave its members equal legal status with the Puritans.

In Virginia and other royal colonies, the church was closely tied to the chartered company and royal colony government, and received political and financial support. Such a church was considered "the Establishment at prayer," reluctant to exercise a prophetic role in criticizing social inequities or wrongs. It also meant that, while those in positions of power were nominal church members (a pew was reserved for the governor), the church had no visible mission impetus toward the poor, the Indians, and those marginal in society. When Morgan Godwyn was dismissed from his post in Potomac Parish for insisting on the baptism and religious instruction of slaves, he was a reminder of the constant presence of dissident voices for a more inclusive church.

Governance of the English churches in America was by lay vestries. Originally intended as meetings of the whole parish, such bodies, usually twelve prosperous white males, quickly became self-perpetuating, controlling the daily life and assets of churches. Although nominal power was in the hands of men, many rarely attended services. "Believing wives" often held the small congregations together, since women and children frequently outnumbered males in attendance, and doubtlessly informed their vestry husbands of views on issues facing the parish, although they would not take their own places as elected vestry members for another three centuries.

Vestries carefully consolidated power over churches. By declaring the parish officially vacant, an illegal but generally uncontested move, in Virginia they could hire clergy on one-year temporary contracts, thus keeping potential dissidents on a short tether. Given the total absence of bishops or any operative church structure beyond the parish, a system of lay, congregational control of the Church of English holdings was created, establishing a precedent for church governance, and with it a tension between its congregational power base and the later claims of an episcopacy. This conflicting location of power was reflected in Bishop William F. Creighton of Washington's advice to his successor two centuries later, "If you are going to use your authority, make sure you have it first."

Throughout this century, the American clergy were largely products of universities in Great Britain or Scotland, and their educational level and personal conduct appears to be little different from counterparts at home. Many became part of planter society, adept at card playing, drinking, horse racing—the predictable diversions of an isolated society—but others faithfully attended to their work of baptizing and teaching, and preaching the Gospel with few books and little interaction with colleagues. To earn a living, many farmed or rented out the church's glebe lands; for salaries were abysmally low, and sometimes, in Maryland, clergy were paid a tithe of parish member's tobacco crops.

ENGLISH PARISH LIFE

By 1660 and the Civil War's end, English parish life reached a low ebb, although it would revive. A generation had grown up never exposed to Prayer Book services, and in some places Puritans had abandoned use of the Lord's Prayer, claiming it was a popish innovation. Life for the lower levels of clergy and laity remained much as it had been in previous centuries. Ill-educated and ill-paid, clergy often supported large families in isolated rural parishes. Frequently they were treated as peasants by wealthy manor owners. A contemporary account described the chaplain leaving the dinner table when the servants did, "picking his teeth, and sighing with his hat under his arm whilst the knight and my lady eat up the tarts and chickens!"[15] Servants and masters made periodic communions at different services; claret was used in the communion cup for ordinary folk, more expensive muscatel for the gentry.

A subtle shift in the parish's place in village life took place. Until now, the parish church was the center of village life. Often the first or most important building constructed in the village, it was maintained by parishioners, for poorly paid clergy could not be expected to sustain its fabric. Historically, each manor was its own independent fiefdom with the church as its administrative seat. Court sessions were held and important records were stored in churches. People gathered to hear news and to lend and borrow money, to report lost cattle or sheep. The town plough was kept at the church, dovecotes were erected for the parish, and the clergy were responsible for the parish bull or boar. "The church was school, storehouse, arsenal, fire-station, and when necessary fortress," Christopher Hill, a historian of the period, observed. "The lantern tower of All Saints, York, was a lighthouse for travelers. Churches served as storehouses and fortifications . . . and during the English civil war they also did duty as prisons, hospitals, stables." Commenting on the social importance of the church then and now, Hill wrote, "Its sacred functions are a residuum. The dusty notices fluttering in the porches of country churches today are a faint reminder of the days when the real life of the community was focused on its one common center."[16]

It would be too easy to dismiss the village clergy of this period and write off the parish's changing role. The church tower pointed to a world beyond the present. Its bell summoned people to the yearly cycle of worship, of seed time and harvest, of winter eventually giving way to spring and the resurrection. As they had for centuries, people came to commemorate the high points of their lives—christenings, marriages, and burials. Their fears and joys were offered in prayer, and the clergy celebrated the sacraments and instructed their congregations. For most parishioners, life continued as before, with the exception of sharply competing demands for loyalty during the Puritan ascendancy, which provoked conflict and the dislocation of many pastors. Finally, by the late seventeenth century, despite swings in national mood, the Church of England had established a unique place, attempting to recover the historic church's teachings and structure while avoiding the excesses of Roman Catholics and Puritans.

The Prayer Book

The Prayer Book did not escape unscathed. Puritans proscribed its use, and devout churchgoers used it secretly during the Commonwealth and Protectorate, until it was restored with the king in 1662. It remained a conservative, prudent, middle-of-the-road volume, inclusive in theology and elegant in language, which allowed it to last until 1928 as the book of choice of high, low, and broad Anglican worshipers. Writing in 1687, Dean Thomas Comber (1645–1699), a supporter of William and Mary, said the Prayer Book was "so comprehensive, so exact, and so inoffensive a Composure; which is so *judiciously contrived* that the wisest may exercise at once their knowledge and devotion; and yet so plain, that the most ignorant may pray with understanding."[17]

Architecture

Despite this century's political hard edges, this was a time of substantial cultural achievement for the Church of England. The ethos of Anglican worship was reflected in church architecture. Following the Great Fire of London in 1666 in which eighty-nine churches and thirteen thousand homes were destroyed by fire, Christopher Wren (1632–1723) built fifty-two new churches. The most dramatic was St. Paul's Cathedral; more representative were smaller churches such as St. James's, Piccadilly, or St. Clement Dane's. Wren's "auditory" churches with clearly visible altars and pulpits in the same room replaced the "two-room" churches of the Middle Ages, with their separate spaces for preaching the word and celebrating the Eucharist. Altars were central, but not dramatic and high up, as in the Gothic tradition, and some pulpits contained sounding boards or wooden hoods to direct speech toward congregations. Wren's churches were unadorned on the outside, and reflected functional, purposeful interior design. Chancel screens were eliminated, as were side chapels; galleries were added to allow more people to fit into smaller spaces. While only nineteen churches or chapels had been built or rebuilt in Elizabeth's time, by 1662 nearly four hundred churches were remodeled and 133 new churches built, even before some of Wren's most significant commissions were executed.[18] Church furnishings were restored, and choirs and organs were incorporated into services.

Music, a Golden Age

This politically and religiously unsettled time produced some of the church's most enduring composers, musicians such as Orlando Gibbons, Henry Purcell, and John Blow. Services at the Chapel Royal under Charles II drew on the country's most talented musicians. Orlando Gibbons (1583–1625) was the last major composer of the English renaissance. A former chorister of King's College, Cambridge, Gibbons became organist at the Chapel Royal and later Westminster Abbey. A Protestant, Gibbons wrote more than forty English anthems, hymn tunes, and settings of the communion service, plus the secular madrigals and motets for which he is famous. Drama and skillfully woven pictorial phrases, plus the use of numerous instruments, characterize his music.

Henry Purcell (1659–1695) stands next to William Byrd as the Church of England's second great composer of premodern times. An organist at the Chapel Royal, Purcell became keeper of the king's wind instruments and in his short life was a prolific composer of operas such as *Dido and Aeneas* and *The Fairy Queen* and anthems such as "Hear My Prayer, O Lord" and "Thou Knowest, Lord, the Secrets of Our Hearts," performed at Queen Mary's funeral. Most of Purcell's sacred music was written while he was still in his twenties. The seventy anthems reflect a range of emotions, from intimate passages to monumental works like the great anthem "My Heart Is Inditing," written for the coronation of James II and scored for eight-part choir and strings. When Charles II was restored to the throne, Purcell depicted him in an anthem as King David, and in many works departed from Cranmer's "one-note-for-every-syllable" principle for religious works, often resembling operatic arias in places.

John Blow (1649–1708) was a less dramatic composer of sacred music.

Organist at Chapel Royal and Master of the Children at St. Paul's Cathedral, he became organist at Westminster Abbey at Purcell's death. The author of nine complete services and almost a hundred English anthems, he wrote many eight-part anthems with delicate contrapuntal harmonies. English-language hymns by Blow included George Herbert's "Let All the World in Every Corner Sing," (present tune: *Augustine*) Thomas Ken's (1637–1711) "Awake My Soul and with the Sun" (tune: *Morning Hymn*), and Samuel Crossman's (1624–1683) "Jerusalem on High" and "My Song Is Love Unknown" (present tune: *Love Unknown*). Gradually, these and other popular hymns were collected in books and they became a major part of English spirituality.

The Puritans, themselves a musical people, did away with polyphonic Latin and English mass settings, burned music manuscripts and disbanded cathedral and college choirs. Elaborately built pipe organs were hacked apart or moved to private homes (including Cromwell's) or to taverns. Their slogan was "the Bible and nothing but the Bible" and Puritan musical taste was for often-lugubrious metrical psalm settings. A few lasting hymns emerged from this period, but most of the period's religious music was decidedly inferior to the earlier work of composers like Byrd and Gibbons.

A CENTURY OF RELIGIOUS WRITINGS

A distinct perspective on life and faith was articulated by some of the Church of England's most enduring voices during this century. Loosely called Caroline Divines, these writers on divinity during the reigns of Charles I and Charles II saw little of one another and were rarely influenced by one another's writing. Articulate conservatives in the tradition of Jewel and Hooker, they were both apologists for the monarchy and produced some of the century's most probing, imaginative theological works. Writing against a background of the Civil War and Commonwealth, by their holiness of life and literary skills they helped give the struggling church confidence and definition. As church figures, they carved out a position between the two competing systems of Rome and the Continental Reformation; as academics, they found answers to many contemporary problems in the teachings of the early church.

By far the greatest writers during this period, however, were two non-Anglicans, John Milton and John Bunyan. Milton (1608–1674) was a strong supporter of the Puritan cause and secretary to the Republican government during the interregnum. Milton abandoned his youthful interest in ordination in the Church of England because of what he regarded as the "tyranny" of Archbishop Laud. His *Paradise Lost*, the greatest epic poem in the English language, was written when he was old and blind; it established his worldview in language that endured long after the sermons and pamphlets of the time disappeared. Milton in "Lycidas" attacked "swan-eating and Canary-sucking" prelates whose only concern was to eat and drink while "the hungry sheep look up and are not fed." John Bunyan (1628–1688), author of over sixty works, was an unlettered Baptist lay preacher whose *Pilgrim's Progress* (1676) became the best-known allegorical work of its kind in the English language. Written in prison, inspired by a dream, it is a journey to the promised land. Characters such as Sloth, Obstinate, Mr. Worldy Wiseman, Prudence, and Chastity became part of English popular culture; the journey to the Heavenly City was symbolic of the human journey.

Jeremy Taylor

This politically disruptive century nevertheless produced some of Anglicanism's most imaginative writers. Jeremy Taylor built on the ideas of Thomas Cranmer. John Donne, George Herbert, and Thomas Traherne won lasting places as creative artists. John Locke became a formative political theorist of the structure of the state and its relation to the church. The career of Jeremy Taylor (1613–1667) was closely tied with that of his patron, William Laud, bishop of London, then Archbishop of Canterbury. Laud arranged for Taylor's appointment to a parish church in the London diocese, but his tranquil life was shattered in 1640 when a mob demanded the episcopacy's abolition and Laud was sent to the Tower and executed in 1645. Taylor, after a brief imprisonment, went into exile in Wales, where he was fortunate to secure a chaplaincy on the estate of Richard Vaughan, earl of Carbery. Here, in the secluded protection of Golden Grove, Taylor spent a decade and wrote some of his most lasting works, including two widely circulated books for the laity, *Holy Living* and *Holy Dying*. Both described practical steps toward the sanctification of life. With the monarchy's restoration in 1660, Taylor was made a bishop in Ireland, where much of his time was spent dealing with the stubborn Presbyterian clergy ensconced there, until his death in 1667.

In this passage he describes the lark's flight in language suggesting the soul's flight to God:

For so have I seen a lark rising from his bed of grass and soaring upwards sings as he rises, and hopes to get to heaven, and climb above the clouds; but the poor bird was beaten back with the loud sighings of an eastern wind, and his motion made irregular and unconstant, descending more at every breath of the tempest, than it could recover by the liberation and frequent weighing of his wings; till the little creature was forced to sit down and pant, and stay till the storm was over, and then it made a prosperous flight, and did rise and sing as if it had learned music and motion from an Angel as he passed sometimes through the air about his ministries here below.[19]

Taylor redefined the meaning of sacraments for contemporary audiences buffeted by post-Reformation debates. In a commentary on the Eucharist as a past and future event commemorating Christ's sacrificial death and anticipating the Second Coming, he moves beyond doctrines of his time. The Eucharist, for Taylor, is more than a remembered meal in the Protestant tradition or a reenactment of Christ's death, as represented in Catholic thought. It is a once-and-future event:

Here the Lord appears to us in a feast, which is a time of innocent delight. The glory of God is set forth unto us in that which our senses apprehend for sweetness and pleasure, as I appoint unto you a Kingdom—that you may eat and drink at my table, which is translated from bodily pleasure to spiritual, that in the heaven of blessedness the soul shall feed continually as at a banquet, of which we have now a taste in the kingly provision of Christ's supper. It is a Kingly feast, although imparted in a little pittance of bread and wine; yet it is most costly and precious, in that which it signifies, than Solomon and all his court had for their diet by day. We are brought to eat at the King's table as Mephibosheth was, like one of the King's sons. For he that broke bread and gave it to the apostles, gives it to us as our High Priest, though he be in heaven. Wherefore the spirit saith write: blessed are they that are called to the marriage-supper of the Lord.[20]

It would be a mistake to confuse Taylor's deep sacramental interest with support of the Roman Catholic Church. Taylor disagrees with those who "conclude that it must be done by submission to an infallible guide; this must do it or nothing: and this is the way of the church of Rome; follow but the pope and his clergy, and you are safe, at least as safe as their warrant can make you. Indeed, this was a very good way, if it were a way at all; but it is none; for this can never end our controversies." Taylor argued that no such guide exists, nor is one needed, and " they who pretend to be this infallible guide are themselves infinitely deceived."[21]

John Donne

John Donne (1571–1631) was brought up in the Roman Catholic faith, his uncle being leader of a Jesuit mission to England. Trained as a lawyer at Lincoln's Inn, he was appointed to several diplomatic missions, was ordained in the Church of England in 1615, and became dean of St. Paul's Cathedral in 1621. A man-about-town in his youth, he secretly married his patron's niece, bringing down familial wrath on the couple, who then lived in poverty supported largely by the generosity of friends. Donne was an ambitious courtier until his ordination at age forty-four. An ambassadorship to Venice or a high position in the Virginia Company were his goals, but King James urged him to enter the church instead, something Donne resisted, for those around the king often made fun of the church and its clergy. Even after agreeing to ordination, Donne sought the King's assurances that he would be provided with a lucrative sinecure. Donne became a Chaplain-in-Ordinary, which allowed him to hold two livings simultaneously, and his friends at court eventually added other livings to his string. The crowning post was the dean's position at St. Paul's Cathedral, which the author secured after a prestigious appointment as reader at Lincoln's Inn.

Donne's life and writings reflect the agonies of his age. The Roman Catholic and Protestant ways were in conflict. For Catholics, redemption came via the church and its sacraments; for Protestants, the doctrine of justification by faith alone was strong at this time. Faith was a gift from God, so the argument ran, bestowed freely without any action or good works done by the Christian. An inscrutable God selected those who would be saved. A person always hoped for salvation, prayed for it, and worried about it. This tension is reflected in Donne's "Holy Sonnets" and in some of his love poems, where his distraught soul longs for God and salvation.

His wife died young, and most of the children died in infancy. Donne's own health was weak, and death and illness seep constantly into his poetry and sermons. Best known as a poet and mystic, Donne's inner life is fully exposed in his lengthy sermons, which often took one or two hours to deliver, and which fill ten printed volumes.

George Herbert

George Herbert (1593–1633), a prolific writer of religious poetry and prose, died at age forty. His poems about the church—"The Temple" and a longer prose work, *A Priest to the Temple, Or, The Country Parson, His Character and Rule of Holy Life*—describe the spiritual world of that quintessential staple of the Church of England, the country parson.

The tranquil, ordered pace of Herbert's devotional life was the opposite of England's political unrest of the time in which he wrote. Son of a politically prominent family, he was named University Orator at Cambridge in 1620, a position that could have led him to further advancement with the crown. Herbert was briefly a member of Parliament, and for a while considered a career in politics, but sought ordination instead after several years of indecision, apparently because he felt himself deeply unworthy of the calling. He married Jane Danvers in 1629. We know little about her, except that she appeared with Herbert daily at 10:00 A.M. and 4:00 P.M. for Morning and Evening Prayers, along with three nieces from a deceased sister. Herbert found fulfillment in the life of a country parson, serving two churches near the Welsh border—the parish church of Fugglestone St. Peter and the chapel of Bemerton St. Andrew until his death in Bemerton rectory on March 1, 1633, only three years after his ordination.

Herbert was often ill, and at times depressed and given to frequent mood swings; his works, especially the poems, openly chronicle his struggles with God and his numerous personality conflicts. At least five poems are called "Affliction." While anthologies often include the author's more serene works, such as "The Call," the range of his writing demonstrates that it is possible to have deep conflicts both with God and within one's self and honestly still find a peaceful resolution of such disturbing issues. Over 170 poems, written during a lengthy period, but given final shape in Herbert's later years, are structured around the Life of Christ and the liturgical year, and draw heavily on biblical and natural images. In a poem like "Aaron" and "The Collar" the twin themes of struggle and struggle's resolution in surrender to Christ are enunciated. A similar conflict, serenely resolved, is described in "The Flower," in which the polarities of winter and spring, hell and heaven, death and life, atrophy and growth are juxtaposed. The writer, aware of his own mortality, concludes:

> And now in age I bud again,
> After so many deaths I live and write;
>   I once more smell the dew and rain,
> And relish versing: Oh my only light,
>   It cannot be
>   That I am he
>   On whom thy tempests fell all night.[22]

Nicholas Ferrar

Nicholas Ferrar (1593–1637) founded the Little Gidding family monastic experiment. A successful businessman and partner in the Virginia Company, Ferrar abandoned a prosperous career, declining an important ambassadorship just before leaving London. In 1626 Ferrar, his extended family, and servants set off for the distant town of Little Gidding in Huntingdonshire, near Cambridge, where thirty-some persons restored the church in an old manor house. After he arrived in the isolated rural region, the family spent several days cleaning out the small manor church, used most recently as a hay barn and pigsty. Ordained a deacon by Archbishop Laud, Nicholas presided over the many family services for over a decade until his death.

Services were based heavily on Bible readings and memorization and recitation of psalms. The chapel was tastefully adorned with cedar-wood furnishings and blue cloth hangings, and a Eucharist was celebrated monthly by a nearby vicar. Ferrar introduced a daily round of prayer, the extended family rising each morning at 4:00 A.M. and praying in alternating groups daily for fifteen minutes at the beginning of each hour. At night vigils, between 9:00 P.M. and 1:00 A.M., two people recited the Psalter in turn while kneeling. The community also created schools and devoted themselves to good works among the region's poor and sick. Thrice weekly the family prepared twenty gallons of gruel, which was distributed to the needy. Ferrar died in 1637 at age forty-five, and Little Gidding was sacked during the civil war. Cromwell's soldiers devastated the place, smashing the organ, burning it and papers on a massive bonfire, where they roasted sheep stolen from the manor farm, and then hauled off the simple but attractive furnishings Ferrar had carefully assembled.

A Puritan, meaning to be critical of Little Gidding, wrote:

> I observed the Chapel in general to be fairly and spaciously adorned with herbs and flowers, natural and artificial, and upon every pillar along both sides of the chapel . . . tapers. The half-pace was all covered with tapestry, and upon that half-pace stood the Altar-like table, with a rich carpet hanging very large on the half-pace, and some plate, and a chalice and candlesticks . . . a laver and cover all of brass, cut and carved with imagery work . . . and the cover had a cross erected on it.[23]

In the late twentieth century there has been a revival of interest in Ferrar and the household he created, encouraged in part by T.S. Eliot, who named the last of his *Four Quartets* "Little Gidding."

Thomas Traherne

No discussion of the seventeenth-century English Church would be complete without considering the metaphysical poet Thomas Traherne (1637?–1694), whose most enduring works were not discovered until three centuries after his death, and whose writings became a major influence on modern writers on creation-and-religion issues. (The remnants of his library were bought at a street bookstall in the late nineteenth century, and his poems passed through several hands until they were finally published several years later.) A student at Oxford University, he was both a rector of small rural churches and private chaplain to Sir Orlando Bridgman, Lord Keeper of the Seals. Traherne, a precursor of later generations of nature poets, wrote works describing the beauties of God's universe and the innocence of childhood. If his work suggests Wordsworth and Blake, the influence of contemporaries like George Herbert and Henry Vaughan is evident as well. In the posthumously published *Centuries of Meditation* Traherne wrote:

> The corn was orient [rising toward the sky—*ed.*] and immortal wheat, which never should be reaped, nor was ever sown. I thought it had stood from everlasting to everlasting. The dust and stones of the street were as precious as gold: the gates were at first the end of the world. The green trees when I saw them first through one of the gates transported and ravished me, their sweetness and unusual beauty made my heart leap, and almost mad with ecstasy, they were such strange and wonderful things.[24]

Elsewhere he wrote in a similar vein:

> You will never enjoy the world aright till the Sea itself floweth in your veins, till you are clothed with the heavens, and crowned with the stars: and perceive yourself to be the sole heir of the whole world, and more so, because men are in it who are everyone sole heirs as well as you. Till you can sing and rejoice and delight in God, as misers do in gold, and Kings in scepters, you will never enjoy the world.[25]

John Locke

The convergence of religious thought with other disciplines in the late seventeenth century was represented in John Locke (1632–1704), who combined Christian faith with the new inquiries into science and political thought. Locke's *Essay Concerning Human Understanding* was published in 1690. His *The Reasonableness of Christianity as Delivered in the Scriptures* followed in 1695, in which Locke argued that faith must be followed by good works and that religious truth is easily discernible through reason. Rejecting dogmatism, Locke introduced the idea of probability into religious discourse; it was probable that the human soul existed, and with the twin tools of reason and probability he constructed a method of approaching the great religious questions of his time. Locke did not believe in original sin, but in a Messiah, whose teachings were discernible through the reasonableness of scriptures. A student of the Bible, Locke rejected Puritans' efforts to build beliefs on single Bible verses taken out of context. He wrote, "We must look into the drift of the discourse, observe the coherence and connection of the parts, and see how it is consistent with itself, and other parts of Scripture, if we will conceive it right."[26]

Locke's religious writings represented a bridge between Christian belief and the new advances of scientific thought. He sharply challenged traditional Platonist belief about the presence of "innate ideas," arguing that all ideas emerge from experience and are discoverable through reason. Locke believed that the existence of God could be discerned through reason and that God, in turn, gave humanity laws for the conduct of life. Locke's schema recognized that religious knowledge was obtainable according to reason, against reason, and above reason. The author also espoused doctrines of religious toleration and support for free inquiry far ahead of his time. While he excluded atheists and Roman Catholics, believing both were dangerous to society in different ways, he argued for a national church with a creed encompassing enough to allow people of sharply divergent viewpoints to exist together in the same body. Human understanding was too limited, he argued, for any one person, such as a pope or a denominational leader, to impose his beliefs on others. Revolutionary in its time, such a viewpoint moved far beyond this epoch's rigid Puritanism, doctrinaire Roman Catholicism, or Church of England intransigence.

Locke's conceptual approaches bridged disciplines; he quickly saw the compatibility of science and religion and that faith and reason represent different ways of viewing reality. The Christian religion, the meaning of words, education, economics, politics, philosophy, psychology, and rule of law were all subjects of his scrutiny. Additionally, Locke practiced medicine briefly, spent several years on the Continent, and served with the Board of Trade. Plagued by asthma all his life, the bachelor Locke lived for fourteen years in the manor house of Otes in Essex, the county seat of Sir Francis Masham and the Masham family. Increasingly meditative in his later years, the philosopher died in 1704, reciting psalms with Lady

Masham and her daughter, in his words "in perfect charity with all men, and in sincere communion with the whole church of Christ, by whatever names Christ's followers call themselves."

SUMMARY

Despite the difficulties it faced, the Church of England survived this troubled century intact and well positioned for the future. Prolonged warfare was devastating, but by century's end new intellectual currents stirred that would affect the church far more in the time ahead than had recent conflicts. The work of the Caroline Divines and the Cambridge Platonists and their successors provided a blueprint for the cooperation of science and religion. The Cambridge Platonists, a group of philosophical divines, flourished from 1633 to 1688 at Cambridge, where they constantly advocated tolerance and comprehension within the church and with the academic world. The power struggle over the divine right of kings, important in this century's initial decades, receded as political power passed gradually to Parliament. For the person in the pew, the reasons for attending church at the century's end were not different from those at its beginning. Now that bishops, priests, and the Prayer Book were restored, life resumed with its usual patterns of worship and social interaction at the village church. Into its second century as an independent entity, the church had not only survived but, in writers like George Herbert, Jeremy Taylor, and John Locke, had produced original voices articulating its own distinctive position. The Church of England was launched.

READINGS

George Herbert

The Country Parson described a rural vicar's life in idealized language; Herbert's personal religious struggles are laid bare in his poetry, and this prose work is his idea of how the Country Parson should live. The book combines evangelical fervor and Catholic reverence for sacraments. A work of profound spirituality grounded in the Book of Common Prayer, it was written at a unique moment when the Church of England emerged from the shadows of its Roman Catholic past, while giving its own stamp to Reformation ideas. Herbert wrote the book, "that I may have a Mark to aim at," but, in an approach increasingly characteristic of Anglican writing, it sets parameters, yet remains open-ended. It reflects a deep awareness of the changes of the liturgical year, and of the progression of Christ's life. Readers several centuries later will find it an inviting work for the spiritual journey.

In Herbert's view, the Country Parson's role is nothing less than the sanctification of his own life, his family, and the village. Izaak Walton said of Herbert, "and some of the meaner sort of his parish did so love and reverence Mr. Herbert that they would let their plough rest when Mr. Herbert's Saints'-Bell rung to prayers, that they might offer their devotions to God with him."[27] Here is Herbert describing the Parson's life:

The Country Parson is exceeding exact in his Life, being holy, just, prudent, temperate, bold, grave in all his ways. And because the two highest points of Life, wherein a Christian is most seen, are Patience, and Mortification; Patience in regard of afflictions, Mortification in regard of lusts and affections, and the stupefying and deading of all the clamorous powers of the soul, therefore he hath thoroughly studied these, that he may be absolute Master and commander of himself, for all the purposes which God hath ordained him. . . . Neither is it for the servant of Christ to haunt Inns, or Taverns, or Ale-houses. . . . Country people (as indeed all honest men) do much esteem their word, it being the Life of buying, and selling, and dealing in the world; therefore the Parson is very strict in keeping his word, though it be to his own hindrance. . . . The Parson's yea is yea, and nay nay: and his apparel plain, but reverend, and clean, without spots, or dust, or smell; the purity of his mind breaking out, and dilating itself even to his body, clothes, and habitation."[28]

The center of the Parson's life is the study and preaching of the Bible and prayer. There is almost no mention of church organization in the thirty-seven categories Herbert finds important to discuss in the Country Parson's life. Of the Parson's prayer life Herbert says:

The Country Parson, when he is to read divine services, composeth himself to all possible reverence; lifting up his heart and hands, and eyes, using all other gestures which may express a hearty and unfeigned devotion. This he doth, first, as being truly touched and amazed with the Majesty of God, before whom he then presents himself; yet not as himself alone, but as presenting with himself the whole Congregation, whose sins he then bears, and brings with his own to the heavenly altar to be bathed, and washed . . . in Christ's blood. . . . His voice is humble, his words treatable [distinct—ed.] and slow; yet not so slow neither, as to let the fervency of the supplicant hang and die between speaking, but with a grave liveliness, between fear and zeal, pausing yet pressing, he performs his duty." Among the people he "exacts of them all possible reverence, by no means enduring either talking, or sleeping, or gazing, or leaning, or half-kneeling, or any other undutiful behavior." The congregation should "answer aloud both Amen, and all other answers, which are on the Clerk's and people's part to answer; which answers also are to be done not in a huddling, or slubbering fashion, gaping, or scratching the head, or spitting even in the midst of their answer, but gently and pausably, thinking what they say.[29]

A central activity for the Parson is preaching:

The Country Parson preacheth constantly, the pulpit is his joy and his throne. . . . Sometimes he tells them stories, and sayings of others, according as his text invites him; for them also men heed, and remember better than exhortations; which though earnest, yet often die with the Sermon, especially with Country people; which are thick, and heavy, and hard to raise to a point of Zeal, and fervency, and need a mountain of fire often to kindle them; but stories and sayings they will well remember. . . . The character of his sermon is Holiness; he is not witty, or learned, or eloquent, but Holy.[30]

Of the Parson's house he says:

The furniture of his house is very plain, but clean, whole, and sweet, as sweet as his garden can make; for he hath no money for such things, charity being his only perfume. . . . His fare is plain, and common, but wholesome, what he hath is little, but very good; it consisteth most of mutton, beef and veal.[31]

The Church of England was a state church, and Herbert enjoined the Country Parson to be "not only a Pastor, but a Lawyer also, and a Physician. Therefore he endures not that any of his Flock should go to Law; but in any Controversy, that they should resort to him as their Judge."

The Parson equally has a physician's role, if he possesses the skills. A list of home-bred medicines, herbs, salves and poultices is offered, for "our Savior made plants and seeds to teach the people for he was a true householder."[32]

Chapter XIII
The Parson's Church

The Country Parson hath a special care of his Church, that all things there be decent, and befitting his Name by which it is called. Therefore first he takes order, that all things be in good repair; all walls plastered, windows glazed, floors paved, seats whole, firm, and uniform, especially that the Pulpit, and Desk, and Communion Table, and Font be as they ought, for those great duties that are performed in them. Secondly, that the Church be swept, and kept clean without dust, or Cobwebs, and at great festivals strawed, and stuck with boughs, and perfumed with incense. Thirdly, That there be fit, and proper texts of Scripture everywhere painted, and that all the painting be grave, and reverend, not with light colors, or foolish antics. Fourthly, That all books appointed by Authority be there, and those not torn, or fouled, but whole and clean, and well bound; and that there be a fitting, and sightly Communion Cloth of fine linen, with an handsome, and seemly Carpet of good and costly Stuff, or Cloth, and all kept sweet and clean, in a strong and decent chest, with a Chalice, and Cover, and a Stoop, or Flagon; and a Basin for Alms and offerings; besides which, he hath a Poor-man's Box conveniently seated, to receive the charity of well-minded people, and to lay up treasure for the sick and needy. And all this he doth, not out of necessity, or as putting a holiness in the things, but as desiring to keep the middle way between superstition, and slovenliness, and as following the Apostle's two great and admirable Rules in things of this nature: The first whereof is, *Let all things be done decently, and in order:* The second, *Let all things be done in edification* (1 Cor. 14:[26, 40]). For these two rules comprise and include the double object of our duty, God, and our neighbor; the first being for the honor of God; the second for the benefit of our neighbor.

Chapter XIV
The Parson in Circuit

The Country Parson upon the afternoons in the weekdays, takes occasion sometimes to visit in person, now one quarter of his Parish, now another. For there he shall find his flock most naturally as they are, wallowing [active—*ed.*] in the midst of their affairs: whereas on Sundays it is easy for them to compose themselves to order, which they put on as their holy-day clothes, and come to Church in frame [appropriately—*ed.*], but commonly the next day put both off. When he comes to any house, first he blesseth it, and then as he finds the persons of the house employed, so he forms his discourse. Those that he finds religiously employed, he both commends them much, and furthers them when he is gone, in their employment; as if he finds them reading, he furnisheth them with good books; if curing poor people, he supplies them with Receipts, and instructs them further in that skill, showing them how acceptable such works are to God, and wishing them ever to do the Cures with their own hands, and not to put them over to servants. Those that he finds busy in the works of their calling, he commendeth them also: for it is a good and just thing for everyone to do their own business. But then he admonisheth them of two things; first, that they dive not too deep into worldly affairs, plunging themselves over head and ears in carking [anxiety—*ed.*] and caring; but that they so labor, as neither to labor anxiously, nor distrustfully, nor profanely. Then they labor anxiously, when they overdo it, to the loss of their quiet, and health: then distrustfully, when they doubt God's providence, thinking that their own labor is the cause of their thriving, as if it were in their own hands to thrive, or not to thrive. . . . Wherefore neither disdaineth he to enter into the poorest Cottage, though he even creep into it, and though it smell never so loathsomely. For both God is there also, and those for whom God died.

Chapter XXXV
The Parson's Condescending

Most likely "condescending" in this context means "being a part of" local customs and usages. Here Herbert discusses the planting-time ritual of "beating the bounds," the priest and parishioners, singing hymns and psalms on Rogation Sunday, and processing around the parish's boundaries. Disputes between neighbors over land were settled; arrangements were made for baptisms and marriages; the land was blessed; and a generally convivial time was had by all. In the second ancient custom, Herbert recalls a benediction said when a candle was brought into a room. (In an age of electricity, the mystery of light is remote, but for many people, it was and is a symbol of Christ.)

The Country Parson is a Lover of old Customs, if they be good, and harmless; and the rather, because Country people are much addicted to them, so to favor them therein is to win their hearts, and to oppose them therein is to deject them. If there be any ill in the custom, that may be severed from the good, he pares the apple and gives them the clean to feed on. Particularly, he loves Procession [the Rogationtide custom of "beating the bounds"—*ed*.] and maintains it, because there are contained therein four manifest advantages. First, a blessing of God for the fruits of the field: Secondly, justice in the Preservation of bounds: Thirdly, Charity in loving walking, and neighborly accompanying one another: Fourthly, Mercy in relieving the poor by a liberal distribution and largesse, which at that time, ought to be used. Wherefore he exacts all to be present at the perambulation, and those that withdraw, and sever themselves from it, he mislikes, and reproves as uncharitable, and unneighborly; and if they will not reform, presents them. Nay, he is so far from condemning such assemblies, that he rather procures them to be often, as knowing that absence breeds strangeness, but presence love. . . . Another old Custom there is of saying, when light is brought in, God sends us the light of heaven [from an old vesper rite—*ed*.], and the Parson likes this very well; neither is he afraid of praising, or praying to God at all times, but is rather glad of catching opportunities to do them. Light is a great Blessing, and as great as food, for which we give thanks: and those that think this superstitious, neither know superstition, nor themselves.[33]

Jeremy Taylor

In 1649 Jeremy Taylor, while in exile in Wales, published another of the post-Reformation comprehensive guides to moral living, his *Rules of Exercises of Holy Living* and its companion volume, *Holy Dying*. This was another attempt of a Church of England writer to articulate an encompassing statement of belief and its application to daily life for the Christian to whom earlier Roman Catholic dogma would no longer apply, and who found the writings of Luther and Calvin incomplete. Taylor was aware of writing at a difficult time; the High Church royalist party had been thrown from power, the supporters of Cromwell exercised their will. In dedicating the work to his patron, Richard Vaughan, earl of Carbery, Taylor wrote:

I have lived to see religion painted on banners, and thrust out of churches, and the temple turned into a tabernacle, and that tabernacle made into an ambulatory, and covered with skins of beasts and torn curtains, and God to be worshiped, not as He is, the Father of our Lord Jesus

Christ, an afflicted Prince, the King of sufferings; nor as the God of peace; which two appellatives God newly took upon him in the New Testament, and glories in it forever: but He is owned now rather by the Lord of hosts, which title He was pleased to lay aside when the kingdom of the gospel was preached by the Prince of peace. But when religion puts on armor, and God is not acknowledged by His New Testament titles, religion may have in it the power of the sword, but not the power of godliness.[34]

Section I
The First General Instrument of Holy Living, Care of Our Time

God hath given to a man a short time here upon earth, and yet upon this short time eternity depends; but so that for every hour of our life, after we are persons capable of laws and know good from evil, we must give account to the great Judge of men and angels. And this is it which our blessed Savior told us, that we must account for every idle word: not meaning that every word which is not designed to edification, or is less prudent, shall be reckoned for a sin; but that the time which we spend in our idle talking and unprofitable discoursings, that time which might and ought to have been employed to spiritual and useful purposes, this is to be accounted for.

For we must remember that we have a great work to do, many enemies to conquer, many evils to prevent, much danger to run through, many difficulties to be mastered, many necessities to serve, and much good to do, many children to provide for, or many friends to support, or many poor to relieve, or many diseases to cure, besides the needs of nature and of relation, our private and our public cares, and duties of the world which necessity and the providence of God hath adopted into the family of Religion.

God hath given every man work enough to do, that there shall be no room for idleness; and yet hath so ordered the world that there shall be space for devotion: he that hath the fewest businesses of the world, is called upon to spend more time in the dressing of his soul; and he that hath the most affairs, may so order them that they shall be a service of God; whilst at certain periods they are blessed with prayers and actions of religion, and all day long are hallowed by a holy intention.

Idleness is called the sin of Sodom and her daughters, and indeed is "the burial of a living man"; an idle person being so useless to any purposes of God and man that he is like one that is dead, unconcerned in the changes and necessities of the world; and he only lives to spend his time, and eat the fruits of the earth: like a vermin or a wolf; when their time comes they die and perish, and in the mean time do no good; they neither plough nor carry burdens; all that they do either is unprofitable or mischievous.[35]

John Donne

John Donne (1571/2–1631), dean of St. Paul's Cathedral, wrote erotic and sacred verse, plus prayers and sermons. He often preached for two hours. Donne was no popularizer; within the confines of a clear outline there are layers of reworking the same theme from different angles, all designed to lead the hearer to an inescapable conclusion, the need for repentance, amendment of life, and walking with Christ. Like those of Newman two hundred years later, the sermons had an inner consistency and were almost exclusively about the struggle for redemption.

> *"Deaths Duell,*
> *or,*
> *A Consolation to the Soule,*
> *against the dying Life and living*
> *Death of the Body"*

[Preached during Lent, 1630, in the presence of King Charles I at Whitehall.]

Buildings stand by the benefit of their foundations that sustain and support them, and of their buttresses that comprehend and embrace them, and of their contignations that knit and unite them. The foundations suffer them not to sink, the buttresses suffer them not to swerve, and the contignation and knitting suffers them not to cleave. The body of our building is in the former part of this verse. It is this: "He that is our God is the God of salvation"; *ad salutes,* of salvations in the plural, so it is in the original; the God that gives us spiritual and temporal salvation too.

But of this building, the foundation, the buttresses, the contignations are in this part of the verse, which constitutes our text, and in the three divers acceptations of the words among our expositors. "Unto God the Lord belong the issues of death." For first the foundation of this building (that our God is the God of all salvations) is laid in this; that unto this "God the Lord belong the issues of death," that is, it is in his power to give us an issue and deliverance, even then when we are brought to the jaws and teeth of death, and to the lips of that whirlpool, the grave. And so in this acceptation, this *exitus mortis,* this issue of death is *liberatio a morte,* a deliverance from death, and this is the most obvious and most ordinary acceptation of these words, and that upon which our translation lays hold, "the issues from death."

And then secondly the buttresses that comprehend and settle this building, that he that is our God, is the God of all salvation, are thus raised. "Unto God the Lord belong the issues of death," that is, the disposition and manner of our death: what kind of issue and transmigration we shall have out of this world, whether in our perfect senses or shaken and disordered by sickness. There is no condemnation to be argued out of that, no judgment to be made upon that, for however, they die, "precious in his sight is the death of his saints," and with him are "the issues of death," the ways of our departing out of this life are in his hands. And so in this sense of the words, this *exitus mortis,* the issue of death is *liberatio in morte,* a deliverance in death. Not that God will deliver us from dying, but that he will have a care of us in the hour of death, of what kind soever our passage be.

And then lastly the contignation and knitting of this building, that he that is our God is the God of all salvations, consists in this, "Unto this God the Lord belong the issues of death," that is, that this God the Lord having united and knit both natures in one, and being God, having also come into this world, in our flesh, he could have no other means to save us, he could have no other issue out of this world, nor return to his former glory, but by death. And so in this sense, this *exitus mortis*, this issue of death *is liberatio per mortem*, a deliverance by death, by the death of this God, our Lord Christ Jesus. And this is St. Augustine's acceptation of the words, and those many and great persons that have adhered to him.

Our critical day is not the very day of our death but the whole course of our life. I thank him that prays for me when my bell tolls, but I thank him much more that catechises me, or preaches to me, or instructs me how to live. . . . There's my security, the mouth of the Lord has said it, do this and you shall live. But though I do it, yet I shall die too, die a bodily, a natural death. But God never mentions, never seems to consider that death, the bodily, the natural death. God does not say, live well and you shall die well, that is, an easy, a quiet death; but live well here, and you shall live well forever. As the first part of a sentence points well with the last, and never respects, never harkens after the parenthesis that comes between, so does a good life here flow into an eternal life, without any consideration what manner of death we die. But whether the gate of my prison be opened with an oiled key (by a gentle and preparing sickness), or the gate be hewn down by a violent death, or the gate be burned down by a raging and frantic fever, a gate into heaven I shall have, for from the Lord is the cause of my life, and with God the Lord are the issues of death. And further we carry not this second acceptation of the words, as this issue of death is a *liberatio in morte* God's care that the soul be safe, what agonies soever the body suffers in the hour of death.[36]

John Locke

John Locke (1632–1704), son of a Puritan lawyer, wrote during the late seventeenth century, covering most domains of human knowledge known during his time. A king, Charles I, had been murdered, replaced by a Commonwealth form of government. When the monarchy was later restored, a subsequent king, James II, fled in 1688, and a quasi-contractual arrangement brought William of Orange and Mary to the British throne. Puritans, who wanted no return of monarchical power, found this troubling, as did followers of the departed king, for whom the new rulers lacked legitimacy. Deeply rooted in the Church of England's beliefs of this time, Locke hammered out a modern theory of a democratic state, providing a paradigm for democratic government, church–state relations, and a market economy which have endured to modern times, albeit with modifications. Modern theorists have much more information to use and have advanced aspects of Locke's methodology; but few have attempted the comprehensive linkages he saw among disciplines, for his province was nothing less than a science of human knowledge.

From *An Essay Concerning Human Understanding*

There are other ideas, whose agreement or disagreement can not otherwise be judged of but by the intervention of others which have not a certain agreement with extremes, but an *usual* or *likely* one: and in these it is that the *judgment* is properly exercised; which is the acquiescing of the mind, that any ideas do agree, by comparing them with such mediums. This, though it never amounts to knowledge, no, not to that which is the lowest degree of it; yet sometimes the intermediate ideas tie the extremes so firmly together, and the probability is so clear and strong, that *assent* as necessarily follows it, as *knowledge* does demonstration. The great excellency and use of the judgment is to observe right, and take a true estimate of the force and weight of each probability; and then casting them up all right together, choose that side which has the overbalance.

Intuitive knowledge is the perception of the *certain* agreement or disagreement of two ideas immediately compared together.

Rational knowledge is the perception of the *certain* agreement or disagreement of any two ideas, by the intervention of one or more other ideas.

Judgment is the thinking or taking two ideas to agree or disagree, by the intervention of one or more ideas, whose certain agreement or disagreement with them it does not perceive, but hath observed to be *frequent* and *usual*.

By what has been before said of reason, we may be able to make some guess at the distinction of things, into those that are according to, above, and contrary to reason. 1. *According to reason* are such propositions whose truth we can discover by examining and tracing those ideas we have from sensation and reflection; and by natural deduction find to be true or probable. 2. *Above reason* are such propositions whose truth or probability we cannot by reason derive from those principles. 3. *Contrary to reason* are such propositions as are inconsistent with or irreconcilable to our clear and distinct ideas. Thus the existence of one God is according to reason; the existence of more than one God, contrary to reason; the resurrection of the dead, above reason. *Above Reason* also may be taken in a double sense, viz. Either as signifying above probability.[37]

Of Faith and Reason, and Their Distinct Provinces

[The lack of] measures and boundaries between faith and reason . . . may possibly have been the cause, if not of great disorders, yet at least of great disputes, and perhaps mistakes in the world. For till it be resolved, how far we are to be guided by reason, and how far by faith, we shall in vain dispute, and endeavor to convince one another in matters of religion.

Reason, therefore, here, contradistinguished to faith, I take to be the discovery of the certainty or probability of such propositions or truths, which the mind arrives at by deduction made from such ideas, which it has got by the use of its natural faculties; viz., by sensation or reflection.

Faith, on the other side, is in the assent to any proposition, not thus made out by the deduction of reason; but upon the credit of the proposer, as coming from God, in some extraordinary way of communication. This way of discovering truths to men we call revelation. . . . If the provinces of faith and reason are not kept distinct by these boundaries, there will, in matters of religion, be no room for reason at all; and those extravagant opinions and ceremonies that are to be found in the several religions of the world, will not deserve to be blamed. For, to this crying up of faith, in opposition to reason, we may, I think, in good measure ascribe those absurdities that fill almost all the religions which possess and divide mankind. For men having been principled with an opinion, that they must not consult reason in the things of religion, however apparently contradictory to common sense, and the very principles of all their knowledge; have let loose their fancies and natural superstition; and have been by them let into so strange opinions, and extravagant practices in religion, that a considerate man cannot but stand amazed at their follies, and judge them so far from being acceptable to the great and wise God, that he cannot avoid thinking them ridiculous, and offensive to a good sober man. So that in effect religion, which should most distinguish us from beasts, and ought most peculiarly to elevate us, as rational creatures, above brutes, is that wherein men often appear most irrational, and more senseless than the beasts themselves.[38]

Second Treatise on Government
Of Political or Civil Society

Man being born, as have been proved, with a title to perfect freedom and an uncontrolled enjoyment of all the rights and privileges of the law of Nature, equally with any other man, or number of men in the world, hath by nature a power not only to preserve his property—that is, his life, liberty, and estate, against the injuries and attempts of other men, but to judge of and punish the breaches of that law in others, as he is persuaded the offense deserves, even with death itself, in crimes where the heinousness of the fact, in his opinion, requires it. But because no political society can be, nor subsist, without having in itself the power to preserve the property, and in order thereunto punish the offenses of all those of that society, there, and only there, is political society where every one of the members hath quitted this natural power, resigned it up into the hands of the community in all cases that exclude him not from appealing for protection to the law established by it.

Wherever, therefore, any number of men so unite into one society as to quit every one his executive power of the law of Nature, and to resign it to the public, there and there only is a political or civil society. And this is done wherever any number of men, in the state of Nature, enter into society to make one people one body politic under one supreme government: or else when any one joins himself to, and incorporates with any government already made. For hereby he authorizes the society, or which is all one, the legislative thereof, to make laws for him as the public good of the society shall require, to the execution whereof his own assistance (as to his own decrees) is due. And this puts men out of a state of Nature into that of a commonwealth, by setting up a judge on earth with authority to determine all the controversies and redress the injuries that may happen to any member of the commonwealth.

Hence it is evident that absolute monarchy, which by some men is counted for the only government in the world, is indeed inconsistent with civil society, and so can be no form of civil government at all. For the end of civil society being to avoid and remedy those inconveniences of the state of Nature which necessarily follow from every man's being judge in his own case, by setting up a known authority to which every one of that society may appeal upon any injury received, or controversy that may arise, and which every one in the society ought to obey. Wherever any persons are who have not such an authority to appeal to, and decide any difference between them there, those persons are still in the state of Nature. And so is every absolute prince in respect of those who are under his dominion.[39]

4

The Eighteenth Century

Sir, the pretending to extraordinary revelations and gifts of the Holy Ghost
is a horrid thing, a very horrid thing.
                              —*Bishop Butler to John Wesley (August 1739)*

I F A MUSEUM STAGED AN EXHIBIT on the Anglican ethos, the eighteenth-
century collection could be visited quickly, for it represented an interlude
between the major attractions, loosely called "The Formative Years" and
"Modern Times." No single theme or figure emerged around which to
build the display. Walls might be devoted to earnest Queen Anne, the
poet Oliver Goldsmith, and writers such as Bishop Butler, William Law,
and John and Charles Wesley, and some of the latter's hymns would be
played as representative music of the period. Filling out the space would
be scenes of town and country life, the churches and their clergy—the
overall impression would be of an agreeable world untroubled by change.

Notwithstanding, eighteenth-century English religious life reflected
some of the church's most creative figures at a time when society was at
its most dissolute. Hogarth's engravings and Defoe's verbal portraits brilliantly satirized English society in an era of hereditary city and country
gentlemen, most of whom were born to lands and money, had little education, did not travel, and for whom religion meant little. For such people, life was endless morning rounds of riding to the hunt, afternoon card
playing, followed by long evening suppers and the whist table. Personal
morals were lax and a debauched and dissolute lifestyle was common for
many. It was popular entertainment to watch inhabitants of mental institutions or observe a public hanging, much as later generations might
watch weekend football games. Notwithstanding, the age produced

Jonathan Swift's *Gulliver's Travels* and Daniel Defoe's nonconformist work *Robinson Crusoe*, and the poetry of another nonconformist, William Blake. Methodism, still part of the Church of England, claimed hundreds of thousands of followers. Philanthropic activity flourished by the century's end; hospitals were built throughout the country and almsgiving to the poor was everywhere encouraged. The institutional church emerged, less tied to the crown than before, with new energy from lay leadership and with a sense of global mission that would make it an increasingly international presence. The American church received its first bishop, and in 1742 Thomas Thompson, a Cambridge cleric, arrived in the Cape Coast, later called Ghana, in West Africa, initially holding services at the home of a traditional chief. Three converts studied for ordination in England; two died there, but the third returned and worked as a pastor for fifty years. The overseas church was launched, albeit in embryonic form.

CHURCH–STATE RELATIONS: THE NEW MONARCHS

If church life was at a low level for much of this century, court life was no higher. To begin with, most clergy had taken an oath to support the king, but the monarch who claimed their allegiance, James II, was a Roman Catholic who had not formally abdicated the crown but fled hastily to France, dropping the royal seals in the Thames River during his 1688 departure. His successor, William of Orange, was a Protestant little interested in church affairs. A Dutch Calvinist, he found the doctrinal and political nuances of English Protestants bewildering and not worth much time. After two centuries of intense church–state sparring, the Church of England now found itself with a disinterested monarch. Political leadership of the church passed to Parliament, its day-to-day governance to bishops, its intellectual leadership to the universities.

Church–state relations improved during the brief reign of Queen Anne (1702–1714), who gave "Queen Anne's Bounty," a portion of royal revenues, about seventeen thousand pounds a year to improve clergy salaries. A devout church member, Anne received communion monthly and took an active interest in the lot of poor clergy. Her strategy was to begin by augmenting the lowest salaries by ten pounds a year, gradually supporting those still under fifty pounds. But after her death, church–state relations declined with the four Hanoverian Georges, who ruled from 1714 until 1830. George I (1714–1717) and his son, George II (1717–1760), were nominal Lutheran converts to Anglicanism, but neither was interested in religion. Church building slacked off, and from 1717 on church convocation ceased to meet, leaving the church without a legislative body or a national clergy voice. With Parliament's growing power, two distinct political factions emerged—Tory and Whig—which eventually became the Conservative and Liberal parties. Originally followers of James II and later Queen Anne, Tories drew strength from Church of England supporters from among the country gentry. The Whigs, named for cattle drivers, a seventeenth-century term of derision for Scottish Presbyterians, supported Parliament against the crown. Their strength came from merchants and the landed gentry. Closely allied to the Hanoverian monarchs, from 1714 onward for the next fifty years, Whigs dominated British politics as the earlier era of the high church–Stuart monarchy coalition passed into history. The Church of England remained the official state church, but its bishops no longer played the influential political role they had in the past.

THE FRENCH AND AMERICAN REVOLUTIONS

The American Revolution of 1776 and French Revolution of 1789 were watershed moments in history, and while their impact was limited in England, both affected the Church of England in important ways. England had never established an episcopate in America, although proposals had surfaced as early as 1713, and the issue of episcopal governance came to a head when armed conflict broke out in 1776. Loyalist clergy, whose numbers were considerable, included prayers for the king in their services, resulting in many churches being closed and clergy fleeing to Canada or England. Clergy who supported the American Revolution were left in place, but without a bishop. Because of the Revolution, the American church's desire to have its own bishop was denied, since an American bishop could not be expected to take a loyalty oath to the Crown. As a result, Samuel Seabury, the first American bishop, was consecrated in Scotland by three Scottish prelates. Seabury, a Connecticut loyalist, had originally made the three-thousand-mile trip by ship to London, but British bishops declined to consecrate him. Seabury then journeyed north across the border where three Non-Juror bishops proceeded with the service in Aberdeen on November 14, 1784. Parliament finally passed an act allowing English bishops to consecrate American bishops without the loyalty oath. This resulted in William White of Pennsylvania and Samuel Provoost of New York journeying to London to become bishops in 1786. America now had enough bishops for the customary three to conduct an episcopal ordination. The American church was launched. While elsewhere missionaries established lasting presences in the Caribbean, the United States, and Canada, the East India Company opposed missionary work, preferring to leave native populations as they were. A 1793 directors' resolution said "the sending of missionaries into our eastern possessions is the maddest, most extravagant, and most unwarrantable project that was ever proposed by an enthusiastic lunatic."[1]

The French Revolution split England into two camps: those such as the young William Wordsworth, who welcomed it as a way of overcoming long-standing injustices, and others such as Edmund Burke, whose horror at its excesses was chronicled in his *Reflections on the Revolution in France* (1791). England watched as French enthusiasm for reform turned quickly into murder and terror. Consequently, England's nascent reform efforts were stifled for a generation. Always suspicious of what was happening in France, the insular British looked with repugnance on the French Revolution's excesses, including the plundering of churches and the murdering of clergy. Given this climate, any effort to improve the lot of England's Roman Catholics and dissenters was suspended, and public attention to the slave trade's evils was diverted until the next century. For the government, religion became a means of preventing revolution and when Parliament voted a million pounds for church building in 1818, its primary purpose was to create social stability and prevent unrest. Notwithstanding, English reform voices were heard, although their impact would not come until the next century.

Edmund Burke (1729–1797) articulately defined church–state relations. Burke called the church "a great national benefit, a great public blessing . . . its existence or non-existence is of course a thing by no means indifferent to the public welfare." With the French Revolution at his back, he said of the English: "they do not consider their church establishment as convenient, but as essential to their state. . . . They consider it as the foundation of their whole constitution, with which, and with every part of which, it holds an indissoluble union. Church and state are ideas inseparable in their minds, and scarcely is the one ever mentioned without mentioning the other."[2]

CLERGY LIFE

Given low educational standards and poor pay, it is easy to understand why many eighteenth-century clergy were not held in high regard. Dependent on the manor lords for their living, many in society's upper ranks were "fox-hunting vicars," some appearing in church in riding apparel under clerical robes. Many preached a weekly sermon on piety and moral obligations, but otherwise made few efforts at good works or influencing community life. Well-endowed church livings generally went to a manor lord's younger sons, since the first son inherited the estate. This prevented regular clergy without independent means from rising to better-paying positions and contributed to the low quality of clerical life. Possibly more than half the ten thousand parishes in eighteenth-century England were in the hands of absentee clergy. There were far too many clergy for the handful of well-paying jobs, and those who sought advancement tied their fortunes to political patrons they believed helpful. At the end of the eighteenth century, of the 11,600 benefices in England and Wales, bishops and cathedral chapters controlled the patronage to about 2,500 livings, the Crown held 1,100 livings; and Oxford and Cambridge universities and public schools held title to another six hundred places. Over five thousand church positions paid less than fifty pounds a year, but fortunate holders of multiple posts could accumulate an income of over five hundred pounds a year. Such discrepancies in income and standing bred jealousy among clergy. The curate in Tobias Smollet's *Roderick Random* (1748) calls his vicar "an old fool" who held two livings worth four hundred pounds each "while poor I am fain to do all his drudgery, and ride twenty miles every Sunday to preach; for what? Why, truly for twenty pounds a year."[3]

As in the past, clergy related to or married into noble or wealthy families could accumulate several parishes, called "livings," where they collected annual tithes but rarely visited, hiring the cheapest possible replacements, sometimes for a meager five pounds a year. Seeking a better position for a poor curate, a petitioner informed a bishop "I only throw a letter, like a lottery ticket, into a wheel, where it may possibly turn up a *small* prize; or from a possibility you may transfer it into some other ecclesiastical wheel, where small prizes may bear a greater proportion to blanks than in your own."[4]

Tithes remained the main source of clerical income, the "Great Tithe" being a portion of the harvest; the "Lesser Tithe," extracted from the results of farming and gardening, was more difficult to collect. Country parsons were entitled to a glebe, a piece of land for their use, usually consisting of several acres of farmland, but not all clergy had such possibilities. Poorer clergy, lacking money to raise their families or buy books, supplemented meager income by teaching and farming. For the more affluent, newspaper advertisements offered profitable livings "situated in fine sporting country" with generous opportunities to hunt and fish. Some hunted and fished, some followed scholarly pursuits; a writer of the period recommended star-gazing as "a proper, and perhaps the most proper of all possible recreations for a clergyman." James Austen, brother of Jane, himself a country clergyman, advised colleagues to acquire "an extensive and accurate knowledge of all sporting matters" to assure a place at the squire's table and to acquire a decent position, "For nothing is more certain than a good shot has often brought down a comfortable vicarage, and many a bold rider lept into a snug rectory."[5]

Clergy wrote seeking positions even before the incumbent was dead, as in a frequently cited letter to the duke of Newcastle, one of the patronage system's most skilled manipulators; "I think it my duty to acquaint your Grace that the Archbishop of York lies a-dying, and, as all here think, cannot possibly live beyond tomorrow morning, if so long; upon this occasion of two vacancies, I beg, I hope, I trust your Grace's kindness and goodness will be shown to one who has long solicited your favor."[6] James Woodforde's *Diary of a Country Parson* carefully chronicles the life of one of the better-situated clergy who, while lacking a theological mind, set a good table, gave regularly to the poor, entertained graciously, and was in turn a staple of local society. It would be too easy to dismiss people like Woodforde; they were uncomplicated believers who sought to communicate their faith and lead respectable lives, but zeal for the Lord's house came nowhere near consuming them. A commentator on Hanoverian England's religious life has written, "Even in its worthiest representatives it lacked originality, poetic sensibility, and prophetic insight; in justice we must concede that it possessed solid scholarship, unwearied industry, practical sagacity, and sober piety."[7]

Still, there were exceptions to the general picture, humble and devout clergy, some learned in biblical languages and studies, many with fine minds. They contributed to the growing body of Anglican religious writings and, by their lives and examples, demonstrated what the church might be. A historian of the period said of the clergy, "They were robust in thought and vigorous in expression, but the range of their sympathies was circumscribed. They equated what was reasonable with what commended itself to common sense. Emotion was suspect and 'enthusiasm' anathema. . . . Their sermons were rational rather than mystical in tone, ethical rather than dogmatic in content. Nevertheless, they recognized that a licentious age had to be confronted with the claims of morality, and they pressed its demands on a generation none too ready to listen."[8]

The clerical picture in Oliver Goldsmith's "The Deserted Village" (1770) may be of the poet's brother or his father, both members of the clergy. In any case, it is like a Constable landscape, a lasting portrait of a segment of this period's religious life.

> A man he was to all the country dear,
> And passing rich with forty pounds a year.
> Remote from towns he ran his godly race,
> Nor e'er had chang'd, nor wish'd to change, his place;
> Unpractis'd he to fawn, or seek for power,
> By doctrines fashion'd to the varying hour;
> Far other aims his heart had learn'd to prize,
> More skill'd to raise the wretched than to rise.
> His house was known to all the vagrant train,
> He chid their wanderings, but reliev'd their pain;
> The long-remember'd beggar was his guest,
> Whose beard descending swept his aged breast;
> The ruin'd spendthrift, now no longer proud,
> Claim'd kindred there, and had his claims allow'd;
> The broken soldier, kindly bade to stay,
> Sat by his fire, and talk'd the night away;
> Wept o'er his wounds, or, tales of sorrow done,
> Shoulder'd his crutch, and show'd how fields were won.
> Pleas'd with his guests, the good man learn'd to glow,
> And quite forgot their vices in their woe;
> Careless their merits or their faults to scan,
> His pity gave ere charity began.
>
> At church, with meek and unaffected grace,
> His looks adorn'd the venerable place;
> Truth from his lips prevail'd with double sway,
> And fools who came to scoff remain'd to pray.[9]

BISHOPS

As in prior centuries, clergy had little contact with bishops—this would not change until roads and railroads made transportation easier in the mid-nineteenth century, although Methodist lay and clerical preachers moved steadily across the country on foot or by horse. A considerable educational and income barrier separated parish parsons and bishops, and the latter were resident much of the year in London as members of the House of Lords. Most visited dioceses only during summer months. A 1730s description of the bishop of Gloucester ties together several themes of the age:

> he resides as much as any bishop in his diocese in the year, and keeps a very generous and hospitable table, which makes amends for the learning he is deficient in. However, though no great scholar nor a deep man, he is a very frequent preacher; and this, with his zeal for the government, good humor, and regular life, makes him very well liked by the government and all that know him.[10]

Dioceses were large, and most bishops visited only a sampling of parishes. Bishops had little contact with ordinands; if candidates could not arrange a time for ordination with their bishops they were often given Letters Dimissory commending the bearer "to be ordained Deacon (or Priest) by any bishop of this realm of England who should be willing to ordain him."[11] Confirmations were mass events, assembling from five hundred to a thousand candidates in many places, resulting in considerable confusion. There are reports of younger clergy, unknown to the bishops, being asked to kneel with parishioners for the episcopal laying on of hands, and an account of a confirmation at Bury St. Edmunds reported three or four elderly women who were confirmed every time the bishop came to town, their position being you cannot have too much of a good thing.[12] To avoid repeated confirmations, some dioceses required tickets from parish clergy for all candidates presented, but when hundreds and sometimes thousands of persons were confirmed, accurate counting was impossible. (From May to September 1709, the bishop of Lincoln confirmed 12,800 persons in twenty-six services.)[13] Archbishop Gilbert of York "went around the whole rail at once, laid his hand upon the head of every person severally, and when he had gone through the whole then he drew back to the Communion Table and in as audible and solemn a manner as he could, pronounced the prayer over them all."[14]

It was said that if a bishop of the period "rose by the weight of his character," this defied "all rules of gravity and experience." Hannah More, a contemporary writer on society and spirituality, in a letter to her sister, described a gathering at the London residence of the bishop of St. Asaph's:

Conceive to yourself one hundred and fifty or two hundred people met together, dressed in the extremity of fashion; painted as red as bacchanals; poisoning the air with perfumes; treading on each other's gowns; making the crowd the blame; not one in ten able to get a chair; protesting they are engaged to ten other places; and lamenting the fatigue they are not obliged to endure; ten or a dozen card tables crammed with dowagers of quality, grave ecclesiastics and yellow admirals; and you have an idea of an assembly.[15]

REGULAR SERVICES

Morning and Evening Prayer were the accustomed services in most parishes, with a quarterly Eucharist. Sermons were long and pedantic; some preachers read printed sermons by well-known authors, and others paid to have sermons written for them. An impoverished Samuel Johnson earned two guineas per sermon as a ghost writer. Clergy were enjoined from showing enthusiasm in preaching or conducting services; contemporary manners forbid displays of emotion while preaching. "Dull, duller, and dullest are a sufficient critical vocabulary to describe their merits," a student of the period said of eighteenth-century church services.[16] Liturgical innovation was not a feature of this age. Sermons were mostly about personal morality, drawn from the creeds and the Ten Commandments, which were often painted on boards hung by the pulpit, and pointed to as norms for personal behavior. Much energy went into examining the new scientific doctrines—the thought of Newton, Pascal, or Descartes. Skepticism and rationalism were widespread, and God, the deists' eternal clock-maker, was unlike the God of earlier and later ages.

John Tillotson, Archbishop of Canterbury from 1691 to 1694, was a student of the early church and a reformer who sought to alleviate abuses of the church patronage system, for which he encountered considerable opposition. His sermon drawn from the text "His commandments are not grievous," presaged Margaret Thatcher's political platform:

Two things make any course of life easy; present comfort and satisfaction and the assurance of a future reward. Religion gives part of its reward in hand, the present comfort and satisfaction of having done our duty; and for the rest it offers us the best security that heaven can give. Now these two must needs make our duty very easy; a considerable reward in hand, and not only the hopes but the assurance of a far greater recompense hereafter.[17]

Church organization reflected local social organization. The largest and best located pew box belonged to the lord of the manor, and its sides were high enough to provide comfort, warmth, and occasional refreshment. The poor generally filled in at the rear of the church, and in some fashionable churches tipping the usher to obtain a good seat was a regular practice.

An eighteenth-century Sunday in the country is described by Joseph Addison in *The Spectator* (1711):

> I am always very well pleased with a country Sunday and think if keeping the seventh day holy were only a human institution, it would be the best method that could have been thought of for the polishing and civilizing of mankind. It is certain the country people would soon degenerate into a kind of savages and barbarians, were there not such frequent returns of a stated time in which the whole village meet together with their best faces and their cleanliest habits, to converse with one another upon different subjects, hear their duties explained to them, and join together in adoration of the Supreme Being. Sunday clears away the rust of the whole week, not only as it refreshes in their minds the notions of religion, but as it puts both the sexes upon appearing in their most agreeable forms and exerting such qualities as are apt to give them a figure in each village.[18]

MUSIC

As for music, metrical psalms were cheerlessly sung by most congregations, although hymns were gradually introduced—some have called this "the Golden Century of English hymnody." In rural churches, accompaniment was provided not by organs but by bands of minstrels seated in the church's elevated west end gallery where they sang and played on brass and stringed instruments—oboes, clarinets, guitars, drums, and flutes. These self-taught illiterate local musicians played with more vigor than precision and engaged in raucous arguments among themselves or with clergy or parishioners during the service. Parishes without organs used wooden pitch-pipes, played by the parish clerk to start singing. Hand-turned barrel organs were common, and a well-endowed church might have several removable cylinders, each containing ten or twelve tunes, including hymn tunes and popular songs.

The drabness of the age was lifted by the music of William Croft (1678–1727), William Boyce (1711–1779), and Samuel Wesley (1766–1837). Worship at this time contained creative sparks that would ignite later in this century and in the next. Isaac Watts (1674–1748), a non-conformist, was a prolific hymn text writer, with over six hundred compositions to his credit. A dissenting clergy member, his *Divine Songs for Children* was highly popular for over a century, and the Church of England, always with an eye toward borrowing good hymn texts and tunes from whatever source, appropriated "O God, Our Help in Ages Past" (tune: *St. Anne*), "When I Survey the Wondrous Cross" (tune: *Rockingham*), and "Jesus Shall Reign Where'er the Sun" (tune: *Duke Street*), among others. In short, except for hymns, the eighteenth century was a time of little musical innovation in the church. No new musical forms evolved, nor did any composers of genius appear on the scene. The best musical offerings came from foreigners; George Frederic Handel lived in England, where he wrote the "Messiah."

Deism and Skepticism

New intellectual currents were prevalent during this century. Skepticism was popular among intellectuals, and deism held sway as a philosophical system. Deism is not easy to define, for it never became a systematic school of thought. A main deist work was John Toland's (1670–1722) *Christianity not Mysterious* (1696), which makes the case for what is natural and reasonable in Christianity, arguing against revelation and the supernatural. Some deists separated the Creator from the rest of creation; for others, neither God nor divine revelation was beyond the province of human reason. Others believed in Divine Providence, but not in an afterlife; still others accepted the truth of natural religion, but not of revelation. In short, deists, borrowing heavily from the new scientific language available to them, could argue that faith and the supernatural had no place in religion, that rational thought employing the scientific method was adequate for people to hold to as a belief system. Although nominally Christian, it made few demands on people, appealing to reason and the study of nature as revealed through reason. The popular religion of many clergy was penetrated by such beliefs. Fanny Price in Jane Austen's *Mansfield Park* reflects the spirit of an age, when, gazing out a window on a clear moonlit night, she says:

> Here's harmony! Here's repose! . . . When I look out on such a night as this, I feel as if there could be neither wickedness nor sorrow in the world; and there certainly would be less of both if the sublimity of Nature were

more attended to, and people were carried more out of themselves by contemplating such a scene.[19]

Centuries later, deism's defects are apparent. Deism regarded religion as being primarily a system of carefully linked ideas and a code of moral precepts. What was missing was the historic essence of the Christian faith as being founded on a personal tie with a living God, redemption from sin, and a victory over the forces of evil and discord through the incarnation, atonement, and resurrection of Christ.

JOSEPH BUTLER
Analogy of Religion

As might be expected, there was a strong reaction against deism, producing, among other works, Joseph Butler's influential study *Analogy of Religion, Natural and Revealed, to the Constitution and Course of Nature* (1736). Butler (1692–1752) was a convert from Presbyterianism to the Church of England. In addition to being a leading critic of deism, his practical studies of ethics were widely influential in the period between the demise of Puritanism and the rise of Methodism. A shy, retiring bachelor, more at home at his writing desk than in social settings, Butler held several significant appointments: he was preacher at Rolls Chapel, London, which stood on the site of the Public Record Office, and in 1725 he moved to Stanhope, the "golden rectory" of the north. There he published *Fifteen Sermons Preached at the Rolls Chapel* (1726), followed by the *Analogy of Religion* in 1736, just after his appointment as Clerk of the Closet to Queen Caroline. The queen, impressed with Butler's sermons of an earlier era, asked if he was dead. The archbishop of York cryptically replied, "No, Madam, he is not dead, but he is buried." After returning to London, Butler was a mentor to the queen and her circle, meeting with her for two hours each evening. At her deathbed she asked that Butler be given a good position. The bereaved monarch, George II, vowed he would never marry again, only have mistresses, and rewarded Butler with the bishopric of Bristol, the church's poorest diocese. The new prelate was allowed to keep income from the Stanhope rectory, which he relinquished in 1740 on becoming dean of St. Paul's, a position he held for the next decade. Declining an offer of the primacy, he accepted the Diocese of Durham instead, a post he held until his death in 1752.

Generous in his giving, but of saturnine disposition, Butler was per-

sonally and philosophically opposed to any displays of emotion or enthusiasm in religion. He is remembered for his famous observation to John
Wesley in August 1739, "Sir, the pretending to extraordinary revelations
and gifts of the Holy Ghost is a horrid thing, a very horrid thing." Wesley was preaching then in the open air to miners near Bristol. Butler, who
later gave five hundred pounds for a church for miners, confronted him
over congregations being seized with trembling during sermons and over
Wesley preaching in his diocese without episcopal permission. Wesley
made a lucid plea that, not being diocesan clergy, but ordained a Fellow
of a College, he had "an indeterminate commission to preach the word
of God in any part of the Church of England." Unmoved, Butler said,
"You have no business here . . . therefore I advise you to go hence." In
this confrontation between the religion of the heart and the religion of
the mind no compromise was possible.[20]

Butler wrote in the interlude between Puritanism and Methodism, the
hundred-year period when "the sovereign court of reason" prevailed.
Galileo's astronomical theories, Harvey's discovery of blood circulation,
and Gilbert's experiments with magnetism resulted in an age when people believed that the truths of nature, God, and science could be pried
open by the human mind. Butler entered the lists to prove that historic
Christianity and the new science were compatible. An intellectual historian, Ernest Campbell Mossner, wrote, "what Locke is to philosophy,
what Newton is to science, what Burke is to politics, Butler is to theology."[21] The age demanded a voice to present Christianity in a way compatible with the new learning. Writing in the *Spectator*, Joseph Addison
wanted to bring "philosophy out of closets and libraries, schools and colleges, to dwell in clubs and assemblies, at tea-tables and in coffee-
houses."[22] "I renew my affectionate request," wrote Thomas Sprat,
bishop of Rochester in 1667, "that the Church of England . . . encourage experiments, which will be to our Church as the British oak is to our
empire, an ornament and defense to the soil wherein it is planted."[23]

The heart of Butler's thought is contained in the *Rolls Chapel* sermons.
These dense meditations were aimed at providing practical advice on
ethics combining biblical teaching with Butler's insights into what would
later be called psychology. The key to Butler's system is a five-part schema
composed of *appetites*, the desire to satisfy physical cravings, and *passions*,
the desire to fulfill mental or emotional urges. They compete with *benevolence*, concern for the welfare of others, and *self-love*, looking after one's
own needs and interests. At the pinnacle is *conscience*—the "voice of
God"—weighing good and evil, judging between competing emotions,

offering humanity a way of moral conduct. For the rest of his life Butler reworked this pentagonal structure into various combinations whenever the analysis of human motives and actions was needed.

Simple as this construct may appear to later ages, it was impressive in its time, representing a frontal attack on the deists and their mechanistic universe, and on Hobbes, who argued that self-love was the driving principle to all human conduct and that civil government was the way to contain it. For Butler, the new science could be incorporated into the old faith. He reoriented the Christian philosophy of his time in a new direction. Consistently taking the high road in an era fraught with polemics, Butler offered a practical system of ethics and natural theology characterized by moderation, reason, and moral suasion. A product of the Reformation, he argued that both the Bible and conscience are gifts of God and that faithfulness to scripture does not preclude the believer from following the dictates of conscience.

WILLIAM LAW
A Serious Call to a Devout and Holy Life

William Law (1686–1761), in *The Case for Reason* (1731), argued that reason has limits and needs to be supplemented with faith to reach truth. Law was also a mystic, and his two works *Christian Perfection* (1726) and *A Serious Call to a Devout and Holy Life* (1728) became widely accepted devotional classics, influencing such figures of the next generation as Samuel Johnson and John and Charles Wesley. Like Bunyan, Law used allegorical figures to depict virtue and vice, stressing right conduct, systematic devotion, and an all-encompassing spirituality infusing both the person and society. Constant appeals for simplification of life and focus on direct contact with God made Law attractive to Quakers and those on the margins of or outside formal church structures.

Law belonged to the high church clergy faction loyal to the Stuarts as England's divine right monarchs. Refusing to take an oath of allegiance to George I, who came from the Hanover line, he became a "Non-juring" clergy, part of a segment of the Church of England that continued until the late eighteenth century. Deprived of any possibility of a university or church post, Law earned a living as a tutor, private chaplain, and writer. The Non-Jurors, those who would not pledge loyalty to William and Mary, believing it conflicted with their previous oaths to James II, are an interesting footnote to history. Their numbers included several hundred clergy, including the Archbishop of Canterbury and several bishops who refused to follow the new monarchs. The Non-Jurors looked to the past, a splinter political movement sworn to uphold the divine right of hereditary kings, a belief the Whig historian Macaulay called "superstition as stupid and degrading as the Egyptian worship of cats and onions."[24]

SAMUEL JOHNSON'S RELIGION

The religious life of the brilliant essayist and lexicographer Samuel Johnson (1709–1784) vividly represents one person's religious quest in this century. In some ways, Johnson's life was a Job-like pilgrimage common to any century; but much of its prayer language was cast in an eighteenth-century idiom. Johnson, the son of a Lichfield bookseller, was a man of brilliant but erratic learning, whose business failed, leaving the family destitute. Johnson's mother held narrow, conventional religious beliefs; her vivid pictures of hell and damnation inculcated a lifelong sense of guilt in the young Johnson, something he struggled vainly to overcome during most of his seventy-six year life. James Boswell, his devoted chronicler of later years, compared Johnson's mind to the Coliseum in Rome and Johnson to a gladiator who fiercely battled wild beasts, driving them back to their dens, but not killing them, for they only return later. A sickly youth who nearly died at birth, Johnson for a time lost sight in one eye and always had difficulty seeing with the other. Deaf in one ear, his face scarred by smallpox, he was the butt of savage jeers from other children and of students when he attended Oxford. (He was forced to withdraw after a thirteen-month stay, as his father could not afford the fees.) When he was young, Johnson's parents took him to London, where the royal chaplains prayed over him, and Queen Anne touched him, people believing the royal touch had thaumaturgical powers. No miraculous healing occurred, and Johnson continued deeply aware of his infirmities all his life. He remained a religious person throughout; his diaries are full of self-examination and prayers, plus resolutions to attend church and communion, which Johnson rarely followed. Johnson married a widow in 1735, about the time he gained employment as a satirist for the *Gentleman's Magazine*, a London mass circulation publication. Johnson was a voracious reader, with a generous, open nature despite his difficulties. His London literary reputation rose gradually; from 1747 to 1755 he edited the *Dictionary of the English Language*, while writing essays for the

Tattler and *Spectator* and other publications. In 1762 a patron of the arts established a pension of three hundred pounds a year for Johnson, providing him, at age fifty-three, with his first steady income.

Skeptical and rational in temperament, as befit the times, Johnson increasingly claimed the Christian religion in response to his depression and quest for a meaning to life. He wrote of "the sorrow inherent in humanity" and "the pain of being a man," concluding "the business of life was to work out our salvation." An avid reader of the Book of Common Prayer, he copied phrases from it into his own writings. Johnson went to his parish, St. Clement Danes, on New Year's Day; on March 28, the day his wife died; on his own birthday, September 18; and on Easter Sunday. On Easter, Johnson carefully composed a prayer before attending church, repeating parts of it frequently during the service. Much of Sunday was otherwise spent in Bible study or in the study of biblical languages. Johnson was widely read in the early church fathers and in contemporary writers, works such as William Law's *A Serious Call to a Devout and Holy Life*. Charitable in his giving, Johnson sometimes left pennies in the hands of poor children sleeping on the streets and was generous with his small income.

Serenity came to Johnson in his final illness, and his last recorded prayer reflects a tranquillity rarely shown in his life:

> Almighty and most merciful Father, I am now, as to human eyes it seems, about to commemorate for the last time, the death of thy son Jesus Christ, our Savior and Redeemer. Grant, O Lord, that my whole hope and confidence may be in his merits and in thy mercy: forgive and accept my late conversion, enforce and accept my imperfect repentance; make this commemoration of him available to the confirmation of my faith, the establishment of my hope, and the enlargement of my Charity, and make the Death of thy son Jesus effectual to my redemption. Have mercy upon me and pardon the multitude of my offenses. Bless my friends, have mercy upon all men. Support me by the Grace of thy Holy Spirit in the days of weakness, and at the hour of death, and receive me, at my death, to everlasting happiness, for the sake of Jesus Christ. Amen.[25]

HANNAH MORE

Hannah More (1745–1833) was both an articulate Christian and a figure in London's most fashionable eighteenth-century literary circles. Edmund Burke, David Garrick, and Joshua Reynolds were all contemporaries, and she was equally familiar with the members of the Clapham Society, including William Wilberforce and other Evangelicals and social reformers. She wrote a tract called *Village Politics,* in which Jack Anvil, the village blacksmith, and Tom Hook, the local stone mason, argue the positions of Edmund Burke and Tom Paine. The author of novels, poems, and plays, More founded a successful school in Bristol and came to London to live with the Garricks. Fluent in four languages, she wrote plays and poetry as well. Her poem "Bas Bleu" describes the "bluestocking clubs" for women that were formed in response to the spread of men's coffee houses. More's prose style combines a lucid, practical exposition of what it means to be a Christian with witty observations about London life. From the considerable royalties of her publishing more than twenty books, she contributed to many Christian societies, including schools for the poor. An anonymous tract she wrote, *The Importance of the Manners of the Great to General Society,* published in 1788, went through several printings. In the 1780s Hannah and a sister founded a school in the rural town of Cheddar; its doors opened to 140 children, and within a few years attendance at the parish church rose from a handful to over five hundred persons. The movement soon spread to other churches as well, and many schools were founded in the region. Next she turned to a series of tracts, including brief stories, ballads, Sunday readings, and instructional material. Selling for under a penny each, the tracts sold over two million copies by 1796. In a time of widespread tract literature, much of it critical of church and state, these were gentle stories, calling citizens to act with decorum and those in authority to take their moral responsibilities toward others seriously.[26]

JOHN WESLEY AND THE METHODISTS

Mid-century England's torpor was shaken by a thunderbolt religious Europe had not seen since the days of Luther. John Wesley, one of nineteen children of an Anglican clergy family, was born in 1703 in Epworth rectory. At Oxford he joined with a group called "Methodists," a gathering of intense young men who regulated their lives by methodical prayer, Bible study, and discipline. Close followers of the Prayer Book, they attended communion weekly, and, in an age of slovenly religious practice, were models of zealous devotion. Wesley received communion twice a week all his life.

In 1738 Wesley, age thirty-five, by now ordained in the Church of England, underwent a religious experience, described in his journal:

> In the evening [May 24—*ed.*] I went very unwillingly to a society in Aldersgate Street, where one was reading Luther's preface to the *Epistle to the Romans.* About a quarter to nine, while he was describing the change which God works in the heart through faith in Christ, I felt my heart strangely warmed. I felt that I did trust in Christ, Christ alone, for salvation; and an assurance was given me that he had taken away *my* sins, even *mine,* and saved me from the law of sin and death.

Taking the world as his parish, Wesley set out on horseback to preach wherever he found listeners. Wesley, like Luther, was empowered by his discovery of the doctrine of justification by faith. For Wesley, this meant that an individual, informed by the Holy Spirit, would suddenly realize that his or her sins were forgiven and salvation assured through Christ's atoning death. "I then testified openly to all there what I now first felt in my heart," he wrote, thus launching one of Christendom's great missionary endeavors.[27]

The sentiment conveyed in John Wesley's conversion experience is expressed in his brother Charles's hymn:

> Come sinners to the gospel feast;
> Let every soul be Jesu's guest;
> Ye need not be left behind,
> For God hath bidden all mankind.
>
> Sent by my Lord, on you I call:
> The invitation is to all:
> Come all the world; come, sinner, thou!
> All things in Christ are ready now.[28]

Charles Wesley, John's brother, was the great hymn writer, whose several thousand texts include such enduring favorites as "Love Divine, All Loves Excelling," "Let Saints on Earth in Concert Sing," and "Jesu, Lover of My Soul." Writing about the spirituality of the early Methodist hymns, Evelyn Underhill observed:

> In those early Methodist hymns which spread through England the forgotten treasures of Christian spirituality, expressed in language which the simplest worshipper could understand, we find reminiscences of all the masters of adoring worship, Catholic and Protestant alike; from St. Augustine to the Quietists. Though on the ethical side the Methodist standard was austere, all was penetrated by their passionate delight in God, the ador-

ing abandonment to His Will and Purpose, the sense of a direct and enabling relationship with the living Christ. In the greatest of these hymns, especially those of Charles Wesley, we can recognize the fervor and realism which swept the country to re-kindle the smoldering devotional life.[29]

In fifty-two years John Wesley is estimated to have delivered forty thousand sermons and traveled over 225,000 miles to all parts of England, Scotland, Ireland, and Wales. A person of tireless energy, his dedication to his work was unwavering, and he spoke to small rural gatherings or to miners emerging at the end of their shifts, often giving three or four hour-long sermons a day. Wesley's zeal and advocacy meant that London pulpits were denied him, and gangs of ruffians interrupted services, throwing stones at him, sometimes instigated by local Anglican vicars. Within a short time, Wesleyan societies were formed to care for their members, and the movement grew. In church government, it developed a strong, centralized structure with maximum lay participation, especially in running the growing number of local congregations.

For several years, the societies saw themselves pumping new blood into the Church of England, but as their numbers expanded and steely indifference or hostility continued to greet them, Methodists created an independent denomination. By the time of Wesley's death in 1791, possibly seventy thousand persons in Great Britain and Ireland considered themselves Methodists; their numbers swelled to over three hundred thousand members within half a century, more than four percent of the country's adult population.[30] Wesley always saw his work supplementing, not replacing, the Church of England, and he died a loyal member of that church, urging his followers, "be Church of England men still; do not cast away the peculiar glory which God hath put upon you and frustrate the design of Providence, the very end for which God raised you up." Wesley's sermon book contained the lines, "I preach as never sure to preach again, and as a dying man to dying men." His was a life void of self-gratification; his vital energies were in going about the countryside, saving souls and preaching to congregations great and small. At a time of lethargy and indifference in the Church of England, he brought energy and warmth to religion and taught people the immediacy of God's love.

Relationships between the Methodists and the established church became acute over the question of ordinations. From 1760 on, demands grew for the laying on of hands from among the hundreds of lay ministers the movement generated. Meeting refusals from the Church of England, in 1785 a reluctant Wesley began to ordain his own clergy, creating a break with the established church. With any sign of flexibility or accommodation, the Church of England could have both kept this extra-ordinary figure and his followers as part of its fold and been enriched by their contribution, but no such offer was ever tendered. Even such a lead-ing figure as reform-minded Bishop Joseph Butler of Bristol, as noted above, once said to Wesley, "Sir, the pretending to extraordinary revela-tions and gifts of the Holy Ghost is a horrid thing, a very horrid thing."[31] Additionally, the Convocations, the periodic meetings of church govern-ment, had been suspended for many years, so there was no possibility of the whole church considering issues raised by the Wesleyan movement. The Church of England lost a great opportunity, the damage from which it is yet to resolve fully.

ANGLICAN EVANGELICALS

As might be expected, there was a reaction against the late eighteenth century's theological barrenness and against the Hanoverian Church's dissipated worldliness. Under the influence of the Methodists, an Evan-gelical movement formed within the Anglican Church, largely led by lay persons. One writer called Evangelicals "the moral cement of English life,"[32] and Evangelicals quickly translated belief into action.

This century's final decades were also a time of widespread church philanthropy, led by Evangelical laity. The Society for the Promotion of Christian Knowledge (S.P.C.K.) was founded in 1698 by Thomas Bray (1656–1730), who also established the Society for the Propagation of the Gospel (S.P.G.) in 1701. Bray had been the Church of England Com-missary for the colony of Maryland, recruiting missionaries for Philadel-phia, Pennsylvania, where the number of church members increased from fifty to seven hundred. Bray also organized over eighty parish libraries, and the Society distributed Bibles and tracts and established charity schools. By 1704 fifty-four charity schools functioned in London; within a decade the number increased to one thousand, often in conjunction with individual parishes throughout England. Between 1719 and 1750 five general hospitals were built in London; when one foundling hospital opened, more than a hundred baskets, each with an unwanted baby, were hung at the entrance gate. Societies for the Reformation of Manners spread, attracting church members and Dissenters, instigating thousands of court cases for swearing, drunkenness, and related misdemeanors.[33]

Hospitals were founded, as were institutes for the blind and deaf. The Royal Humane Society was chartered in the 1770s, and across the country charity schools and Sunday schools expanded, led by lay persons seeking to reform manners. Toward the century's end, the Society for the Discharge and Relief of Persons Imprisoned for Small Debts helped reform debtor's prisons and secure the release of over fifteen thousand persons. Penal reform became a national cause. While there was much enthusiasm for the Sunday schools and charity schools, there was also vocal opposition to them. Some leaders feared that the newly educated would be susceptible to radical ideas and would no longer be content with their humble place in society.

The Anglican Evangelicals were strong proponents of almsgiving, family prayers, and works of faith, and from these Christian groups many social reform movements originated, such as William Wilberforce's antislavery crusade. Wilberforce (1759–1883) was a philanthropist, a parliamentarian, and in 1787 founder of a society for the reformation of manners. He became increasingly interested in the slavery question, fortified by activity of the Clapham Sect, an Evangelical lay group, and frequent Bible reading. Wilberforce the politician played a major role in Parliament's abolishing the slave trade, which came when the House of Lords finally passed such a bill in 1807. The Emancipation Act of 1833 was even more comprehensive, completely abolishing slavery. The Clapham Sect, of which Wilberforce was a leader, was a loosely organized band of affluent Evangelicals, mostly living near and worshiping in the Clapham parish church near London. Politically conservative, their reading of the Bible convinced them that a Christian must do good works, including eradicating slavery, educating the poor through Sunday schools, and expanding foreign missions. Clapham Sect members lived in the same affluent neighborhoods and were connected by marriage or moved in similar social circles. During the early nineteenth century, they exercised influence in Parliament and in the press out of all proportion to their numbers.

In affluent homes, a daily service was conducted in the family chapel or dining room, led by the head of the house, with wife, children, relatives, and servants in attendance. Samuel Butler, in *The Way of All Flesh*, paints a devastating portrait of a hypocritical head of household, disinterested servants, and impatient family members anxious for this exercise in "parlor religion" to end. Such prayers, however, and the continual testimonies of the Evangelicals who led them or participated in the services contributed directly to revitalizing the Church of England. All participants were reminded they must give an account of what they have done with their talents on Judgment Day. In reaction against the long, emotionless sermons of their time, Evangelicals placed great store in the conversion experience, believing that salvation came to a person at a particular moment, often accompanied by demonstrations of fainting or rapture. The leading exponent of this brand of religion was George Whitefield, originally a friend of Wesley but soon a rival. An unstable and erratic personality, Whitefield had an electrifying pulpit style, which attracted many people to him. The reverse side of such personalism in religion is that Evangelical belief contributed little that was new to religious thought. Its focus was largely on confronting sinners. The intensity of such "religion of the heart" meant that it did not always connect with church traditions and the numerous avenues to greater religious understanding provided through books and universities or other spiritual traditions. At its worst, such a personal, emotional religion could turn narrow and intolerant.

The Evangelical movement left an enduring impact on the church, one still evident two centuries later. With its emphasis on personal faith, affirmed through Bible reading and demands for good works, the Evangelicals created a small but vocal stratum of church members determined to effect Christian change in the world around them. And the numbers of persons attending church increased as a result of contact with itinerant preachers or more regular preaching missions. The abolition of slavery, improved conditions for factory workers, prison reform, education for slum children, and missionary societies abroad were all part of the Evangelical agenda. So were the spread of Christian philanthropy and the expansion of missionary work at home and abroad.

An important figure in the Evangelical revival was Selina, countess of Huntingdon (1709–1791), who extended the preaching missions to the upper echelons of British society. Selina was a strong personality, raising money for a ministerial training college and many chapels, naming and dismissing pastors, and determining the content of services with an enthusiasm that would tolerate no opposition. Several regular clergy were also drawn to the movement, such as William Cowper (1731–1800), writer of the hymns "O for a Closer Walk with God" and "There Is a Fountain Filled with Blood," and the former captain of a slave ship John Newton (1725–1807), who contributed, "Glorious Things of Thee Are Spoken," "How Sweet the Name of Jesus Sounds," and "Amazing Grace!"

The Evangelicals' program contributed to a serious reform movement among church members, aimed at such specific targets as Prayer Book revision, greater freedom for clergy to interpret the Bible and creeds, and greater freedom for non-Establishment and Roman Catholic clergy. Most of their reforms were rejected—the timing of their introduction coincided with the French Revolution—but within a generation they would be reintroduced and passed.

In a passage reflective of Evangelical piety, Samuel Wesley, then an impoverished Oxford undergraduate, described an encounter with a poor youth:

> It being the height of winter and a very severe one, I walked out in the morning alone and as I went musing along in an unfrequented path near the riverside I saw a little boy about some seven or eight years old, lying under a hedge and crying bitterly, I went up to him and asked the reason. He told me that two days before his father died, his mother having been dead several years and left none in the house but himself and a little sister about ten years old, without any victuals or money, that they had stayed at home all the next day but none took care of them or brought them any relief. That they resolved in the morning she should go a-begging in their own parish about a mile or two from Oxford, and he would go to the city and try what they could get to keep themselves alive; accordingly he told me he got up as soon as it was day and walked towards Oxford but being weak through a long ague [fever—*ed.*] and want of meat was forced to lie down there and could go no further. I confess I was touched with the boy's story, I raised him from the ground to which his clothes were almost frozen and rubbed his limbs, benumbed and almost dead with the cold till he could make a shift to go, then I pulled out my two pence—all the stock I had in the world—and gave it him seeing him in greater extremity than I was myself with which he went overjoyed into the town and bought a two penny loaf which he carried home to his sister.[34]

SUMMARY

"The church," wrote Bishop William Warburton, "like the Ark of Noah, is worth saving; not for the sake of the unclean beasts and vermin that almost filled it, and probably made most noise and clamor in it; but for the little corner of rationality that was as much distressed by the stink within as by the tempest without." Despite the difficulties, including widespread public indifference, American and French revolutions, and disinterested royalty, the church produced several outstanding figures, people like the Wesleys, Hannah More, and William Wilberforce. Notwithstanding, complacency reigned, and the church and its leaders were rarely major players in political or cultural life. There were economic reasons for this, demonstrated in the general poverty and low status of the clergy, but the reason lay deeper. Basically, until this century, the church was dependent on its symbiotic relationship with the crown. It generally defended the monarchy from attack, which required a coherent doctrine of church–state relations. In the past, this setting spawned a climate where works on distinctly Church of England spirituality and ecclesiology were created, as during the reigns of Henry VIII and Elizabeth and at the time of the Caroline Divines, but the new eighteenth century monarchs imported from Germany lacked either religious or intellectual interests, and the church was now left to find its own place in society. It took the Church of England much of the century to do this, and the great concerns were not the nature of the church, its sacraments or governance, but personal morality in a profligate age. With his customary rhetorical flourish Edmund Burke found a positive place for the church in the eighteenth century:

> If you think it to be an invaluable blessing, a way fully sufficient to nourish a manly, rational, solid, and at the same time humble piety; if you find it well fitted to the frame and pattern of your civil constitution; if you find it a barrier against fanaticism, infidelity, and atheism; if you find that it furnishes support to the human mind in the afflictions and distresses of the world, consolation in sickness, pain, poverty, and death; if it dignifies our nature with hope of immorality, leaves inquiry free, whilst it preserves an authority to teach, where authority only can teach, *communia altaria, aeque ac patriam, diligite, colite, fovete* [the church, like the country, cultivates, loves, protects—*ed.*].[35]

READINGS

William Law

William Law's (1686–1761) work contributed to the eighteenth century's Evangelical revival. From 1727 to 1737 Law lived in the household of Edward Gibbon in Putney, near London, as tutor to the famous historian's father. In 1729 he published *A Serious Call to a Devout and Holy Life*, which, like John Bunyan's *Pilgrim's Progress*, written a half-century earlier, became a post-Reformation religious classic. Unconcerned about his dress, he was described in later life as going about "in a pair of stockings that a ploughman would not have picked off a dunghill." Written for an upper-class audience, the book detailed how Christians could live virtuous lives; the language was pithy, filled with aphorisms and characters similar to those appearing in Restoration dramas, although Law had a strong aversion to the stage. Its thumbnail sketches are miniature portraits of predictable period types. The worldly businessman, the fashion-conscious fop, the money-counting clergy, the fashion-conscious woman, all were memorable characters, given Latin names like Miranda (wonderful) and Flavia (extravagant). Austin Warren, a scholar of the period, has written, "Among these, there are very few persons downright evil, and but a very few who are wise and saintly; most of them are at neither pole but in between . . . it is these compromisers, ordinary, normal, well-adjusted members of society, who are Law's chief and most effective butts."[36]

From *A Serious Call to a Devout and Holy Life*
Chapter 7

How the imprudent use of an estate corrupts all the tempers of the mind and fills the heart with poor and ridiculous passions through the whole course of life, represented in the character of Flavia.

Flavia and Miranda are two maiden sisters that have each of them two hundred pounds a year. They buried their parents twenty years ago, and have since that time spent their estate as they pleased.

Flavia has been the wonder of all her friends for her excellent management in making so surprising a figure in so moderate a fortune. Several ladies that have twice her fortune are not able to be always so genteel and so constant at all places of pleasure and expense. She has everything that is in fashion, and is in every place where there is any diversion. Flavia is very orthodox, she talks warmly against heretics and schismatics, is generally at church, and often at the Sacrament. She once commended a sermon that was against the pride and vanity of dress, and thought it was very just against Lucinda, whom she takes to be a great deal finer than she need be. If anyone asks Flavia to do something in charity, if she likes the person who makes the proposal or happens to be in a right temper, she will toss him half a crown or a crown, and tell him if he knew what a long milliner's bill she had just received he would think it a great deal for her to give. A quarter of a year after this, she hears a sermon upon the necessity of charity; she thinks the man preaches well, that it is a very proper subject, that people want much to be put in mind of it; but she applies nothing to herself because she remembers that she gave a crown some time ago when she could so ill spare it.

As for poor people themselves, she will admit of no complaints from them; she is very positive they are all cheats and liars and will say anything to get relief, and therefore it must be a sin to encourage them in their evil ways.

Flavia would be a miracle of piety if she was but half so careful of her soul as she is of her body. The rising of a pimple in her face, the sting of a gnat, will make her keep her room two or three days, and she thinks they are very rash people that don't take care of things in time. This makes her so overcareful of her health that she never thinks she is well enough, and so overindulgent that she never can be really well. So that it costs her a great deal in sleeping draughts, in spirits for the head, in drops for the nerves, in cordials for the stomach, and in saffron for her tea.

Thus lives Flavia; and if she lives ten years longer, she will have spent about fifteen hundred and sixty Sundays after this manner. She will have wore about two hundred different suits of clothes. Out of this thirty years of her life, fifteen of them will have been disposed of in bed; and of the remaining fifteen, about fourteen of them will have been consumed in eating, drinking, dressing, visiting, conversation, reading and hearing plays and romances, at operas, assemblies, balls, and diversions. For you may reckon all the time that she is up thus spent, except for about an hour-and-a-half that is disposed of at church most Sundays in the year. With great management, and under mighty rules of economy, she will have spent sixty hundred pounds upon herself, bating only some shillings, crowns, or half crowns that have gone from her in accidental charities.

I shall not take upon me to say that it is impossible for Flavia to be saved; but this much must be said, that she has no grounds from scripture to think she is in the way of salvation. For her whole life is in direct opposition to all those tempers and practices which the gospel has made necessary to salvation.

She might have been humble, serious, devout, a lover of good books, an admirer of prayer and retirement, careful of her time, diligent in good works, full of charity and the love of God, but that the imprudent use of her estate forced all the contrary tempers upon her.

Now though the irregular trifling spirit of this character belongs, I hope, but to few people, yet many may here learn some instruction from it and perhaps see something of their own spirits in it.

For as Flavia seems to be undone by the unreasonable use of her fortune, so the lowness of most people's virtue, the imperfections of their piety and the disorders of their passions is generally owing to their imprudent use and enjoyment of lawful and innocent things.[37]

John Wesley

A Plain Account of Genuine Christianity (1753) is a comprehensive statement of John Wesley's belief, aimed at converting readers. Although Wesley was conversant with classical Christian authors and languages, his work is the opposite of the scholarly, meditative writings of an earlier generation of Anglican divines. Wesley's writing is focused clearly on the reader's amendment of life from worldliness to holiness.

Section I

1. I would consider, first, who is a Christian indeed? What does that term properly imply? It has been so long abused, I fear, not only to mean nothing at all, but what was far worse than nothing, to be a cloak for the vilest hypocrisy, for the grossest abominations and immoralities of every kind, that it is high time to rescue it out of the hands of wretches that are a reproach to the human race, to show determinately what manner of man he is to whom this name of right belongs.

2. A "Christian" cannot think of the Author of his being without abasing himself before him, without a deep sense of the distance between a worm of earth and him that *sits on the circle of the heavens*. In his presence he sinks into the dust, knowing himself to be less than nothing in his eye and being conscious, in a manner words cannot express, of his own littleness, ignorance, foolishness. So that he can only cry out, from the fullness of his heart, "O God, what is man? What am I?"

5. Above all, remembering that God is love, he is conformed to the same likeness. He is full of love to his neighbor: of universal love, not confined to one sect or party, nor restrained to those who agree with him in opinions, or in outward modes of worship, or to those who are allied to him by blood or recommended by nearness of place. Neither does he love only those that love him, or that are endeared to him by intimacy of acquaintance. But his love resembles that of him whose mercy is over all his works. It soars above all these scanty bounds, embracing neighbors and strangers, friends and enemies: yes, not only the good and gentle but also the froward, the evil, the unthankful. For he loves every soul that God has made, every child of man, of whatever place or nation. And yet this universal benevolence does in nowise interfere with a peculiar regard for his relations, friends, and benefactors, a fervent love for his country and the most endeared affection to all men of integrity, of clear and generous virtue.

15. This is the plain, naked portraiture of a Christian. But be not prejudiced against him for his name. Forgive his particularities of opinion and (what you think) superstitious modes of worship. These are circumstances but of small concern and do not enter into the essence of his character. Cover them with a veil of love and look at the substance: his tempers, his holiness, his happiness. Can calm reason conceive either a more amiable or a more desirable character?

Is it your own? Away with names! Away with opinions! I care not what you are called. I ask not (it does not deserve a thought) what opinion you bare of, so you are conscious to yourself that you are the man whom I have been (however faintly) describing.

Do not you know how you ought to be such? Is the Governor of the world well pleased that you are not?

Do you not at least desire it? I would to God that desire may penetrate your inmost soul and that you may have no rest in your spirit 'til you are not only almost but together a Christian![38]

While John Wesley was often thought of as preaching for several hours a day, then moving on to other places to seek conversions, he spent many hours in personal prayer, and wrote often about self-examination and the quest for personal holiness. The following excerpt is from the Scheme of Self-Examination Wesley and his associates used while at Oxford. The minute detail into which they explore their own depths rivals the Spiritual Exercises of St. Ignatius of Loyola and other great writers of that genre.

A Scheme of Self-Examination
Used by the First Methodists at Oxford

Sunday—Love of God and Simplicity:
Means of which are, Prayer and Meditation

1. Have I been simple and recollected in everything I said or did? Have I (a) been simple in everything, that is, looked upon God, my Good, my Pattern, my one Desire, my Disposer, Parent of Good; acted wholly for him; bounded my views with the present action or hour? (b) Recollected? That is, has this simple view been distinct and uninterrupted? Have I, in order to keep it so, used the signs agreed upon with my friends, wherever I was? Have I done anything without a previous perception of its being an exercise or a means of the virtue of the day? Have I said anything without it?

3. Have I duly used ejaculations? That is, have I every hour prayed for humility, faith, hope, love, and the particular virtue of the day? Considered with whom I was the last hour, what I did, and how? With regard to recollection, love of man, humility, self-denial, resignation, and thankfulness? Considered the next hour in the same respects, offered up all I do to my Redeemer, begged his assistance in every particular, and commended my soul to his keeping? Have I done this deliberately, not in haste, seriously, not doing anything else the while, and fervently as I could?

4. Have I duly prayed for the virtue of the day? That is, have I prayed for it going out and coming in? deliberately, seriously, fervently?

6. Have I duly meditated? Every day, unless for necessary mercy, (a) From six, &c., to prayers? (b) From four to five? What was particular in the providence of this day? How ought the virtue of the day to have been exerted upon it? How did it fall short? (Here faults.) (c) On Sunday, from six to seven, with Kempis? From three to four on redemption, or God's attributes? Wednesday and Friday, from twelve to one, on the Passion? After ending a book, on what I had marked in it?[39]

Charles Wesley

Charles Wesley was a prolific writer of hymns. In the preface to his 1780 handbook he notes, "In these hymns there is no doggerel, no botches, nothing put in to patch up the rhyme, no feeble expletives. (b) Here is nothing turgid or bombast on the one hand, nor low and creeping on the other. (c) Here are no *cant* expressions, no words without meaning. . . . (d) Here are (allow me to say) both the purity, the strength, and the elegance of the English language—and at the same time the utmost simplicity and plainness, suited to every capacity." The following hymn, "Love Divine, All Loves Excelling" (1747), expresses the Wesley brothers' deep belief in the presence of the Holy Spirit within individual lives and in society. Far more than a moment of individual inspiration, the work of the Holy Spirit is to "Finish then thy new creation," to prepare humanity for the end of history and the Second Coming.

> Love divine, all loves excelling,
>   Joy of heaven, to earth come down,
> Fix in us thy humble dwelling.
>   All thy faithful mercies crown!
> Jesu, thou art all compassion,
>   Pure unbounded love thou art;

Visit us with thy salvation!
    Enter every trembling heart.
Come almighty to deliver,
    Let us all thy grace receive;
Suddenly return, and never,
    Never more thy temples leave.
Thee we would be always blessing,
    Serve thee as thy hosts above,
Pray, and praise thee without ceasing,
    Glory in thy perfect love.
Finish then thy new creation,
    Pure and spotless let us be;
Let us see thy great salvation
    Perfectly restored in thee;
Changed from glory into glory,
    Till in heaven we take our place,
Till we cast our crowns before thee,
    Lost in wonder, love, and praise.

James Woodforde, Diarist

For over forty years, from 1758 to 1803, James Woodforde held a number of curacies in Oxford, Somerset, Weston, and Norfolk. His record of his daily life has become a valuable document in English social history, a unique slice of life of English country life before the Industrial Revolution. Woodforde was an energetic country parson, sending veal broth and baskets of meat and vegetables to the poor of his parish, dining with the gentry, and keeping a well-laden table for those who visited him. An income of four hundred pounds a year allowed him to support a niece and keep several servants, and to live well. The French and American revolutions, social change, and theological controversy all elude Woodforde, who set after large hares with his skilled greyhounds, Dutchess, Hector, and Reach'em. There is no hypocrisy in his writing or person; his was not an acute theological mind, or even an interesting one, but he did like people, was hospitable, and exercised his office faithfully and with probably more competence than many contemporaries.

1778

    Jan. 6. We breakfasted, dined, supped and slept again at home. Sukey's sister breakfasted here and then went home. I did not speak one word to her, as she came unasked. Bill went out a shooting again this morning and he brought home only 4 Blackbirds. Gave Bill this evening for powder and shot 2/6.

Jan. 19. . . . This being the day for the Queen's Birth Day to be kept Bill fired my Blunderbuss 3 Times, each charge three Caps of Powder with a good deal of Paper and Tow on it. I fired him off in the evening with 3 Caps of Powder also.

Jan. 27. . . . Mr. Du Quesne called on me this morning and stayed with me some time, he told me that a Meeting of the Nobility, Gentry and Clergy of the county of Norfolk would be held tomorrow Morn' at the Maid's Head at Norwich for opening a Subscription to advance a Regiment in these critical Times for the King. He asked me if I should be there, which I promised.

Mar. 1. . . . Read Prayers and Preached this morning at Weston. Neighbor Gooch's Father was taken very ill today and thought to be dying. I sent him Tent Wine and in the afternoon went and saw him and read Prayers by him. He desired to have the Sacrament administered to him which I told him I would do it to Morrow morning. Poor Gooch has been an invalid for many years. His Pulse I thought was pretty regular, he had been convulsed in one of his hands, but talked pretty cheerful and well. My Clerks' Wife Jane Smith got immensely drunk I hear today.

Mar. 2. . . . Poor Neighbor Gooch died this morning at about 7 o'clock. I was quite surprised to hear of it indeed, as he did not appear to me yesterday near his latter end. I hope that his Intention was to receive the sacrament this morning, that his Will be, to the Supreme Being, taken as if the Deed had been done.

April 15. . . . We breakfasted, dined, supped and slept at home. Brewed a vessel of strong Beer today. My two large Piggs, by drinking some Beer grounds taken out of one of my Barrels today, got so amazingly drunk by it, that they were not able to stand and appeared like dead things almost, and so remained all night from dinner time today. I never saw Piggs so drunk in my life, I slit their ears for them without feeling.

April 16. We breakfasted, dined supped and slept again at home. My 2 Piggs are still unable to walk yet, but they are better than they were yesterday. They tumble about the yard and can by no means stand at all steady yet. In the afternoon my 2 Piggs were tolerably sober.

April 18. . . . Between 5 and 6 in the evening I took a ride to Honingham and buried one Willen late a schoolmaster there and who died very sudden being taken as he came from Durham. His son and Daughter attended him to the grave and were much concerned for their Father. Pray God comfort them. None but those that have lost their Parents can feel that sorrow which such an event generally produces.

1779

Jan. 1st. . . . I breakfasted, dined, supped and slept again at home. This morning very early about 1 o'clock a most dreadful storm of wind with Hail and Snow happened here and the Wind did not quite abate till the evening. A little before 2 o'clock I got up, my bedstead rocking under me, and never in my life that I know of, did I remember the Wind so high or of so long continuance. I expected every Moment that some part or other of my House must have been blown down, but blessed by God the whole stood, only a few Tiles displaced. My Servants also perceived their Bedsteads to shake. Thanks be to God that none of my People or self were hurt. My Chancel received great damage as did my Barn. The Leads from my Chancel were almost all blown off with some Parts of the Roof. The North West Window blown in and smashed all to pieces. The East Window also damaged but not greatly. The North W: Leads on the top of the Church also, some of them blown up and ruffled, besides 2 windows injured. . . . In the evening the Wind abated and was quite calm when I went to bed about 11 o'clock. Since what happened this morning, I prolonged the Letter I designed to send to my sister Pounsett to relate what had happened here by the storm. And this evening sent it to her by Mr. Cary. As the year begins rather unfortunate to me, hope the other Parts of it will be as propitious to me.

April 11. . . . Between 11 and 12 o'clock this morning I went to Church and publickly christened Mr. Custance's child of Ringland, it had been privately named before, and the name of it was Hambletom Thomas. . . . There were Coaches at Church. Mr. Custance immediately after the Ceremony came to me and desired me to accept a small Present; it was wrapped up in a Piece of white Paper very neat, and on opening of it, I found it contained nothing less than the sum of 4.4.0 He gave the Clerk also 0.10.6.

May 15. . . . Bled my three Horses this morning, 2 quarts each.

May 18. . . . Mr. Howes and Wife and Mrs. Davy, Mr. Bodham and his Brother, and Mr. De Quesne all dined and spent the afternoon and part of the evening with us today. I gave them for dinner a dish of Maccarel, 3 young Chicken boiled and some Bacon, a neck of Pork roasted and a Gooseberry Pye hot. We laughed immoderately after dinner on Mr. Howe's being sent to Coventry by us for an Hour. What with laughing and eating hot Gooseberry Pye brought on me the Hiccups with a violent pain in my stomach which lasted till I went to bed. At Cards Quadrille this evening—lost 0.2.6.[40]

5

The Nineteenth Century

I do not want to force any one to like it; nor do I care a sixpence for it as a piece of fine composition. I never called it "an excellent liturgy" in my life, and hope I never shall. But it has helped me to see more of the love of God and the bonds by which men are knit to each other, and to feel more hope as to those whom I should naturally regard as foes, than any other book except the Bible. It is my protection and the protection of the Church against Anglicanism and Evangelicalism and Liberalism and Romanism and Rationalism, and till these different devils cease to torment us, I will, with God's help, use this shield against them.

—F. D. Maurice on *The Book of Common Prayer*

THE FINAL DECADES OF the eighteenth century represent a watershed in world history—the Industrial Revolution. Within a few short years, rural England's topography was altered; the island of bucolic villages and small farms was replaced by one with large enclosed fields and factories. A distinct class of factory owners and workers emerged, and new configurations of space and distance changed the way people had thought and moved about for centuries. It was a revolutionary time and many of the political, economic, and societal problems church and state confront globally today emerged then, such as the place of women and children, the question of fair wages and equitable working conditions, population growth, urban crime, pollution, medical and quality-of-life problems, and the place of immigrants and migrants moving to the bleak new factory towns. "Drunk for a penny. Dead drunk for two pence. Clean straw for nothing" was a sign in front of London ginshops. Sports such as dog fighting and bearbaiting were brutal, executions at Tyburn provided entertainment. Villagers flocked to large cities' slums, hoping for employment, but often lived illiterate, wretched lives. Frederick Engels described living conditions for the poor in Manchester in 1844:

This chaos of small one-storied, one-roomed huts, in most of which there is no artificial floor, kitchen, living and sleeping-room all in one. In such a hole, scarcely five feet by six, I found two beds—and such bedsteads and beds!—which, with a staircase and chimney-piece, exactly filled the room. . . . Everywhere before the doors refuse and offal; and any sort of pavement that lay underneath could not be seen, but only felt, here and there, with the feet. . . . The whole side of the Irk is built in this way.[1]

England's population grew, a million more persons between 1700 and 1750, to about six million persons, nine million by the century's end, much of it in urban areas. Demands for food increased and crop rotation and planting seeds in rows instead of scattering them randomly allowed an increase in agricultural production. Large landowners used the new demands for food and new technologies to enclose their lands. By 1760 over three hundred thousand acres of land were fenced off; within the next four decades an additional three million acres were enclosed and the open-field system of the past, allowing peasant farmers a degree of mobility and freedom, came to an end. Cottagers were often forced into poverty or servitude. Few had legal titles to land, some held small family plots, but, deprived of former rights to pasture cows or raise geese and pigs on the common or to gather fuel in neighboring underbrush, sold their holdings and worked as laborers on large farms. The agricultural revolution's scarifying effects were as lasting as those of the Industrial Revolution.

It was the Age of Steam, as depicted in J. M. W. Turner's paintings, the landscape "of dark, satanic mills" of William Blake's poems. Technological change came first and most dramatically to the textile industries, especially in weaving, spinning, and cotton production. Improvements in the mining of coal and production of steel, largely through the use of steam engines, dramatically changed those industries. Such technologies gradually made their way around the globe.

Industrial capitalism found its voice in Adam Smith, whose *Wealth of Nations* was published in 1776 and went through five editions in the author's lifetime. Smith expounded a theory of *laissez faire*, "let alone" capitalism. The less regulation the better; natural economic laws would control the market. Smith wrote, "the patrimony of a poor man lies in the strength and dexterity of his hands; and to hinder him from employing this strength in what manner he thinks proper without injury to his neighbor, is a plain violation of this most sacred property."[2] Smith provided the capitalistic system's moral justification, the rationale for a harsh, competitive world.

A Slowly Responding Church

Indifference and incomprehension are two words describing the Church of England's attitude toward the swift social change then enveloping English society. While there were devout holy people in places, the institutional Church of England was complacent. Anglican bishops and clergy were often too closely aligned with the establishment. Clergy are usually deficient in expounding economic theory, and the Industrial Revolution produced sermons blaming their plight on the poor and exhorting those trampled by industrial and agricultural change to pull themselves up by their bootstraps. Parson Dale in Edward Bulwer-Lytton's *"My Novel!"* preached a sermon with sentiments heard frequently during this period, "If there were no penury and no pain, what would become of benevolence, of charity, of the blessed human pity, of temperance in the midst of luxury, of justice in the exercise of power."[3]

It took decades for the Church of England to emerge from its "fat slumbers" (Edward Gibbon) and for voices of social conscience to arise in any numbers. When John Hodgson, vicar of Jarrow, called public attention to a mining disaster where ninety-two parishioners lost their lives, an outcome was the invention of the safety lamp for miners. Other clergy spoke out against the hours and working conditions of children and a "Chaplain to the Metropolitan Trades Union" was appointed. Strange as it may seem to a later age, one of the most grievous charges that could be levied against the clergy of this era was showing *enthusiasm*, meaning zeal for a cause, of which Methodism was the prime example. In toasting a newly consecrated bishop, an Archbishop of Canterbury remarked, "Remember, my Lord Bishop, that your Primate on the day of your consecration defined your duty for you:—that duty is to put down enthusiasm and to preach the Gospel."[4] Understandably, a widely used text for sermons at this time was, "let your moderation be known unto all men" (Phil. 4:5).

The Bishops

The bishops, from whom leadership might be expected, were closely aligned with the political establishment. Futile is the search for one of their number to articulate a religious response to the Industrial Revolution, the expansion of empire, or the rise of scientific thought as a quasi religion of its own. Bishops were either of the aristocracy or closely allied to it. Venality was rampant; the bishop of Llandaff spent twenty-five of the thirty-four years of his episcopacy as a farmer in the Lake District, rarely visiting the impoverished Welsh diocese, although collecting incomes from sixteen livings. An Archbishop of Canterbury appointed a twelve-year old grandson to a post paying nearly a thousand pounds a year. Meanwhile, a few bishops received princely sums. The bishop of Winchester reportedly drew an income of fifty thousand pounds, the bishop of Ely, thirty thousand.

Bishops had huge dioceses, some parts of which they rarely visited. When one archbishop of York appeared for confirmations, the vergers called out "Silence for the Archbishop," after which the prelate ascended the Minster pulpit, extended his hands over the sea of people below, and pronounced the words of confirmation once. In the Diocese of Ely, mass confirmations were held at the cathedral once every four years. Sometimes oranges were sold in the cathedrals where such mass services were performed, and the nearby public houses were ready with food and drink for the congregations as they left the place of worship.

The bishops showed no leadership in reform of the church or society; most resisted it when the 1831 Reform bill was first raised in the House of Lords. Twenty-one votes of the forty-one-vote majority opposing the bill came from bishops. (Only two bishops voted for the bill.) When such news reached the countryside, riots occurred at bishops' palaces and prelates were burned in effigy. One bishop kept a disguise handy in case he had to flee. The Archbishop of Canterbury was jeered and pelted with cabbage stocks by a mob which applauded when a speaker urged converting the cathedral into a stable.[5]

CLERGY LIFESTYLES

Great disparities were reflected in clerical lifestyles, from relatively afflu-ent southern rectories to the north, where many clergy lives differed little from the rural and industrial poor. Notwithstanding, nineteenth-century clergy salaries were higher than previously. Improved agricultural meth-ods had proportionally increased tithe income, and Queen Anne's Bounty, turning over a segment of royal revenues to benefit the incomes of poorer clergy, had been a fillip to improving clergy stipends. The his-torian Peter Virgin wrote, "A third of the clergy in 1830 earned over

£400 a year from their benefices, while a further third did not manage to make as much as £200 a year. The ecclesiastical incomes of most of these poor incumbents were in the range of £60-£180 a year, putting them on the same level as the emerging lower middle class—teachers, clerks, shop-keepers, and the like."[6]

Many clergy were like Mr. Quiverful in Anthony Trollope's *Barchester Towers*, whose family increased while his salary remained pitifully static. A few clergy continued collecting incomes from their livings after they had moved to India or the Caribbean, but these were exceptions. It is esti-mated that in 1812 nearly three-fifths of the clergy were not resident in their parishes.[7] Lamenting the clergy's generally low educational level, a contemporary description says, "The country clergy are constant readers of the *Gentleman's Magazine*, deep in the antiquities of the signs of inns, speculations as to what becomes of swallows in winter, and whether hedge-hogs, or other urchins, are most justly accused of sucking cows dry at night."[8]

The broader picture, however, was by no means drab. There were many pious clergy, and in places, holy persons, preaching, teaching, visit-ing the sick, burying the dead, instructing young people in the faith, and giving food and clothing to the poor and advice to all who sought it. In an era before the spread of hospitals and doctors, the vicar often kept the parish medicine box; some started schools and alms-houses, many wrote letters for their parishioners. Clergy numbers included able scholars and writers; names such as Lewis Carroll (Charles Dodgson) and Thomas Malthus, are only two that come to mind.

Tithes collected from the local parish remained the main source of clerical income, causing resentment among the nonfaithful and non-Anglicans, and no small amount of evasion among nominal parishioners. A cleric writing in 1825 described the annual collections in his parish:

> The farmers of my Parish are now in the midst of their hop-gathering; but they all complain how much they have suffer'd by a destructive fly, which attack'd them before they had risen half-way up their poles. This Circum-stance prognosticates to me many long Faces on St. Luke's Day when they pay me my Tithes. But I may expect their countenances to brighten a little over the Punch-Bowl after an ample Dinner which I always set before them. The music of their sovereigns and Crown pieces, not to mention the pleasing whispers of their Five-pound notes in piano, will help keep up the spirits of me and my Curate at the Table of our Morning Business.[9]

Parenthetically, from the mid-nineteenth century on, that characteristic institution the "squarson" declined, spoiled by the Oxford Movement's emphasis on holiness, which triggered a rethinking of the priestly role and the growth of a more professional bar. Squire and parson had long been combined in the same person, and in 1831 possibly a quarter of the magisterial bench was composed of clerical JPs, although the numbers would soon decline precipitously. Clergy sat as local judges in landlord–tenant, minor criminal, poor law relief, and wage and contract disputes. There were winners and losers in each legal case, and the local jurist's role conflicted with the clergy's religious obligations; mercy and justice did not sit down well together. In 1831 one in every six clergymen was a magistrate; such persons made good incomes and lived as the gentry, riding to the hunt—critics called them "mighty nimrods of the cloth." Entertaining at bounteous tables, they were skilled at card games and parlor conversation. As might be expected, such well-entrenched persons were among those most resistant to reform appeals.

The "typical" country church at century's end differed little from the "typical" country church in the century's opening years; it would be neither markedly high nor low. Victorian liturgical reforms would have reached it, chiefly in adding many brass fixtures, including rails and basins, and through the addition of a larger, raised altar. Memorial stained glass windows became a feature of the age, and lecterns, litany desks, and raised pulpits were common. Clergy led prayers from the side instead of facing congregations. Surpliced choirs grew in numbers and pipe organs proliferated.

THE CLAPHAM SECT AND WILLIAM WILBERFORCE'S ANTI-SLAVERY CAMPAIGN

Public lethargy notwithstanding, there were stirrings of conscience within the church, represented by the prominent antislavery group the Clapham Sect, named for the place where members met, the Clapham parish church, then outside London. Members included a small circle of distinguished lawyers, bankers, writers, and philanthropists, affluent, well-placed leaders of society. Given to frequent prayer meetings, Bible reading, and self-examination, their leader was William Wilberforce (1758–1833), the leading opponent of slavery in Great Britain. Wilberforce, a member of Parliament, wrote a well-received devotional work, *Practical View of the Prevailing Religious Systems of Professed Christians in the Higher and Middle Classes in this Country contrasted with Real Christianity* (1797), but he is best remembered, as is the Clapham Sect, for calling attention to slavery and championing its abolition. The group also supported the Bible Society, the Church Missionary Society, and the educational and charitable work of Hannah More. John Wesley encouraged Wilberforce in a 1791 letter:

> Unless God has raised you up for this very thing, you will be worn out by the opposition of men and devils. But if God be for you, who can be against you? Are all of them together stronger than God? Oh, be not weary of well doing! Go on, in the name of God and in the power of his might, till even American slavery (the vilest that ever saw the sun) shall vanish away before it.
>
> Reading this morning a tract written by a poor African, I was particularly struck by that circumstance that a man who has a black skin, being wronged or outraged by a white man, can have no redress; it being a "law" in all our colonies that the oath of a black against a white goes for nothing. What villainy is this?[10]

Wilberforce and his group encountered fierce opposition from their own class, which regarded slavery as an economic necessity. Merchants, shippers, and planters supported the slave trade, since English mills depended on West Indies' plantations for raw cotton, and plantations required steady, cheap slave labor. The slave trade worked via a triangular shipping route. Cheap cotton goods and iron wares, such as kettles and needles, were transported from England to Africa, where the goods were traded for slaves. Life on the slave ships was terrible, and many people died on the infamous "Middle Passage" from Africa to the West Indies, after which the ships returned to England filled with sugar, tobacco, and raw cotton.

Wilberforce appealed to English peoples' consciences, his main argument being an unyielding and oft-repeated moral conviction about the horrors of slavery. In addition to Parliament, the Clapham antislavery group spoke at public gatherings, and even distributed soup plates with a Negro on the bottom and a slogan, "A man and a brother." On February 23, 1807, the House overwhelmingly voted the slave trade illegal; in 1833 slavery was abolished throughout the British dominions.

In addition to antislavery groups, the century's first three decades saw the proliferation of benevolent societies, whose membership covered the spectrum of church thought, opening schools and spreading the gospel at home and abroad. Cheap Bibles were printed for mass distribution, and new translations were authorized by the British and Foreign Bible Society for lands where Protestant missionaries were active.

Educational reform came through figures such as Thomas Arnold (1795–1842), Rugby's legendary headmaster, who died at age forty-six, worn out from his efforts. Arnold also preached muscular Christianity, building Christian character in men and boys. *The Manliness of Christ* was a popular book of the period, written by Thomas Hughes, otherwise remembered for *Tom Brown's School Days*. A strong sense of duty was instilled in pupils, and Arnold made his elite boys' school a Christian universe in miniature. Religion permeated every aspect of society; even the smallest boy had a contribution to make. The whole society, Arnold believed, would be reformed by Christian-inspired education. Nor was this effort uncritical of the establishment. In *Politics for the People*, Charles Kingsley, a Victorian cleric and author, wrote, "We have used the Bible as if it was a mere special constable's handbook—an opium dose for keeping beasts of burden patient while they were being overloaded—a mere book to keep the poor in order. . . . Instead of being a book to keep the poor in order, it is a book, from beginning to end, written *to keep the rich in order*."[11] New universities loosened the tight hold of the ancient colleges of Oxford and Cambridge. If the curricula of Oxford and Cambridge were musty and out-of-date, their structures were even more anachronistic. No dissenter could take a degree at Cambridge, and at Oxford subscription to the Thirty-Nine Articles was part of the matriculation process. College fellows were required to be in orders, and daily attendance at chapel was recorded.

A CLIMATE OF REFORM
AND THE REFORM ACT OF 1832

The Reform Act of 1832 was a turning point in British political and social life, but even before its passage the Church of England was subject to both external and internal reforms. External reforms came from a series of parliamentary acts. The Clarendon Code of 1661, which had given the Church of England an almost total hold on governmental positions, was repealed in 1828, allowing nonconformists legitimate places in public life. It ended the long-established belief, dating to the times of Hooker and the Elizabethan Settlement, that church and state were really one.

Now it was accepted that a person could be a good citizen without belonging to the Church of England, or to any church. A year later a landmark Catholic Emancipation Bill was passed, allowing Roman Catholics to stand for Parliament. Increasingly, the church fended for itself, to stand or fall as the place where the Good News was preached and works of justice and mercy performed.

Later changes were equally far-reaching. In 1835 Parliament established an Ecclesiastical Commission, which produced sweeping reform recommendations, including an overhaul of church finances and organization. New dioceses were created in the heavily industrial areas of Yorkshire and Lancaster; some clergy salaries were increased, relieving in part inequities between affluent and less affluent clergy. The number of endowed places in cathedrals was reduced, and savings were applied toward salaries of poorer diocesan clergy. An 1836 Tithe Act based clergy compensation on the amount of a fixed rent rather than clergy having to solicit each individual parishioner for a tenth of their income for the church. An 1868 bill abolished compulsory church rates; the care and maintenance of parish churches now fell to individual congregations. Roman Catholics and Methodists were no longer required to pay for the upkeep of Church of England buildings they never frequented. Church convocations, suspended for political reasons in 1717, were revived in the 1850s.

By 1854 Church of England membership was no longer required for admittance to Oxford or Cambridge universities, and in 1871 the religious test for college fellowships was abolished. One cleric lamented excessively:

> Oxford, I fear, has seen her best days. Her sun has set and for ever. She never more can be what she has been—the great nursery of the Church. She will become a cage of unclean beasts at last. Of course we shall not live to see it; but *our great-grandchildren will:* and the Church (and Oxford itself) will rue the day when its liberties and its birthright were lost by a licentious vote of a *no longer Christian* House of Commons. (Italics in original.)[12]

The structure of church government devised by the Church of England and later most of its overseas provinces contained a contradiction never satisfactorily resolved. Basically, it tried to amalgamate an ecclesiastical structure of bishops, priests, and deacons with a parliamentary one of a legislative body and committees. The resultant institution was neither sacred nor structurally efficient, yet it somehow endured, allowing conflicts to surface, resolutions to be passed, budgets to be voted and appointments to be made. Members complained about the institution's obvious shortcomings, and there were periodic efforts to tinker with it. Yet, like one of the brass and iron machines of an earlier era displayed in the British Museum, it worked with a force and energy of its own. No one could repair it by tampering with the design, although each generation's inventors suggested ways to start over and build a better structure.

THE OXFORD MOVEMENT

The major reform effort within the church at this time was unrelated to the social ferment engulfing England. The Oxford Movement (1833–1854) was essentially the work of a handful of brilliant academic clerics, writing largely for one another, seeking to return the Church of England to its Catholic past, in liturgy, theology, and spiritual life. Although some of its members were personally active in campaigns against slavery and poor working conditions in urban areas, it was in no sense a social betterment effort, nor did it spend much time disputing the Evangelicals. The Catholic past and an attraction for Rome were all-consuming, until the movement's leading light, John Henry Newman (1801–1890), converted to Roman Catholicism in 1845, by which time the movement's program had long been enunciated.

The movement began in July 1833 with a sermon by John Keble (1792–1866), professor of poetry and a saintly figure, on the nature and authority of the church. Keble responded to a House of Commons bill cutting the number of Anglican bishops in Ireland and appointing a reform commission. The issue became an ecclesiastical turf question for Keble, who showed little interest in the irreligion of the rich or the plight of the poor, the injustices of criminal laws or the absence of public education for the rural and urban masses. Calling the sermon "National Apostasy," he argued that the church was a divine institution and that the bishops were successors to the apostles, not subject to parliamentary realignment. Legislative tampering with church structure, it followed for Keble, was a serious sin separating the nation from God.

These Oxford dons and their followers were of two minds on how to renew and reform the church. Some were for "more of the same," seeking to return the church to what it was in the time of the Caroline Divines. Others were more aggressive, launching a series of "Tracts for the Times," carefully argued scholarly documents written by movement participants primarily for each other, although they received wider circulation and influenced the national debate on church reform as well. With titles such as "Thoughts on the Ministerial Commission," "The Catholic Church," and "Thoughts on Alterations in the Liturgy," they enthusiastically examined most aspects of religious life in ninety essays. As the movement found its identity, tracts became longer, adding copious quotations from early church figures. By 1834 more than fifty of the documents, cheaply printed for mass distribution, were in circulation. Newman wrote on the Church of England as the *via media* (Nos. 38, 41), a position he rescinded with his conversion to Rome.

Neither grounded in the current realities of industrial Britain nor forward-looking, the Tractarians recreated the early church as they understood it—the font of authority and holiness—and had only scorn for the Reformation. Hurrell Froude, a follower of Newman, said, "The Reformation was a limb badly set—it must be broken again in order to be righted." Newman, writing of the apostolic succession, urged readers to "[e]xalt our Holy Fathers, the Bishops, as the Representatives of the Apostles, and the Angels of the Churches; and magnify your office, as being ordained by them to take part in their Ministry."[13] Worldly prelates, like Dr. Proudie in Anthony Trollope's *Barchester Towers*, would be both embarrassed by and suspicious of Newman's positions. Predictably, the tracts enraged Evangelicals, and the war at Oxford was fought with such weapons as denials of appointment, threats to withhold degrees, and suspension of preaching rights for alleged doctrinal deviation. Three positions emerged, one favoring closer ties with Rome, a strictly Protestant position, and one supporting Anglicanism as a middle way between extremes. The subtleties of the third position were lost, however, on inflammatory Protestants who wanted no commerce with the "Scarlet Woman" of Rome, and those increasingly attracted to Rome, for whom the Reformation was a distasteful interlude in an otherwise triumphal march. And there were other bishops and clergy who were content to manage their estates and lamented public controversy.

A STATIC THEOLOGY

"Their actual theology was static," a writer on the Tractarians observes, "Except for Newman and Ward they had not much theology in the strict and proper sense. They had an immense knowledge of the Faith, its history, its traditional exegesis, its moral implications, but they were not constructive theologians."[14]

Several side effects sprang from the Oxford Movement. The study of patristics and liturgy grew, as did enthusiasm for church ritual. Original Oxford Movement participants preached in black gowns and academic hoods, as was the custom of the day, and showed little interest in ceremony. Often such change resulted in protests and riots, with cries that the clergy were enacting "the mummeries of superstition" and leading their flocks toward Rome. A court case held the use of eucharistic vestments legal, as were crosses, as long as they were kept off the altar. Disputes over the use of candles and elevating the communion host found their way into courts. A Public Worship Regulation Act was passed in 1874 to reduce litigation over church doctrine and ceremony. An Anglo-Catholic society, the English Church Union, was founded in 1869 to defend prosecuted priests against legal charges. An Evangelical group, the Church Association, incorporated a few years later to step up the prosecutions. The Association, known to opponents as "The Persecution Society," claimed sixty favorable court decisions. Infrequently, priests were jailed for violating prohibitions against the use of ritual. One such liturgical donnybrook occurred in 1844 in a Cambridge church, St. Sepulchre's Church, then undergoing restoration. Parishioners replaced the wooden communion table with a stone altar, against the desires of the rector and church wardens. Charges and countercharges were exchanged until the century's end, and in 1888, Edward King (1829–1910), the saintly bishop of Lincoln, was tried before the Archbishop of Canterbury on charges of violating Prayer Book norms. King was acquitted; the court allowed two lighted candles to be set on the Holy Table during the service, even if not needed for light, permitted the chalice mixed with wine and water, and allowed the celebrant to face eastward during the service, although his back was to the congregation, and to sing the *Agnus Dei* after the prayer of consecration. Controversy is never far from the surface when Anglicans of different ceremonial traditions meet, and this sort of dispute was frequent between loyalists of the high church and other camps.

Some people found the Tractarians offensive, either too close to Roman Catholicism or overly zealous about issues of little interest to parishioners in the pew, but there is no question that the intellectual ferment unleashed by the Oxford Movement shaped the tenor of discussions in the Church of England for much of this century and beyond. Seen in a broader perspective, the Oxford Movement triggered a lively discussion on various contradictory issues. While emotions ran high and tempers flared, all sides eventually gained from the controversy. Disputants were required to think through their positions, marshal arguments, and search for new evidence and reasons for their statements. A brisk purposefulness worked its way into the discourse of Evangelicals and high church followers; to participants, if not the general public, the church was a far livelier place than it had been for much of the previous century. J. R. H. Moorman has written, "the tracts and their writers and supporters left their mark not only on the University but on the Church as a whole, on its theology, its worship, its whole life. Ideas had been planted which in time were to transform the whole face of the Anglican Communion at home and overseas. The Church could never be the same again."[15]

To this writer at least, the Oxford Movement's contributions were decidedly mixed, something less than the Anglican Counter-Reformation it sometimes has been called. Its emphasis was on personal holiness and returning the church to the sacred way. Despite individual significant ministries in the slums of London by individual Anglo-Catholic priests, including Pusey, it rarely spoke to the gross social and economic inequities produced by the Industrial Revolution. Far from suggesting greater avenues for the unity and cooperation of denominations, the Tractarians were oblivious to these issues, as they were to questions of church governance, beyond a veneration of bishops. And in the intellectual debates raging in the early nineteenth century among scientists, historians, biblical critics, and other scholars, it contributed little but an appeal to return to the past.

THE OXFORD MOVEMENT IN AMERICA

"What was counted High once is Low now," stated William R. Wittingham, professor of Ecclesiastical History at General Theological Seminary in New York.[16] The main English influence on the American church in the nineteenth century was in response to the Oxford Movement. When the din and clangor had subsided decades later, the liturgy, doctrine, and outlook of the American church differed considerably from what it had been in the 1830s. The Oxford Movement's most fertile reception was among the High Church party, established as a vocal minority in several major cities, including at the General Theological Seminary in New York, and in the midwestern "Biretta Belt," extending roughly from Chicago to the Great Plains, including the Nashotah House seminary, a center of Anglo-Catholic worship. Additionally, many prominent American bishops had studied in England and were exposed to the movement, which they inwardly digested with various results.

Yet the situation in the two countries was considerably different; for instance, if the Oxford Movement proponents in Great Britain sought a closeness with Rome to affirm the catholicity of the Anglican Church, many Americans saw in the emphasis on the apostolic succession proof of an independent Protestant church whose historic credentials were now affirmed.

Strong opposition was voiced against the Oxford Movement as well, cast often in the sharp polemical language of the period. Some low church bishops suggested that the Tractarians should speedily complete their journey across the Tiber. Bishop Moore of Virginia cautioned that the movement "threatened a revival of the worst evils of the Romish system." Another critic called the *Tracts* "meat . . . putrid to the bone."[17] The polarities were evident. If the Anglo-Catholic extreme was what would be called "nosebleed high" the spectrum's other end was not inaccurately described as "snake low."[18]

Yet, over time, even enemies of the Oxford Movement began to adopt, albeit in modified form, some of its beliefs and practices. A few clergy accepted everything from Roman fiddle-back chasubles to recitation of the rosary, others were content to hold communion services more frequently. Stone altars facing east replaced wooden communion tables, pulpits gave way to lecterns, and European-designed stained glass windows replaced vistas of the heartland with visions of the saints. Statues multiplied, candles proliferated, the Eucharist became the mass. Acolytes and vergers found a permanent place in the liturgy, and even in places that were not high church, processions with surpliced choirs appeared. Organists, choir directors, and church musicians became a permanent feature of the ecclesiastical landscape. As was the case in England, the monastic movement was launched. Indigenous orders, such as the Order of the Holy Cross, sprang up, and groups like the Society of St. John the Evangelist were directly traceable to founding houses in England.

It would be erroneous to consider the High Church party interested only in ritualism and self-preservation. Its most fervid advocates tried to lead a holy life, and it always had a minority strain deeply committed to social action. Some of its clergy became "slum priests," living among the poor and participating in groups like the Church Association for the

Advancement of the Interests of Labor, which bore resemblances to the English Guild of St. Matthew. Comparing the two traditions, David L. Holmes has written:

> Though the original emphasis of both Anglo-Catholicism and evangelical-ism called for a life of prayer, discipline, and devotion, the significant issues in later decades often revolved around candles, titles, and ecclesiastical millinery. Slavery, child labor, twelve-hour workdays, and impoverished lives were just outside the doors of Episcopal churches. But for many years questions of matters of church style and worship dominated the concerns of many Episcopalians.[19]

The balance sheet on the Oxford Movement's influence in America was mixed. A decidedly high church ritualistic movement was established in America, but its numbers were never large and it never claimed a majority position in the American Church. Still, if the intense energy of the Anglo-Catholics did not triumph, they still significantly influenced the beliefs, texture, and color of the American Church.

JOHN HENRY NEWMAN, FROM OXFORD TO ROME

Edward Bouverie Pusey (1800–1882), a Hebrew scholar, and John Henry Newman were the Oxford Movement's most visible leaders. Newman was brought up in a conventionally pious household but experienced a conversion to Evangelical Anglicanism during adolescence. This gave him direction and determination that lasted all his life and is reflected in his sermons, which "preach for a conversion." Newman was a prolific, skilled, and imaginative writer and authored twenty-four of the ninety tracts. He wrote many hymns, including such popular favorites as "Lead, Kindly Light" and "Praise to the Holiest in the Height." Newman's Sunday afternoon Oxford sermons, delivered to large congregations when he was vicar of St. Mary's Church (1828–1843), are among the finest products of this century's religious writing. The sermons are long, tightly argued, and were delivered by Newman from written texts. (He abandoned the use of prepared drafts after his conversion to Roman Catholicism, following the practice of Catholic preachers.) A repetitive theme is the quest for perfection of life. "Be you content with nothing short of perfection" is a reechoing theme throughout the sermons. Void of illustrative material, they do not discuss history; most belong to the "cure of the soul" category and show penetrating psychological insights long before psychology was developed as a field or the relationship of religion and psychology was a scholarly discipline. A listener described Newman the preacher:

> Action in the common sense there was none. His hands were literally not seen from the beginning to the end. The sermon began in a calm, musical voice, the key slightly rising as it went on; by and by the preacher warmed with his subject, till it seemed as if his very soul and body glowed with suppressed emotion. The very tones of his voice seemed as if they were not his own. There are those who, to this day, in reading many of his sermons, have the whole scene brought back before them. The great church, the congregation all breathless with expectant attention, the gaslight just at the left hand of the pulpit, lowered that the preacher might not be dazzled: themselves, perhaps standing in the half-darkness under the gallery.[20]

There is little that is distinctly Anglican in Newman's sermons. While the quest for spiritual perfection is part of the Anglican religious search, Newman's continual focus on doctrine, discipline, obedience, and authority as indispensable to the religious life, fails to accept a world where different emphasis is possible and diverse approaches to the search for Christ are valid. Newmen spent his life like an archaeologist examining the writings of early church figures; the Reformation was an aberration in history, a buoy to be steered away from. Newman's mastery of the English language is unrivaled among sermon writers, and his quest for holiness, his ability to both link biblical analysis with moral problems, and his psychological insight into human evil and human frailty assure his place in intellectual history.

In his early tracts Newman argued, "Popery must be destroyed: it cannot be reformed." He urged readers, "Choose your side." The Church of England, he argued, had escaped the corrupting influences of both Romanism and Protestantism and remained unsullied in the great tradition of the apostolic church. In 1839 Newman changed his position, influenced by a Roman Catholic argument that the Anglican Church was a schismatic church, just as the Donatist church had been in fourth-century North Africa. (Bishop Donatus had broken with Rome in a doctrinal and power struggle.) At about this time Newman formulated the concept of "Development," by which he argued that divine revelation was progressive. If the church had strayed from the ways of Catholic truth in the early church, by the Counter-Reformation it had not only corrected its wanderings but was fully the receptacle of God's truth, so the argument went.

Although he was increasingly arguing himself toward Roman Catholicism, Newman was stuck with having excoriated that body in earlier tracts defending the Thirty-Nine Articles. He set about correcting this in Tract 90, the result of which produced such sparks that no more tracts were published. Newman's agile line of argument was what a lawyer might take hoping to reverse a previously filed brief. He said the issue was not the basic teachings, which remained sound, but distortions that had grown up around them. Not basic doctrine, but the errors of its interpreters were the problem. This was not Newman at his best, but it served its purpose. Moorman says, "Much of the tract is no doubt special pleading unworthy of a great mind."[21]

Newman retired to a village outside Oxford, where he built a semi-monastic community of followers. Increasingly disenchanted with the Church of England, he resigned his position in St. Mary's Church. After a sermon, "The Parting of Friends," he dropped his Oxford master's hood over the communion rail and walked out. On October 8 he wrote, "I am this night expecting Father Dominic the Passionist. . . . He does not know of my intention; but I mean to ask of him admission into the One Fold of Christ."[22]

Newman's Roman Catholic years were often disappointing. Although he lived for an additional forty-five years, his most productive intellectual period was behind him, and he never regained the prominence he once enjoyed. Skilled papal bureaucrats did not share power with the newly arrived nor welcome Newman into the church's inner circles. Conflict was inevitable with the Roman Catholic leader in Britain, Cardinal Manning, himself a convert from the Church of England, who tried to expunge all aspects of the English faith and tradition from Catholic practice. An assignment to the wilds of Ireland to found a university consumed several years for Newman, whose base of operations then shifted to Birmingham. Shortly before his death he was made a cardinal, in part a reward for his supporting the pope. Newman's devotion remained steadfast and his loyalty to Rome unswerving, but the inescapable conclusion is, here was a talent wasted.

It is interesting to speculate as to whether or not Newman was ever really at home in the Church of England. Although he was active in its ministry for many years, Newman never was comfortable with ambiguity and the lack of a clear central authority, such as Rome offered. His quest was a search for such finality, and he found it, although at a costly price, which included the absence of the intellectual freedom and congenial university setting in which his best work was produced. A student of the period has written, "He lacked the willingness to suspend judgment, to recognize the role that doubt may play even in a confident and living faith, to be content with the kind of assurance that the Church of England offers, and to believe that there are many questions to which God in His wisdom has given no clear and incontestable answer."[23] A touching scene from Newman's letters describes the aging cleric visiting his former friend, Keble, at the latter's vicarage near Southampton while Newman was heading for vacation on the Isle of Wight. Neither recognizes the other, and there is the added complication of Pusey having shown up as well:

> As we three sat together at one table, I had as painful thoughts as I ever recollect, though it was a pain, not acute, but heavy. There were three old men, who had worked together vigorously in their prime. This is what they have come to—poor human nature—after 20 years they meet together round a table, but without a common cause, or free outspoken thoughts— but, though kind yet subdued, and antagonistic in their mode of speaking, and all of them with broken prospects.

(Their meeting lasted four hours, and after a meal the bell rang for Pusey to take the evening service. Newman left.)

> Just before my time for going, Pusey went to read the Evening Service in Church, and I was left in the open air with Keble by himself. . . . We walked a little way, and stood looking in silence at the Church and Churchyard, so beautiful and calm. Then he began to converse with me in more than his old tone of intimacy, as if we had never been parted, and soon I was obliged to go.[24]

By the mid-nineteenth century three general tendencies had emerged in the Church of England, representing "high," "low," and "broad" church constituencies. Considerable overlap of belief existed among, and within, the three groups, and differences often depended as much on style as substance. The high church is the easiest to identify, basically those who emerged from the Oxford Movement, stressing the church's lineage to Catholic Christianity represented by episcopate, priesthood, and sacraments. Low church members were generally Evangelicals, emphasizing right conduct and good works and according a "low" place to episcopate, priesthood, and sacraments. Between these relatively narrowly defined positions on the band came a "broad" middle spectrum of

belief and practice whose members were unaccepting of too-precise theological definitions and categorizations, arguing that Anglicanism's
strengths lay in a broad, flexible stance on noncreedal questions. Proponents of the middle ground urged the church to extend its grasp to welcome most orthodox dissenters. In his short but meteoric life, Thomas
Arnold, cited above as an educational reformer, challenged the church, in
Principles of Church Reform (1833). He asked if the church could become
"a Church thoroughly national, thoroughly united, thoroughly Christian, which should allow great varieties of opinion, and of ceremonies,
and forms of worship, according to the various knowledge, and habits,
and tempers of its members, while it truly held one common faith, and
trusted in one common Savior and worshipped one common God."[25]

SAMUEL TAYLOR COLERIDGE

One of the most influential broad church members was the English poet
and philosopher Samuel Taylor Coleridge (1772–1834). He gained the
admiration of many younger clergy for having emerged as an articulate lay
church leader after weathering the ordeals of rationalism, youthful unbelief, Unitarianism, and the onslaughts of German philosophy and scientific
and biblical criticism. Thomas Arnold, and F. D. Maurice, both of whom
he influenced, and their broad church contemporaries did not spring *de novo*
on mid-century England. Their antecedents were seventeenth-century
divines who sought to broaden high church positions and make common
cause with the Puritans. Their successors were twentieth-century figures
such as William Temple and Michael Ramsey, whose breadth of view and
sense of proportion offered contending church factions possibilities of
finding unity. Like Maurice a few years later, Coleridge was an impressionistic, not a systematic, thinker, who called himself an "Inquiring
Spirit." Many of his most perceptive insights were lengthy comments
penned in the margins of his own or borrowed books.

A romantic, the young Colerdige swam the New River fully clothed to
improve his stamina, was briefly infatuated with the French Revolution,
quit Cambridge to join the 15th Dragoons under the name of Silas
Tomkyn Comberbache, became an opium addict, and published poetry
such as "The Rime of the Ancient Mariner" and "Kubla Khan." After
abandoning thoughts of becoming a Unitarian minister, he spent his final
decades as a devout member of the Church of England. (Both his father
and one of his sons were Church of England clergy.) Coleridge was a life-

long friend of another romantic poet, William Wordsworth, and his sister, Dorothy, and the trio visited Germany in 1798, where Coleridge stayed nine months, learned the language, and studied German philosophers, poets, and theologians.

Nineteenth-century Church of England interest in Luther is traceable directly to Coleridge, who was able to battle the invasion of German biblical criticism and philosophy, which he had studied firsthand and could refute by an appeal to Luther's writings and to a religious faith not threatened by new scientific theories. In his *Letters* he writes "In this doctrine my soul can find rest: I hope to be saved by faith—not by my faith but by the faith of Christ in me." Coleridge extolled Luther's doctrine of justification by faith and argued in such works as *Lay Sermons* (1816), *Aids to Reflection* (1824), his most popular prose volume, and *Confessions of an Inquiring Spirit* (1840) that Luther was the successor to St. Paul.

Coleridge deeply admired Luther, sometimes calling him "the German Son of Thunder," "dear Luther, "heroic Luther," or "Thou rare black swan." Aquatic bird imagery reappears in Coleridge, who once said the Reformers took "the goose by the neck and set the knife to the throat" of false papal claims; elsewhere he writes "Yes! heroic Swan, I love thee even when thou gabblest like a goose; for thy geese helped save the Capitol." Still, Coleridge's Reformation was anything but a sentimental period; he once called it "a necessary evil" in history, a time to combat the papal antichrist which subverted church authority while invoking Christ's name. No wonder Newman said his views took "a liberty which no Christian can tolerate"[26]

F. D. MAURICE AND CHRISTIAN SOCIALISM

Newman is often pointed to as the Church of England's most original thinker during the nineteenth century, but that distinction really belongs to a less well known figure, F. D. Maurice. Frederick Denison Maurice (1805–1872), a Unitarian who converted to the Church of England, was an independent and original writer who defies easy categorization, for his interests were equally lively in biblical studies, liturgy, philosophy, and social issues. Maurice linked Christian belief with social reform, worship with political action. Well aware of the Oxford Movement writers, he never joined their numbers, correctly believing they minimized the Protestant contribution to the Church of England. Maurice was professor of divinity at King's College, London, but lost his post in 1853 for holding heretical views, having urged people to reject the doctrine of eternal punishment for sinners. Maurice started evening courses at a Working Man's College, and many prominent scholars donated time freely to this cause. Writers such as John Ruskin and Dante Gabriel Rossetti were among the teachers. Maurice also helped found Queen's College for the education of women in 1848 and from 1846 to 1860 held the prestigious chaplaincy of Lincoln's Inn, for which incumbents were selected by the law community for their ability as preachers. (Maurice had taken his original Cambridge degree in civil law, and later served as editor of a London literary chronicle before obtaining advanced degrees in classics and divinity.)

Maurice's social and theological views were enunciated in 1837 in *The Kingdom of Christ, or Letters to a Quaker concerning the Principles, Conceptions and Ordinances of the Catholic Church,* in which he argued that Christ created a kingdom without class lines, rich or poor, oppressed or oppressor. Among the many followers of Maurice was Charles Dodgson, better known as Lewis Carroll, but Dodgson, an Oxford cleric and mathematician, wrote little on religion and steered clear of the doctrinal controversies raging about him.

Writing to a fellow Christian socialist in 1852, Maurice said:

> [M]y business, because I am a theologian, and have no vocation except for theology, is not to build, but to dig, to show that economy and politics . . . must have a ground beneath themselves, that society is not to be made anew by arrangements of ours, but is to be regenerated by finding the law and ground of its order and harmony, the only secret of its existence, in God. . . . The Kingdom of Heaven is to me the great practical existing reality which is to renew the earth and make it a habitation for blessed spirits instead of for demons.[27]

More a prophet than a systematic thinker, Maurice's creativity darted across several disciplines; in calling himself a "digger" rather than a "builder," he meant his constant forays into the Christian past were the wellsprings of his contemporary inspiration. Maurice said that the Christian Socialist movement meant the church must engage in a conflict with "the unsocial Christians and the un-Christian Socialists."[28] Naturally, Tory believers were vehement in their opposition to what Maurice and his followers were doing, but by the century's second half a new vision of the church's relationship to industrial society was taking shape. Action groups were formed such as the Church of England Total Abstinence Society, the Church Penitentiary Association, the Young Men's Christian Association, the Christian Social Union, the Church Lads' Brigade, Boy

Scouts, Girl Scouts, and similar groups, founding soup kitchens or working with orphans, the unemployed, and prostitutes. By 1873 the Church Congress, an unofficial association of Anglican Church members that gathered periodically between 1861 and 1938, discussed what position the church should take toward strikes and the labor movement. Some clergy lived among the poor, such as the Christian socialist Stewart Hancock, who described the *Magnificat* as "the Hymn of the Social Revolution." Stewart Duckworth Headlam (1847–1924), founded a high church social action group, the Guild of St. Matthew, in 1877, combining Maurice's theological outlook with what remained of the Tractarian movement. It was Maurice's fusion of worship and social action that created a common ground for church members of diverse tendencies.

Maurice's "Christian socialism" was tame compared to the sort of thing Karl Marx argued in his *Communist Manifesto*, published in London in 1848. Maurice called socialism "the science of partnership" and attacked Adam Smith's *laissez-faire* capitalism: "The true law of the universe is that man is made to live in community: men realize their true nature when they cooperate with one another as children of God and brothers in Christ."[29] Compared to later socialist experiments, Maurice's views were mild, advocating education for workers, economic cooperatives, and an awareness of the church's part in realizing the gospel's social implications. Elsewhere, in his *Theological Essays*, Maurice established clearly differing roles for church and state: "The Church is, therefore, human society in its normal state; the world, that same society irregular and abnormal. The world is the Church without God; the Church is the world restored to its relation with God, taken back by him into the state for which He created it. Deprive the Church of its Center and you make it into a world."[30] Drawing on Hooker's earlier work, in particular *The Laws of Ecclesiastical Polity,* for Maurice the kingdom of Christ is both a political and a religious kingdom, where the Church of England is not expected to exist forever as a separate entity, but as an agent of ecumenism, sharing with others its commitment to Christ, as learned through the Bible, tradition, and reason.

Maurice was Anglicanism's most original, comprehensive mind in this century, a figure who invites comparison with Hooker. He wrote about holiness and sacraments, as did Newman, but his lively mind was attracted to other subjects as well. In nearly forty printed volumes his brilliant insights are often buried in sermons, lectures, and articles of no lasting relevance. A far more comprehensive figure than is usually thought of, Maurice wrote equally about the incarnation, Christ's entry into human history through the nativity, the kingdom of God realized in society, and the sacramental life necessary to sustain the latter.

Maurice believed that the kingdom was revealed in the sacraments of baptism and the Eucharist, and in Prayer Book worship. Worship was inseparable from social action; without worship, social action was like the activity of a political party, but in the context of a prayerful life fed by worship, it proclaimed the kingdom. Maurice wrote:

> The worshipper has found that object to which the eyes of himself and all creatures were meant to be directed, in beholding which they attain the perfection of their being, while they lose all the feeling of selfish appropriation which is incompatible with perfection. They gaze upon Him who is the all-embracing Love, with whom no selfishness can dwell, the all-clear and distinguishing Truth, from which darkness and falsehood flee away; and they are changed into the same image, and their praises are only the responses to the joy with which He looks upon His redeemed Creation and declares it very good.[31]

CHARLES GORE AND *LUX MUNDI*

The mid-century church could have gone two ways, toward being an isolated Anglo-Catholic enclave on one side, or toward a more populous Evangelical majority on the other, with a sharp division between the two camps. That it retained its position as a *via media* is largely due to the efforts of a single figure who bridged both traditions, Charles Gore (1853–1932). (It is interesting to speculate what might have happened had Gore, the Church of England's pivotal figure at this time, accepted an offer to become headmaster of St. Paul's School, Concord, New Hampshire. The fierce energy and intellectual brilliance he poured out for half a century in England might have been concentrated on running a school in America instead.)

Gore was a contradictory personality, dogmatic yet doubting, a zealot for the priesthood of all believers, which he inherited from Luther, yet a champion of apostolic succession. Gore never brought these disparate strains together in a theological system; his best arguments appeared in material repeated and reworked over fifty years in books, sermons, and articles that were, like F. D. Maurice's writings, fashioned for particular audiences.

By mid-century the Oxford Movement had run its course; a gap was created with Newman's departure for Rome; new challenges were on the horizon, such as movements of political reform, the intellectual challenge of German biblical criticism, and the advances of science, most of which the Tractarians had left untouched. Gore was born of a titled family and in comfortable circumstances, which left him self-assured in dealing with any audience. An Oxford-educated theologian, he became principal of Pusey House, Oxford, a student center and high church gathering place. Skilled as an administrator, forceful as a preacher, deeply pastoral in contacts with others, Gore was a canon of Westminster and founder of the Community of the Resurrection, a monastic order for men; he became successively bishop of Worcester, Birmingham, and Oxford, until his resignation in 1919.

Archbishop Michael Ramsey wrote: "He was prophetic . . . though a character and indeed a face which seemed to recall the Hebrew prophets in moral intensity and in nearness to God's righteousness and compassion. To hear him recite the psalms in the daily service was to feel oneself listening to the psalmist himself."[32]

The younger Gore was regarded by Oxford Movement remnants as a radical, but in later life he appeared to a new generation of church leaders as a rigid conservative. Gore often said, "I am profoundly convinced with a certainty that is unshakable," but he never disclosed his method of reaching such certainties. Notwithstanding, his impressive voice and prelate's bearing left little doubt where he was coming from. Gore called himself a liberal Catholic, but his liberalism was nothing like political liberalism—in using the word Gore meant his interests and beliefs were considerably broader than those of what remained of the Oxford Movement's successor generation. Gore joined a band of young Oxford clerical intellectuals who were much influenced by Maurice and German criticism. Called the Holy Party, they resembled Wesley's Holy Club of an earlier era and stayed together from 1875 to 1917, exercising a profound influence on the church. Once he joined, Gore became the group's "pope" and from their liberal Catholic deliberations came the Christian Social Union, the formative volume of theological essays *Lux Mundi*, which went through twelve editions in 1889, and later the monastic Community of the Resurrection (1892).

Aware of doubts and difficulties facing intellectuals toward the century's end, Gore tried in *Lux Mundi* and other writings to reconcile the twin systems of religious and scientific authority by clarifying their boundaries. *Lux Mundi* was a typical Church of England theological compendium, a collection of essays resulting from numerous conversations among peers. Some of the church's most insightful works emerge from such periodic collections of articles probing various theological, historical, and ethical topics, for example, *Essays and Reviews* (1860), *Foundations* (1912), *Essays Catholic and Critical* (1926), and *Soundings, or Essays Concerning Christian Understanding* (1962). In the absence of an Anglican Luther, Calvin, Tillich, or Moltmann, and given the lack of any authoritative doctrinal role from councils of bishops or Archbishops of Canterbury, these essay collections gave basic religious questions shape and definition in crucial periods of church history, even if they are personal explorations of issues and not doctrinal pronouncements *ex cathedra*.

An Anglo-Catholic in devotional practice and theology, through unflagging energy and force of personality Gore called the church's attention to social injustice and urban problems. *Lux Mundi* became the most discussed religious volume of its era. In it Gore and other Oxford essayists attempted "to succor a distressed faith by endeavoring to bring the Christian Creed into its right relation to the modern growth of knowledge, scientific, historic, critical; and to modern problems of politics and ethics." If skeptics believed the book did not go far enough, traditional Evangelicals and high church adherents were distressed that it moved far beyond frontiers acceptable to them, especially by appearing to elevate Christ's humanity at the expense of his divinity.

A year later, in the Bampton lectures at Oxford, Gore expanded his views of the incarnation, again to the chagrin of traditionalists. Gore fixed on the problem of reconciling Christ's humanity and divinity. Using the phrase from St. Paul in Philippians 2:7 that "he emptied himself and took upon him the form of a servant," the theologian argued that the earthly Christ accepted all human limitations, shared the knowledge available at the time in which he lived, was subject to temptation, and abandoned any claims to divine omniscience, his divinity being hidden in his humanity while on earth. Predictably, the lectures created controversy, for Gore made no claims of biblical inerrancy or the church's infallibility, but the lectures bridged the worlds of faith and social action, scholarly criticism and belief in ways that would hold for much of the next century. Other authors argued the compatibility of evolution with Christian belief. They pushed the intellectual boundaries of the Catholic movement farther than it had been until now.

As a founder of the Christian Social Union, Gore argued that it was a "monstrous misuse" of Christ's saying "My kingdom is not of this world" to exclude the church from social action. "We deny the verity of the Incarnation in its principle if we deny the Christian spirit the privilege, aye, and the obligation to concern itself with everything that interests and touches human life."[33] Believing the democratic ideals of liberty, equality, and fraternity were of divine origin, Gore argued that such concepts could easily be corrupted because "the *vox populi* can so easily lend itself to the purposes of the evil one."[34] His prophetic side was revealed in what he called a "permanently troubled social conscience" which found political fulfillment in a religious-based socialism that had nothing in common with Marxism. "We shall not get a perfect society. We are not fools," he wrote in dismissing utopian solutions.[35] "Sonship and brotherhood," not economic and class issues, were the pillars of Gore's social theory. In *Christ and Society* Gore described the relationship between religion and social action as being the proposition:

> [t]hat Jesus Christ is really the Savior and redeemer of Mankind, in its social as well as its individual life and in the present world as well as in that which is to come: and that there lies upon those who believe in Him a responsibility which cannot be exaggerated to be true to the principles which He taught, and by all available means to bring them to bear upon the whole life of any society of which they form a part, especially when it professes the Christian name.[36]

A contemporary English theologian, Paul Avis, in a study of Gore's thought, concluded: "In the work of Charles Gore Christian doctrine entered the age of criticism unimpaired and in its wholeness. There is no reductionism in Gore's thought. Anglican theology retains its integrity, its catholicity of truth, its coherence, its checks and balances: deity and humanity, grace and nature, revelation and reason, transcendence and immanence, judgment and mercy. In this respect Gore is a model for us today."[37]

THE MIDDLE YEARS
"Swept with Confused Alarms of Struggle and Flight"

Despite the growth of skepticism and atheism, Victorian England was a largely religious country; church attendance was higher per capita than it would be a century later; family prayer and Bible reading at home were widespread; in rural areas the parish church remained the center of village life; and in cities the church became a formidable social voice. Mainstream Anglicanism was largely Protestant in tenor, the main services being Morning and Evening Prayer, with communion typically once or twice a year—although monthly communion came to be more common

in Wesley's wake. For many Victorians, the struggle was between duty
and pleasure: duty was the high calling—to queen, country, firm, and
family; the pursuit of pleasure could lead to perdition. The Ten Commandments, hung on painted panels behind the altar in many churches,
were for many churchgoers at least as important as the creeds.

Yet, beneath the surface, conventional Christian belief was challenged
by writers from Matthew Arnold to John Stuart Mill, George Eliot to
Thomas Carlyle. A clear statement of mid-century skepticism was contained in Matthew Arnold's *Dover Beach:*

> The Sea of Faith
> Was once, too, at the full, and round earth's shore
> Lay like the folds of a bright girdle furl'd.
> But now I only hear
> Its melancholy, long, withdrawing roar,
> Retreating, to the breath
> Of the night-wind, down the vast edges drear
> And naked shingles of the world.
>
> Ah, love, let us be true
> To one another! for the world, which seems
> To lie before us like a land of dreams,
> So various, so beautiful, so new,
> Hath really neither joy, nor love, nor light,
> Nor certitude, nor peace, nor help for pain;
> And we are here as on a darkling plain
> Swept with confused alarms of struggle and flight,
> Where ignorant armies clash by night.[38]

Science came into its own as an intellectual discipline; political theory
emerged as a branch of learning separate from theology. The literature of
lost faith and the number of doubting persons also grew with the century,
driven by the spread of scientific thought and biblical scholarship from
Germany that questioned an earlier age's placid assumptions. Science and
religion could be compatible, and the church could only gain from biblical scholarship, but none of this was immediately evident, nor was it an
issue for many conventional worshipers for whom such questions were
remote. Ironically, the first rumblings of dissent came from geologists,
whose work with rock samples dated the world much older than tradi-
tionally accepted dates for the Garden of Eden.

The spiritual climate of mid-century Britain is skillfully portrayed by
Alfred Lord Tennyson in his epic poem *In Memoriam.* Driven to writing
it by the death of a close friend, the Poet Laureate reflected on Divine

Providence and human fallibility and mixed both with his concern for the impact of science on the quality of national life. Humanity, nature's "last work, who seem'd so fair" is about to "Be blown about the desert dust, Or seal'd within the iron hills." Tennyson reflected the era's skepticism: "There lives more faith in honest doubt, Believe me, than in half the creeds." The poet's faith finally wins out over doubt:

> Strong Son of God, immortal Love,
>   Whom we that have not seen Thy face,
>   By faith and faith alone embrace,
> Believing where we cannot prove.[39]

Despite the questioning, Victorians' faith remained strong, although the number of adherents declined sharply. An 1851 census, the first of its kind to include religious questions, estimated the population at eighteen million people, five million of them attending Anglican churches. Methodists were the next largest group with 1.5 million members. There were 300,000 Roman Catholics, 800,000 Independents, which included Congregationalists, and 600,000 Baptists.[40] By the century's end, however, only about 20 percent of Londoners attended church regularly. Increasingly, Sunday church services competed with sporting events and family outings, and the church lost members.

The mid-century church in England was far more active in society than in the previous century. Guilds, associations, and other parish and national organizations multiplied; parochial work was more carefully planned; clergy were better educated than before. Mr. Slope in *Barchester Towers*, says:

> It is not only in Barchester that a new man is carrying out new measures and carting away the useless rubbish of centuries. The same thing is going on throughout the country. Work is now required from every man who receives wages; and they who have to superintend the doing of the work, and the paying of the wages, are bound to see that this rule is carried out. New men, Mr. Harding, are now needed, and are now forthcoming in the church, as well as in other professions.[41]

Interest in church decoration, for which the word "sacramentality" was devised, was characteristic of this age. Choir stalls, lecterns, bishops' chairs, and new altars were carved in Gothic-inspired designs. New stained glass windows were commissioned. Moorman wrote, "walls were covered with stencilled designs; ornaments appeared on all sides; acres of damask and embroidery, and tons of brass and marble were carried into the churches; new floors were put down, steps were raised, old woodwork destroyed. Scarcely a church in England escaped the attention of the Victorian 'reformers.'"[42]

Interest in ritual was strong, and volumes with titles like *The Priest's Prayer Book* went through several editions. Post-Tractarians developed a wide range of altar and private devotions; there were more frequent celebrations of the Eucharist, extensive ceremonies, and decorative chancels. The Stations of the Cross hung about churches; black academic gowns gave way to colorful eucharistic vestments; chanting spread and sometimes incense appeared; and within a few decades the use of ritual expanded, and many churches adopted eucharistic vestments, candles on the altar, a sung service, and a robed choir.

MUSIC

Nineteenth-century church reforms affected music as well. Sebastian Wesley, Samuel's son, in 1849 published a reform plan that called for every cathedral to have a core of twelve paid choral members, a salaried organist, and a full-time music copyist. Parish music was at a low ebb; to the minstrels of an earlier era were added a scattering of village choirs, often augmented by the "compulsory scream" of orphans, "charity" children, and Sunday schools before special music for children's voices became widespread. Church music was largely a local affair. Choirs had little training, and even when one of their number went off for schooling, the resultant repertoire on their return changed little from what it had been for decades.

The transition from old to new church music was depicted in Thomas Hardy's *Under the Greenwood Tree* (1872), a work set in a nineteenth-century village. A new vicar, whom the villagers described as "one o' these up-country London ink-bottle chaps," brings a harmonium with him to Mellstock parish. Such instruments, like barrel organs, replaced the long-established church choir and instrumentalists and their bass viols, fiddles, clarinets and brass instruments. "The zeal of these bygone instrumentalists must have been keen and staying, to take them, as it did, on foot every Sunday after a toilsome week through all weathers to the church which often lay at a distance from their homes," Hardy wrote.[43] The vicar, when asked by the musicians why the gallery orchestra will be disbanded, tells them, "I see that violins are good, and that an organ is good; and when we introduce the organ it will not be that fiddles were bad, but that an organ was better."[44] Hardy, a village fiddler who played for such orchestras, wrote:

> The music on Christmas mornings was frequently below the standard of church-performances at other times. The boys were sleepy from the heavy exertions of the night, the men were slightly wearied; and now, in addition to these constant reasons, there was a dampness in the atmosphere that still further aggravated the evil. Their strings, from recent exposure to the night air, rose whole semitones, and snapped with a loud twang at the most silent moment; which necessitated more returning to the back of the gallery, and made the gallery throats quite husky with the quality of coughing and hemming required for tuning it. The vicar looked cross.[45]

In a poignant closing scene, "The old choir, with humbled hearts, no longer took their seats in the gallery" now filled with school children "but were scattered about with their wives in different parts of the church. Having nothing to do with conducting the service for almost the first time in their lives they all felt awkward, out of place," listening to the solo organist but concluding "the simpler notes they had been wont to bring forth were more in keeping with the simplicity of their old church than the crowded chords and interludes it was her pleasure to produce."[46]

Two outcomes of the Oxford Movement were a greater interest in a sung service, especially the psalms and choral responses, and a desire to establish skilled parish choirs along lines until now limited to cathedrals. The number of church choirs grew, and nineteenth-century church music was a distinct improvement on music of the previous century. Notwithstanding, Kenneth R. Long concluded, "in spite of frivolous melodies, juicy harmonies, jog-trot rhythms and lamentable taste, in spite of second-hand quasi-operatic style, brass band type accompaniments and a strong whiff of parlor balladry, this music usually avoided the most heinous fault of all—that sheer stultifying dullness which so often blighted eighteenth century music, especially the Service settings."[47]

The mid-century produced a great number of hymns, representing both Anglo-Catholic and Evangelical traditions. More than 269 different hymnals were in use by the 1870s. Oxford Movement interest in the early church resulted in the revival of many ancient hymns, often in new musical settings, and many new works were added, for example, John Chandler's (1806–1876) "On Jordan's Bank" (tune: *Winchester New*) and Frederick Oakeley's (1802–1880) "O Come, All Ye Faithful" (tune: *Adeste fideles*). John Mason Neale (1818–1866) translated Latin hymns such as "All Glory, Laud and Honor" and "The Royal Banners" (tune: *Vexilla Regis prodeunt*, plainsong). The Evangelical outpouring included H. F. Lyte's (1793–1847) "Praise My Soul, the King of Heaven" (tune: *Lauda anima*), Henry Alford's (1810–1871) "Come, Ye Thankful People, Come" (tune: *St. George's, Windsor*), and Charlotte Elliott's (1789–1871) "Just as I Am" (tune: *Woodworth*). Predictably, both sides called for a hymnal that would contain the best offerings of music then being produced. The result was *Hymns Ancient and Modern*, originally an Anglo-Catholic work that found general acceptance—more than 4.5 million copies were in print by 1868. The book contained 386 hymns drawn from various sources and became a staple of Anglican worship for the coming century. Its content included Newman's "Lead, Kindly Light, amid the Encircling Gloom" (tune: *Lux Benigna*) and the Anglican Evangelical H. F. Lyte's most representative of all Victorian hymns, "Abide with Me, Fast Falls the Eventide" (tune: *Eventide*). More upbeat were "Crown Him with Many Crowns" (tune: *Diademata*) by Matthew Bridges (1800–1894) and Bishop Reginald Herber's (1783–1826) great trinitarian hymn "Holy, Holy, Holy, Lord God Almighty!" (tune: *Nicaea*). A few American hymns made their way into English hymnals, including W. P. Merrill's (1867–1954) "Rise Up, O Men of God" (tune: *Festal Song*) and John Greenleaf Whittier's (1807–1892) "Dear Lord and Father of Mankind" (tune: *Rest*). Many hymns were addressed to children, including Christina Rossetti's (1830–1894) "In the Bleak Mid-winter" (tune: *Cranham*). Samuel Sebastian Wesley (1810–1876), grandson of Charles Wesley, the hymn writer, was a leading cathedral organist and composer, who produced almost thirty anthems, several communion settings and numerous hymns, of which "The Church's One Foundation" (tune: *Aurelia*) is among the best-known.

Kenneth R. Long notes that words count for little in Victorian church music, texts often being squeezed into two- and four-bar phrases, producing, at their worst, lyrics such as the following:

> [H]e's our best bul-, he's our best bul-
> He's our best bulwark still
>
> And catch the flee-
> And catch the fleeting hour
>
> (and) Oh for a man-, Oh for a man-
> Oh for a mansion in the sky.[48]

Notwithstanding, three exceptional choral composers appeared to turn the Victorian tide: Sir Hubert Parry (1848–1918), whose best music was written in the nineteenth century, Sir Charles Villiers Stanford (1852–1924), and Charles Wood (1866–1926). Parry was both professor of music at Oxford and director of the Royal College of Music, and a composer of several anthems for large choirs, organ, and orchestra. His eight-part coronation anthem "I Was Glad" (1902) became well known, as did "At the Round Earth's Imagined Corners" and "My Soul, There Is a Country." Stanford's output of over two hundred works included more than forty choral compositions, including his "Magnificat in G," the motet "Beati quorum," and his "Gloria in excelsis," among this century's most lasting examples of Anglican church music. Charles Wood was a student of Stanford's and eventually his successor at Cambridge, and much of his music was written for the exceptionally able Cambridge university choirs he knew and frequently conducted. Wood wrote about thirty anthems and twenty evening services, in addition to communion settings and a "St. Mark's Passion."

F. W. ROBERTSON, PROPHETIC PREACHER

The church grew steadily through most of this century, despite the buffeting by its intellectual challengers. Many clerics believed that the historic faith could be reconciled with the intellectual challenges it faced in this or any age. One such person, a follower of F. D. Maurice, but like Maurice too original to classify easily, was F. W. Robertson (1816–1853). In the brief span of his thirty-seven years, Robertson won an enduring place in the modern history of the Church of England for his sermons. An Oxford graduate who learned the entire New Testament in English and Greek, Robertson served as assistant in churches in Winchester and Cheltenham, and, for five years as incumbent in Brighton, where he was famous as a preacher before dying from a painful brain tumor, spending his last six months in a shuttered room. Prominence came posthumously as his scant output of one hundred sermons was published in many editions. Many of them were in fragmentary form, but they gained a wide audience and deserve a lasting place for the freshness of their language and the author's courage in treating controversial and difficult subjects in a comprehensive way.

Born into a military family, Robertson, too, had hoped for a soldier's career, but ill health prevented it. The preacher drew numerous images from military history or from the life of the seaside community where he lived. Speaking of the inevitability of people sinning if they do not have moral principles to which they adhere, he compared them, "exactly as if a ship were deserted by the crew, and left on the bosom of the Atlantic with every sail set and the wind blowing. No one forces her to destruction, yet on the rocks she will surely go, just because there is no pilot at the helm."[49]

A lively intelligence and brilliant stylist, Robertson was a prophetic figure, soundly biblical, yet candid and imaginative; he confronted Victorian England's intellectual currents, believing the Christian faith could welcome the discoveries of science, history, and the fine arts. Robertson helped restore the humanity of Jesus to contemporary religion in the aftermath of the distant, mechanical God of the deists. He lamented those whose rigidity of views on Christ's divinity "have petrified it into a theological dogma without life or warmth":

> Feel with Him when He looked round about Him in anger, when He vindicated the crushed woman from the powerless venom of her ferocious accusers; when He stood alone in the solitary Majesty of Truth in Pilate's judgment-hall; when the light of the Roman soldiers' torches flashed on Kedron, in the dark night, and He knew that watching was too late; when His heart-strings gave way upon the Cross. Walk with Him through the Marriage Feast. See how the sick and weary come to Him instinctively; how men, when they saw Him, felt their sin, they knew not why, and fell at His feet; how guilt unconsciously revealed itself, and all that was good in men was drawn out and they became higher than themselves in His presence. Realize this. Live with Him until He becomes a living thought—ever present—and you will find a reverence growing up which compares with nothing else in human feeling.[50]

Robertson's thought was incarnational, but for him the God who entered history in the person of Jesus was fully human, a rarely expressed ideal in the preaching of that time.

> We shrink from believing that He really felt the force of temptation. Or that the forsakenness of the Cross and the momentary doubt have parallels in our human life. . . . But thus we lose the Savior. For it is well to know that He was Divine; but if we lose that truth we should still have a God in heaven. But if there has been on this earth no real, perfect human life, no love that never cooled, no faith that never failed, which may shine as a lodestar across the darkness of our experience. A light to light amidst all convictions of our own meanness and all suspicions of others' littleness, why, we may have a religion, but we have not a Christianity. For if we lose Him as Brother, we cannot feel Him as a Savior.[51]

The young cleric also addressed many of the day's social issues, including the conflict between the rights of property owners and those of laborers. He declared it is "a social falsehood that wealth constitutes superiority, and has a right to the subordination of inferiors." Robertson reminded his hearers, "Whoever helps to keep alive that ancient lie of upper and lower, resting on the distinction not on official authority or personal wealth, but on wealth or title, is doing his part to hinder the establishment of the Redeemer's Kingdom."[52]

REVIVAL OF MONASTIC MOVEMENTS

With the second half of the nineteenth century came the revival of monastic orders in the Church of England, more numerous for women than for men, since it was easier for men to become priests, a possibility denied women. The Anglican Sisters of Mercy worked among the poor, sheltering women, teaching children, and preparing the dead for burial. The Society of St. Margaret in East Grinstead (1855) worked among the rural poor; the Community of St. Mary the Virgin at Wantage (1848) ran schools; the Community of St. John the Baptist in Clewer (1851) worked among unmarried mothers. In each case, works of mercy were fortified by a deep religiosity, fed by corporate worship, centered on the Eucharist and daily offices. The Community of St. Mary at the Cross, Edgware (1865), recited the daily offices in Latin and practiced exposition and Benediction of the Blessed Sacrament, a liturgical rite borrowed from Rome.

The Society of St. John the Evangelist for men was founded in Cowley, England, in 1865; the Community of the Resurrection in Mirfield, Yorkshire, in 1882 (after a stay in Oxford); the Society of the Sacred Mission of Keltham, Newark, in 1894; and the Society of the Divine Compassion, in 1894, in Plainstow, London. In the twentieth century came the Anglican Benedictines of Nashdom, in 1914, and the Society of St. Francis of Cerne, Abbas, in 1921. Many of the male communities became extinct, a handful went over to Rome, and some remained, solid in their prayer life and good works, less bountiful in their membership. Of eighty-two female communities, twenty-one became extinct; none crossed the Tiber; and the rest remained.[53] Many of these monastic houses and convents made an impressive contribution to the church's theology, liturgy, and mission life, and became centers for retreats and conferences. Then and now, they were models of merciful works among the poor and outcast, did much to elevate the dignity of destitute people, especially women and children, and set norms of Christian behavior and standards for Christian worship.

CHARLES DARWIN, SCIENCE AND RELIGION

Science was to this age what theology had been to earlier centuries, providing a comprehensive system of beliefs, the assurance of certainty, and a universality of application. Several works on natural history had cracked open the biblical literalism of the Genesis creation myths, but in 1859 Charles Darwin published his monumental *Origin of Species* and in 1871 *The Descent of Man*, revolutionizing England's intellectual landscape. Instead of a separate creation of each species, Darwin made a case for natural selection, a gradual evolution of species in response to adaptation to their environment. Humanity, he argued, represented the highest form of such development, an improvement on the anthropoid apes from which humans emerged over the millennia. The shock waves Darwin's work produced still have not settled everywhere, but were even more disturbing in their time. A Victorian, when confronted with Darwin's findings, said, "I hope they are not true, and if they are, I hope people will have the decency not to talk about them in public." Later generations of Christian intellectuals could see the compatibility of scientific and religious teachings, but few such figures were evident in the 1870s and 1880s. Benjamin Disraeli received warm support for his 1864 remark to an Oxford religious group, "The question is this—Is man an ape or an angel? My lord, I am on the side of the angels," but such comments proved little. While many active church members regarded any questioning of faith as heretical, many scholars welcomed the scientific study of the Bible and contributed solidly to bridging the gap between science and religion. This was also a productive time in biblical studies. The Revised Version of the Bible appeared in the 1880s; numerous biblical commentaries and studies followed toward the century's end.

German and French linguistic and archaeological scholarship questioned the Bible's historical content. The era saw many works about the earthly life of Jesus. In theological language this was the religion of the incarnation rather than of the atonement, emphasizing Christ's humanity and earthly life rather than his suffering. Celebrations of Christmas were widespread after mid-century, and the birth stories attracted increasing interest; Christmas carols proliferated, Dickens's *Christmas Carol* was published in 1843, and holiday feasts and good cheer became staples of English life, spreading plum pudding and Christmas trees to the ends of the empire.

OVERSEAS MISSIONS

The nineteenth century was the great century of British overseas expansion, and if the sun never set on the British Empire, it likewise never set on the missionary works of the Church of England, as overseas dioceses proliferated, the Bible was translated into local languages, and missionaries, teachers, and medical practitioners went abroad for the church. Regular voyages by iron ships left British ports for countries around the world. Great numbers of persons departed home to seek fortunes abroad, to serve as colonial administrators, in the military, with trading companies, or as missionaries and teachers. In the year 1888 it was estimated that nearly twelve million people had gone abroad during the past seventy years, and that 250,000 were leaving the British Isles each year.[54] By 1882 seventy-two new dioceses were scattered throughout the world from North America and the West Indies to India and Africa.

A problem was that the Church of England expanded overseas, but never satisfactorily solved sharing the episcopal office with overseas dioceses until well into the nineteenth century. Since the Church of England was a state church, new bishops were expected to exercise a role as state representatives. An Act of 1786 provided for the church to consecrate as bishops persons "being Subjects or Citizens of countries out of His Majesty's dominions" but it was rarely used. By the mid-1850s, however, there was strong sentiment for overseas expansion, a Colonial Bishoprics Fund was created, and gradually independent overseas dioceses formed, leading to an eventual loosely organized Anglican Communion.

The overseas church was largely the work of Evangelicals. Calcutta was the first of the overseas bishoprics, founded in 1814; Australia in 1836, Cape Town in 1847, Singapore in 1855, Melanesia in 1861, China in 1872, Rangoon in 1877, Jerusalem and the East (refounded) in 1886. The Protestant Episcopal Church in the United States was organized in 1789, but even by 1830 it was no more than thirty thousand communicants, largely limited to the eastern seaboard; by the 1840s several bishoprics were established in the West Indies. A diocese was formed in Hong Kong in 1849; the Church of the Province of New Zealand adopted its constitution in 1857; the Province of Canada in 1862. A constitution for the Church of the Province of South Africa was realized in 1870. In 1864 an African and freed slave, Samuel Adjai Crowther, then ministering in Nigeria, became the first non-European Anglican consecrated a bishop for Africa. Groups such as the Universities' Mission to Central Africa and the Church Missionary Society established the church in east and central Africa.

Until the age of expansion there had been little talk of overseas missions, or of a worldwide church, but such a body in fact evolved. Missionaries pushed through African jungles and Arctic wastes, learned the languages of India, and braved pestilential climates to create schools, hospitals, and churches. Some were killed; others contracted debilitating diseases; but by the century's end a global missionary presence was assured. It would be erroneous, however, to paint a picture of untrammeled conquest. While in places like East Africa the number of new Christians was large, Christians were always a distinct minority in India and Japan, where local peoples found the missionary hospitals and schools often more attractive than churches.

Some missionaries became skilled linguists and others wrote pioneering studies of local customs, but a source of constant friction was the missionaries' cultural imperialism, their frequent intolerance of local habits, and their disinterest in traditional values of the peoples with whom they now lived. English liturgical practices and clerical dress were exported, as were English music and architecture, resulting in such incongruities as a neo-Gothic cathedral with small lancet windows and thick brick walls being placed by the seashore in Accra, Ghana, or indigenous bishops in gaiters, traditional English riding dress. While there were always impressive exceptions, not all missionaries were on a comparable cultural footing with the country's leaders, understood their aspirations, and knew their histories. Thus converts, in India for instance, came from the poor and outcast, admirable from a gospel viewpoint, but not as a matter of establishing long-term influence among the leaders of local societies.

The picture of missionary expansion, however, was by no means a triumphal journey. Disease and martyrdom claimed their numbers. For example, James Hannington became bishop of Eastern Equatorial Africa in 1884, and began a tragic voyage toward Uganda. He wrote on July 22:

> The outlook is gloomy. . . . Starvation, desertion, treachery, and a few other nightmares and furies hover over one's head in ghostly forms, and yet in spite of it all, I feel in capital spirits. Let me beg every mite of spare prayer. You must uphold my hands, lest they fall. If this is the last chapter of earthly history, then the next will be the first page of the heavenly—no

blots and smudges, no incoherence, but sweet converse in the presence of the Lamb.

He was held prisoner by a regional king near the Uganda border and wrote:

> 28th. 7th day. A terrible night; first with noisy, drunken guard, and secondly with vermin, which have found out my tent and swarm. I don't think I got one hour's sleep, and woke with fever fast developing. O Lord, do have mercy on me, and release me! I am quite broken down and brought low. Comforted by reading 27th Psalm. Fever developed very rapidly . . . soon was delirious.

> Evening. Fever passed away. Word came that Mwanga [the king—*ed.*] had sent three soldiers, but what news they bring they will not yet let me know. Much comforted by the 28th Psalm.

> 29th (8th day). I can hear no news, but was held up by the 30th Psalm, which came with great power. A hyena howled near me last night, smelling a sick man. I hope it is not to have me yet.

Shortly thereafter the bishop and his fifty porters were led out and were killed. Widespread persecution of Christians followed, many being killed or sold to Arab slavers.[55]

By the beginning of the twentieth century, grave difficulties were perceived by some in the effort to transmit Western Christianity to people in very different cultures and backgrounds. The difficulties deeply challenged a young English missionary in North China, Roland Allen (1868–1947), who sought to drastically change the entire colonial and paternalistic system of mission governance. Returning to England, he devoted the rest of his life to writing about missionary questions and visiting missionary sites in various parts of the world. He argued that indigenous peoples should be given control of their own churches and the responsibility of supporting them. He also proposed that they identify their own spiritual leaders and present them to their bishops for ordination. Their devotion and commitment to the Christian gospel and the confidence of their friends and neighbors would be their qualification for ordination, rather than the academic study of Western literature. He proposed that many such clergy should earn their livings by secular work, as St. Paul did in the New Testament. In the latter part of the twentieth century, Allen's writings have won increasingly serious attention and his ideas have been successfully put into practice for some years in Alaska, and more recently in a number of other locations. The needs and opportunities of mission fields are thus beginning to influence the home churches.

READINGS

Francis Kilvert

Francis Kilvert (1840–1889), whose published diaries belong to the handful of English clergy accounts deserving a lasting place as literature, spent most of his life in obscure parishes near the Welsh border. He did not have a living of his own until two years before his untimely death, and he died a month after his marriage. A meticulous diary keeper, Kilvert's twenty-two volumes covering the last nine years of his life can be compared in literary quality to the works of Dorothy Wordsworth or to John Constable's paintings. Like Jane Austen, he was a keen observer of life about him, especially rural England in the days before the Industrial Revolution's impact reached far southwestern villages and valleys.

Saturday, Easter Eve, 16 April, 1870

I awoke at 4:30 and there was a glorious sight in the sky, one of the grand spectacles of the Universe. There was not a cloud in the deep wonderful blue of the heavens. Along the Eastern horizon there was a clear deep intense glow neither scarlet nor crimson but a mixture of both. This red glow was very narrow, almost like a riband and it suddenly shaded off into the deep blue. Opposite in the west the full moon shining in all its brilliance was setting upon the hill beyond the church steeple. Thus the glow in the east bathed the church in a warm rich tinted light, while the moon from the west was casting strong shadows. The moon dropped quickly down behind the hill bright to the last, till only her rim could be seen sparkling among the tops of the orchards on the hill. The sun rose quickly and the rays struck red upon the white walls of Penllan, but not so brilliantly as in the winter sunrisings. I got up soon after 5 and set to work on my Easter sermon getting two hours for writing before breakfast.

At 11 I went to the school. Next I went to Cae Mawr. Mrs. Morrell had been very busy all the morning preparing decorations for the Font, a round dish full of flowers in water and just big enough to fit into the Font and upon this large dish a pot filled and covered with flowers all wild, primroses, violets, wood anemones, wood sorrel, periwinkles, oxlips and the first blue bells, rising in a gentle pyramid, ferns and larch sprays drooping over the brim, a wreath of simple ivy to go round the stem of the Font, and a bed of moss to encircle the foot of the Font in a narrow band pointed at the corners and angles of the stone with knots of primroses. . . . Found the schoolmaster and a friend staying with him just going out to get moss and carrying the East window-sill board from the Church to the school to prepare it for tomorrow with the text "Christ is Risen" written in primroses upon moss. Shall I ever forget that journey up the hill to Cefn y Blaen in this burning Easter Eve, under the cloudless blue, the scorching sun, and over the country covered with a hot dim haze?

When I started for Cefn y Blaen only two or three people were in the churchyard with flowers. But now the customary beautiful Easter Eve Idyll had fairly begun and people kept arriving from all parts with flowers to dress the graves. Children were coming from the town and from neighboring villages with baskets of flowers and knives to cut holes in the turf. The roads were lively with people coming and going and the churchyard a busy scene with women and children and a few men moving about among the tombstones and kneeling down beside the green mounds flowering the graves. An evil woman from Hay was dressing a grave (Jane Phillips). I found Annie Dyke standing among the graves with her basket of flowers. A pretty picture she would have made as she stood there with her pure fair sweet grave face and clustering brown curls shaded by her straw hat and her flower basket hanging on her arm. It was her birthday today. I always tell her she and the cuckoos came together. So I went home to get a little birthday present I had been keeping for her, which I bought in the Crystal Palace in January, a small ivory brooch, with the carved figure of a stag. I took the little box which held it out into the churchyard and gave it to her as she was standing watching while the wife of one of her father's workmen, the shepherd, flowered the grave that she came to dress, for her.

More and more people kept coming into the churchyard as they finished their day's work. The sun went down in glory behind the dingle, but still the work of love went on through the twilight and into the dusk until the moon rose full and splendid. The figures continued to move about among the graves and to bend over the green mounds in the calm clear moonlight and warm air of the balmy evening.

At 8 o'clock there was a gathering of the Choir in the Church to practice the two anthems for tomorrow. The moonlight came streaming in broadly through the chancel windows. When the choir had gone and the lights were out and the church quiet again, as I walked down the Churchyard alone the decked graves had a strange effect in the moonlight and looked as if the people had laid down to sleep for the night out of doors, ready dressed to rise early on Easter morning. I lingered in the verandah before going to bed. The air was as soft and warm as a summer night, and the broad moonlight made the quiet village almost as light as day. Everyone seemed to have gone to rest and there was not a sound except the clink and trickle of the brook.

Palm Sunday, 24 March, 1872

A snowy Palm Sunday. Mr. Venables went to Bettws in a dense snow-storm. In the afternoon I had the happiness to have all the poor people to myself. None of the grand people were at Church by reason of the snow. So of course I could speak much better and more freely.

After service I went up to the Bird's Nest to see old Meredith. Further up I stopped and turned to look at the view. I saw what I thought was a long dazzling white and golden cloud up in the sky. Suddenly I found that I had been gazing at the great snow slopes of the Black Mountain lit up by the setting sun and looking through the dark storm clouds. It was a sublime spectacle, the long white rampart dazzling in its brilliancy and warmed by a golden tinge standing high up above the clear dark line of the nearer hills taking the sunshine, and bathed in glory. Then in the silence Hay Church bell for evensong boomed suddenly out across the valley.

Saturday, 5 January, 1878

Speaking of . . . the kneeling and weeping of the oxen on old [calm—ed.] Christmas Eve (tonight) Priscilla said, "I have known old James Meredith 40 years and I have never known him far from the truth, and I said to him one day, 'James, tell me the truth, did you ever see the oxen kneel on old Christmas Eve at the Weston?' And he said, 'No, I never saw them kneel at the Weston but when I was at Hinton at Staunton-on-Wye I saw them. I was watching them on old Christmas Eve and at 12 o'clock the oxen that were standing knelt down upon their knees and there they stayed kneeling and moaning, the tears running down their faces.'"[56]

John Henry Newman

His eight volumes of sermons are among John Henry Newman's most enduring contributions to writings on spirituality. Most were delivered to university congregations on Sunday afternoons at St. Mary's Church, Oxford. They resemble contemporary French or earlier treatises on cure of the soul. Newman's driving interest was the quest for holiness, and he set out to instruct audiences in how to achieve it. The sermons, called *Parochial and Plain Sermons,* are focused and practical; sections from one could easily replace sections of another. Newman frequently quotes from the Bible to illustrate points, but his desire was for hearers to strip away every impediment to a life of holiness. "Is not holiness the result of many patient, repeated efforts after obedience, gradually working on us, and first modifying and then changing our hearts?" His sermons are filled with psychological insights, although he lived and wrote in an era before psychology was a fully developed science; in one sermon he wrote "how mysteriously little things are in this world connected with great; how single moments, improved or wasted, are the salvation or ruin of all-important interests." Thus, "That little deed, suddenly exacted of us, almost suddenly resolved on and executed, may be as a gate into the second or third heaven."

Worship, a Preparation for Christ's Coming
(Advent)

"Thine eyes shall see the King in His beauty: they shall behold the land that is very far off."—Isaiah 33:17

Year after year, as it passes, brings us the same warnings again and again, and none perhaps more impressive than those with which it comes to us at this season. The very frost and cold, rain and gloom, which now befall us, forebode the last dreary days of the world, and in religious hearts raise the thought of them. The year is worn out; spring, summer, autumn, each in turn, have brought their gifts and done their utmost; but they are over, and the end is come. All is past and gone, all has failed, all has sated; we are tired of the past; we would not have the seasons longer; and the austere weather which succeeds, though ungrateful to the body, is in tone with our feelings, and acceptable. Such is the frame of mind which befits the end of the year; and such the frame of mind which comes alike on good and bad at the end of life. The days have come in which they have no pleasure; yet they would hardly be young again, could they be so by wishing it. Life is well enough in its way; but it does not satisfy. Thus the soul is cast forward upon the future, and in proportion as its conscience is clear and its perception keen and true, does it rejoice solemnly that "the night is far spent, the day is at hand," that there are "new heavens and a new earth" to come, though the former are failing; nay, rather that, because they are failing, it will "soon see the King in His beauty," and "behold the land which is very far off." These are feelings for holy men in winter and in age, waiting, in some dejection perhaps, but with comfort on the whole, and calmly though earnestly, for the Advent of Christ.

And such, too, are the feelings with which we now come before Him in prayer day by day. The season is chill and dark, and the breath of the morning is damp, and worshipers are few, but all this benefits those who are by profession penitents and mourners, watchers and pilgrims. More dear to them than loneliness, more cheerful than severity, and more bright than gloom, than all those aids and appliances of luxury by which men nowadays attempt to make prayer less disagreeable to them. True faith does not covet comforts. It only complains when it is forbidden to kneel, when it reclines upon cushions, is protected by curtains, and encompassed by warmth. Its only hardship is to be hindered, or to be ridiculed, when it would place itself as a sinner before its Judge. They who realize that awful Day when they shall see Him face to face, whose eyes are as a flame of fire, will as little bargain to pray pleasantly now, as they will think of doing so then.

One year goes and then another, but the same warnings recur. The frost or the rain comes again; the earth is stripped of its brightness; there is nothing to rejoice in. And then, amid this unprofitableness of earth and sky, the well-known words return; the Prophet Isaiah is read: the same Epistle and Gospel, bidding us "awake out of sleep," and welcome Him "that cometh in the Name of the Lord"; the same Collects, beseeching Him to prepare us for judgment. Oh, blessed they who obey these warning voices, and look out for Him whom they have not seen, because they "love His appearing!"

We cannot have fitter reflections at this Season than those which I have entered upon. What may be the destiny of other orders of beings we know not;—but this we know to be our own fearful lot, that before us lies a time when we must have the sight of our Maker and Lord face to face. We know not what is reserved for other beings; there may be some, which, knowing nothing of their Maker, are never to be brought before Him. For what we can tell, this may be the case with the brute creation. It may be the law of their nature that they should live and die, or live on an indefinite period, upon the very outskirts of His government, sustained by Him, but never permitted to know or approach Him. But this is not our case. We are destined to come before Him; nay, and to come before Him in judgment; and that on our first meeting; and that suddenly. We are not merely to be rewarded or punished, we are to be judged. Recompense is to come upon our actions, not by a mere general provision or course of nature, as it does at present, but from the Law-giver Himself in person. We have to stand before His righteous Presence, and that one by one. One by one we shall have to endure His holy and searching eye. At present we are in a world of shadows. What we see is not substantial. Suddenly it will be rent in twain and vanish away, and our Maker will appear. And then, I say, the first appearance will be nothing less than a personal intercourse between the Creator and every creature. He will look on us, while we look on Him.

Now, when this state of the case, the prospect which lies before us, is brought home to our thoughts, surely it is one which will lead us anxiously to ask, Is this all that we are told, all that is allowed to us, or done for us? Do we know only this, that all is dark now, and all will be light then; that now God is hidden, and one day will be revealed? That we are in a world of sense, and are to be in a world of spirits? For surely it is our plain wisdom, our bounden duty, to prepare for this great change;—and if so, are any directions, hints, or rules given us *how* we are to prepare? "Prepare to meet thy God," "Go ye out to meet Him," is the dictate of natural reason, as well as of inspiration. But *how* is this to be?

Now observe, that it is scarcely a sufficient answer to this question to say that we must strive to obey Him, and so to approve ourselves to Him. This indeed might be enough, were reward and punishment to follow in the mere way of nature, as they do in this world. But, when we come steadily to consider the matter, appearing before God, and dwelling in His presence, is a very different thing from being merely subjected to a system of moral laws, and would seem to require another preparation, a special preparation of thought and affection, such as will enable us to endure His countenance, and to hold communion with Him as we ought. Nay, and, it may be, a preparation of the soul itself for His presence, just as the bodily eye must be exercised in order to bear the full light of day, or the bodily frame in order to bear exposure to the air.

And what is true of the ordinary services of religion, public and private, holds in a still higher or rather in a special way, as regards the sacramental Ordinances of the Church. In these is manifested in greater or lesser degree, according to the measure of each, that Incarnate Savior, who is one day to be our Judge, and who is enabling us to bear His Presence then, by imparting it to us in measure now. A thick black veil is spread between this world and the next. We mortal men range up and down it, to and fro, and see nothing. There is no access through it into the next world. In the Gospel this veil is not removed; it remains, but every now and then marvelous disclosures are made to us of what is behind it. At times we seem to catch a glimpse of a Form which we shall hereafter see face to face. We approach, and in spite of the darkness, our hands, or our head, or our brow, or our lips become, as it were, sensible of the contact of something more than earthly. We know not where we are, but we have been bathing in water, and a voice tells us that this is blood. Or we have a mark signed on our foreheads, and it spake of Calvary. Or we recollect a hand laid upon our heads, and surely it had the print of nails in it, and resembled Him who with a touch gave sight to the blind and raised the dead. Or we have been eating and drinking; and it is not a dream surely, that One fed us from his wounded side, and renewed our nature by the heavenly meat He gave. Thus in many ways He, who is Judge to us, prepares us to be judged,—He who is to glorify us, prepares us to be glorified, that He may not take us unawares; but that when the voice of the Archangel sounds, and we are called to meet the Bridegroom, we may be ready.[57]

F. D. Maurice

Maurice does not make for easy reading, although he is among Anglicanism's most creative theological voices. Cranmer wrote lucidly on the issues of his time, such as the Prayer Book and the Sacraments. Andrewes, Jewell, and Donne had seasons of brilliance. Newman was by far the Church of England's best prose stylist and unexcelled as a writer on holiness and the richness of the early church. Maurice exceeded them all in range of subject matter attempted and prophetic relevance to the church. But Maurice's insights are episodic, arresting passages buried in sermons and lectures on dated topics. Newman had a constant Oxford audience for his best work; Maurice moved among various academic and church positions in London and Cambridge, which deprived him of a regular congregation until his later years. And at a time when German systematic theology was emerging, Maurice's approach went in the opposite direction; he was an episodic rather than a systematic thinker.

Sometimes his messages emerge as "hints," a word Maurice used often. He employed the Socratic method, and reworked the same material several times. It is not for nothing Maurice called himself "only a digger" whose task was "metaphysical and theological grubbing."[58] His prose style was not memorable, and his irenic, charitable temperament contrasts with the sharpness of his polemics. Maurice belonged to no school of thought, and generally distanced himself from all proponents in a controversy, with the result that he was generally left alone in his own corner in a dispute.

The Book of Common Prayer

I do not want to force any one to like it; nor do I care a sixpence for it as a piece of fine composition. I never called it "an excellent liturgy" in my life, and hope I never shall. But it has helped me to see more of the love of God and the bonds by which men are knit to each other, and to feel more hope as to those whom I should naturally regard as foes, than any other book except the Bible. It is my protection and the protection of the Church against Anglicanism and Evangelicalism and Liberalism and Romanism and Rationalism, and till these different devils cease to torment us, I will, with God's help, use this shield against them.[59]

Church Parties

Above all, we must never be tempted to that greatest of all sins, the forming of a new party for the sake of displacing or overcoming existing parties. That temptation will present itself in ten-thousand forms. The Evil Spirit will come as an Angel of Light. He will tell us that it is not a new party we are to construct—that would be very wicked—but a protest against all parties; in fact, a larger Church, a freer and more expansive Christianity. Accursed sophist! *We* construct a Church! *We* lay a broader foundation for Humanity than God has laid in his Son! *We* invent a more comprehensive Gospel than the Gospel of the Ascension, that he has gone up on high, leading captivity captive, glorifying our Nature at the right-hand of his Father! Such an experiment would concentrate all the arrogance and unbelief of former sects into one grand, devilish scheme for our self-exaltation. The Society we assisted in forming would be the Society of the AntiChrist. No, brethren! In this sense of attempting to compete with parties, or imitate them, or supersede them, we must let them wholly alone. In another sense, we must never let them alone; we must be continually tormenting them. The Apostles did not uproot the sect of the Pharisees, but they preached the corner-stone of Humanity."[60]

Baptism, the Sacrament of Constant Union

Baptism asserts for each man that he is taken into union with a divine Person, and by virtue of that union is emancipated from his evil *Nature*. But this assertion rests upon another, that there is a society for mankind which is constituted and held together in that Person, and that he who enters this society is emancipated from the *world*—the society which is bound together in the acknowledgment of, and subjection to, the evil selfish tendencies of each man's nature. But, further, it affirms that this unity among men rests upon a yet more awful and perfect unity, upon that which is expressed in the *Name* of the Father, the Son, and the Holy Ghost. Lose sight of this last and deepest principle, and both the others perish.[61]

The Eucharist

Communion with God, in the largest and fullest sense of that word, is not an instrument of attaining some higher end, but is itself the end to which he is leading his creatures, and after which his creatures, in all kingdoms, and nations, and languages—by all their schemes of religion, by all their studies of philosophy, by art, by science, by politics, by watching, by weeping, by struggling, by submitting, by wisdom, by folly, in the camp and in the closet, in poverty and riches, in honor and in shame, in health and sickness, are secretly longing and crying, and without which they cannot be satisfied.[62]

Bible

"The Bible," we are told sometimes, "gives us such a beautiful picture of what we should be." Nonsense! It gives us no picture at all. It reveals to us a fact; it tells us what we actually are; it says, "this is the form in which God created you, to which he has restored you, this is the work which the Eternal God, the God of truth and love, is continually carrying on within you."[63]

There is no book which speaks so much of shepherds and their flocks, of the most ordinary doings of families, or nations and laws, and wars; of all that we are wont to call vulgar and secular things. You might call the subject matter of the greater part of the Book of Genesis, the disputes between brothers, and the famines which afflicted Palestine and Egypt . . . the subject matter of all the books of the Old Testament, the various fortunes of an Eastern people. . . . Must we not then say that the Revelation or unveiling of the divine or supernatural, if it is made at all, is made *through* these relations of ordinary daily life? Is not this the great characteristic of the Book, the one which, if we take it to be the record of a continuous Revelation, prepares us for the full manifestation in the Son of Man?[64]

The Nation

Destroy national characteristics, reduce us merely into one great society, and whether the bond of that society is a pope, or an emperor, or a customs-union, the result is the same. A living God is not feared or believed in; he is not the center of that combination; his name or the name of a number of Gods may be invoked in, but his presence is not that which holds its different elements together. Therefore let us be sure that if we would ever see a real family of nations, such as the prophets believed would one day emerge out of the chaos they saw around them, a family of nations which shall own God as their Father and Christ as their elder Brother, this must come from each nation maintaining its own integrity and unity.[65]

A National Church should mean a Church which exists to purify and elevate the mind of a nation; to give those who make and administer and obey its laws, a sense of the grandeur of law and of the source whence it proceeds; to tell the rulers of the nation, and all the members of the nation, that all false ways are ruinous ways, that truth is the only stability of our time or of any time. It should exist to make men tremble at the voice of God speaking to them in their consciences, to tell them what he is telling them will be proclaimed before the universe, that every deed which men wish to hide shall be brought forth into the clear and open day. This should be the meaning of a national Church; a nation wants a Church for these purposes mainly; a Church is abusing its trust if it aims at any other or lower purposes.[66]

The Danger of Sects

I think the Church of England is the witness in our land against the sect principle of "forming churches" which is destroying us and the Americans too. . . . As long as we think we can form churches we cannot be witnesses for a Humanity and for a Son of man. We cannot believe that we do not choose him, but that he chooses us and sends us to bear witness of his Father and of him. Everything seems to me involved in this difference. I admit that the English Church is in a very corrupt, very evil condition. I am not afraid to own that, because I believe it is a Church and not a sect. The sect feeling, the sect habit, is undermining it. The business of us who belong to it is to repent of our sectarianism and to call our brothers to repent, to show that we have a ground on which all may stand with us.[67]

Unity

I believe that the language of some excellent persons, who say, we must not give up truth for the sake of unity, though it contains a valuable meaning, is yet far less sound than it appears to be; for I see that truth is suffering every day and hour from the absence of unity.[68]

Church of England

The Church should rejoice in its unique history not because it separates us from men to the left and to the right, but because it enables us to do each justice; not because it gives us the right to despise either, but the privilege of learning from both; not because it tempts us to copy portions of the systems of one or the other, but because we can see from it that each has something better than a system; not because it cherishes in us a love of theoretical wavering, but because it provides us with a basis of practical certainty; not because it makes us satisfied with our exclusive nationality, but because by not abandoning that nationality we become witness of a bond and center for all.[69]

Charles Gore

Charles Gore and other Oxford intellectual clerics of the Holy Party each summer spent a month in the country, where they would take over a vicarage while its incumbent went on vacation. The young clergy took the round of daily services, had a good time, and talked extensively about church issues. Out of their deliberations came *Lux Mundi, A Series of Studies in the Religion of the Incarnation* (1899) edited by Gore, their "pope." Using the theme of the incarnation, the presence of God in history through the person of Jesus the Christ, the remarkable series of essays quickly went through several editions and created a sensation. The authors tried to bridge traditional faith with modern scholarship and in doing so created an intellectual firestorm that endured for decades.

Gore's study of "The Holy Spirit and Inspiration" was among the work's most controversial essays. In it Gore described the Holy Spirit at work in creation, as reflected in the Old and New Testaments. He said it is not necessary to hold that the Old Testament narratives are literal accounts and that Jesus, in referring to them, did so with the intellectual limitations of a human being of his time. Thus, while Jesus revealed God's character and purpose through his divinity, in his humanity he made no claim to anticipate all human knowledge, past, present, and future. Jesus' comments about the Old Testament are thus spoken from the perspective of a teacher of his period. Gore saw Jesus' self-limitation as *kenōsis*, an "emptying" of his powers allowing him to function as a human subject to natural forces while still being the Son of God, third person of the Trinity. While his perspective was generally acceptable to his contemporaries and helped fuse the new scientific knowledge and biblical criticism with conventional religion, it was more than many Anglo-Catholics and Evangelicals could accept. They produced a flurry of books, pamphlets, and sermons in response to *Lux Mundi*, to the initial puzzlement of its authors.

The Holy Spirit and Inspiration

The appeal to "experience" in religion, whether personal or general, brings before the mind so many associations of ungoverned enthusiasm and untrustworthy fanaticism that it does not easily commend itself to those of us who are most concerned to be reasonable. . . . The fact is that in current appeals to experience the fault, where there is a fault, lies not in the appeal but in the nature of the experience appealed to. What is meant by the term is often an excited state of feeling, rather than a permanent transformation of the whole moral, intellectual and physical being of man. Or it is something which seems individual and eccentric, or something confined to a particular class of persons under special conditions of education or of ignorance, or something which other religions besides Christianity have been conspicuous for producing. When a meaning broad and full, and at the same time exact enough, has been given to experience, the appeal is essential to Christianity, because Christianity professes to be not a mere record of the past, but a present life, and there is no life where there is no experience.

The Fathers of the Christian Church appealed in this way to experience, because Christianity, as they knew, is essentially not a past event, but a present life, a life first manifested in Christ, and then perpetrated in His Church. Christianity is a manifested life,—a thing, therefore, like all other forms of life, known not in itself, but by its effects, its fruits, its results. Christianity is a manifested life, and it is this because it is the sphere in which the Spirit, the Life-giver finds His freest and most unhindered activity. . . . The Spirit is life; that is His chief characteristic.

Of the work of the Holy Spirit in the Church we may note four characteristics.

1. It is *social*. It treats man as a "social being" who cannot realize himself in isolation. For no other reason than because grace is the restoration of nature, the true, the redeemed humanity is presented to us as a society or Church.

2. But none the less on account of this social method *the Spirit nourishes individuality*. The very idea of the Spirit's gift is that of an intenser life. Intenser life is a more individualized life, for our life becomes richer and fuller only by intensification of personality and character.

3. Thirdly, the Spirit claims for His own, and *consecrates the whole of nature*. One Spirit was the original author of all that is; and all that exists is in its essence very good. It is only sin which has produced the appearance of antagonism between the Divine operation and human freedom, or between the spiritual and the material. Thus the humanity of Christ, which is the Spirit's perfect work, exhibits in its perfection how every faculty of

human nature, spiritual and physical, is enriched and vitalized, not annihilated, by the closest conceivable interaction of Divine Energy.

4. But the unity of the spirit and the flesh, of faith and experience, of God and the world, is certainly not an accomplished fact. . . . Thus if the Church was to maintain the unity of all things, it could only be by laying great stress upon the ravages which sin has wrought, and upon *the gradualness of the Spirit's method* in recovery. . . . It is because of this gradualness of the Spirit's method that it lays so great a strain on human patience. The spiritually minded of all ages have tended to find the visible Church a very troubled and imperfect home.

III. Hitherto nothing has been said about that part of the Holy Spirit's work which is called the inspiration of Scripture.

The Church is not tied . . . by any existing definitions. We cannot make any exact claim upon any one's belief in regard to inspiration, simply because we have no authoritative definition to bring to bear. . . . Those of us who believe most in the inspiration of the Church will see a Divine Providence in this absence of dogma, because we shall perceive that only now is the state of knowledge such as admits of the question being legitimately raised . . . our Lord uses the time before the flood to illustrate the carelessness of men before His own coming. He is using the flood here as a typical judgment, as elsewhere He uses other contemporary visitations for a like purpose. In referring to the flood He certainly suggests that He is treating it as typical, for he introduces circumstances—"eating and drinking, marrying and giving in marriage"—which have no counterpart in the original narrative. Nothing in his use of it depends on its being more than a typical instance.

There are, we notice, other occasions when our Lord asked questions which cannot be made the basis of positive propositions. It was in fact part of His method to lead men to examine their own principles, without at the time suggesting any positive conclusion at all. It may also fairly be represented, on a review of our Lord's teaching as a whole, that if He had intended to convey instruction to us on critical and literary questions, He would have made His purpose plainer. It is contrary to His whole method to reveal His Godhead by any anticipations of natural knowledge. The Incarnation was a self-emptying of God to reveal Himself under conditions of human nature and from the human point of view. We are able to draw a distinction between what He revealed and what He used. He revealed God, His mind, His character, His claim, within certain limits His Threefold

Being; He revealed man, his sinfulness, his need, his capacity; He revealed His purpose of redemption, and founded His Church as a home in which man was to be through all the ages reconciled to God in knowledge and love. All this He revealed, but through, and under conditions of, a true human nature. Then He *used* human nature, its relation to God, its conditions of experience, its growth in knowledge, its limitations of knowledge. He feels as we men ought to feel; He sees as we ought to see. We can thus distinguish more or less between the Divine truth which He reveals, and the human nature which He uses. Now when he speaks of the "sun rising" He is using ordinary human knowledge. He willed so to restrain the beams of deity as to observe the limits of the science of His age, and He puts Himself in the same relation to its historical knowledge. Thus He does not reveal His eternity by statements as to what has happened in the past, or was to happen in the future, outside the ken of existing history. He made His Godhead gradually manifest by His attitude towards men and things about Him, by His mortal and spiritual claims, by His expressed relation to His father, not by any miraculous exemptions of Himself from the conditions of natural knowledge in its own proper province. Thus the utterances of Christ about the Old Testament do not seem to be nearly definite or clear enough to allow of our supposing that in this case he is departing from the general method of the Incarnation, by bringing to bear the unveiled omniscience of the Godhead, to anticipate or foreclose a development of human knowledge.

For, without doubt, if consistently with the entire loyalty to our Lord and His Church, we can regard as open the questions specified above, we are removing great obstacles from the path to belief of many who certainly wish to believe, and do not exhibit any undue skepticism. Nor does there appear to be any real danger that the criticism of the Old Testament will ultimately diminish our reverence for it.[70]

F. W. Robertson

F. W. Robertson's small output of sermons went through many editions in the late nineteenth and early twentieth centuries, and merits a place in any anthology of English religious thought. "The Message of the Church to Men of Wealth" is excerpted below. This sermon makes a strong case for personal property and emphasizes the importance of right relationships between management and workers, but also raises acute questions about the proper use of wealth.

The Message of the Church to Men of Wealth
[Preached June 15, 1851]

1. Sam. Xxv. 10, 11.—"And Nabal answered David's servants, and said, Who is David? And who is the son of Jesse? There be many servants now-a-days that break away every man from his master. Shall I then take my bread, and my water, and my flesh that I have killed for my shearers, and give it unto men whom I know not whence they be?"

I have selected this passage for our subject this evening, because it is one of the earliest cases recorded in the Bible in which the interests of the employer and the employed—the man of wealth and the man of work—stood, or seemed to stand, in antagonism to each other.

The history of the chapter is briefly this. Nabal, the wealthy sheep-master, fed his flocks in the pastures of Carmel. David was leader of a band of men who got their living by the sword on the same hills,—outlaws, whose excesses he in some degree restrained, and over whom he retained a leader's influence. A rude, irregular honor was not unknown among those fierce men. They honorably abstained from injuring Nabal's flocks. They did more: they protected them from all harm against the marauders of the neighborhood. By the confession of Nabal's own herdsmen, "they were a wall unto them both by night and day, all the time they were with them keeping their flocks."

And thus a kind of Right grew up,—irregular enough, but sufficient to establish a claim on Nabal for remuneration of these services; a new claim, not admitted by him; reckoned by him an exaction, which could be enforced by no law, only by that law which is above all statute—law, decided according to emergencies—an indefinable, instinctive sense of Fairness and Justice. But as there was no law, and each man was to himself a law, and the sole arbiter of his own rights, what help was there but that disputes should rise between the wealthy proprietors and their self-constituted champions, with exaction and tyranny on the one side, churlishness and parsimony on the other? Hence a fruitful and ever fresh source of struggle: the one class struggling to take as much, and the other to give as little, as possible. In modern language, the Rights of Labor were in conflict with the Rights of Property.

The Message of the Church to the Man of Wealth

The message of the Church contains those principles of Life which, carried out, would, and hereafter will, realize the Divine Order of Society. The revealed Message does not create the facts of our humanity: it simply makes them known. The Gospel did not make God our Father: it authoritatively reveals that He is so. It did not create a new duty of loving one another: it revealed the old duty which existed from eternity, and which must exist as long as humanity is humanity. . . . Now, this is the very truth revealed in the Incarnation. David, Israel's model king,—the king by the grace of God, not by the conventional rules of human choice,—is a shepherd's son. Christ, the king who is to reign over our regenerated humanity, is humbly born—the poor woman's Son. That is the Church's message to the man of wealth; and a message which, it seems, has to be learned afresh in every age. . . . Whoever helps to keep alive that ancient lie of upper and lower, resting the distinction not on official authority or personal worth, but on wealth and title, is doing his part to hinder the establishment of the Redeemer's kingdom.

Now, the Church of Christ proclaims that truth in baptism. She speaks of a kingdom here in which all are, as spirits, equal. She reveals a fact. She does not affect to create the fact. She says, not hypothetically: "This child *may* be the child of God if prevenient grace has taken place, or if hereafter he shall have certain feelings and experiences"; nor, "Hereby I create this child magically, by supernatural power, in one moment, what it was not a moment before"; but she says, authoritatively: "I pronounce this child the child of God, the brother of Christ, the First-born, the son of Him who has taught us by His son to call Him *our* Father, not *my* Father. Whatever that child may become hereafter in fact, he is now, by right of creation and redemption, the child of God. Rich or poor, titled or untitled, he shares the spiritual nature of the second Adam, the Lord from Heaven."

To conclude. Doubtless, David was wrong: he had no right even to redress wrongs thus. Patience was his divine appointed duty; and, doubtless, in such circumstances we should be very ready to preach submission, and to blame David. Alas! We, the clergy of the Church of England, have been only too ready to do this: for three long centuries we have taught submission to the powers that be, as if that were the only text in Scripture bearing on the the relations between ruler and the ruled. Rarely have we dared to demand of the powers that be, justice of the wealthy man, and of the titled, duties. We have produced folios of slavish flattery upon the Divine Right of Power. Shame on us! We have not denounced the wrongs done to weakness: and yet, for one text in the Bible which requires submission and patience from the poor, you will find a hundred which denounce the vices of the rich;—in the writings of the noble old Jewish prophets, that, and almost that only;—that in the Old Testament, with a deep roll of words that sound like Sinai thunders; and that in the New Testament, in words less impassioned and more calmly terrible from the apostles and their Master:— and woe to us, in the great day of God, if we have been the sycophants of the rich, instead of the Redressers of the poor man's wrongs:—woe to us if we have been tutoring David into respect to his superior, Nabal, and forgotten that David's cause, not Nabal's, is the cause of God![71]

6

The Twentieth Century

Wimsey scrambled to his feet and looked around.

At first glance he felt himself sobered and awe-stricken by the noble proportions of the church, in whose vast spaces the congregation—though a good one for so small a parish in the dead of a winter's night—seemed almost lost. . . . Then his gaze, returning to the nave, followed the strong yet slender shafting. . . . And there, mounting to the steep pitch of the roof, his eyes were held entranced. . . . Incredibly aloof, flinging back the light in a dusky shimmer of bright hair and gilded outspread wings, soared the ranked angels, cherubim and seraphim, choir over choir, . . . floating face to face uplifted.

"My God!" muttered Wimsey, not without reverence. And he softly repeated to himself: "He rode upon the cherubims and did fly; He came flying upon the wings of the wind."

—*Lord Peter Wimsey worships in Fenchurch St. Paul,*
from Dorothy Sayers, The Nine Tailors

FEW ENGLISH HISTORY TEXTS consider the twentieth-century Church of England worth a separate index entry. Although religious issues had dominated English history for previous centuries, after the Age of Reform the church played a reduced role in British institutional life. Kings conspired with their Archbishops of Canterbury in earlier epochs, but when the archbishop asked to see the prime minister during a national crisis in the 1970s, the prime minister replied that his calendar did not allow for a meeting with the primate. The church's political influence declined, and so did the number of clergy and laity. Redundant London churches became restaurants and antique shops, but the picture was anything but one of unqualified loss. Despite decreased numbers, church life remained vigorous, and this century produced some of Anglicanism's most influential minds, such as William Temple, Evelyn Underhill, T. S. Eliot, and Michael Ramsey. If the Church of England's role diminished at home, it grew abroad. Anglicanism was now established as a global institution, with autonomous provinces in Asia, Africa, the Middle East, and the Americas, many into their second or third generation of corporate life. They drew on an Anglican heritage and the Church of England effectively shared its experience with sister churches, primarily through periodic bishops' meetings at Lambeth conferences. Not much was truly new in the content of this century's Anglican religious thought, but by now it was a spiritually rich, complex past that lay open for new generations of Christians to examine and select from in shaping their own lives and institutions. This did not represent an appeal to nostalgia, or a retreat from difficult times, but finding in the past a source of renewal, a sharing of previous problems and conflicts with some suggestion toward their resolution. T. S. Eliot's often-cited lines from "Little Gidding" echo this sentiment:

> And the end of all our exploring
> Will be to arrive where we started
> And know the place for the first time.

Simultaneous with the Anglican Communion's global spread was the ecumenical movement's growth. Formerly warring churches came into regular contract; insurmountable doctrinal differences were frankly discussed; the level of discourse was raised, and the extent of cooperation enlarged. The century's final years displayed a church that, despite vicissitudes, had faithfully lived out its mission role and, while seemingly static in numbers and influence at home, registered a global impact and was looked on increasingly as a source of guidance and spiritual fulfillment by generations of new Christians who in turn, contributed to its broadening influence. The road to globalism, however, did not come easily; two wars and decades of international political conflict stood in its way.

Two Wars and the Great Depression

Two world wars, a devastating national strike, and the Great Depression contributed to the church's declining place in England's national life. World War I tore a gash across world history; an age ended, another began. Deep cynicism pervaded most segments of society after the war, and profound bitterness about human nature was widespread, reflected in the writings of a generation of young authors, as, for example, Robert Graves. To the church, emerging from a long, relatively comfortable Victorian Age, there was little in its past to prepare it for the horrors of modern warfare. The war naturally encouraged a heightened spirit of nationalism, and many preachers painted it as a great crusade, a "holy war," the forces of light against the forces of darkness. For others, the prolonged war caused many persons to abandon, or at least deeply question, their religious faith. Atheism, agnosticism, and cynicism flourished; they would be prevalent intellectual forces for the rest of the century.

War was followed by the General Strike of 1926, and the Great Depression, with its consequent unemployment and poverty. The Labor movement grew in Great Britain; trade union membership almost doubled to eight million between 1913 and 1919, and fifty-nine Labor Members of Parliament swept into office in 1919. The Church of England had few ties with labor and only a handful of its clergy ever addressed social and political issues affecting the working masses. The church came late to the moral questions raised by industrial society. Church attendance declined, and organized religion increasingly ceased to be part of public life. Parishes relied on smaller numbers of the faithful to hold programs and finances together.

When the Great Depression began with the New York stock market collapse of October 24, 1929, it set in motion global shock waves that resulted in the collapse of industries, massive unemployment, and political disruption quickening the ascendancy of fascist governments in many countries. No sooner were World War I and the Great Depression's devastation overcome than the world experienced the conflagration of World War II. As the Hitlerian war machine swept through Europe, establishing concentration camps and gas chambers in its wake, many European Christians, including those in Britain, saw it as a clear battle between good and evil, even clearer than in World War I. Additionally, there was widespread contact between the German Confessing Church, represented by figures such as Dietrich Bonhoeffer (1906–1945), a Lutheran pastor in the resistance to Hitler, and Anglicans such as Bishop George Bell (1881–1958), a leader of the ecumenical movement. (Shortly before Bonhoeffer was executed in the final days of World War II, he asked a fellow prisoner to contact the bishop of Chichester, "Tell him that for me this is the end but also the beginning.")

England experienced nightly bombing raids, and the country was mobilized to repel an expected German invasion. In 1941 a young curate's wife, describing the inferno that destroyed both her parish church and the House of Commons, wrote of:

> the beams blazing furiously and then falling one by one, until the Altar caught alight and seemed to fold up and die before our eyes. The church burnt with white hot flames. It was a dreadful sight, and though we tried hard in the beginning to get the fire under control, we failed hopelessly. The windows had gone, the wind changed its direction and fanned the flames to even greater heights. We could hear the cries of pigeons in the tower but we found it impossible to reach them. The Great Bells fell.[1]

CLERICAL LIFE

The history of clerical life in this century is a picture of declining numbers and influence. Salaries improved, but influence in the community did not. Adrian Hastings, a historian of the modern church, described clerical life in the 1930s at a time when more than five thousand stipends paid less than four hundred pounds a year:

> The village parson, neither Anglo-Catholic nor Evangelical, neither ambitious nor discontented, remained a common figure throughout the land, more rooted locally than the bishops, more representative than anyone else of a tolerant indigeneity of Christian tradition. . . . Many a vicar could only make up for his lack of theological expertise, professional training and loss of social status with a double share of the rather nebulous Christianity of the public-school: "Take God on the rugger field." Cricket, rowing, fishing, railway timetables, a little Plato, bell ringing: wonderful sidelines, but rather pathetic if they became too central to a priest's mind. The Oxford and Cambridge boat race could be seen as the sacramental focus of much clerical fellowship—so much part of being nice and gentlemanly and rather ineffectual in worldly terms, of never quite growing up.[2]

By 1971 the number of Oxford or Cambridge graduates among the clergy had fallen from 40 percent a few decades earlier to 16 percent, and 57 percent had no degrees. "The large vicarages had been sold," Hastings added. "Cricket playing was no longer much of a clerical characteristic. The new vicar was living in a comfortable but insignificant house—not necessarily near the church—with an assured but limited income. The image of the gentleman was gone. The vicar had almost ceased to be a figure of fun, but he had also almost ceased to be a public figure at all."[3] Worship styles varied from high church Italian, to "British

Museum" moderately ceremonial, to low church, close to what would be encountered in Presbyterian or Congregational churches.

There was a ground swell movement for revising the Prayer Book, the current version of which had been in use for centuries. Many people believed the old rubrics were too restrictive and the book's general outlook too penitential and gloomy. Many chaplains returning from World War I hoped for a book with more varied prayers suitable to the real-life situations they and their parishioners faced. Others wanted inclusion of prayers for labor, missions, and national life. After several years in which high church and Evangelicals sparred, a new Prayer Book to supplement, not replace, the 1661 book, was passed in church convention in 1927 by 517 votes to 133. The Revised Prayer Book Measure then went to Parliament, where it was defeated in the House of Commons, 238 to 205. English innate fears of popery, dissension within the church ranks, and a dithering bench of bishops doomed the vote to defeat. The effects were not entirely negative. Profiting from the debate, some churches in the expanding Anglican Communion used research done for Prayer Book reform to improve their own new Prayer Books, including India, South Africa, and the West Indies. At the same time, many parishes tried liturgical experiments, inspired by Continental liturgical reforms. A heightened interest in the Eucharist as the main act of Sunday worship was central to liturgical reform; for an increasing number of churches, this became a parish family communion followed by a breakfast or social hour. Sermons were shorter; Christian education classes multiplied.

As the century progressed, Church of England clergy were in more frequent, friendly contact with colleagues of other denominations. The old hostilities and suspicions abated, and in universities and some theological colleges persons from different denominations met one another. Evangelicals showed greater interest in high church attention to the beauty of worship; high church parishes became interested in biblical scholarship and social action. While stylistic differences remained, they no longer carried the heavy emotional baggage of the century's opening years.

THE BRITISH–AMERICAN CONNECTION

Toward the end of the 19th century, a church historian assessed the reciprocal interplay of the American and British churches on each other, comparing the process to the coming together of two rivers. In a period metaphor:

> when these tributaries merge into the broad stream they lose their distinctive colors. But this fusion was not effected at once. In some instances, a tributary stream acts as does the Blue Nile in the great rivers of Egypt. It keeps its color and its especial density in the midst of the flood with which it moves. But all, sooner or later, merge themselves so entirely into the common current that only something like a chemical analysis will discover the several contributions.[4]

A century later, it is useful to see where they merged—in the social gospel, civil rights, prayer book revision, theology and culture, and church union—and where they went their separate ways, bearing in mind the subject matter's inherent fluidity. For instance, there would be communality of action in what was called the social gospel, the demands that the church speak to the plight of the working classes. Despite having deep upper-class roots in both countries, both the Church of England and the Protestant Episcopal Church in the United States gave strong support to labor and social justice issues. William Temple was considered a traitor to his class in England for many of his statements and sermons in defense of the working poor. The Christian Social Union in both countries was a lively advocate for social reform. Almost fifty Episcopal bishops were members of the Church Association for the Advancement of the Interests of Labor, which used incarnational theology to urge changes in working conditions in sweatshops and living conditions in tenements. In some parishes, Labor Sunday, the Sunday before Labor Day, was observed in the Episcopal Church. Frances Perkins, the first woman cabinet member in America, was Secretary of Labor and an active Episcopalian and advocate for Franklin Roosevelt's New Deal, with its Social Security Act (1935) and Fair Labor Standards Act (1938).[5]

The Episcopal Church, as might be expected, reflected polarities of viewpoints on these issues. At one Church Congress in 1874 the poor were admonished, "Be content with your wages; work for what you can get, but work. . . . Deserve more, and in the Lord's good time, you will get more. . . . Whatever you suffer here from the injustice of others will turn to your account hereafter."[6] Although slow to react, the American bishops in 1889 said in a pastoral letter, "It is a fallacy in social economics, as well as in Christian thinking, to look upon the labor of men and women and children as a mere commercial commodity to be bought and sold as an inanimate and irresponsible thing."[7]

But communality of action was not always evident. On numerous issues, such as civil rights, women's ordination, a more inclusive place for persons of single-sex orientation, and on liturgical reform and updating the Prayer Book and hymnal, the American church, fueled by its own forces, was in the forefront of change decades before the Church of England.

During the twentieth century, the Prayer Book in America underwent two revisions, as did the hymnal. (The 1928 English Prayer Book remained the country's official Prayer Book, approved by Parliament, although several Alternative Services were in use toward century's end.) The original American Prayer Book remained largely intact from revolutionary times until 1928, when, after fifteen years of study, a new book was approved, against the loud minority voices, present in every generation, which argued that no change was desirable since the Prayer Book, like the Ten Commandments, had been delivered seemingly by Moses from a cloud on Mount Sinai. The 1928 Prayer Book was an imaginative document for its time. Numerous new collects (short prayers) were added, including prayers For Our Country and For Social Justice. The ponderously wordy earlier communion rite was shortened and a hauntingly beautiful Order for Use at the Burial of a Child was added. A new *Hymnal* had been approved recently, trimming over a hundred works that had fallen into disuse and adding selections from both the early church and the Reformation, including Luther's "A Mighty Fortress." Numerous melodies, more appropriate for Victorian parlor recitals, were replaced by more tasteful and substantive creations.

Then again in 1979 the General Convention, responding to a much-changed society, adopted a new Prayer Book for the church, retaining the skeleton of the earlier work, but shifting its emphasis, giving much more prominence to the baptismal process, reducing the emphasis on fatalism and death, and focusing more on the resurrection. A companion hymnal was soon issued; like the new Prayer Book, it was the subject of over a decade's work by representative scholars and pastors, extensively tested in parishes, and carefully introduced in clinics and training programs. Despite some residual grousing, most church members came to accept both Prayer Book and hymnal as being solidly grounded in the faith and offering numerous possibilities for creative worship in tasteful words and music.

In the domain of theology and culture, the Church of England was a constant creative influence on the church in America and elsewhere through figures such as C. S. Lewis, Dorothy Sayers, and Evelyn Underhill, and theologians or religious writers such as Austin Farrer, George Macquarrie, John Polkingham, and Susan Howich. Whether T. S. Eliot was an American or English author could be the subject of numerous doctoral dissertations. What is important here is that none of these figures stands alone; each drew on and used copious illustrations from the Anglican past. Thus, a reading of Evelyn Underhill will bring an acquaintance with a string of English mystics; Eliot provides a pipeline to the Caroline Divines; and Polkingham to earlier writers on science and religion. Familiarity with almost any major Anglican literary or theological figure of the twentieth century leads directly to a living heritage of articulate predecessors, which helps comprise a distinctly Anglican ethos.

In efforts toward wider unity of churches, both the English and American churches were active, often making common cause. Although they had few concrete results to show for it at century's end, they did open rich possibilities for dialogue in a climate of reduced hostilities. Reunion efforts with the Methodists in England failed, and similar explorations with the Presbyterians in the United States went nowhere. Like the parting of the Red and Blue Niles, a Polish pope and women's ordination in the Episcopal and Anglican churches put at least a temporary halt on any closer prospects for Roman Catholic–Anglican unity, but an Episcopalian–Lutheran agreement in 2000 on common ministry created new possibilities for interaction between both denominations in the United States.

Both American and British leadership was evident in the major church unity conferences during this century, and gradually, in places like Edinburgh, Geneva, Stockholm, and Lausanne, the members of the wider Christian community came to know one anothers' leaders, explore traditions, and plan common projects. If William Temple's is the first name commonly associated with the ecumenical movement, no less deserving is that of the American bishop, Charles Henry Brent, a missionary bishop in the Philippines and senior military chaplain, who provided both a rationale and practical planning for Episcopal Church participation in such ventures. Brent, an action-oriented prelate, was a prophetic voice as well, as when he wrote:

> The unity of Christendom is not a luxury but a necessity. The world will go limping until Christ's prayer that all may be one is answered. We must have unity, not at all costs, but at all risks. A unified church is the only offering we dare present to the coming of Christ, for in it alone will He find room to dwell.

If it is a prophecy that the gates of hell shall not prevail against the Church, it is also prophecy that the Church divided against herself will fall. Disorder in the Church is more terrible than feuds in the family or civil war in the State. If war is an evil in national life, it is a thousand fold greater evil in Church life.[8]

WILLIAM TEMPLE AND MICHAEL RAMSEY

Two exceptionally able leaders were called to be Archbishops of Canterbury in the twentieth century. William Temple was archbishop only from 1942 to 1944 but was already established as a brilliant intellect and forceful commentator on public issues by then. Temple, bishop of Manchester and later archbishop of York, was acceptable to all major tendencies of Anglicanism. One of the church's most articulate discussants of social issues, he wrote, as early as 1908:

If Christianity is to be applied to the economic system, an organization which rests primarily on the principle of competition must give way to one which rests primarily on cooperation. The question of the competitive principle is driven down in the Labor market, so that men compete against each other for the right to work which is the right to live. Go and see it at work in the London Docks. If one man is to secure the means of feeding himself and his family, he must be depriving another. Is that an exhibition of Brotherhood?

As citizens we are guilty of a whole system of oppression: it is there: we tolerate it, and so become responsible for its results. There is nothing inevitable in it: it is all the result of human choices. I do not mean that anyone deliberately put it there; it is the greatest fluke in creation. But it is the net result of innumerable human choices, and by human choices it can be modified. Here lies our duty—and our guilt.[9]

Temple was a classmate at Rugby and Oxford of R. H. Tawney, a socialist and economic historian, who wrote *Religion and the Rise of Capitalism* (1926) and several Labor Party manifestos. Tawney stressed, and Temple agreed, that society could be Christian while emphasizing social needs rather than individual ones. While at Manchester he helped mediate the 1926 coal miners strike, bringing him workers' respect. His book *Essays in Christian Politics* contained a rationale for the church's attempts to translate the gospel in a social and political setting. The archbishop's socialist utterances would appear, to a later generation schooled in

Marxist-Leninist thought, mild, hortatory, lacking revolutionary appeal, yet calling the church's attention to the plight of the disadvantaged and those suffering from social ills.

Temple was short and stocky, but of rocklike temperament, a person of inner serenity and sureness, with a ready laugh and an intense gaze. The prelate was interested equally in social action, philosophy, the League of Nations, and the ecumenical movement. A natural leader and vigorous and articulate speaker, he made his mark on any field in which he entered. George Bernard Shaw said of him, "An Archbishop of Temple's enlightenment is a realized impossibility." Temple combined a gift of quickly seizing the most important points about an issue with an intuitive skill in bridging academic disciplines. At best he called the church and its people to bold, new vision, but sometimes he overextended himself, taking on more projects than he could reasonably complete. His optimistic temperament and sheltered public school upbringing did not expose him to a world of tragedy or evil. As a youth Temple participated in what was then known as "social work among the poor." He was fond of quoting a character in *Rugby,* a period school novel, who says "so we filled the little blighters up to the teeth, and then they hooked it back to the slums."[10] Still, no figure of this century was more active in stirring the church to action on so many issues. In 1938 Temple ended a decade's chairmanship of the Archbishops' Commission on Christian Doctrine with publication of a landmark volume, *Doctrine in the Church of England.* This was an attempt by religious leaders representing diverse doctrinal strains to make common cause on the Church of England's basic beliefs. While eclipsed in later generations, the book has much to commend it in providing basic Anglican formularies about the sources and authority of doctrine, the church and sacraments, the future life, and the meaning of sin. In a church short on doctrine beyond the basic statement of the creeds and the Prayer Book's content, it is a valuable document which could profitably be updated for the whole church today.

Although Temple wrote many volumes in response to philosophical issues of special interest to academics of his age, one of his most enduring works is *Christianity and the Social Order,* written in 1942 at the height of World War II and two years before his death. Here Temple set out his larger vision of the church and its relation to society. He observed that most of the church's work and witness is done by Christian people in the workplace, set at tasks having no discernible church connection. Calling Christianity "the most avowedly materialist of all the great world religions," Temple called for a sacramental view of the universe, "both of its material and of its spiritual elements, that there is given hope of making human both politics and economics and of making effectual both faith and love."[11]

Chairman of the Edinburgh Conference on Faith and Order in 1937, Temple was a central figure in most other pre–World War II ecumenical gatherings. A participant at one such gathering described the archbishop:

> He led us into the chapel of the school where we were meeting for our closing devotions. As he opened his Bible . . . the whole atmosphere changed. There was no mistaking the fact that in heart and soul we were being lifted up into the realm where he habitually dwelt. We knew then whence came the courtesy, the patience, the love of justice, and the calm strength with which he had led us into order out of the chaos of our controversies.[12]

Of the ecumenical movement Temple said:

> The unity of the Church is something more than unity of ecclesiastical structure, though it cannot be complete without this. . . . The unity which the Lord prays His disciples may enjoy is that which is eternally characteristic of the Triune God. It is therefore something more than a means to an end, even though that end may be the evangelization of the world; it is in itself the one worthy end of all human aspiration; it is the life of heaven. . . . Before the loftiness of that hope and calling our little experience of unity and fellowship is humbled to the dust. Our friendships, our reconciliations, our unity of spirit in Church gatherings, or in missionary conferences— beautiful as they are, are sometimes even wonderful in comparison with our habitual life of sectional rivalries and tensions, yet how poor and petty they appear in the light of the Lord's longing.[13]

John 17:11 provided the grounding for Temple's ecumenical activity, "Holy Father, keep them in thy name which thou hast given me, that they may be one. Even as we are one." Temple called it, "perhaps the most sacred passage ever in the four Gospels."[14] The archbishop was in his early sixties when gout, which had plagued him since childhood, took his life. His ideas are those of the British upper classes with a social conscience, vigorous, compassionate and at times simplistic. But Temple was a deeply committed Christian as well, someone who translated his initially vague notions of social justice and ecumenism into realities. Death cut him down, but he left an amazingly intact body of ideas for future generations, providing a framework linking social justice and ecumenical ministries with mainstream Anglicanism.

Of the Archbishops of Canterbury, Michael Ramsey stands out as the century's second towering figure. A theologian, Ramsey, who would have preferred a life of writing and teaching, was increasingly called to church leadership positions, first as bishop of Durham, then as archbishop of York, finally as Archbishop of Canterbury from 1961 to 1974. His first book, *The Gospel and the Catholic Church* (1936), represented an advancement from the rigid Anglo-Catholicism of the post–Oxford Movement era. Ramsey was well versed in contemporary theology, and his own early years, spent in a nonconformist family, gave him a broader perspective than many occupants of Augustine's chair enjoyed. Adrian Hastings writes, "He had to be, far more than his predecessors, a pilgrim, exploring the way forward for himself also, rather than presiding from some central and assured position."[15] A striking figure in cope and miter, he was every inch the archbishop in an era when the church was sorely tested. Ramsey's gifts of intellect and spirituality were matched by an utter lack of pomposity and disinterest in the trappings of office; during solemn ceremonies, in an era before lapel microphones, he sometimes whistled softly to himself or hummed "Turn back, O Man, forsake thy foolish ways." Ramsey traveled widely and, over a thirteen-year primacy, built on his predecessors' support of the ecumenical movement and the global presence of Anglicanism. Since he was first of all a theologian, his work was buttressed by an intellectual depth not always evident in church leaders. *The Gospel and the Catholic Church* was followed by *The Church of England and the Eastern Orthodox Church: Why their Unity is Important* (1946), *The Glory of God and the Transfiguration of Christ* (1949), *F. D. Maurice and the Conflicts of Modern Theology* (1951), *From Gore to Temple: The Development of Anglican Theology between "Lux Mundi" and the Second World War, 1889–1939* (1960), and *God, Christ and the World: A Study in Contemporary Theology* (1969). In addition, he published several volumes of essays. Ramsey's writing is erudite yet accessible, meditative, and biblically grounded. It also shows a keen awareness of contemporary issues and writers, the liberation theologians of Latin America, American theologians such as Harvey Cox and Arthur Vogel and European writers such as Teilhard de Chardin and Dietrich Bonhoeffer. He became acquainted with the American church through months spent at Nashotah House, a midwestern seminary, each year in retirement.

Ramsey was born into a Congregationalist home, and his own tendencies were distinctly Anglo-Catholic. Yet, as Archbishop of Canterbury, he worked hard for a union with the Methodist church, a proposal defeated in 1971 by an inadequate vote supporting the merger. A 75-percent vote of both bodies was needed for acceptance of the union plan; the Methodists produced such a majority, but the Church of England mustered only a 65-percent majority, and the proposal died. Ramsey had worked hard for the merger. If it had come off, it would have ended a two-century schism and resulted in mutual recognition of their ministries and sacraments, followed by a service of reconciliation, after which some Methodists would be consecrated bishops by Anglican bishops and future Methodist ordinations would be by bishops in the apostolic succession. Answering critics on both sides, Ramsey told the Canterbury diocesan convention in 1968:

> I know that I am a priest and a bishop in the historic order, referred to in our Prayer Book as coming down from the apostles' time. I know that Methodist ministers are ministers of the Word and sacrament used by Christ and they have been for many, many years. I know that their ministry is not identical with the historic episcopate and priesthood, but I am unable to define precisely what the relative value of the two is. I am frankly agnostic about a great deal of the Methodist ministry, knowing that it is not identical with my own, but also being perfectly certain that they are not just laymen. . . . In this laying on of hands with prayer I would be asking God through his Holy Spirit to give to the Methodist ministry what He knows they need to make their ministry identical with ours as presbyters and priests in the church of God. It would be perfectly clear what was being asked for, the equalization of our ministries. . . . What would it mean receiving that laying on of hands? I would mean this. I believe that I am a priest and bishop in the Church of God. Nothing can make me more so. But I do believe that my ministry will have a very new significance and authority as a result of this Anglican-Methodist union, and I pray that God will give me that enrichment and significance through receiving the laying on of hands from the Methodist president and his colleagues.[16]

No Archbishop of Canterbury was more interested in the Christian East than Ramsey. Refugee believers and professors had made their way to England since the 1917 Russian Revolution, and Ramsey had met them through the Fellowship of St. Alban and St. Sergius, an Anglican–Orthodox society. The beauty of the Orthodox liturgy, the mystery of its spirituality, and a respect for its writings about the early church were all of interest to Ramsey. In 1949 he wrote:

> The history of the Eastern theology of the Transfiguration confronts us with some of the deeper divergencies between Eastern and Western Christianity. The East has dwelt upon the cosmic effects of the redemption wrought by Christ, and has viewed the Christian life in terms of our participation within the new creation. It is an outlook mystical rather than moral. The West, moral rather than mystical in its emphasis, has dwelt

rather upon the justification and sanctification of human lives, sometimes slipping into a moralism or legalism which misses the cosmic context in which the Christian life is set. . . . While some Western expositors have asked what moral and practical lessons are to be learnt from the event, the East has often been content simply to rejoice in the glory which Mount Tabor sheds upon Christ, Christians and all creation. . . . Nowhere is the ethos of eastern orthodoxy far from the themes which the Transfiguration embodies.[17]

He exchanged visits with the ecumenical patriarch Athenagoras and traveled to the Soviet Union and invited its metropolitan, Alexei, to visit Britain in 1964, the first Russian patriarch to make such a visit. However, Ramsey's tenure as archbishop coincided with one of the darkest periods of the Cold War, and there was little he could do beyond providing encouragement to churches under communism. In March 1965 the archbishop went to Rome as guest of Pope Paul VI. After full and frank talks in the Sistine Chapel and in the papal library, they held a common worship service in the historic church of St. Paul-Without-the-Walls, where St. Paul reportedly was buried. Following the service, Paul VI removed the diamond and emerald episcopal ring the people of Milan had presented him as archbishop, and gave it to Ramsey, who wore it until his death.

The larger meaning of Ramsey's episcopate is that a deeply prayerful person, an almost monastic temperament, led the Anglican Communion for over a decade during a difficult time. Most of Ramsey's major writings continue in print and gain a gradually widening audience. His appreciation of Catholicism and Orthodoxy, his carefully crafted reflections on the incarnation, atonement, transfiguration, resurrection, and on such topics as worship and the episcopacy are among the church's most lucid expositions of these questions in this or any century.

EVELYN UNDERHILL

If Temple and Ramsey were twentieth-century Anglicanism's leading theologians, Evelyn Underhill (1875–1941) can lay claim to being its most enduring writer on spirituality. Two of her forty books, *Mysticism* (1911) and *Worship* (1936), were major contributions to twentieth-century Christian thought, and she also wrote many original religious essays and more than 350 articles. She became increasingly popular in the 1920s and 1930s as a conductor of retreats and a spiritual director, setting a pattern many women and men of later generations would emulate. Underhill was born to comfortable circumstances and married a barrister with a successful practice. From the pleasant book-lined study of an eighteenth-century row house in an attractive London suburb, she wrote a steady stream of books and articles. Yearly trips to Italy as a young woman introduced her to the romantic side of Roman Catholicism, and she came close to joining that church until a papal condemnation of modernism and the objections of her husband made such a move impossible. Her parents were only nominally pious and her husband did not possess her interest in religion. The couple were devoted to each other, shared a common enthusiasm for sailing, and entertained frequently across class and vocational lines. Yet Underhill remained guarded about her personal life and thoughts, although she carried on a voluminous correspondence over decades with some of the leading religious figures of the time, including her sometime spiritual director, Baron Frederick Von Hügel, a German lay theologian living in London. Twice weekly she visited eight poor families in North Kensington, which gave her "a sense of expansion and liberation." Having no children of her own, she was pleased to be with these families and especially the children, "such nice and friendly appealing little creatures, like tiny flowers in those grimy places."[18]

Attracted to Roman Catholicism yet unable to accept it, she progressively found in Anglicanism a spiritual home—she once called the Church of England "a respectable suburb of the city of God." The static parishes of London's suburbs held little attraction for her, but in places like the Pleshey Retreat House, built on an ancient church site in Essex, she found inner peace and solace. Her growing attraction toward the church in which she was baptized was undramatic, she saw it as largely a matter of where she could serve God best, and that was "where He has put me." Hers was an ordered life, tranquil on the surface, lacking the evident peaks and valleys such a romantic temperament would suggest; her emotional fire and energy were kindled at her writing desk.

The latest biblical scholarship and debates of institutional religion were of little interest to Underhill, and the author's most lasting works are about the inner search for meaning. Reading her books, it is useful to have in mind the sensitive young lady, visiting Italy with her mother, coming upon churches and processions, serene cloisters and monastic gardens, frescos and chapels, a visual, poetic world free of doctrinal controversy.

Drawing on the recently emerging science of psychology, and compiling hundreds of illustrations from the lives of European mystics for the first time in one place in English, *Mysticism* was a brisk-moving, energetically argued narrative carefully shaped by the author, based on her own extraordinary reading of the texts. It became, to Underhill's surprise and delight, a popular success. By 1930 it was in its twelfth edition, and many more would come. The book's point of departure was human experience, the universal search for truth, propelled by the desire of humans to know and to love. Like peeling layers from an onion, she approached a definition of mysticism. It was:

> not an opinion: it is not a philosophy. It has nothing in common with the pursuit of occult knowledge. On the one hand it is not merely the power of contemplating Eternity: on the other, it is not to be identified with any kind of religious queerness. It is the name of that organic process which involves the perfect consummation of the Love of God: the achievement here and now of the immortal heritage of man. Or, if you like it better— for this means exactly the same thing—it is the art of establishing his conscious relation with the Absolute.[19]

Later she called mysticism "the science of ultimates, the science of union with the Absolute, and nothing else." The mystic is "the person who attains to this Union, not the person who talks about it. Not to *know about* but to *Be*, is the mark of the real initiate."[20]

Mysticism was followed in 1936 by Underhill's second major volume, *Worship*, which was similar in structure to the earlier work. This time she examined a variety of worship forms, calling each a cathedral of the human spirit. With the artistic eye of a sensitive, habitual tourist of religious institutions, she described the salient characteristics of Judaism, Catholicism, Orthodoxy, Anglicanism, and various forms of Protestantism. When she died in 1941, Evelyn Underhill had joined a remarkable group of writers of the 1920s and 1930s who contributed significantly to the vitality of the Anglican spiritual tradition.

C. S. LEWIS

The lack of any single founding figure or source of doctrine means that in each century Anglicanism has profited from various articulate pilgrims of the faith, lay and clerical, female and male, many of whom chronicled their quest in essays, plays, and fiction, in addition to more formal religious writings. In considering the Anglican ethos in the twentieth century, it is important to look at a cluster of such fiction writers whose major works were produced from the 1930s to the 1960s, figures like C. S. Lewis, T. S. Eliot, Dorothy Sayers, and Charles Williams. For many later-twentieth-century Christians, the Oxford don C. S. Lewis (1898–1963) was the single most important source of enlightenment on their religious journey. He opened the doors of the Christian faith to seekers, as in opening the wardrobe through which the children entered the magic kingdom of Narnia. In book after book—more than sixty titles, *The Screwtape Letters, Mere Christianity, The Problem of Pain, The Four Loves, Miracles, The Great Divorce, Surprised by Joy*, and the Narnia chronicles—Lewis found fresh language for those on the spiritual journey. Likewise, parts of his emotional life were laid bare in his books and journals, including his own encounters with marriage, pain, and death in later life. From his Ulster Protestant upbringing he was grounded in the evangelical side of Anglicanism, and from his immersion in early English literature he was acquainted with its Catholic aspects. Lewis was too original an intelligence to be claimed by any party; the pull of the past was strong for him, and in works like the allegorical Narnia books he placed himself firmly in the great tradition of classical fabulists of English spirituality. Hastings wrote of his combining "rationally acute but uncompromising faith with scholarship, imaginative creativity and a natural social conservatism in a way very satisfying to many a young searcher after wisdom."[21] Lewis taught English literature at Oxford and Cambridge; many readers, knowing only his popular religious books, were surprised to find that this was the same Lewis who wrote *English Literature in the Sixteenth Century Excluding Drama* (1954), a lively, opinionated volume in the Oxford History of English Literature series, which ruffled the feathers of traditionalist academics, as did most of what Lewis wrote.

Like others of his era, Lewis was attracted to rediscovering the Christian past. Partly this was traceable to his scholarly interests; partly it is because the safe, secure, imaginative world of childhood he knew was brutally severed at age nine with his mother's death. In *The Lion, the Witch, and the Wardrobe* (1950), the exit through the wardrobe's back to a mythical land was symbolic of Lewis's quest for the lost kingdom of childhood.

In the late 1920s and early 1930s Lewis, an atheist as an undergraduate, became an active, believing Christian. Lewis was deeply influenced by G. K. Chesterton's *Everlasting Man* and James Frazer's *Golden Bough*, a compendium on world mythology. He wrote, "All that stuff of Frazer's about the Dying God. Rum thing. It almost looks as if it had really happened once."[22] Lewis was at that time a close friend of J. R. R. Tolkein, who both taught English at Oxford and was writing his Hobbit books. Tolkein argued that, while the Christ story could be received by some persons as myth, Christians accepted it as reality, since it happened once in history. The "story" comes first, Lewis argued, doctrines come later and are extracted from the "myth." Such concepts, and whatever else was going on inside Lewis, coalesced during an outing to a provincial zoo. Referring to the earlier conversation with Tolkien and another friend, Lewis wrote in *Surprised by Joy*, "when we set out I did not believe that Jesus Christ is the Son of God, and when we reached the zoo I did." Lewis was thirty-three at the time, and from then until his death over three decades later in 1963 he poured out a steady stream of books, poems, children's fables, scholarly works, and Christian apologetics. One of the most widespread early successes was *The Screwtape Letters,* the witty letters from a senior to a junior devil. The problem of evil is treated through various human portraits, touched with exaggeration and satire to make a point. In one exchange the Devil speaks of Jesus:

> He's a hedonist at heart. All those fasts and vigils and stakes and crosses are only a façade. Or only like foam on the sea shore. For at sea, out in His sea, there is pleasure, and more pleasure. He makes no secret of it; at His right hand are "pleasures for evermore." Ugh![23]

World War II was a productive period for Lewis. Some RAF chaplains asked him to deliver a series of broadcast talks for troops. The result was *Mere Christianity*, a book for a nonacademic audience. Lewis was oblivious to newly developing strains of biblical scholarship, and sacraments like baptism and the Eucharist go unmentioned in his work. Hastings has written:

> it remains something of a paradox that, while a chief characteristic of the Christian revival of the mid-century was precisely the liturgical and sacramental movement, Lewis—the most powerful single voice in that revival—was almost void of interest in the liturgy and silent about the sacraments. It may well be that his most lasting literary achievement will prove to be the Narnia stories and the almost mystical *Till We Have Faces:* the work of his autumnal maturity. In the latter's Greek context and the mythical Narnia, Lewis seems best to escape the inhibiting consequences of doctrinal precision.[24]

In 1948 Lewis was soundly defeated in an Oxford debate and changed the focus of his religious writing as a result. His antagonist was a Christian philosopher, Elizabeth Anscombe, who attacked the philosophical underpinnings of his recent book, *Miracles* (1947). Lewis turned from writing popular works of Christian apologetics and focused his creative energies instead on children's stories, which contain some of his richest religious insights. *The Lion, The Witch and the Wardrobe* (1950), using the crucifixion-resurrection theme as its basis, is the major work of his later period. Narnia, the magic kingdom, is destroyed, then restored for eternity. This time the children and their parents enter Narnia because they are all killed in a railway accident; previously the children explored Narnia through the back of a wardrobe.

His final years should have been his happiest ones, but that was not to be. The Lewis household was a dysfunctional place inhabited by Lewis's alcoholic brother, Warnie, who never grew up emotionally. And until her death in 1951, Mrs. Janie Moore, mother of a dead soldier-friend of Lewis, lived with the brothers in a complex relationship. Next came Joy Gresham, an impoverished American writer, and her two children. Lewis, rapturously in love, married the woman he described as a "battle-axe" in 1957, shortly before her death from cancer in 1959. It was then that Lewis wrote one of his most arresting books, *A Grief Observed* (1961). Until then, most of Lewis's religious works were about Christian experience from the outside; this work chronicled his encounter with love, pain, and death from the inside. "No one ever told me that grief felt so like fear," the book opened. In sections it resembles the dark psalms, in others the book of Job. "Can a mortal ask questions which God finds unanswerable?" he asks, Job-like. Also, "my idea of God is not a divine idea. It has to be shattered time after time. He shatters it Himself. He is the great iconoclast. Could we not say that this shattering is one of the marks of His presence?"[25] The book, which Archbishop Trevor Huddleston called "a profoundly religious and theological document," was published under the pseudonym N. W. Clark by Faber & Faber, the publishing house then headed by T. S. Eliot. Ironically, Lewis and Eliot never got along well. Theirs was a frosty relationship, although both came as strangers to England and found in Anglicanism the grounds for expressing their religious faith in creative language.

T. S. ELIOT

From St. Louis, Missouri, by way of Harvard University, T. S. Eliot (1888–1965) came to England, where he became well known as a poet and essayist of the interwar and postwar period. Eliot, a devout Anglo-Catholic, also worked as a banker, pioneering in what would later be called foreign exchange, and a publisher. His baptism in 1927 shocked his atheistic and agnostic friends. The temper of the times was reflected in Virginia Woolf's observation:

> I have had a most shameful and distressing interview with dear Tom Eliot, who may be called dead to us all from this day forward. He has become an Anglo-Catholic believer in God and immortality, and goes to church. I was shocked. A corpse would seem to me more credible than he is. I mean, there's something obscene in a living person sitting by the fire and believing in God.[26]

Sir Herbert Read recalled once staying over at the Eliots to discuss articles for *The Criterion*, a literary journal that lasted from 1922 to 1929:

> I woke early and presently became conscious that the door of my room, which was on the ground floor, was slowly and silently being opened. I lay still and saw first a hand and then an arm reach around the door and lift from a hook the bowler hat that was hanging there. It was a little before seven o'clock and Mr. Eliot was on his way to an early communion service. It was the first intimation I had of his conversion to the Christian faith.[27]

Bothered by the "unsettled society" that was America, Eliot, like other American intellectuals of that time, preferred the "settled society" of England with its traditions, customs, and hierarchy. Raised a Unitarian, Eliot was a humanist agnostic for many years, while searching for a faith, until his baptism at age thirty-nine in 1927, the same year he became a British subject. He attended St. Stephen's, Kensington, where he was vicar's warden. *The Idea of a Christian Society* (1939) and *Notes Towards the Definition of Culture* (1948) contain the fullest expression of his views on history and society. Eliot's essays are less lasting than his poems, and in the latter the twentieth-century quest for meaning finds its resolution in the earlier spirituality of English religious writers. Neither the Reformation nor the Oxford Movement interested Eliot, and his articles were enthusiastic advocacy pieces, Anglo-Catholic and royalist in outlook, defending traditional Western civilization as he understood it. His writings also mirrored the anti-semitism of British upper classes. While Eliot's plays, such as *Murder in the Cathedral* (1935), *The Family Reunion* (1939), *The Cocktail Party* (1950), and *The Elder Statesman* (1959), state his religious position, often in didactic language, in his poetry, heavily influenced by earlier mystics and classical poets, like Dante and the Metaphysical Poets, Eliot is one of the modern era's most enduring voices. *The Waste Land* (1922), *Ash Wednesday* (1930), *Four Quartets*

(1944) deserve a place in any anthology of twentieth-century religious classics.

DOROTHY L. SAYERS

While Dorothy L. Sayers (1893–1957) was best known as author of the Lord Peter Wimsey detective stories, she was also a major writer of religious plays and essays, some ranking among the best examples of their kind in the twentieth century. Born in Oxford, where her father was headmaster of Christ Church Choir School, she was brought up in a loving, cultured setting, one like the historic country parish of Fenchurch St. Paul in *The Nine Tailors*, a mystery with highly evocative representations of contemporary English church life. Her description of change-ringing, central to the book, resulted in The Campanological Society of Great Britain inviting her to be their vice-president. In one scene inside the church,

> the Rector, with the electoral roll-call of the parish in his hand, was numbering his flock. He was robed and stoled, and his anxious old face had taken on a look of great pastoral dignity and serenity. . . . Into the ringing chamber . . . streamed light and sound from the crowded church. The Rector's voice, musical and small, came floating up, past the wings of the floating cherubim: "Lighten our darkness. . . ."[28]

For many years she worked with an advertising agency; she was married to a handsome journalist whose own career declined as hers took off, causing friction in the marriage. A son from an earlier relationship, born out of wedlock, lived with a cousin in Cambridge, but Dorothy doted on him with letters, presents, and, when possible, visits. Her preferences were toward the high, liturgical church, and, like many intellectuals, she attended All Saints, Margaret St., when in London. In the mid-1930s Canterbury Cathedral revived the ancient custom of staging religious dramas in churches, a creative tradition that had lain dormant for centuries. T. S. Eliot produced *Murder in the Cathedral* in 1935; Charles Williams staged *Thomas Cranmer of Canterbury* in 1936; Dorothy L. Sayers's *The Zeal of Thy House* in 1937 assured her place among the leading religious writers of her time.

Out of the tensions of her own life's blunt edges and her creative energies, Sayers produced a constant stream of carefully crafted works. Like the works of Charles Williams, whom she knew, T. S. Eliot, and C. S. Lewis, a contemporary, her writing represents a brilliant, imaginative restating of the orthodox Christian faith for modern readers. Although she was born to the rectory, her own religious writings did not appear until she was in her forties, including a popular series of radio dramas, of which *The Man Born to Be King* was the best known, and the influential volume *The Mind of the Maker*, which explores the relationship between the Christian doctrine of the Trinity and the artistic creative process. Her basic argument was that "all three persons of the Trinity are essentially concerned in creation," a process duplicated in human creative activity as The Book as You Think It, The Book as You Write It, and The Book as They Read It.[29]

Although *The Man Born to Be King* series was a national event, widely listened to on radio, it did not escape controversy. Fundamentalists and biblical literalists objected to her use of Cockney accents and common speech among characters in the biblical narrative, causing her to write the BBC's Director of Religious Broadcasting:

> I am frankly appalled at the idea of getting through the Trial and Crucifixion scenes with all the "bad people" having to be bottled down to expressions which could not possibly offend anybody. I will not allow the Roman soldiers to use barrack-room oaths, but they must behave like common soldiers hanging a common criminal, or where is the point of the story? Nobody cares . . . nowadays that Christ was "scourged, railed upon, buffeted, mocked, and crucified," because all those words have grown hypnotic with ecclesiastical use. But it does give people a slight shock to be shown that God was flogged, spat upon, slugged in the jaw, insulted with vulgar jokes, and spiked up on the gallows like an owl on a barn-door. That's the thing the priests and people did—has the Bishop forgotten it?[30]

Orthodox and patriotic in traditional ways, she had a strong social conscience as well. In a speech on work and economics, she said:

> Nothing has so deeply discredited the Christian Church as her squalid submission to the economic theory of society. . . . I believe, however, that there is a Christian doctrine of work, very closely related to the doctrines of the creative energy of God and the divine image in man. The modern tendency seems to be to identify work with gainful employment; and this is, I maintain, the essential heresy at the back of the great economic fallacy which allows wheat and coffee to be burnt and fish to be used for manure while whole populations stand in need of food. . . . If man's fulfillment of his nature is to be found in the full expression of his divine creativeness, then we urgently need a Christian doctrine of work, which shall provide,

not only for proper conditions of employment, but also that the work shall be such as a man may do with his whole heart, and that he shall do it for the work's sake.[31]

There was a prophetic tinge to her religious commentaries. Sayers was the opposite of Evelyn Underhill; mysticism meant little to her. "Where the intellect is dominant it becomes the channel of all other feelings. The 'passionate intellect' is really passionate. It is the only point at which ecstasy can enter. I do not know whether we can be saved by the intellect, but I do know that I can be saved by nothing else." She once wrote that neither "inner light" nor "spiritual experience" was a meaningful term for her and that:

> [o]f all the presuppositions of Christianity, the only one I really have and can swear to from personal inward conviction is sin. About that I have no doubt whatever and never have had. Neither does any doctrine of determinism or psychological maladjustment convince me in the very least that when I do wrong it is not I who do it and that I could not, by some means or other, do better.[32]

Her religious writings are not fully developed, and Sayers came to them late in her career. It is idle to speculate, but, had she chosen theology rather than French as the focus of her youthful creativity, she might have been the Anglican church's most lucid voice in this century, a figure certain to rival Newman in an earlier age.

RONALD BLYTHE, RELIGIOUS DIARIST

The English tradition of the religious diarist, of whom Parson James Woolforde and Francis Kilvert are perhaps the best-known examples, is continued in the twentieth century by Ronald Blythe, novelist, poet, prolific diarist, and author of *Akenfeld*, an account of village life. Blythe depicts the harsh but beautiful world of rural England, specifically the three East Anglia parishes where he has long served, Wormingsford, Mount Bures, and Little Horkesley. "It gets harder and harder in rural life," he writes, "to keep liturgy and everyday experience in meaningful rotation, to keep worship out of the theme park, to get a chilly wisp of November into the church." Nature and the liturgical year combine in this passage:

> The Palm Sunday procession was made from church to church, singing, of course, St. Theodulf's magnificent hymn, Gloria, laus et honor, over and

over again. He was one of Charlemagne's poet-bishops and, they say, the inventor of parish education and a keen advocate of beautifully illustrated Gospels. His hymn shows him a master of exultation. By rights we should surge up to the church, then into it, singing it, and all very grandly—"To thee now high exalted, our melody we raise." Just one week after his triumphal entrance, the risen Lord walked in a garden, a simple quiet place where the tombs were made. The spiritual as well as the natural movement of these March-April days is immense and irresistible. We are swept along, though far from mindlessly. There is planting, there is purpose, there is intelligence.[33]

MUSIC

After a long period of mediocre musical production, twentieth-century England sparkled with an outpouring of exceptional musicians writing secular and religious works, composers such as Ralph Vaughan Williams, Gustav Holst, Herbert Howells, Benjamin Britten, William Walton, and the non-Anglican Erik Routley, to name only a few. The spread of radio broadcasts and recordings helped diffuse the work of these and other composers and make high-quality representations of historic music available as well. Noteworthy were the annual Christmas Eve broadcasts of lessons and carols from Kings College, Cambridge, and the work of the Royal School of Church Music in training and education.

Ralph Vaughan Williams (1872–1958) was deeply influenced by Tudor music, as in his "Fantasia on a Theme by Thomas Tallis" (1910). English folk tunes and Genevan psalm tunes were widely used in his work, which included fifty choral works, including the popular "Five Mystical Songs" (1911), "Fantasia on Christmas Carols" (1912), and "Prayer to the Father in Heaven" (1948). Benjamin Britten (1913–1976) was attracted to the music of Henry Purcell. His "War Requiem" (1962) and "A Ceremony of Carols" (1942) are well known, as is his work for children, "Noye's Fludde" (1958).

Hymns Ancient and Modern, first published in 1861, was revised in 1904 and 1950, and remained a middle-of-the-road volume. The more comprehensive and musically interesting *English Hymnal*, first appearing in 1906, became a staple of twentieth-century Anglican worship, especially for its liturgical settings. Vaughan Williams, a prolific composer and researcher of folk music traditions, was the music editor, and Percy

Dearmer was the general editor. Dearmer, vicar of St. Mary's, Primrose Hill, London, was a foremost liturgical scholar, whose volume *The Parson's Handbook* became the clerical equivalent of Emily Post's guide to good manners for generations of Anglican clergy. Church of England worship also benefited from revisions in Methodist, Presbyterian, and other denominational hymnals, and by the general elevation of musical standards through specialized faculties, choir schools, and musical festivals. Never had the church's musical life been richer; never had its numbers, in proportion to total population, been lower. At the century's end, however, it could safely be said that music remained one of the major contributors to creating a distinctly Anglican ethos.

ANGLICAN COMMUNION, THE LAMBETH CONFERENCE

The Church of England gradually expanded its ties with its overseas sister churches and in the process adopted a global perspective on many issues central to church life. What evolved, apart from the work of specific missionary societies, was a series of periodic global bishops' conferences. In September 1867 the first such Lambeth Conference was held, attracting seventy-six bishops, many of whom stayed until December to discuss church issues. By 1888 the Lambeth Conference attracted 145 bishops, by 1968, 462 prelates from all over the world. Described as "a commonwealth of Churches without a central constitution . . . a federation without a federal government,"[34] these global meetings of bishops, held at ten-year intervals, became a regular feature of a church increasingly aware of its international role. The meetings were not synods or formal church councils with any legal standing, and they did not define doctrine; they were times for collegial exchange. One bishop-participant wrote:

> The pronouncements of the Fathers have only rarely reached the level of classic inspiration; there has been a tendency to verbiage, to pious locutions, to superficial handling of grave themes. The Conference, like most ecclesiastical assemblies, has not always been able to resist the temptation to pass resolutions on every conceivable subject. Yet it is doubtful whether any similar assembly in modern times has put on record so much sense and so little nonsense, or shown such sensitiveness to the movement of the times through which it has lived.[35]

The role of the Archbishop of Canterbury in such gatherings was symbolic. As successor to the seat of St. Augustine, the position held high prestige and historic importance, but little real power.

In 1920 the Lambeth Conference produced one of its most successful documents, "An Appeal to All Christian People." After acknowledging the role all Christian bodies have played in the current sad state of divisions, it called for a church "within whose visible unity all the treasures of faith and order, bequeathed as a heritage by the past to the present, shall be possessed in common, and made serviceable to the whole body of Christ." The document then suggested a formula for Christian unity; the Lambeth Quadrilateral of 1888, which is a variation of the earlier Chicago Quadrilateral of 1886, drawn from the work of William Reed Huntington, an American priest, in his book *The Church Idea, an Essay Toward Unity* (1870).[36] The four tenets are the following:

A. The Holy Scriptures of the Old and New Testaments as "containing all things necessary to salvation," and as being the rule and ultimate standard of faith.

B. The Apostles' Creed, as the Baptismal Symbol; and the Nicene Creed, as the sufficient statement of the Christian Faith.

C. The two Sacraments ordained by Christ Himself—Baptism and the Supper of the Lord—ministered with unfailing use of Christ's Words of Institution, and of the elements ordained by Him.

D. The Historic Episcopate, locally adapted in the methods of its administration to the varying needs of the nations and peoples called of God into the Unity of His Church.

The Lambeth drafters realized that the question of church order, in particular the role of bishops, would be a sore point on church union. They were willing to negotiate a mutual recognition of each other's ministerial orders in cases where unity was achieved. The goal was not absorption of other bodies, but a fresh vision of a multifaceted church moving ahead. "We do not ask that any one Communion should consent to be absorbed in another. We do ask that all should unite in a new and great endeavor to secure and to manifest to the world the unity of the Body of Christ for which He prayed."[37]

Increasingly, representatives from other Christian denominations were given observer status, and nonepiscopal consultants played a major role as resource leaders. At the 1988 Lambeth Conference, twenty-seven primates, heads of independent provinces, were present among the 525 bishops from around the world. Africa sent 175 bishops to the conference; Asia and South America were represented by large delegations as well. The Anglican Communion was clearly an international body, its membership now predominately nonwhite. The shift in sentiment from a national to an international perspective was expressed by an African bishop who told the Church of England, "We do not want you to be our mother—be our sister."[38]

"We must never make the survival of the Anglican Communion an end in itself"

"Exclusiveness is not a characteristic of the City of God," Archbishop of Canterbury Robert Runcie said in his opening address to the 1998 Conference, aptly called, "The Nature of the Unity We Seek." Runcie's text was the vision of the new heaven and new earth, the holy city, the New Jerusalem in the book of Revelation (cf. Rev. 21:22–27), where the gates of the city are never shut. Speaking of the "broken and divided world" in which the bishops live, Runcie described:

> the wounds of Southern Africa and Uganda, Sudan and Ethiopia; the wounds of the Philippines, Korea, and Sri Lanka; of Nicaragua, El Salvador, Argentina; of Jerusalem and the Middle East; the wounds of Ireland; the great global wounds of distrust between east and west, and the increasing disparity between North and South. Look at each other as human beings bearing the marks of human brokenness. But look at each other as fellow citizens of the heavenly city, and as those who are thus constituted within Christ's Church as a sign of hope for the whole human race, the bearers of the gospel of reconciliation.[39]

Runcie was no sentimentalist, using the past as apron strings to tie the worldwide body to outdated traditions. "We must never make the survival of the Anglican Communion an end in itself, the Churches of the Anglican Communion have never claimed to be more than a part of the one holy catholic and apostolic Church. Anglicanism, as a separate denomination, has a radically provisional character which we must never allow to be obscured." Reminding the bishops that "dispersed authority" was a characteristic of Anglicanism, he said they "may indeed wish to discuss the development of more solid structures of unity and coherence. But I for one would want their provisional character made absolutely clear; like tents in the desert they should be capable of being easily dis-

mantled when it is time for the Pilgrim people to move on."[40] No worldwide system of church government ever emerged from the Lambeth
Conferences, nor was the possibility suggested, and no universally arrived
at statements of doctrine resulted from its deliberations. What did evolve
was a concept of the universal church. If, for most of its existence, the
parish was the church's basic unit, with horizons limited to a village or a
few hills, by the century's end that had changed. Christians in England
might pray for the struggling church in the Sudan; a diocese in Latin
America might send a missionary offering to Africa; the church in Australia might support refugee work in southeast Asia. The preaching and
diplomacy of Desmond Tutu, archbishop of Capetown, attracted worldwide attention to Africa, as had the earlier writings of Trevor Huddleston,
a Community of the Resurrection missionary monk and later an archbishop, and Alan Paton, writer and lay leader, who publicized the horrors
of apartheid to a global community. (Huddleston visited Tutu when the
latter was hospitalized as a child, affirming the latter's interest in pursu-
ing a religious vocation.) Travelers from America might find themselves
welcomed in an Anglican church in Madrid or Brussels. While most
Anglicans' loyalty would remain with their home parish, perspectives
would never be quite the same, for a new world had intruded on them,
that of a global church. By the early 1990s the Anglican Communion
contained approximately seventy million members in five hundred dioceses, thirty thousand parishes and sixty-four thousand congregations
united in twenty-nine self-governing churches. England had the largest
membership, twenty-five million nominal members, Nigeria was next
with five million; Australia had nearly four million; Southern Africa and
the United States of America roughly 2.5 million members each. This
global presence, whose greatest growth was in the nonwhite world, was
equaled in geographic distribution only by the larger Roman Catholic
Church. Much of the church's growth was in Third World countries,
comprising twenty of the twenty-nine member churches.

While periodic Lambeth Conferences remained the primary vehicle for
inter-Anglican communication, they were supplemented in 1958 with a
small permanent office eventually becoming the Anglican Consultative
Council. Meeting every two or three years, the sixty-nine-member council is an advisory board composed of lay and clerical membership, presided over by the Archbishop of Canterbury. A Nigerian high court judge
was its first chairman, and subsequent leadership roles passed to American, Asian, Caribbean, and United Kingdom members. With annual meetings of its standing committee, the council provides constant monitoring

of information about global religious matters, ecumenical affairs, and shared information among member churches of the Anglican Communion. It thus fills a void left between the ten-year Lambeth meetings.

HESITANT STEPS TOWARD UNITY

After centuries of heated conflict, during the twentieth century Christian churches made hesitant steps toward unity. The late-nineteenth-century Student Christian Movements in various countries were precursors of the ecumenical movement, which William Temple called "the great new fact of our time." The movement emerged gradually from the 1910 Edinburgh International Missionary Conference. In the dull interwar decades, ecumenical contacts provided both excitement and fresh horizons for a generation of Church of England leaders and ties with the world overseas. After they returned home following the Edinburgh Conference, the Chinese Christian delegation cabled the conference organizers, "Hang on to co-operation like grim death," presaging both the importance of global contacts and their perils as well. No super church resulted from these conferences, but former antagonists gathered periodically, prayed together, issued declarations, and engaged in ongoing dialogue. There were severe impediments, Protestant suspicions, and Roman Catholic declarations, for example, Leo XIII's 1896 bull *Apostolicae Curae,* which declared "ordinations performed according to the Anglican rite are utterly invalid and altogether void."[41] Contacts with the Orthodox Church grew and following World War I the Fellowship of St. Alban and St. Sergius was founded, drawing on Anglicans interested in Eastern Orthodoxy and the growing Russian exile community in London and Paris. During the 1930s international conferences examined theological differences and brought Christians together, including German Christians threatened by the growing Nazi movement. Gathered under the banner of Life and Work and Faith and Order movements, the ecumenical representatives met in places like Oxford, Edinburgh, Stockholm, and Lausanne, and in classic European resort towns; out of such contact the World Council of Churches emerged in 1948. At that time representatives of 147 churches from forty-four different countries met in Amsterdam. (The number of members grew gradually to over three hundred churches.) Western Christians gradually came to see fellow believers from churches in Asia, Africa, and Latin America not as colonial subjects but as partners in a worldwide mission. The World Council of Churches, permanently housed in Geneva, did much to promote substantive encounters among Christians. It encouraged an informed international laity, and its promotion of annual weeks of Christian Unity each January brought denominations into prayerful contact with one another. While sharp doctrinal and cultural differences existed, at least personal suspicions and denominational hostilities were defused. However, the World Council of Churches' bright promise was considerably dulled in the century's later years as it increasingly took partisan political positions, often reflecting the politics of its German and Scandinavian social democratic leadership. Notwithstanding, Christians from all over the world continued to meet and ask what practical steps they could take toward unity despite their pronounced differences.

Roman Catholic relations improved when John XXIII became pope. The Archbishop of Canterbury, Geoffrey Fisher, visited the pope in Rome in 1960. The Church of England was invited to send observers to the Vatican Council called by John XXIII, and in 1966 Archbishop Michael Ramsey was received by Pope Paul VI in a joint service, from which emanated an Anglican–Roman Catholic International Commission, which in the 1970s produced agreed-upon statements on the Eucharist, ministry and ordination, and church authority. A papal visit to Canterbury in 1982 and the Archbishop of Canterbury's return visit to Rome in 1989 helped build an atmosphere of trust. This careful, hesitant, and qualified work, however, reached a plateau, if not a setback, as within the Anglican communion women priests and bishops were ordained and official Roman Catholic interest cooled considerably. This, and the cautious, conservative pontificate of John Paul II left moves toward unity in suspension. In any case, there was no reversion to the bad old days of mutual suspicion and distrust, name calling and recriminations; the Northern Ireland syndrome in Roman Catholic–Anglican relations had been avoided.

It is difficult to say exactly what the ecumenical movement means. No new encompassing church structure emerged from it, yet its impact on changing styles of worship was real, and greater reunion with Methodist, and Lutheran churches was a reality, as were the unified Church of South India and the United Church of Canada. The absence of negatives is to its credit. Anglicans and other denominations are generally more tolerant of one another than before; clergy and lay support groups often cross confessional lines and on social action projects, such as housing or feeding the poor, there is genuine cooperation. "That all may be one" is still a distant goal, but at least the underpinnings of unity are more evident now than in the past. It is unthinkable that the church would regress to the hostility and factionalism so characteristic of its earlier history.

A FINAL, FUTURE WORD

An aspect of the Anglican ethos is that, while Anglicanism has its own distinctive history, it gradually adapts its practices as it interacts with other denominations, Roman Catholics, Orthodox, and more conventional Protestant groups. The shifts are subtle, the addition of an Orthodox prayer here, or of a hymn from the charismatic movement there, perhaps the reading of a Roman Catholic author by a seminary class. This suggests a church constantly aware of its position in a wider context, graced with flexibility allowing it to bend with the winds of change without being uprooted. Another image might be of an organism retaining its basic structure while adapting to changes in its environment, seasonal or permanent.

Toward the century's end, Adrian Hastings wrote:

> Within the church almost every possible movement seems to have been tried and found just a little wanting. A trouble with modern culture is the sheer speed with which it goes through things. . . . The church opening upon the 1990s may, quite possibly, so far as it still creatively exists, be in better heart for having no such "movement" or pin-up figure upon which to focus devotion. . . . In place of the long, decaying old denominational consciousness . . . one senses the development of an almost taken-for-granted ecumenical consciousness.

There is also the "absolute provisionality of all our structures, movements, and whatever."[42]

Self-critical church members sometimes announce the eminent demise of their church, yet it endures. At times a faction breaks off, as in the women's ordination controversy within the American church; such splinter groups usually atrophy and wither, while the church regroups and goes on. My own observation is that the church is at its worst when it becomes self-congratulatory and prideful of its tolerance and flexibility. When the church is inward-looking and self-satisfied, it displays narcissism at its worst. Bishop Stephen Neill has written of the Anglican churches:

> With their own diversity and variety of traditions, they reach out in all directions, can find themselves at home with all manner of Churches, and

can to some extent serve as interpreters to one another of widely divided Churches both within and outside the ecumenical fellowship. On the other hand, the non-Anglican Churches are sometimes driven to distraction and infuriation by the uncertainties of Anglican action and the indefinable quality of Anglican thought. . . . Comprehensiveness has its drawbacks as well as its advantages.[43]

Anglicans in advocating a *via media* have avoided entering into the fullest depths of either Catholicism or Protestantism, and their emotional and doctrinal highs and lows as well. If the Anglican tradition has in any respect excelled, it has been in providing conditions that allow ordinary Christians to freely practice their devotional life and find a meaning to life, while functioning fully within the world. And when it is content with church buildings, choirs, and community standing, it will always be pulled up short by the crucified Christ and the Suffering Servant of Second Isaiah, horribly disfigured and rejected by this world's powers and principalities. When the Anglican Church looks to the margins of society, and to the world's brokenness, its complacency is challenged and its comfortable image of "the Conservative Party at prayer" gives way to gospel faithfulness. New times bring new issues. With the passion once reserved for placing the English Bible in the hands of laity, or in opposing slavery, waves of post–World War II Anglicans opposed apartheid and racial discrimination, welcoming people of color into full membership in the church. Then came a greater role for women, leading to their ordination to priesthood and episcopacy, and an exploration of the contribution women make to the fullest life of the church. The next question became a wider inclusion of persons of single-sexual orientation, gays and lesbians, into church life and ministry, and a consequent exploration of the depths and mystery of human sexuality and human community. A global church, at the same time, explored the environment as an issue of religious concern, and the economic disparities between North and South, the question of disarmament and the arms trade in the post–Cold War era plus the wisdom of limiting rapid population growth through contraception. Scientific advances brought with them global ethical questions, ranging from genetic engineering to assuring the quality of life of aging populations or making adequate nutrition available to the young. The list grows, and the church's position is not always crystalline; honest Christians may interpret difficult issues differently. Sometimes rational voices prevail, but the letters-to-the-editor columns of church publications are filled with their share of bile and invective.

"The whole desire of the Church has been to offer the fullness of God's help to every soul but never to dictate to any soul precisely how that soul may best receive the benefit," William Temple wrote in *Essays in Christian Politics*, adding, "It sets a high standard for the individual member. No doubt it involves comparative failure for very many who might, by a more strict and more military discipline, have been led to a fuller use of all the means of grace than in fact they practice under the Anglican system."[44]

The Anglican presence has shown its toughness and resiliency, difficult to adequately measure with statistics or canonical texts. It will always display tension between its polarities, the worldly and the mystical, between the prayers of devout laity and the work of power-conscious prelates, between high, low, and broad church. Other Anglican opposites include the academic and practical, English roots and overseas applications, the ordered call to a round of daily prayer and social tensions resulting in conflict and martyrdom. Another distinctly English contribution to the Anglican ethos is a respect for the past, for traditions and institutions embodying them, mixed with a passion for freedom and stubborn individuality. But the past's virtues, the example of Becket, Cranmer's prose, Andrewes's spirituality, or Temple's vision, must be made available to contemporary church members in Singapore and the Sudan, southern Brazil and northern Canada, if the church fulfills its ministry to be the Israel of God.

Out of the busy interaction of diverse elements has come an Anglican ethos, different in each century as issues, institutions, and personalities differ. There is no reason to doubt its future. Its ultimate worth is measured not by numbers or proximity to seats of power but by its following the divine will as disclosed in history through Christ's continual presence in the church. Its legacy, represented only partly by the readings selected for this volume, combines depth and vision. In each century the unpredictable happened: personalities emerged from relative obscurity to either define an era or lead the church in new directions. Some, like Henry VIII, had an immediate impact; others, like Julian of Norwich, were a more cumulative, long-term presence. Richard Hooker, John Wesley, Charles Gore, Michael Ramsey, Evelyn Underhill, Desmond Tutu—the list is long and varied. Like individual pieces of glass in a large rose window, their impact is augmentative, depending on where the observer stands in relation to the object. Possibly what the historian considers uncertainty, surprise in human events, or even apparent defeat, might be viewed as the

Holy Spirit at work, moving about like a wind, difficult to capture, impossible to see, but nevertheless permanently changing lives and institutions.

Readings

C. S. Lewis

Probably more English-speaking Christians have been attracted to the writings of C. S. Lewis (1898–1963) than to any other modern writer on religious topics. In literary history, children's stories, fables such as the Narnia tales, and books on specific topics, such as love, pain, psalms, and prayer, Lewis has attracted a global audience. The first excerpt below is from his famous *Screwtape Letters,* in which a senior devil advises a junior devil on how to lead a Christian to hell, in this case by abandoning the wider idea of the church for loyalty to a faction within it, such as the low or high church factions, for example: "I think I warned you before that if your patient can't be kept out of the Church, he ought at least to be violently attached to some party within it." *The Horse and His Boy,* one of the Narnia chronicles, provides the second excerpt, in which Shasta, a youthful orphan, and Aravis, daughter of a chief from a different region, undertake a pilgrimage-adventure, during which Shasta encounters Aslan, the lion and Christ-figure, which results in his own painful growth and self-discovery.

The Screwtape Letters
XVI

My Dear WORMWOOD,

You mentioned casually in your last letter that the patient has continued to attend one church, and one only, since he was converted, and that he is not wholly pleased with it. May I ask what you are about? Why have I no report on the causes of his fidelity to the parish church? Do you realize that unless it is due to indifference it is a very bad thing? Surely you know that if a man can't be cured of churchgoing, the next best thing is to send him all over the neighborhood looking for the church that "suits" him until he becomes a taster or connoisseur of churches.

The reasons are obvious. In the first place the parochial organization should always be attacked, because, being a unity of place and not of likings, it brings people of different classes and psychology together in the kind of unity the Enemy desires. The congregational principle, on the other hand, makes each church into a kind of club, and finally, if all goes well, into a coterie or faction. In the second place, the search for a "suitable" church makes the man a critic where the Enemy wants him to be a pupil. What He wants of the layman in church is an attitude which may, indeed, be critical in the sense of rejecting what is false or unhelpful, but which is wholly uncritical in the sense that it does not appraise—does not waste time in thinking about what it rejects, but lays itself open in uncommenting, humble receptivity to any nourishment that is going. (You see how groveling, how unspiritual, how irredeemably vulgar He is!) This attitude, especially during sermons, creates the condition (most hostile to our whole policy) in which platitudes can become really audible to a human soul. There is hardly any sermon, or any book, which may not be dangerous to us if it is received in this temper. So pray bestir yourself and send this fool the round of the neighboring churches as soon as possible. Your record up to date has not given us much satisfaction.

The two churches nearest to him, I have looked up in the office. Both have certain claims. At the first of these the Vicar is a man who has been so long engaged in watering down the faith to make it easier for a supposedly incredulous and hard-headed congregation that it is now he who shocks his parishioners with his unbelief, not vice versa. He had undermined many a soul's Christianity. His conduct of the services is also admirable. In order to spare the laity all "difficulties" he has deserted both the lectionary and the appointed psalms and now, without noticing it, revolves endlessly round the little treadmill of his fifteen favorite psalms and twenty favorite lessons. We are thus safe from the danger that any truth not already familiar to him and his flock should ever reach them through Scripture. But perhaps your patient is not quite silly enough for this church—or not yet?

At the other church we have Fr. Spike. The humans are often puzzled to understand the range of his opinions—why he is one day almost a Communist and the next not far from some kind of theocratic Fascism—one day a scholastic, and the next prepared to deny human reason altogether—one day immersed in politics, and, the day after, declaring that all states of this world are *equally* "under judgment." We, of course, see the connecting link, which is Hatred. The man cannot bring himself to preach anything which is not calculated to shock, grieve, puzzle, or humiliate his parents and their friends. A sermon which such people could accept would be to him as insipid as a poem which they could scan. There is also a promising streak of dishonesty in him; we are teaching him to say "The teaching of the Church is" when he really means "I'm almost sure I read it in Maritain or someone of that sort." But I must warn you that he has one fatal defect: he really believes. And this may yet mar all.

But there is one good point which both these churches have in common—they are both party churches. I think I warned you before that if your patient can't be kept out of the Church, he ought at least to be violently attached to some party within it. I don't mean on really doctrinal issues; about those, the more lukewarm he is the better. And it isn't the doctrines on which we chiefly depend for producing malice. The real fun is working up hatred between those who *say* "mass" and those who *say* "holy communion" when neither party could possibly state the difference between, say, Hooker's doctrine and Thomas Aquinas', in any form which would hold water for five minutes. And all the purely indifferent things—candles and clothes and what not—are an admirable ground for our activities. We have quite removed from men's minds what that pestilent fellow Paul used to teach about food and other unessentials—namely, that the human without scruples should always give in to the human with scruples. You would think they could not fail to see the application. You would expect to find the "low" churchman genuflecting and crossing himself lest the weak conscience of his "high" brother should be moved to irreverence, and the "high" one refraining from these exercises lest he should betray his "low" brother into idolatry. And so it would have been but for our ceaseless labor. Without that the variety of usage within the Church of England might have become a positive hotbed of charity and humility.

Your affectionate uncle,
SCREWTAPE[45]

The Horse and His Boy
From Book 5 in the *Chronicles of Narnia*
The Unwelcome Fellow Traveler

Shasta discovered that someone or somebody was walking beside him. It was pitch dark and he could see nothing. And the Thing (or Person) was going so quietly that he could hardly hear any footfalls. What he could hear was breathing. His invisible companion seemed to breathe on a very large scale, and Shasta got the impression that it was a very large creature. And he had come to notice this breathing so gradually that he had really no idea how long it had been there. It was a horrible shock.

It darted into his mind that he had heard long ago that there were giants in these Northern countries. He bit his lip in terror. But now that he really had something to cry about, he stopped crying.

The Thing (unless it was a Person) went on beside him so very quickly that Shasta began to hope he had only imagined it. But just when he was becoming quite sure of it, there suddenly came a deep, rich sigh out of the darkness beside him. That couldn't be imagination! Anyway, he had felt the hot breath of that sigh on his chilly left hand. . . .

"Who are you?" he said, scarcely above a whisper.

"One who has waited long for you to speak," said the Thing. Its voice was not loud, but very large and deep.

"Are you—are you a giant?" asked Shasta.

"You might call me a giant," said the Large Voice. "But I am not like the creatures you call giants."

"I can't see you at all," said Shasta, after staring very hard. Then (for an even more terrible idea had come into his head) he said, almost in a scream, "You're not—not something *dead*, are you? Oh please—please do go away. What harm have I ever done you? Oh, I am the unluckiest person in the whole world."

Once more he felt the warm breath of the Thing on his hand and face. "There," it said, "that is not the breath of a ghost. Tell me your sorrows."

Shasta was a little reassured by the breath: so he told how he had never known his real father or mother and had been brought up sternly by the fishermen. And then he told the story of his escape and how they were chased by lions and forced to swim for their lives and of all the dangers in Tashbaan and about his night among the Tombs and how the beasts howled at him out of the desert. And he told about the heat and thirst of their desert journey and how they were almost at their goal when another lion chased them and wounded Aravis. And also, how very long it was since he had had anything to eat.

"I do not call you unfortunate," said the Large Voice.

"Don't you think it was bad luck to meet so many lions?" said Shasta.

"There was only one lion," said the Voice.

"What on earth do you mean? I've just told you there were at least two the first night and—."

"There was only one: but he was swift of foot."

"How do you know?"

"I was the lion." And as Shasta gaped with open mouth and said nothing, the Voice continued. "I was the lion who forced you to join with Aravis. I was the cat who comforted you among the houses of the dead. I was the lion who drove the jackals from you while you slept. I was the lion who gave the Horses the new strength of fear for the last mile so that you should reach King Lune in time. And I was the lion you do not remember who pushed the boat in which you lay, a child near death, so that it came to shore where a man sat, wakeful at midnight, to receive you."

"Then it was you who wounded Aravis?"

"It was I."

"But what for?"

"Child," said the Voice, "I am telling you your story, not hers. I tell no-one any story but his own."

"Who *are* you?" asked Shasta.

"Myself," said the Voice, very deep and low so that the earth shook: and again "Myself," loud and clear and gay: and then the third time "Myself," whispered so softly you could hardly hear it, and yet it seemed to come from all round you as if the leaves rustled with it.

Shasta was no longer afraid that the Voice belonged to something that would eat him, nor that it was the voice of a ghost. But a new and different sort of trembling came over him. Yet he felt glad too.

The mist was turning from black to gray and from gray to white. This must have begun to happen some time ago, but while he had been talking to the Thing he had not been noticing anything else. Now, the whiteness around him became a shining whiteness; his eyes began to blink. Somewhere ahead he could hear birds singing. He knew the night was over at last. He could see the mane and ears and head of his horse quite easily now. A golden light fell on them from the left. He thought it was the sun.

He turned and saw, passing beside him, taller than a horse, a Lion. The horse did not seem to be afraid of it or else could not see it. It was from the lion that the light came. No-one ever saw anything more terrible or beautiful.

Luckily Shasta had lived all his life too far south in Calormen to have heard the tales that were whispered in Tashbaan about a dreadful Narnian demon that appeared in the form of a lion. And of course he knew none of the true stories about Aslan, the great Lion, the son of the Emperor-over-sea, the King above all High Kings in Narnia. But after one glance at the Lion's face he slipped out of the saddle and fell at its feet. He couldn't say anything, and he knew he needn't say anything.

The High King above all kings stooped towards him. Its mane, and some strange and solemn perfume that hung about the mane, was all around him. It touched his forehead with its tongue. He lifted his face and their eyes met. Then instantly the pale brightness of the mist and the fiery brightness of the Lion rolled themselves together into a swirling glory and gathered themselves up and disappeared. He was alone with the horse on a grassy hillside under a blue sky. And there were birds singing.[46]

T. S. Eliot

Eliot was an Anglo-Catholic who attended mass each morning when in London. His poetry shows influences of the Book of Common Prayer, mystics such as Julian of Norwich, and a deep awareness of the English religious past, as in "Little Gidding," the site of Nicholas Ferrar's short-lived lay monastic establishment, portrayed in Eliot's *Four Quartets*. The poem "Journey of the Magi" draws heavily on the imagery of Lancelot Andrewes; it can be compared to a Renaissance painting on the subject.

> "A cold coming we had of it,
> Just the worst time of the year
> For a journey, and such a long journey:
> The ways deep and the weather sharp,
> The very dead of winter."
> And the camels galled, sore-footed, refractory,
> Lying down in the melting snow.
> There were times we regretted
> the summer palaces on slopes, the terraces,
> And the silken girls bringing sherbet.
> Then the camel men cursing and grumbling
> And running away, and wanting their liquor and women,
> And the night-fires going out, and the lack of shelters,
> And the cities hostile and the towns unfriendly
> And the villages dirty and charging high prices:
> A hard time we had of it.
> At the end we preferred to travel all night,
> Sleeping in snatches,
> With the voices singing in our ears, saying
> That this was all folly.
>
>   Then at dawn we came down to a temperate valley,
> Wet, below the snow line, smelling of vegetation;
> With a running stream and a water-mill beating the darkness,
> And three trees on the low sky,
> And an old horse galloped away in the meadow.
> Then we came to a tavern with vine-leaves over the lintel,

Six hands at an open door dicing for pieces of silver,
And feet kicking the empty wine-skins.
But there was no information, and we continued
And arriving at evening, not a moment too soon
Finding the place; it was (you may say) satisfactory.

All this was a long time ago, I remember,
And I would do it again, but set down
This set down
This: were we led all that way for
Birth or Death? There was a Birth, certainly,
We had evidence and no doubt. I have seen birth and death,
But had thought they were different; this Birth was
Hard and bitter agony for us, like Death, our death.
We returned to our places, these Kingdoms,
But no longer at ease here, in the old dispensation,
With an alien people clutching their gods.
I should be glad of another death.[47]

Evelyn Underhill

A conductor of retreats and a prolific writer on spirituality, Evelyn Underhill was a major figure in articulating the Anglican ethos during the twentieth century. Her book *Worship,* first published in 1936, was an
encompassing survey of Christian worship's multiple characteristics,
including its roots in Judaism, and the evolution of the worship patterns
of major Christian traditions, Catholic and Protestant. This excerpt is
from a final chapter on "The Anglican Tradition":

The peculiar character of Anglicanism arises in part from the operation
of history; the conflict within her own borders, both before and after her
cultus took form, of Puritan and Catholic ideals. But it is also a true expression of certain paradoxical attributes of the English mind: its tendency to
conservatism in respect of the past, and passion for freedom in respect of
the present, its law-abiding faithfulness to the established custom, but
recoil from an expressed dominance; its reverence for the institutions which
incorporate its life, and inveterate individualism in the living of that life; its
moral and practical bent. All these characteristics can be studied in any
rural parish at the present day; and all spring to attention whenever either
an innovator or an authoritarian threatens to disturb the ancient ways. For

the English mind will neither have too much authority nor too much novelty; it will love the past, and frequently turn back to it, but will insist on interpreting the lessons of the past in its own way. It will accept the duty of an ordered worship, but resist mere ceremonial for its own sake. It will listen with respect to its spiritual teachers, but will not tolerate interference with the liberty and deep reserve of the individual soul. The short treatise "On Ceremonies" inserted in the First Prayer Book of Edward VI and still retained in the Book of Common Prayer is here a matchless expression of the national mind; its conviction that "innovation and newfangledness . . . is always to be eschewed," that "order and quiet discipline" are desirable qualities conducing to the glory of God, its democratic demand that the ceremonies used in public worship shall be at no point "dark or dumb" but "so set forth that every man may understand what they do mean and what use they do serve," its desire to steer such a course between those "addicted to their old customs" and those that would "innovate all things," as shall "please God and profit them both"—a problem which the national church has never perfectly solved.

Again, as this same document makes plain to us, the English mind is always inclined to assume that a primary object of ordered worship is the edifying of the congregation. Such worship chiefly exists to "stir up the dull mind of man to the remembrance of his duty to God"; for we tend as a race to give works priority over faith, to equate religion with goodness, and to estimate worship by its this-world effects in terms of the moral will, rather than by its power of lifting up the mind and heart unto God. This spiritual temper, which is still characteristic of the piety of rural England, did not spring into existence at the Reformation. It is fundamental to the national character; and Cranmer knew well what note to his fellow-countrymen the edifying quality of his "godly and descent order" of daily prayer. . . . It is this characteristic response of the English soul to the demand of God to which Anglican worship at its best gives stylized expression; and to which in its periodic revivals it always returns. On the whole, it is a response which leans more to the prophetic and Biblical than to the liturgic and sacramental side of the Christian cultus. The hymn-singing and Bible reading, the moral emphasis, which the English mind considers to be essential parts of worship, are not mere legacies of the Reformation; nor is it by chance that the Church of England has been content to use for centuries a dislocated Eucharistic canon, but has carefully revised her lectionaries and constantly added to her repertory of hymns. Not the supernatural mystery, but the homely side of man's relation to the Transcendent, his here-and-now dependence and moral obligation, is developed here.[48]

Charles Williams

Poet, essayist, novelist, playwright, critic, and editor, Charles Williams is difficult to categorize, but he was among the most articulate English religious voices of the first half-century. An enthusiastic, almost hypnotic lecturer, Williams was short, thin, and in endless motion. He worked as an editor for Oxford University Press and, when it moved from Amen Corner to Oxford during World War II, got to know T. S. Eliot and C. S. Lewis, whose *Allegory of Love* he edited for publication. Williams wrote several theological novels including *The Place of the Lion, Descent into Hell,* and *All Hallows Eve,* in which the supernatural and natural worlds commingle.

Williams did as much as any writer to make the Anglican ethos explicable in fiction. In his novel *Descent into Hell,* Peter Stanhope, a Christian playwright encounters Pauline Anstruther, a resident of the town near London where they both live in the 1930s, and who acts in one of his plays. Pauline is frightened by the increasingly frequent appearances of a *Doppelgänger,* her ghostly double. Stanhope offers to help her by bearing her fear and fright, a statement in fiction of the Christian idea of the Atonement, God bearing the difficulties of God's people, thus allowing Christians to bear each other's burdens as well.

Pauline sat back in her chair, and her arms lay along its arms. A rehearsal was taking place in the ground of the Manor House, and she had ended her part in the first act. . . . Stanhope sits near her and, in the course of conversation asks,

"Will you tell me what it is that bothers you?"

She said, "It sound too silly. . . . I have a trick," she said steadily, "of meeting an exact likeness of myself in the street." And as if she hated herself for saying it, she turned sharply on him. "There!" she exclaimed. "Now you know. You know exactly. And what will you say?"

Her eyes burned at him; he received their fury undisturbed, saying, "You mean exactly that?" and she nodded. "Well, it's not unknown. Goethe met himself once—on the road to Weimar, I think. But he didn't make it a habit. How long has this been happening?"

"All my life," she answered. "At intervals—long intervals, I know. Months and years sometimes, only it's quicker now. O, it's insane—no one could believe it, and yet it's there."

"It's your absolute likeness?" he asked.

"It's me," she repeated. "It comes from a long way off, and it comes up towards me, and I'm terrified—terrified—one day it'll come on and meet me. It hasn't so far; it's turned away or disappeared. But it won't always; it'll come right up to me—and then I shall go mad or die."

"Why?" he asked quickly, and she answered at once, "Because I'm afraid, dreadfully afraid."

"But," he said, "that I don't quite understand. You have friends; haven't you asked one of them to carry your fear?" "Carry my fear!" she said, sitting rigid in her chair, so that her arms, which had lain so lightly, pressed now into the basket-work and her long firm hands gripped it as if they strangled her own heart. "How can anyone else carry my fear? Can anyone else see it and have to meet it?"

Still, in that public place, leaning back easily as if they talked of casual things, he said, "You're mixing up two things. Think a moment, and you'll see. The meeting it—that's one thing, and we can leave it til you're rid of the other. It's the fear we're talking about. Has no one ever relieved you of that? Haven't you ever asked them to?"

She said: "You haven't understood, of course. . . . I was a fool. . . . Let's forget it. Isn't Mrs. Perry efficient?"

"Extremely," he answered. "And God redeem her. But nicely. Will you tell me whether you've any notion of what I'm talking about? And if not, will you let me do it for you?"

She attended reluctantly, as if to attend were an unhappy duty she owed him, as she had owed others and tried to fulfill them. She said politely, "Do it for me?"

"It can be done, you know," he went on. "It's surprisingly simple. And if there's no one else you care to ask, why not use me? I'm here at your disposal, and we could so easily settle it that way. Then you needn't fear it, at least, and then again for the meeting—that might be a very different business if you weren't distressed."

"But how can I not be afraid?" she asked. "It's hellish nonsense to talk like that. I suppose that's rude, but—."

"It's no more nonsense than your own story," he said. "That isn't; very well, this isn't. We all know what fear and trouble are. Very well—when you leave here you'll think to yourself that I've taken this particular trouble over instead of you. You'd do as much for me if I needed it, or for any one. And I will give myself to it. I'll think of what comes to you, and imagine it, and know it, and be afraid of it. And then, you see, you won't." . . . "It's so easy," he went on, "easy for both of us. It needs only the act. For what can be simpler than for you to think to yourself that since I am there to be troubled instead of you, therefore you needn't be troubled? And what can be easier than for me to carry for a little while a burden that isn't mine?"

She said, still perplexed at a strange language: "But how can I cease to be troubled? Will it leave off coming because I pretend it wants you? Is it your resemblance that hurries up the street?

"It is not," he said, "and you shall not pretend at all. The thing itself you may one day meet—never mind that now, but you'll be free from all distress because that you can pass on to me. Haven't you heard it said that we ought to bear one another's burdens?" . . . "To bear a burden is precisely to carry it instead of. If you're still carrying yours, I'm not carrying it for you—however sympathetic I may be. And anyhow there's no need to introduce Christ, unless you wish. It's a fact of experience. If you give a weight to me, you can't be carrying it yourself; all I'm asking you to do is to notice that blazing truth. It doesn't sound so difficult."

"And if I could," she said. "If I could do—whatever it is you mean, would I? Would I push my burden on to anybody else?"

"Not if you insist on making a universe for yourself," he answered. "If you want to disobey and refuse the laws that are common to us all, if you want to live in pride and division and anger, you can. But if you will be part of the best of us, and live and laugh and be ashamed with us, then you must be content to be helped. You must give your burden up to someone else, and you must carry someone else's burden. I haven't made this universe and it isn't my fault. But I'm sure this is a law of the universe, and not to give up your parcel is as much to rebel as not to carry another's. You'll find it quite easy if you let yourself do it."[49]

Dorothy L. Sayers

Although Dorothy L. Sayers was a well-known essayist and playwright, some of her most perceptive religious writing comes in her detective stories, in *The Nine Tailors* in particular, which brought her an offer of the presidency of England's leading bell-ringing society. Her East Anglia rectory childhood is recalled when Lord Peter Wimsey visits Fenchurch St. Paul to savor the old church's details and watch a change-ringing that inadvertently contributes to a death. Wimsey's tour of the church and his reflections on it are a vivid statement of the Church of England ethos derived from the history, architecture, and worship of many historic landmark village churches:

Wimsey scrambled to his feet and looked around.

At first glance he felt himself sobered and awe-stricken by the noble proportions of the church, in whose vast spaces the congregation—though a good one for so small a parish in the dead of a winter's night—seemed almost lost. The wide nave and shadowy aisles, the lofty span of the chancel arch—crossed, though not obscured, by the delicate fan-tracery and crenellated molding of the screen—the intimate and cloistered loveliness of the chancel, with its pointed arcading, graceful ribbed vault and five narrow east lancets, led his attention on and focused it first upon the remote glow of the sanctuary. Then his gaze, returning to the nave, followed the strong yet slender shafting that sprang fountain-like from floor to foliated column-head, spraying into the light, wide arches that carried the celestory. And there, mounting to the steep pitch of the roof, his eyes were held entranced with wonder and delight. Incredibly aloof, flinging back the light in a dusky shimmer of bright hair and gilded outspread wings, soared the ranked angels, cherubim and seraphim, choir over choir, from corbel and hammer-beam floating face to face uplifted.

"My God!" muttered Wimsey, not without reverence. And he softly repeated to himself: "He rode upon the cherubims and did fly; He came flying upon the wings of the wind."

Mr. Hezekiah Lavender poked his new colleague sharply in the ribs, and Wimsey became aware that the congregation had settled down to the General Confession, leaving him alone and agape upon his feet. Hurriedly he turned the leaves of his prayer-book and applied himself to making the proper responses. Mr. Lavender, who had obviously decided that he was either a half-wit or a heathen, assisted him by finding the Psalms for him and by bawling every verse loudly in his ear.

". . . Praise Him in the cymbals and dances: praise Him upon the strings and pipe."

The shrill voices of the surpliced choir mounted to the roof, and seemed to find their echo in the golden mouths of the angels.

"Praise Him upon the well-tuned cymbals; praise Him upon the loud cymbals."

"Let everything that hath breath praise the Lord."[50]

William Temple

Although his tenure as Archbishop of Canterbury was only two years, 1942–1944, William Temple (1881–1944) was a prolific writer of philosophy, biblical studies, and social commentaries. Active in the Workers' Educational Association and the Student Christian Movement, he served as headmaster of Repton, rector of St. James's, Piccadilly, before becoming archbishop of York in 1929. Many of his social commentaries, such as those contained below, originated as lectures or addresses.

From Christianity and the Social Order

It is sometimes supposed that what the Church has to do is sketch a perfect social order and urge men to establish it. But it is very difficult to know what a "perfect social order" means. Is it the order that would work best if we were all perfect? Or is it the order that would work best in a world of men and women such as we actually are? If it is the former, it certainly ought not to be established; we should wreck it in a fortnight. If it is the latter, there is no reason for expecting the Church to know what it is.

There is no such thing as a Christian social idea, to which we should conform our actual society as closely as possible. We may notice, incidentally, about any such ideals from Plato's *Republic* onwards, that no one really wants to live in the ideal state as depicted by anyone else. Moreover, there is the desperate difficulty of getting there. When I read any description of the Ideal State and think how we are to begin transforming our own society into that, I am reminded of the Englishman in Ireland who asked the way to Roscommon "Is it to Roscommon you want to go?" asked the Irishman. "Yes," said the Englishman; that's why I asked the way." "Well," said the Irishman, "if I wanted to go to Roscommon, I wouldn't be starting from here."

But though Christianity supplies no ideal in this sense, it supplies something of far more value—namely, principles on which we can begin to act in every possible situation. All Christian thinking, and Christian thinking about society no less than any other, must begin not with man but with God. The fundamental conviction is that God is the creator of the world which could not begin or continue except by His will. The world is not necessary to God in the same sense God is necessary to the world; for if there were no God, there would be no world; but if there were no world, God would be just what He is—only (presumably) about to make the world.

Each individual is born into a family and a nation. In his maturity he is very largely what these have made him. The family is so deeply grounded in nature and the nation in history that anyone who believes in God the Creator and as providence is bound to regard both as part of the divine plan for human life. Their claims have to be adjusted to one another, and so have the claims of the several families within each nation and of the several nations in the family of mankind. But any ordering of society which impairs or destroys the stability of the family stands condemned on that account alone; and any ordering of international life which obliterates the freedom of the several nations to develop their own cultural traditions is also condemned. The aim within the nation must be to create a harmony of stable and economically secure family units; the aim of the world as a whole must be to create a harmony of spiritually independent nations which recognize one another as reciprocally supplementary parts of a richly harmonious fellowship.

Such a harmony would be the earthly counterpart and "first fruits" (as St. Paul might call it) of the perfected Kingdom of God. It would supply the school, training the citizens of that Kingdom—of which the full life cannot be known under earthly conditions, for it is a fellowship of the servants of God in all generations alike with Him and with one another.[51]

Michael Ramsey

In *The Gospel and the Catholic Church*, Michael Ramsey, Archbishop of Canterbury, makes a strong case that the impasse among Christians over church order can find its resolution in the death and resurrection of Christ. As Christians die to self and are raised with Christ, there may be a way out of their collective brokenness. Since Ramsey wrote the book in 1936, a great deal of discussion has taken place among Christian groups and, while the steps toward organic unity are not extensive, at least a healthy dialogue takes place among most divided groups.

The Church and the Passion

The relevance of the Church of the Apostles consisted not in the provision of outward peace for the nations, nor in the direct removal of social distress, nor yet in any outward beauty of the Church itself, but in pointing to the death of Jesus the Messiah, and the deeper issues of sin and judgment—sin in which the Christians had shared, judgment under which they stood together with the rest of mankind. In all this the Church was scandalous and unintelligible to men, but by all this and nothing else it was relevant to their deepest needs.

For the relevance of the Church can never be any easier than was the relevance of the Messiah. He provoked questionings and doubts among many of the wisest and holiest of His race. He perplexed those who looked to Him as a national leader, as a reformer, a prophet, a teacher and a healer, and even as Messiah; for He abandoned His useful and intelligible works in Galilee in order to bring God's Kingdom by dying on the Cross. "There was no beauty in him that we should desire him." And the life beset by the "whys?" and "wherefores?" of good and sensible men ended with the terrible question-mark of the cry of desolation on the Cross, "My God, My God, why has thou forsaken me?" . . . His Church on earth is scandalous, with the question-marks set against it by bewildered men and with the question-mark of Calvary at the center of its teaching; yet precisely there is the power of God found, if only the Christians know whence they come and wither they go. They are sent to be the place where the Passion of Jesus Christ is known and where witness is borne to the Resurrection from the dead. Hence the philanthropist, the reformer, the broad-minded modern man can never understand, in terms of their own ideals, what the Church is or what it means. Of course it is scandalous, of course it is formed of sinners whose sinfulness is exposed by the light of the Cross, of course there is an awful question-mark at its center. These things must needs be, if it is the Body of Christ crucified and risen from the dead.

Ecclesia Anglicana

Amid the convulsions of religion in Europe in the sixteenth century the English church had a character and a story which is hard to fit into the conventional categories of Continental Christianity. The Anglican was and is a bad Lutheran, a bad Calvinist, and certainly no Papist. His church grew into its distinctive position under the shelter of the supremacy of the English King, and its story is bound up with the greed and the intrigues of Tudor statesmen. . . . Yet this church of England cannot be explained in terms of politics alone. It bore a spiritual witness, if only by linking together what Christians elsewhere had torn asunder—the Gospel of God, which had made the reformers what they were, and the old historical structure which the Reformers as a whole had rejected but without which the Gospel itself lacks its full and proper expression. The impact of Luther and Calvin was felt in the Anglicanism of the latter half of the sixteenth century, and is seen not only in the Thirty-Nine Articles but in the general return to the scriptures as the ruling element in faith and piety. The Bible was put once more into the hands of the people. Yet the Anglican church appealed to the Bible along lines very different from those of the Lutherans and the Calvinists; for it appealed also to the primitive Church with its structure and tradition, and thus interpreted the Bible in its true context. By refraining from the Lutheran error of giving particular statements of Scripture a domination over the rest, and from the Calvinistic error of pressing the use of Scripture into a self-contained logical system, it saw that Scripture centers simply in the fact of Christ Himself, and that this fact is to be apprehended with the aid of the whole structure and tradition of the Church. Here, therefore, was an appeal to antiquity, coherent and complete, and a faithfulness to lessons of history which the Reformers on the continent were missing.

For while the Anglican Church is vindicated by its place in history, with a strikingly balanced witness to Gospel and Church and sound learning, its greater vindication lies in its pointing through its own history to something of which it is a fragment. Its credentials are its incompleteness, with the tension and the travail in its soul. It is clumsy and untidy, it baffles neatness and logic. For it is sent not to commend itself as "the best type of Christianity," but by its very brokenness to point to the universal church wherein all have died.[52]

Notes

INTRODUCTION

1. Jeremy Taylor, *A Discourse of the Liberty of Prophesying*, Sect. X, 5, in *Works*, ed. Heber, Vol. VIII, pp. 97–98; also Vol. V, p. 498; Vol. XI, p. 485, quoted in H. R. McAdoo, *Anglican Heritage: Theology and Spirituality* (Norwich: Canterbury Press, 1991), 15.

2. Timothy Finn, *Knapworth at War* (1982), 46, quoted in Adrian Hastings, *A History of English Christianity, 1920–1990* (Philadelphia: Trinity Press International, 1991), 666.

3. F. D. Maurice, *Lincoln's Inn Sermons, Kingdom of Christ*, II, pp. 11, 36, quoted in Alex R. Vidler, *F. D. Maurice and Company: Nineteenth Century Studies* (London: SCM, 1966), 193.

CHAPTER 1
FROM EARLIEST TIMES TO THE MIDDLE AGES

1. Oliver Davies and Fiona Bowie, eds., *Celtic Christian Spirituality: Medieval and Modern* (London: SPCK, 1995), 38.

2. Ibid., 128.

3. John T. McNeill, *The Celtic Churches: A History, A.D. 200 to 1200* (Chicago: University of Chicago Press, 1974), 223–24.

4. Davies and Bowie, *Celtic Christian Spirituality*, 34–35.

5. From Cogitosus's *Life of Brigid*, quoted in Davies and Bowie, *Celtic Christian Spirituality*, 64.

6. Quoted from Alexander Carmichael, *Carmina Gadelica*, in Davies and Bowie, *Celtic Christian Spirituality*, 122–23.

7. R. H. Hodgkin, *History of the Anglo-Saxons* (1935), 1:254, quoted in John

R. H. Moorman, *A History of the Church in England,* 3rd ed. (Harrisburg, Pa.: Morehouse Publishing, 1994), 10.

8. *Poems from the Old English,* trans. Burton Raffel, 2nd ed. (Lincoln: University of Nebraska Press, 1964), 40.

9. Quoted from the Old Irish, *Life of Columcille,* in John Mardsen, *The Fury of the Northmen: Saints, Shrines, and Sea-Raiders in the Viking Age, AD 793–878* (New York: St. Martin's Press, A Thomas Dunne Book, 1993), 65.

10. Quoted from Symeon's *History of the Church of Durham,* in Mardsen, *Fury of the Northmen,* 29

11. Mardsen, *Fury of the Northmen,* 179.

12. John Gillingham, "The Early Middle Ages, 1066–1290," in *The Oxford History of Britain,* ed. Kenneth O. Morgan (New York: Oxford University Press, 1993), 177.

13. John R. H. Moorman, *Church Life in the Thirteenth Century* (Cambridge: Cambridge University Press, 1946), 99.

14. Ibid., 276, 338–39.

15. Ibid., 99.

16. Ibid., 153.

17. Quoted in Alec Clifton-Taylor, *The Cathedrals of England* (London: Thames & Hudson, 1986), 73.

18. Moorman, *Church Life,* 135.

19. *Poems from the Old English,* trans. Raffel, 31–34.

20. Quoted from translations by Charles Cotton, *Friends of Canterbury Cathedral* (Cambridge: Cambridge University Press, 1930), 263; *Canterbury* in Clifton-Taylor, *Cathedrals,* 23.

21. Quoted in Clifton-Taylor, *Cathedrals,* 23.

22. Quoted from T. S. R. Boase, *English Art, 1100–1216,* vol. 3 of *Oxford History of English Art* (Oxford: Oxford University Press, 1953), 89; also in Clifton-Taylor, *Cathedrals,* 263.

23. Julian of Norwich, *Revelations of Divine Love,* ed. Halcyon Backhouse with Rhona Pipe (London: Hodder & Stoughton, 1992), 14–15.

24. Ibid., 140.

25. *The Hymnal 1982 According to the Use of the Episcopal Church,* (New York: Church Hymnal Corporation, 1986), No. 370, trans. Cecil Frances Alexander (1818–1895).

26. Bede, *A History of the English Church and People,* trans. Leo Sherley-Price (Baltimore: Penguin Books, 1975), 126–28.

27. Bede, *History,* III.9, Penguin edition, pp. 155–57.

28. *Poems from the Old English,* trans. Raffel, 67.

29. From *The Statesman's Book* of John of Salisbury, trans. John Dickinson, (New York: Alfred A. Knopf, 1927), 64–65, 3–9, 198–200, quoted in *The Traditions of the Western World,* ed. J. H. Hexter (Chicago: Rand McNally, 1968), 220–26.

30. Julian of Norwich, *Revelations of Divine Love*, ed. Backhouse and Pipe, 55–56, 124–26.

CHAPTER 2
THE SIXTEENTH CENTURY

1. Diarmaid MacCulloch, *Tudor Church Militant: Edward VI and the Protestant Reformation* (London: Allen Lane, Penguin Press, 1999), 2.

2. *The Acts and Monuments of John Foxe*, ed. S. R. Cattley (London: R. B. Seeley and W. Burnside, 1837–41), 4:633–36, quoted in Franklin Le Van Baumer, *Main Currents of Western Thought* (New York: Alfred A. Knopf, 1954), 175.

3. A. G. Dickens, *The English Reformation*, The Fortuna Library (London: Collins, 1969), 161.

4. *The Acts and Monuments of John Foxe* (1877), 7:530, quoted in J. R. H. Moorman, *A History of the Church in England*, 3rd ed. (Harrisburg, Pa.: Morehouse Publishing, 1994), 195.

5. Dickens, *English Reformation*, 371.

6. Leah S. Marcus, "Elizabeth the Writer," *History Today* [London] (October 2000): 38.

7. Hallam, *Constitutional History*, 1:224, cf. 225, quoted in Robert K. Faulkner, *Richard Hooker and the Politics of a Christian England* (Los Angeles: University of California Press, 1981), 179.

8. Richard Hooker, *The Laws of Ecclesiastical Polity*, book viii, I, 2, quoted in Horton Davies, *Worship and Theology in England: From Cranmer to Baxter and Foxe, 1534–1690* (Grand Rapids: Eerdmans, 1996), 27–28.

9. Dickens, *English Reformation*, 403.

10. Christopher Hill, *Change and Continuity in 17th-Century England* (New Haven: Yale University Press, 1998), 99.

11. W. H. Frere and W. M. Kennedy, eds., *Visitation Articles and Injunctions of the Period of the Reformation* (London: Longmans, Green & Co., 1910), 2:241–45, quoted in Moorman, *History of the Church in England*, 180–85.

12. From *Injunctions Given by the most reverend Father in Christ, Edmonde . . . in his Metropoliticall visitation of the Province of Yorke* (London, 1571) (*STC* 10375), quoted in David Cressy and Lori Anne Ferrell, *Religion and Society in Early Modern England: A Sourcebook* (New York: Routledge, 1996), 92–93.

13. Frere and Kennedy, eds., *Visitation Articles and Injunctions*, 2:126.

14. Davies, *From Cranmer to Baxter and Foxe*, 365.

15. Louis B. Wright, *Middle-Class Culture in Elizabethan England* (Chapel Hill: University of North Carolina Press, 1935), 228.

16. From Dickens, *English Reformation*, 214, quoted in Christopher Haigh,

English Reformations: Religion, Politics, and Society under the Tudors (Oxford: Clarendon Press, 1993), 161.

17. Dickens, *English Reformation*, 185.

18. Diarmaid MacCulloch, "Cranmer's Ambiguous Legacy," *History Today* 46, no. 6 (June 1996): 23–31; see also Diarmaid MacCulloch, *Thomas Cranmer* (New Haven: Yale University Press, 1996).

19. John Bridges, "A Sermon preached at Paul's Crosse" (1571), quoted in Davies, *From Cranmer to Baxter and Foxe*, 33.

20. Charles P. Price and Louis Weil, *Liturgy for Living* (New York: Seabury Press), 83–85.

21. MacCulloch, "Cranmer's Ambiguous Legacy," 31.

22. C. S. Lewis, *English Literature in the Sixteenth Century Excluding Drama* (Oxford: Oxford University Press, 1954), 221.

23. "Articles of Religion," *Prayer Book and Hymnal* (New York: Church Hymnal Corporation, 1986), 867–78.

24. *Subscriptions*, 79, quoted in Paul Avis, *Anglicanism and the Christian Church* (Minneapolis: Fortress Press, 1989), 264.

25. *The Sermons of Bishop Latimer* and *The Remains of Bishop Latimer* (1884–45) (Printed by the Parker Society in two volumes), quoted in Moorman, *History of the Church in England*, 183.

26. Hugh Latimer, *Works*, 1:306; *Sermons*, 463–64, quoted in Davies, *From Cranmer to Baxter and Foxe*, 248–49.

27. Davies, *From Cranmer to Baxter and Foxe*, I, 248.

28. John Jewel, *The Zurich Letters*, ed. Hastings Robinson, 2 vols. (Cambridge: The Parker Society, 1842–45), 1:55, quoted in John E. Booty, *John Jewel as Apologist of the Church of England* (London: S.P.C.K., 1963), 24.

29. John Jewel, *An Apology of the Church of England*, ed. J. E. Booty (Charlottesville: University of Virginia Press, for The Folger Shakespeare Library, 1963), 135.

30. *The Encyclopedia Britannica*, 11th ed. (New York: Cambridge University Press, 1910), 672. An important recent biography of Hooker in Philip B. Secor's *Richard Hooker, Prophet of Anglicanism* (Toronto: Anglican Book Centre, 2000).

31. Quoted in Davies, *From Cranmer to Baxter and Foxe*, II, xvii.

32. *Orthodox Spirituality and Protestant and Anglican Spirituality*, trans. Barbara Wall (Paris, 1963), 111, quoted in Davies, *From Cranmer to Baxter and Foxe*, 98.

33. *The Preces Privatae of Lancelot Andrewes, Bishop of Winchester, translated with an Introduction and Notes by F. E. Brightman* (New York: Meridian Books, 1961), 60.

34. T. S. Eliot, *For Lancelot Andrewes: Essays on Style and Order* (Garden City, N.Y.: Doubleday, Doran, 1929), 19.

35. C. J. Stranks, *Anglican Devotion: Studies in the Spiritual Life of the*

Church of England between the Reformation and the Oxford Movements (1961), 9, quoted in Davies, *From Cranmer to Baxter and Foxe,* I, 405.

36. Davies, *From Cranmer to Baxter and Foxe,* I, 408.

37. From John Foxe's *Acts and Monuments* (1576) (*STC* 11224), 1661, quoted in Cressy and Ferrell, *Religion and Society in Early Modern England,* 34–35.

38. Lansdowne Mss. 8, f. 16, in Henry Gee, *The Elizabethan Prayer Book* (1902), 164–65, quoted in Moorman, *History of the Church in England,* 217.

39. Henry Gee and William John Hardy, *Documents Illustrative of English Church History* (London: Macmillan, 1910; reprint, New York: Kraus Reprint Corporation, 1966), 269–81.

40. *The Fathers of the English Church; or, a Selection from the Writings of the Reformers and early Protestant Divines of the Church of England,* vol. 3 (London: John Hatchard, 1809), 603–5, 618–19, 622, 636–37.

41. *The Works of Thomas Cranmer,* ed. G. E. Duffield (Appleford, Berkshire, England: Sutton Courtenay Press, 1964), 3–4.

42. *The Fathers of the English Church or, a Selection from the Writings of the Reformers and Early Protestant Divines of the Church of England,* vol. 2 (London: John Hatchard, 1808), 646–49.

43. John Jewel, "Apology of the Church," in *The Fathers of the English Church; or, a Selection from the Writings of the Reformers and early Protestant Divines of the Church of England,* vol. 7 (London: John Hatchard, 1909), 18–19, 26, 28.

44. Richard Hooker, *Of the Laws of Ecclesiastical Polity,* ed. Ronald Bayne (London: Macmillan, 1902), 15, 19, 20–27.

45. Richard Hooker, *Ecclesiastical Polity: Selections,* ed. Arthur Pollard (Manchester: Fyfield Books, 1990), 129–31, 138–39, 146–47, 167–73.

46. *The Private Prayers of Lancelot Andrewes,* ed. Hugh Martin (London: SCM, 1957), 15, 20–21, 40, 110–13.

CHAPTER 3
THE SEVENTEENTH CENTURY

1. Anonymous, The Vicar of Bray, in *The New Oxford Book of English Verse, 1250–1950,* ed. Helen Gardner (New York: Oxford University Press, 1972), 425–27.

2. From *The Kings Majesties Declaration to His Subjects, Concerning Lawfull Sports to be Used* (London, 1633) (*STC 9257*), quoted in David Cressy and Lori Anne Ferrel, *Religion and Society in Early Modern England: A Sourcebook* (New York: Routledge, 1996), 147.

3. H. R. Trevor-Roper, *Archbishop Laud, 1573–1645* (London: Macmillan, 1940), 148.

4. Horton Davies, *Worship and Theology in England: From Cranmer to Baxter and Foxe, 1534–1690* (Grand Rapids: Eerdmans, 1996), II, 13.

5. William Prynne, *Canterburies Doome* (1646), 114f., quoted in Davies, *From Cranmer to Baxter and Foxe*, 19.

6. From Percival Moore, ed., "The Metropolitical Visitation of Archdeacon (sic) Laud," *Associated Architectural Societies Reports and Papers* 29 (1907): 477–534, quoted in Cressy and Ferrel, *Religion and Society in Early Modern England*, 155–57.

7. Trevor-Roper, *Archbishop Laud*, 295.

8. C. V. Wedgwood, *The King's Peace* (1955), 93, quoted in Stephen Neill, *Anglicanism* (New York: Oxford University Press, 1982).

9. From E. H. Evelyn White, ed., "William Dowsing's Destructions," in *Transactions of the Cambridgeshire and Huntingdonshire Archaeological Society* 3 (1914): 77–91, quoted in Cressy and Ferrel, *Religion and Society in Early Modern England*, 184.

10. Kenneth R. Long, *The Music of the Church of England* (London: Hodder & Stoughton, 1971), 205.

11. J. R. H. Moorman, *A History of the Church in England*, 3rd ed. (Harrisburg, Pa.: Morehouse Publishing, 1994), 239.

12. MS Tanner 57, fo. 525, quoted in John Spurr, *The Restoration Church of England, 1646–1689* (New Haven: Yale University Press, 1991), 20.

13. Quoted in Davies, *From Cranmer to Baxter and Foxe*, II, 354–55.

14. Spelling modernized. Quoted in Charles C. Tiffany, *A History of the Protestant Episcopal Church in the United States of America* (New York: Christian Literature Co., 1898), 13–14.

15. J. Eachard, *The Grounds and Occasions of Contempt of the Clergy* (1670), in E. Arber, *An English Garner*, vii, p. 258, quoted in Moorman, *History of the Church in England*, 258.

16. Christopher Hill, *Society and Puritanism in Pre-Revolutionary England*, 2nd ed. (New York: Schocken Books, 1967), 421–24.

17. Thomas Comber, *A Discourse Concerning the Daily Frequenting the Book of Common Prayer* (1687), 13, quoted in Davies, *From Cranmer to Baxter and Foxe*, I, 332.

18. Davies, *From Cranmer to Baxter and Foxe*, II, 32.

19. Jeremy Taylor, *Works*, 4:310, in Jeremy Taylor, *Selected Works*, ed. Thomas K. Carroll (New York: Paulist Press, 1990), 353.

20. Jeremy Taylor, *Selected Works*, ed. Carroll, 55, quoted in T. K. Carroll, *The Caroline Liturgical Renewal—A Puritan Controversy* (Rome: Anselmianum, 1973), 282.

21. Jeremy Taylor, *Selected Works*, ed. Carroll, 357.

22. George Herbert, *The Country Parson, The Temple,* ed. John N. Wall, Jr. (New York: Paulist Press, 1984), 291–92.

23. *The Arminian Nunnery, or A Brief Description and Relation of the late Erected Monastical Place called the Arminian Nunnery at Little Gidding in Huntingdonshire* (1641), 7–8, quoted in Davies, *From Cranmer to Baxter and Foxe,* I, 106.

24. Thomas Traherne, *Centuries,* III, 3, quoted in K. W. Salter, *Thomas Traherne, Mystic and Poet* (London: Edward Arnold, 1964), 22–23.

25. Thomas Traherne, *Centuries,* I, 29, quoted in Salter, *Thomas Traherne,* 71.

26. John Locke, *The Reasonableness of Christianity* (1695), 292, quoted in Moorman, *History of the Church in England,* 256.

27. Izaak Walton, *The Life of George Herbert,* 301–2, quoted in Davies, *From Cranmer to Baxter and Foxe,* I, 103.

28. George Herbert, *The Country Parson, The Temple,* ed. Wall, 56–57.

29. Ibid., 60–61.

30. Ibid., 62–63.

31. Ibid., 69–70.

32. Ibid., 88.

33. Ibid., 74–77, 109.

34. Jeremy Taylor, *Selected Works,* ed. Carroll, 430.

35. Ibid., 430–31, 441–43.

36. John Donne, *Selections from Divine Poems, Sermons, Devotions, and Prayers,* ed. John Booty (New York: Paulist Press, 1990), 173–74, 184–86, 233–35, 244.

37. John Locke, *An Essay Concerning Human Understanding,* ed. Alexander Campbell Fraser (Oxford: Clarendon Press, 1894), 2:408–13.

38. John Locke, *An Essay Concerning Human Understanding* (Chicago: Henry Regnery, 1956), 19–23, 336–37.

39. John Locke, *Treatise of Civil Government,* ed. Charles L. Sherman (New York: Appleton-Century-Crofts, 1937), 5–7, 19, 29, 56–57.

CHAPTER 4
THE EIGHTEENTH CENTURY

1. From H. H. Montgomery, *Foreign Missions* (London: Longmans, Green, 1902), 6, quoted in Roger Lloyd, *The Church of England, 1900–1965* (London: SCM, 1966), 46.

2. Edmund Burke, "Speech on the Petition of the Unitarians," May 11, 1792, and *Reflections on the Revolution in France* (1790), 147–48, quoted in Norman Sykes, *Church and State in England in the XVIIIth Century* (Cambridge: Cambridge University Press, 1934), 331.

3. In T. Smollett, *Roderick Random*, chapter 9; Sykes, *Church and State*, 217; John R. H. Moorman, *A History of the Church in England*, 3rd ed. (Harrisburg, Pa.: Morehouse Publishing, 1994), 286.

4. Mason to Hurd, 26 November 1791, in *Correspondence of Hurd and Mason*, ed. E. H. Pearce and L. Whibley, quoted in Sykes, *Church and State*, 102.

5. James Austen, *Loiterer*, no. 21, quoted in Irene Collins, *Jane Austen and the Clergy* (London: Hambleton Press, 1994), 116.

6. James Austen, *Loiterer*, no. 21, quoted in Collins, *Jane Austen*, 116.

7. Gerald R. Cragg, *The Church in the Age of Reason, 1648–1789* (New York: Penguin Books, 1981), 140.

8. Ibid., 117.

9. Oliver Goldsmith, *The Deserted Village, The Harvard Classics, English Poetry in Three Volumes*, vol. 2, ed. Charles W. Eliot (New York: P. F. Collier & Son, 1910), 512.

10. In *Diary of Viscount Percival, Earl of Egmont*, I, 100. H.M.C. Egmont MSS, quoted in Sykes, *Church and State*, 95.

11. In *Act Book for the Diocese of Gloucester*, 20 Feb. 1768–23 March 1789, Gloucester City Library, 304 (10), quoted in Sykes, *Church and State*, 99.

12. In *A Frenchman in England* (1784), trans. S. C. Roberts (Cambridge, 1933), 86, quoted in Sykes, *Church and State*, 134.

13. Sykes, *Church and State*, 429.

14. In *Life of Dr. Thomas Newton*, quoted in Sykes, *Church and State*, 135.

15. In William Roberts, *The Life of Hannah More with Selections from her Correspondence* (London: Seely, Jackson and Halliday, 1872), 63, quoted in *English Spirituality in the Age of Wesley*, ed. David Lyle Jeffrey (Grand Rapids: Eerdmans, 1994), 5.

16. L. Stephens, *History of English Thought in the Eighteenth Century* (New York, 1902), 2:335–38.

17. In *The Works of the Most Reverend Dr. John Tillotson, late Lord Archbishop of Canterbury: containing Two Hundred Sermons and Discourses, on Several Occasions . . .*, 2 vols. (1742), Sermon 137, "The Life of Jesus Christ consider'd as our Example," 2:241, quoted in Horton Davies, *Worship and Theology in England: From Watts and Wesley to Martineau, 1690–1900* (Grand Rapids: Eerdmans, 1996), III, 56.

18. Joseph Addison, in *The Spectator*, August 9, 1712, quoted in Davies, *From Watts and Wesley to Martineau*, 55.

19. Fanny Price in Jane Austen, *Mansfield Park*, 113, in *The Novels of Jane Austen: The Text Based on Collation of the Early Editions*, ed. R. W. Chapman, 3rd ed., 5 vols. (Oxford, 1823), quoted in Collins, *Jane Austen*, 188–89.

20. Ernest Campbell Mossner, *Bishop Butler and the Age of Reason: A Study in the History of Thought* (New York: Macmillan, 1936), 165–66.

21. Ibid., 240.

22. Joseph Addison, in *The Spectator*, No. 10, March 12, 1711, quoted in Mossner, *Bishop Butler and the Age of Reason*, 15.

23. In Thomas Sprat, *History of the Royal Society* (1667), 374, quoted in Mossner, *Bishop Butler and the Age of Reason*, XII.

24. Gordon Rupp, *Religion in England, 1688–1791* (Oxford: Clarendon Press, 1986), 7.

25. Samuel Johnson, *Diaries, Prayers, Annals*, ed. E. L. McAdam, Jr., with Donald and May Hyde, in *The Yale Edition of the Works of Samuel Johnson* (New Haven: Yale University Press, 1958), 1:4, 17–18, quoted in Charles E. Pierce, Jr., *The Religious Life of Samuel Johnson* (Hamden, CT: Archon Books, 1983).

26. Hannah More, *Strictures on the Modern System of Female Education, Fashionable Christianity*, 2 vols., 2nd ed. (London: T. Cadell, 1799; reprint, New York: Garland, 1974), in *English Spirituality in the Age of Wesley*, ed. David Lyle Jeffrey (Grand Rapids: Eerdmans, 1994), 484–91.

27. John Wesley, in J. H. Overton, *John Wesley* (1891), 61, quoted in Moorman, *History of the Church in England*, 298.

28. *John and Charles Wesley, Selected Prayers, Hymns, Journal Notes, Sermons, Letters and Treatises*, ed. Frank Whaling (New York: Paulist Press, 1981), 179.

29. Evelyn Underhill, *Worship* (New York: Crossroad, 1989), 305.

30. From P. D. Gilbert, *Religion and Society in Industrial England*, table, p. 31, in Peter Virgin, *The Church in an Age of Negligence: Ecclesiastical Structure and Problems of Church Reform, 1700–1840* (Cambridge: James Clarke, 1989), 18.

31. Quoted in James B. Simpson and Edward M. Story, *The Long Shadow of Lambeth X* (New York: McGraw-Hill, 1969), 228.

32. Elie Halévy, *A History of the English People*, 3 vols., 1934, 3:166, quoted in Davies, *From Watts and Wesley to Martineau*, 222.

33. S. C. Carpenter, *Church and People, 1789–1889: A History of the Church of England from William Wilberforce to "Lux Mundi"* (London: S.P.C.K., 1937), 42.

34. Samuel Wesley, in H. A. Beecham, "Samuel Wesley, Senior: New Biographical Evidence," App. Letter, August 22, 1692, in *Renaissance and Modern Studies* (Nottingham: University of Nottingham, 1963), vii, p. 104, quoted in Rupp, *Religion in England*, 301.

35. E. Burke, "Speech on the Petition of the Unitarians," 11 May 1792, 147–48, quoted in Sykes, *Church and State*, 428.

36. Austin Warren, *William Law: Ascetic and Mystic*, in William Law, *A Serious Call to a Devout and Holy Life, The Spirit of Love*, ed. Paul G. Stanwood (New York: Paulist Press, 1978), 16.

37. William Law, *A Serious Call to a Devout and Holy Life, The Spirit of Love*, ed. Paul G. Stanwood (New York: Paulist Press, 1978), 104–9.

38. John Wesley, *A Plain Account of Genuine Christianity* (1753), in *John and Charles Wesley*, ed. Whaling, 107, 176, 227–28, 121–25.

39. Ibid., 85–86.

40. James Woodforde, *The Diary of a Country Parson, 1758–1802* (New York: Oxford University Press, 1978), 137–40, 150–52, 154 157–58.

CHAPTER 5
THE NINETEENTH CENTURY

1. Frederick Engels, in *Conditions of the Working Class in England in 1844,* 51, quoted in S. C. Carpenter, *Church and People, 1789–1889: A History of the Church of England from William Wilberforce to "Lux Mundi"* (London: S.P.C.K., 1933), 314.

2. Adam Smith, *Wealth of Nations,* ed. Cannan, 1:123, quoted in W. E. Lunt, *History of England* (New York: Harper & Brothers, 1938), 585.

3. Richard D. Altick, *Victorian People and Ideas* (New York: W. W. Norton, 1973), 205.

4. Carpenter, *Church and People,* 28.

5. Ibid., 58.

6. Peter Virgin, *The Church in an Age of Negligence: Ecclesiastical Structure and Problems of Church Reform, 1700–1840* (Cambridge: James Clarke, 1989), 94.

7. Carpenter, *Church and People,* 27.

8. Quoted in Carpenter, *Church and People,* 69.

9. In John Lettice to James Plumptre, 3 September 1825, Cambridge University Library, Add. Mss 5866, f.35, quoted in Virgin, *Church in an Age of Negligence,* 43.

10. John Wesley, *A Plain Account of Genuine Christianity* (1753), in *John and Charles Wesley, Selected Prayers, Hymns, Journal Notes, Sermons, Letters and Treatises,* ed. Frank Whaling (New York: Paulist Press, 1981), 170–71.

11. Altick, *Victorian People,* 142–43.

12. In E. M. Goulburn, *Life of Dean Burgon* (1892), 1:283, quoted in Alec R. Vidler, *The Church in an Age of Revolution, 1799 to the Present Day* (New York: Penguin Books, 1971), 139.

13. Quoted in J. R. H. Moorman, *A History of the Church in England,* 3rd ed. (Harrisburg, Pa.: Morehouse Publishing, 1994), 341, Tract 1.

14. Carpenter, *Church and People,* 140.

15. Moorman, *History of the Church in England,* 347.

16. Quoted in David L. Holmes, *A Brief History of the Episcopal Church* (Valley Forge, Pa.: Trinity Press International, 1993), 111.

17. James Thayer Addison, *The Episcopal Church in the United States, 1789–1931* (New York: Charles Scribner's Sons, 1951), 156, 158.

18. Holmes, *Brief History,* 108.

19. Ibid., 109.

20. Quoted in Horton Davies, *Worship in England: From Watts and Wesley to Martineau* (Grand Rapids: Eerdmans, 1996), IV, 306.

21. Moorman, *History of the Church in England*, 345.

22. Quoted in Moorman, *History of the Church in England*, 347.

23. Stephen Neill, *Anglicanism*, 4th ed. (New York: Oxford University Press, 1982), 256.

24. In *The Letters and Diarys of John Henry Newman*, ed. Charles Stephen Dessain, vols. xi–xxii (London: 1961–72), xxii, xxiv, 52, 143, quoted in Ian Ker, *John Henry Newman: A Biography* (New York: Oxford University Press, 1988), 578.

25. T. Arnold, in *Miscellaneous Works*, edition of 1845, p. 279, quoted in Neill, *Anglicanism*, 246.

26. Paul Avis, *Anglicanism and the Christian Church* (Minneapolis: Fortress Press, 1989), 239–44.

27. F. D. Maurice, op. cit., 1:138, quoted in Davies, *From Watts and Wesley to Martineau*, 294.

28. Moorman, *History of the Church in England*, 356.

29. Alec R. Vidler, *F. D. Maurice and Company: Nineteenth Century Studies* (London: SCM, 1966), 96.

30. F. D. Maurice, *Theological Essays* (New York: Harper, 1957), 176–77.

31. In F. D. Maurice, *The Kingdom of Christ*, 1838 edition, 2:300, quoted in Davies, *From Watts and Wesley to Martineau*, IV, 301.

32. Quoted in Paul Avis, *Gore: Construction and Conflict* (Worthing, West Sussex, England: Churchman Publishing, 1988), 5.

33. James Carpenter, *Charles Gore: A Study in Liberal Catholic Thought* (London: Faith Press, 1960), 244.

34. Ibid., 247.

35. Ibid., 249.

36. Charles Gore, *Christ and Society* (New York: Charles Scribner's Sons, 1928), 5.

37. Avis, *Gore*, 115.

38. Matthew Arnold, "Dover Beach," in *Immortal Poems of the English Language*, ed. Oscar Williams (New York: Washington Square Press, 1964), 428–29.

39. Alfred Lord Tennyson, *In Memoriam*, in Davies, *From Watts and Wesley to Martineau*, IV, 196–97.

40. Quoted in Moorman, *History of the Church in England*, 386.

41. Anthony Trollope, in *Barchester Towers* (1857), chapter xii, quoted in Moorman, *History of the Church in England*, 362.

42. Moorman, *History of the Church in England*, 363.

43. Thomas Hardy, *Under the Greenwood Tree, Or the Mellstock Choir*, ed. David White (New York: Penguin Books, 1985), 195.

44. Ibid., 114.

45. Ibid., 72.

46. Ibid., 195.

47. Kenneth R. Long, *The Music of the Church of England* (London: Hodder & Stoughton, 1971), 300–331.

48. Ibid., 337–38.

49. F. W. Robertson, in Series I, Sermon xviii, pp. 91–92, quoted in Davies, *From Watts and Wesley to Martineau*, IV, 321.

50. F. W. Robertson, in Unpublished Sermons, in *The Life and Letters of Frederick W. Robertson*, 2 vols. in 1, ed. Stopford A. Brooke (Boston, 1870), 2:169–70, quoted in Davies, *From Watts and Wesley to Martineau*, IV, 316; see also Frederick W. Robertson, *Sermons,* fourth series, edition of 1898.

51. F. W. Robertson, in Series II, Sermon IX, "The Faith of the Centurion," quoted in Davies, *From Watts and Wesley to Martineau*, II, 316–17.

52. F. W. Robertson, in Series I, Sermon XVII, pp. 189–92, 194, quoted in Davies, *From Watts and Wesley to Martineau*, IV, 319.

53. In Peter F. Anson, *The Call of the Cloister* (1955), Appendix, "List of Religious Communities and Kindred Bodies in the Anglican Communion in Order of Foundation," pp. 590–94, quoted in Davies, *From Watts and Wesley to Martineau*, 135.

54. Moorman, *History of the Church in England,* 404.

55. Quoted in Carpenter, 451–52.

56. *Kilvert's Diary, 1870–1879: Selections from the Diary of the Rev. Francis Kilvert,* ed. William Plomer (New York: Macmillan, 1947), 22–25, 190–91, 374.

57. John Henry Newman, "Worship, a Preparation for Christ's Coming (Advent)," Volume V, Sermon I, in *John Henry Newman, Selected Sermons,* ed. Ian Ker (New York: Paulist Press, 1994), 279–85.

58. Vidler, *F. D. Maurice and Company,* 15.

59. F. D. Maurice, in *Life of F. D. Maurice,* 1:512, quoted in Vidler, *F. D. Maurice and Company,* 23.

60. F. D. Maurice, in *Lincoln's Inn Sermons,* 4:12–13, quoted in Vidler, *F. D. Maurice and Company,* 83.

61. F. D. Maurice, in *Kingdom of Christ,* 1:279, quoted in Vidler, *F. D. Maurice and Company,* 179.

62. F. D. Maurice, in *Kingdom of Christ,* 1:259, quoted in Vidler, *F. D. Maurice and Company,* 121.

63. F. D. Maurice, in *The Prayer-Book and the Lord's Prayer,* 221, quoted in Vidler, *F. D. Maurice and Company,* 145.

64. F. D. Maurice, in *Claims of the Bible,* 27f., quoted in Vidler, *F. D. Maurice and Company,* 147.

65. F. D. Maurice, in *Sermons on the Sabbath-Day,* 93f., quoted in Vidler, *F. D. Maurice and Company,* 165.

66. F. D. Maurice, in *Lincoln's Inn Sermons,* 2:93f., in Vidler, *F. D. Maurice and Company,* 173.

67. F. D. Maurice, in *Life of Frederick Denison Maurice*, 2:299f., quoted in Vidler, *F. D. Maurice and Company*, 195.

68. F. D. Maurice, in *Subscription No Bondage*, 101, quoted in Vidler, *F. D. Maurice and Company*, 197.

69. F. D. Maurice, in *Epistle to the Hebrews*, 126; *The Prayer-Book and the Lord's Prayer*, 159, quoted in Vidler, *F. D. Maurice and Company*, 196.

70. Charles Gore, *Lux Mundi: A Series of Studies in the Religion of the Incarnation*, 13th ed. (New York: Thomas Whittaker, 1890), 263ff.

71. Frederick William Robertson, *Sermons Preached at Trinity Chapel, Brighton*, First Series (Boston: Ticknor and Fields, 1863), 285–87, 292–305.

CHAPTER 6
THE TWENTIETH CENTURY

1. In Joan Veazey, *People at War*, 148, quoted in Adrian Hastings, *A History of English Christianity, 1920–1990* (London: SCM, 1991), 284–385.

2. Hastings, *History*, 70.

3. Ibid., 615.

4. S. D. O'Connell, *History of the American Episcopal Church*, 8th ed. (New York: Thomas Whittaker, 1899), 429.

5. David L. Holmes, *A Brief History of the Episcopal Church* (Valley Forge, Pa.: Trinity Press International, 1993), 129–30.

6. Quoted in James Thayer Addison, *The Episcopal Church in the United States, 1789–1931* (New York: Charles Scribner's Sons, 1951), 283.

7. Ibid., 287.

8. Charles Henry Brent, in Don S. Armentrout and Robert Boak Slocum, *Documents of Witness: A History of the Episcopal Church, 1782–1985* (New York: Church Hymnal Corporation, 1994), 461–62, quoted in Frederick Ward Kates, ed., *Things That Matter: The Best of the Writings of Bishop Brent* (New York: Harper & Brothers, 1949), 38–42.

9. F. A. Iremonger, *William Temple, Archbishop of Canterbury: His Life and Letters* (New York: Oxford University Press, 1948), 94–95.

10. Ibid.

11. William Temple, *Nature, Man, and God* (London: Macmillian, 1924), 478.

12. Iremonger, *William Temple*, 417–18.

13. Ibid., 389–90.

14. Ibid., 389.

15. Hastings, *History*, 533.

16. A. M. Ramsey, address to the Diocesan Convention in Canterbury, Octo-

ber 26, 1968, quoted in Owen Chadwick, *Michael Ramsey: A Life* (Oxford: Clarendon Press, 1990), 339.

17. Arthur Michael Ramsey, *The Glory of God and the Transfiguration of Christ* (London: Longmans, Green, 1960), 135–36.

18. In E. Underhill to F. von Hügel, midsummer 1992, von Hügel–Underhill Collection, quoted in Dana Greene, *Evelyn Underhill: Artist of the Infinite Life* (New York: Crossroad, 1990), 84.

19. Evelyn Underhill, *Mysticism: A Study in the Nature and Development of Man's Spiritual Consciousness* (London: Routledge, 1912), ix.

20. Ibid., 86.

21. Hastings, *History*, 493.

22. In C. S. Lewis, *Surprised by Joy*, 213, quoted in Hastings, *History*, 237.

23. C. S. Lewis, *The Screwtape Letters* (London, 1942), 112.

24. Hastings, *History*, 494–95.

25. C .S. Lewis, *A Grief Observed* (Greenwich, Conn.: Seabury Press, 1963), 7, 52, 55.

26. To Vanessa Woolf, February 11, 1928, in *Letters of Virginia Woolf*, vol. 3, *A Change of Perspective, 1923–1928* (1977), 457–58, quoted in Hastings, *History*, 236.

27. Herbert Read, "T.S.E.—A Memoir," 22, quoted in J. Bradley Hunt Gunter, *T. S. Eliot and Anglicanism: The Man of Letters as Religious and Social Critic*, Ph.D. thesis (Ann Arbor, Mich.: University Microfilms, 1970), 101–2.

28. Quoted in Barbara Reynolds, *Dorothy L. Sayers: Her Life and Soul* (New York: St. Martin's Press, 1993), 241.

29. Quoted in Reynolds, *Dorothy L. Sayers*, 312–13.

30. Quoted in Reynolds, *Dorothy L. Sayers*, 326.

31. Quoted in Reynolds, *Dorothy L. Sayers*, 335.

32. Quoted in Reynolds, *Dorothy L. Sayers*, 367–68.

33. Ronald Blythe, *Word from Wormingford: A Parish Year* (New York: Penguin Books, 1998), 83–84.

34. John Howe, *Highways and Hedges, Anglicanism and the Universal Church* (London: CIO Publishing, for the Anglican Consultative Council, 1985), 14.

35. Stephen Neill, *Anglicanism*, 4th ed. (New York: Oxford University Press, 1982), 365.

36. Ibid., 367–78.

37. Ibid., 369.

38. Vinany Samuel and Christopher Sugden, *Lambeth, a View from the Two-Thirds World* (Harrisburg, Pa.: Morehouse Publishing, 1989), 6.

39. Robert Runcie, *The Unity We Seek*, ed. Margaret Pawley (Harrisburg, Pa.: Morehouse Publishing, 1989), 4–5.

40. Ibid., 7.

41. From H. Bettenson, *Documents of the Christian Church*, 382–83, quoted in J. R. H. Moorman, *A History of the Church in England*, 3rd ed. (Harrisburg, Pa.: Morehouse Publishing, 1994), 408.

42. Hastings, *History*, xxvii, xxviii.

43. Neill, *Anglicanism*, 387.

44. William Temple, *Essays in Christian Politics* (London: Longmans, Green, 1927), 201–2, quoted in Roger Lloyd, *The Church of England, 1900–1965* (London: SCM, 1996), 20.

45. C. S. Lewis, *The Screwtape Letters* (London: HarperCollins, 1959), 81–85.

46. C. S. Lewis, *The Horse and His Boy,* book 5 in *The Chronicles of Narnia* (London: HarperCollins, 1975), 155–60.

47. T. S. Eliot, *The Complete Poems and Plays, 1909–1950* (New York: Harcourt, Brace, 1952), 68–69, 143–45.

48. Evelyn Underhill, *Worship* (New York: Crossroad, 1989), 314–20, 336–37.

49. Charles Williams, *Descent into Hell* (London: Faber & Faber, 1955), 91–98.

50. Dorothy L. Sayers, *The Nine Tailors* (London: New English Library, Hodder & Stoughton, 1988), 30–31.

51. William Temple, *Christianity and Social Order* (London: SCM, printed by Penguin Books, London, 1942), 9, 49–58.

52. Michael Ramsey, *The Gospel and the Catholic Church* (Cambridge, Mass.: Cowley Publications, 1990), 4–5, 204–5, 220, 224–25.

Selected Bibliography

Altick, Richard D. *Victorian People and Ideas.* New York: W. W. Norton, 1973.

Andrewes, Lancelot. *Sixteen Sermons, Chiefly on the Principal Fasts and Festivals of the Church.* London: Thomas Davison, Whitefriars, 1831.

Avis, Paul. *Anglicanism and the Christian Century.* Minneapolis: Fortress Press, 1989.

————. *Gore: Construction and Conflict.* Worthing, West Sussex, England: Churchman Publishing, 1988.

Baxter, Richard. *A Christian Directory.* London: Robert White, 1678. Volume 1 in Franklin Le Van Baumer, *Main Currents of Western Thought.* New York: Alfred A. Knopf, 1954.

Bede. *A History of the English Church and People.* Baltimore, Md.: Penguin Books, 1975.

Blythe, Ronald. *Word from Wormingford: A Parish Year.* New York: Penguin Books, 1998.

Booty, John E. *John Jewel as Apologist of the Church of England.* London: S.P.C.K., 1963.

Carey, John. *John Donne: Life, Mind and Art.* New York: Oxford University Press, 1981.

Carpenter, James. *Gore: A Study in Liberal Catholic Thought.* London: Faith Press, 1960.

Carpenter, S. C. *Church and People, 1789–1889: A History of the Church of England from William Wilberforce to "Lux Mundi."* London: S.P.C.K., 1933.

————. *Eighteenth Century Church and People.* London: John Murray, 1959.

Chadwick, Owen. *Michael Ramsey: A Life.* Oxford: Clarendon Press, 1990.

————. *The Reformation.* Baltimore, Md.: Penguin Books, 1972.

————. *The Victorian Church*, Part I, *1829–1859*, Part II, *1860-1901.* London: SCM, 1992.

Chappell, Paul. *Music and Worship in the Anglican Church, 597–1967.* London: Faith Press, 1968.

The Church of England, c. 1689–c. 1833: From Toleration to Tractarianism. Edited by John Walsh, with Colin Haydon and Stephen Taylor. Cambridge: Cambridge University Press, 1993.

Clifton-Taylor, Alec. *The Cathedrals of England.* London: Thames & Hudson, 1986.

Collins, Irene. *Jane Austen and the Clergy.* London: Hambledon Press, 1994.

Coward, Barry. *The Stuart Age: England 1603–1714.* 2nd edition. New York: Longman, 1994.

Cragg, Gerald R. *The Church in the Age of Reason, 1648–1789.* New York: Penguin Books, 1981.

Cranmer, Thomas. *The Works of Thomas Cranmer.* Edited by G. E. Duffield. Appleford, Berkshire, England: Sutton Courtenay Press, 1964.

Cranston, Maurice. *John Locke: A Biography.* New York: Longmans, Green, 1957.

Cressy, David, and Lori Anne Ferrell, eds. *Religion and Society in Early Modern England: A Sourcebook.* New York: Routledge, 1996.

Cunliffe, Barry. *The Ancient Celts.* New York: Oxford University Press, 1997.

Cust, Richard, and Ann Hughes, eds. *The English Civil War.* New York: Arnold, 1997.

Davies, Horton. *Worship and Theology in England: From Cranmer to Baxter and Foxe, 1534–1690.* Grand Rapids: Eerdmans, 1996.

———. *Worship and Theology in England: From Watts and Wesley to Martineau, 1690–1900.* Grand Rapids: Eerdmans, 1996.

———. *Worship and Theology in England: The Ecumenical Century, 1900 to the Present.* Grand Rapids: Eerdmans, 1996.

Davies, Oliver, and Fiona Bowie, eds. *Celtic Christian Spirituality, Medieval and Modern.* London: S.P.C.K., 1995.

Demers, Patricia. *The World of Hannah More.* Lexington: University of Kentucky Press, 1996.

Dickens, A. G. *The English Reformation.* London: Collins, The Fortuna Library, 1969.

Doctrine in the Church of England, The Report of the Commission on Christian Doctrine Appointed by the Archbishops of Canterbury and York in 1922. London: S.P.C.K., 1952.

Donne, John. *Selections from Divine Poems, Sermons, Devotions, and Prayers.* Edited by John Booty. Classics of Western Spirituality. New York: Paulist Press, 1990.

Doran, Susan, and Christopher Durston. *Princes, Pastors and People: The Church and Religion in England 1529–1689.* London: Routledge, 1991.

Duffy, Eamon. *The Stripping of the Altars: Traditional Religion in England, 1400–1580.* New Haven: Yale University Press, 1992.

Eliot, T. S. *The Complete Poems and Plays, 1909–1950.* New York: Harcourt, Brace, 1952.

The Fathers of the English Church; or a Selection from the Writings of the Reformers and Early Protestant Divines of the Church of England. Volumes II, III, VII. London: John Hatchard, 1808, 1809, 1811.

Faulkner, Robert K. *Richard Hooker and the Politics of a Christian England*. Los Angeles: University of California Press, 1981.

Foxe, John. *Book of Martyrs; or, a History of the Lives, Sufferings, and Triumphant Deaths, of the Primitive as well as Protestant Martyrs*. Hartford, Conn.: Philemon Canfield, 1832.

Frere, W. H. *The English Church in the Reigns of Elizabeth and James I (1558–1625)*. 1904. Reprint, New York: AMS Press.

Gee, Henry, and William John Hardy. *Documents Illustrative of English Church History*. London: Macmillan, 1910. Reprint, New York: Kraus Reprint Corporation, 1966.

Gilley, Sheridin, and W. J. Sheils. *A History of Religion in Britain: Practice and Belief from Pre-Roman Times to the Present*. Cambridge, Mass.: Blackwell, 1994.

Goldsmith, Oliver. *The Works of Oliver Goldsmith*, volume 1. Edited by Peter Cunningham. New York: Harper & Brothers, 1881.

Gore, Charles. *Christ and Society*. New York: Charles Scribner's Sons, 1928.

———. *Lux Mundi: A Series of Studies in the Religion of the Incarnation*. 13th edition. New York: Thomas Whittaker, 1980.

———. *The Sermon on the Mount: A Practical Exposition*. London: John Murray, 1899.

Greene, Dana. *Evelyn Underhill: Artist of the Infinite Life*. New York: Crossroad, 1990.

Gunter, J. Bradley Hunt. *T. S. Eliot and Anglicanism: The Man of Letters as Religious and Social Critic*. Ph.D. thesis. Ann Arbor, Mich.: University Microfilms, 1970.

Guy, John. *Tudor England*. Oxford: Oxford University Press, 1991.

———, ed. *The Tudor Monarchy*. New York: Arnold, 1997.

Haigh, Christopher. *English Reformations: Religion, Politics, and Society under the Tudors*. Oxford: Clarendon Press, 1993.

Hardinge, Leslie. *The Celtic Church in Britain*. London: S.P.C.K., 1972.

Hardy, Thomas. *Under the Greenwood Tree, Or the Mellstock Choir*. Edited by David White. New York: Penguin Books, 1985.

Hastings, Adrian. *A History of English Christianity, 1920–1990*. Philadelphia: Trinity Press International, 1991.

Hill, Christopher. *The Century of Revolution, 1603–1714*. London: Routledge, 1961.

———. *Change and Continuity in 17ᵗʰ-Century England*. 1974. New Haven: Yale University Press, 1991.

———. *Society and Puritanism in Pre-Revolutionary England*. 2nd edition. New York: Schocken Books, 1967.

Hollister, B. Warren. *The Making of England, 55 B.C. to 1399.* Lexington, Mass.: D. C. Heath, 1986.

Holmes, Urban T., III. *What is Anglicanism?* Harrisburg, Pa.: Morehouse Publishing, 1982.

Howe, John. *Highways and Hedges: Anglicanism and the Universal Church.* London: CIO Publishing, for the Anglican Consultative Council, 1985.

Hutton, William Holden. *The English Church from the Accession of Charles I to the Death of Anne (1625–1714).* 1903. Reprint, New York: AMS Press.

Inge, W. R. *Diary of a Dean, St. Paul's, 1911–1914.* New York: Hutchinson, 1949.

Iremonger, F. A. *William Temple, Archbishop of Canterbury: His Life and Letters.* London: Oxford University Press, 1948.

Jewel, John. *An Apology of the Church of England.* Edited by J. E. Booty. The Folger Shakespeare Library. Charlottesville: University of Virginia Press, 1974.

Johnson, Howard A. *Global Odyssey.* New York: Harper & Row, 1963.

Jones, M. G. *Hannah More.* Cambridge: Cambridge University Press, 1952.

Julian of Norwich. *Revelations of Divine Love.* Edited by Halcyon Backhouse with Rhona Pipe. Hodder & Stoughton Christian Classics. London: Hodder & Stoughton, 1987.

———. *Showings.* Edited by Edmund Colledge. Classics in Western Spirituality. New York: Paulist Press, 1978.

Ker, Ian. *John Henry Newman: A Biography.* New York: Oxford University Press, 1988.

Kilvert's Diary, 1870–1879: Selections from the Diary of the Rev. Francis Kilvert. Edited by William Plomer. New York: Macmillan, 1947.

Knox, David Broughton. *Thirty-Nine Articles: The Historic Basis of Anglican Faith.* London: Hodder & Stoughton, 1967.

Law, William. *A Serious Call to a Devout and Holy Life, The Spirit of Love.* Edited by Paul G. Stanwood. New York: Paulist Press, 1978.

Lehmberg, Stanford E. *The Reformation of Cathedrals.* Princeton, N.J.: Princeton University Press, 1988.

Legg, Wickham. *English Church Life: From the Restoration to the Tractarian Movement.* London: Longmans, Green, 1914.

Lewis, C. S. *The Horse and His Boy.* New York: Macmillan, Collier Books, 1975.

———. *The Screwtape Letters.* New York: Macmillan, 1959.

———. *Surprised by Joy, The Shape of My Early Life.* New York: Harcourt, Brace, 1955.

Locke, John. *An Essay Concerning Human Understanding.* Edited by Alexander Campbell Fraser. Oxford: Clarendon Press, 1894.

———. *The Reasonableness of Christianity.* Edited by I. T. Ramsey. Stanford, Calif.: Stanford University Press, 1958.

Long, Kenneth R. *The Music of the English Church*. London: Hodder & Stoughton, 1971.

Lloyd, Roger. *The Church of England, 1900–1965*. London: SCM, 1966.

MacCulloch, Diarmaid. *Thomas Cranmer, A Life*. New Haven: Yale University Press, 1996.

————. "Cranmer's Ambiguous Legacy." *History Today* 46, no. 6 (June 1996).

————. *Tudor Church Militant: Edward VI and the Protestant Reformation*. New York: Allen Lane, Penguin Press, 1999.

Main Currents of Western Thought. Edited by Franklin Le Van Baumer. New York: Alfred A. Knopf, 1954.

Marsden, John. *The Fury of the Northmen: Saints, Shrines, and Sea-Raiders in the Viking Age*. New York: St. Martin's Press, 1993.

Maurice, F. D. *Theological Essays*. New York: Harper, 1957.

Maycock, A. L. *Nicholas Ferrar of Little Gidding*. London: S.P.C.K., 1963.

McAdoo, H. R. *Anglican Heritage: Theology and Spirituality*. Norwich, U.K.: Canterbury Press, 1991.

McCullough, Peter E. *Sermons at Court: Politics and Religion in Elizabethan and Jacobean Preaching*. Cambridge: Cambridge University Press, 1998.

McNeill, John T. *The Celtic Churches: A History, A.D. 200 to 1200*. Chicago: University of Chicago Press, 1974.

Moorman, J. R. H. *Church Life in the Thirteenth Century*. Cambridge: Cambridge University Press, 1946.

————. *A History of the Church in England*. 3rd edition. Harrisburg, Pa.: Morehouse Publishing, 1994.

Morgan, Kenneth O., ed. *The Oxford History of Britain*. New York: Oxford University Press, 1993.

Mossner, Ernest Campbell. *Bishop Butler and the Age of Reason*. New York: Macmillan, 1936.

Neill, Stephen. *Anglicanism*. New York: Oxford University Press, 1982.

Newman, John Henry. "Worship, a Preparation for Christ's Coming (Advent)." Volume V, Sermon I, in *John Henry Newman, Selected Sermons*, edited by Ian Ker. New York: Paulist Press, 1994.

The New Oxford Book of English Verse, 1250–1950. Edited by Helen Gardner. New York: Oxford University Press, 1972.

Norton, William J., Jr. *Bishop Butler, Moralist & Divine*. New Brunswick, N.J.: Rutgers University Press, 1940.

Overton, John H., and Frederic Relton. *The English Church from the Accession of George I to the End of the Eighteenth Century (1714–1800)*. 1906. Reprint, New York: AMS Press.

Page, Robert Jeffress. *Charles Gore, Anglican Apologist*. Ph.D. thesis. Ann Arbor, Mich.: University Microfilms, 1955.

Pierce, Charles E., Jr. *The Religious Life of Samuel Johnson*. Hamden, Conn.: Archon Books, 1983.

Poems from the Old English. Translated by Burton Raffel. Lincoln: University of Nebraska Press, 1964.

Prestige, G. L. *The Life of Charles Gore.* London: William Heinemann, 1935.

Price, Charles P., and Louis Weil. *Liturgy for Living.* New York: Seabury Press, 1979.

The Private Prayers of Lancelot Andrewes. Edited by Hugh Martin. London: SCM, 1957.

Ramsey, Michael. *The Anglican Spirit.* Edited by Dale Coleman. Cambridge, Mass.: Cowley Publications, 1992.

———. *The Glory of God and the Transfiguration of Christ.* London: Longmans, Green, 1960.

———. *The Gospel and the Catholic Church.* Cambridge, Mass.: Cowley Publications, 1990.

Reardon, Bernard M. G. *From Coleridge to Gore: A Century of Religious Thought in Britain.* London: Longman, 1971.

Reynolds, Barbara. *Dorothy L. Sayers: Her Life and Soul.* New York: St. Martin's Press, 1993.

Robertson, Frederick William. *Sermons on Bible Subjects,* Volumes I, II, III. New York: E. P. Dutton, 1906.

———. *Sermons Preached at Trinity Chapel, Brighton.* Boston: Ticknor & Fields, 1863.

Rowell, Geoffrey, ed. *The English Religious Tradition and the Genius of Anglicanism.* Nashville: Abingdon Press, 1992.

Rupp, Gordon. *Religion in England, 1688–1791.* Oxford: Clarendon Press, 1986.

Salter, K. W. *Thomas Traherne: Mystic and Poet.* London: Edward Arnold, 1964.

Sawyer, Peter, ed. *The Oxford Illustrated History of the Vikings.* New York: Oxford University Press, 1997.

Samuel, Vinay, and Christopher Sugden. *Lambeth, a View from the Two Thirds World.* Harrisburg, Pa.: Morehouse Publishing, 1989.

Secor, Philip B. *Richard Hooker: Prophet of Anglicanism.* Toronto: Anglican Book Center, 2000.

Sayers, Dorothy L. *The Nine Tailors.* London: New English Library, Hodder & Stoughton, 1988.

Sharpe, J. A. *Early Modern England: A Social History, 1550–1760.* New York: Arnold, 1997.

Simon, Marcel. *L'Anglicanisme.* Paris: Librairie Armand Colin, 1969.

Simpson, James B., and Edward M. Story. *The Long Shadow of Lambeth X.* New York: McGraw-Hill, 1969.

Spurr, John. *The Restoration Church of England, 1646–1689.* New Haven: Yale University Press, 1991.

Sykes, Norman. *Church and State in England in the XVIIIth Century.* Cambridge: Cambridge University Press, 1934.

Sykes, Stephen. *Unashamed Anglicanism*. Nashville: Abingdon Press, 1995.

Sykes, Stephen, John Booty, and Jonathan Knight. *The Study of Anglicanism*. London: S.P.C.K., 1998.

Taylor, Jeremy. *Jeremy Taylor, Selected Works*. Edited by Thomas K. Carroll. Classics of Western Spirituality. New York: Paulist Press, 1980.

Temple, William. *Christianity and the Social Order*. London: SCM, 1942.

———. *Nature, Man, and God*. London: Macmillan, 1924.

In Tune With Heaven: The Report of the Archbishops' Commission on Church Music. London: Church Publishing House and Hodder & Stoughton, 1992.

Thomas, Keith. *Religion and the Decline of Magic*. New York: Oxford University Press, 1971. Reprint, 1997.

Trevor-Roper, H. R. *Archbishop Laud, 1573–1645*. London: Macmillan, 1940.

Underhill, Evelyn. *Mysticism: A Study in the Nature and Development of Man's Spiritual Consciousness*. London: Methuen, 1912.

———. *Worship*. New York: Crossroad, 1989.

Vidler, Alec R. *The Church in an Age of Revolution, 1799 to the Present Day*. New York: Penguin Books, 1981.

———. *F. D. Maurice and Company: Nineteenth Century Studies*. London: SCM, 1966.

Virgin, Peter. *The Church in an Age of Negligence: Ecclesiastical Structure and Problems of Church Reform, 1700–1840*. Cambridge: James Clarke, 1989.

Wade, Gladys I. *Thomas Traherne*. Princeton, N.J.: Princeton University Press, 1944.

Walsh, John, ed., with Colin Haydon and Stephen Taylor. *The Church of England, c. 1689–c. 1833: From Toleration to Tractarianism*. Cambridge: Cambridge University Press, 1993.

Wesley, John, and Charles Wesley. *John and Charles Wesley, Selected Prayers, Hymns, Journal Notes, Sermons, Letters, and Treatises*. Edited by Frank Whaling. New York: Paulist Press, 1981.

Williams, Charles. *Descent into Hell*. London: Faber & Faber, 1955.

Williams, Penry. *The Later Tudors: England, 1547–1603*. Oxford: Oxford University Press, 1998.

Woodforde, James. *The Diary of a Country Parson, 1758–1802*. New York: Oxford University Press, 1978.

Index